BOOK ONE   Fourth Edition

CENTURY 21

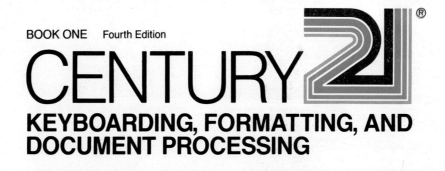

KEYBOARDING, FORMATTING, AND DOCUMENT PROCESSING

T. James Crawford, Ph.D.

Professor of Business
and of Education
Indiana University

Lee R. Beaumont, Ed.D.

Professor of Business, Emeritus
Indiana University of Pennsylvania

Lawrence W. Erickson, Ed.D.

Professor of Education, Emeritus
University of California (LA)

Jerry W. Robinson, Ed.D.

Senior Editor
South-Western Publishing Co.

Arnola C. Ownby, Ed.D.

Professor of Office Administration
and Business Education
Southwest Missouri State University

Published by

SOUTH-WESTERN PUBLISHING CO.

T56   CINCINNATI   WEST CHICAGO, IL   DALLAS   PELHAM MANOR, NY   LIVERMORE, CA

ACKNOWLEDGMENTS

Contributing Authors

Several teachers prepared selected materials for this textbook and correlating laboratory materials and tests. Their names are listed here as evidence of our appreciation of their helpful participation.

Jack P. Hoggatt, Ed.D.
Associate Professor of Business Education and Administrative Management
University of Wisconsin, Eau Claire

John J. Olivo, Jr., Ph.D.
Assistant Professor of Business Education and Office Administration
Bloomsburg (PA) University

Sharon Lund O'Neil, Ph.D.
Associate Professor of Business Education
University of Houston

Jon A. Shank, Ed.D.
Professor of Administrative Management and Business Education
Robert Morris College, Coraopolis (PA)

Donna L. Willard, M.S.
Instructor of Business Education
Great Oaks Joint Vocational School District, Cincinnati

Other Contributors

In addition to the authorship team and editorial staff who prepare and process the manuscript that becomes a textbook, thousands of others contribute in vital ways to the quality of the final product. Among these are teachers and students too numerous to thank individually. We mention these groups here as an expression of appreciation and thanks.

In preparation for this new fourth edition of *Century 21 Keyboarding, Formatting, and Document Processing,* over 5,000 teachers responded to a comprehensive questionnaire sent to a stratified sample of keyboarding/typewriting teachers throughout the country. Their responses weighed heavily in deciding the major changes that have been made in the revision.

Planned changes in course titling and course content were obtained by questionnaire responses from all state and selected city supervisors. The responses helped to guide the changes in the book's title, content, and sequence.

Almost 2,000 teacher interview reports prepared by marketers, editors, and authors during interviews with users of the previous edition were helpful in identifying for revision specific materials that appeared to cause some learning difficulty.

A more limited sample of teachers and students reported specific feedback on selected segments of the textual and teaching/learning support materials in a formal learner verification revision (LVR) study.

Photo Credits

COVER PHOTO and photo in heads on pages iii and RG 1:
© Richard Fukahara/West Light

PHOTO, p. xi, top: IBM Corporation

PHOTO, p. 243: Photo courtesy Colorado Tourism Board

PHOTOS FOR ALL PHASE OPENERS: Melvin L. Prueitt, IS-2, Los Alamos National Laboratory, author of *Art and the Computer,* 1984.

If one were asked to list the terms which best represent the changes that have occurred in the workplace during the past decade, these would likely be among the top twenty: information processing, automation, personal computers, word/data processing, electronics, technology, communication, keyboard(ing), format(ting), text-editing, and document processing. Thus, the information and electronic age has ushered in a whole new vocabulary that permeates personal, professional, and business communication.

At the center of the many changes which the information and electronic age has brought are a wide variety of typewriter-like keyboards and an equal variety of people who operate them. Any learning program designed to prepare students to function knowledgeably and efficiently in the modern world must give attention to the concepts, terminology, and processes that those who use that program are expected to know.

From its title to its index, *Century 21 Keyboarding, Formatting, and Document Processing, Book 1,* Fourth Edition, reflects the changes that are taking place in school curriculums as well as in office systems throughout the country -- and the world. The words in this book's title and contents are deliberately chosen to mirror the language of the modern workplace; for until one understands the language of change, one can only reluctantly accept change itself. Some of the terms are merely different words applied to familiar concepts and processes. Others are new words to name new methods of handling familiar functions.

But whatever the changes in vocabulary, the course of study this book is designed to serve -- keyboarding, typewriting, word processing, or some variant of these -- still has three major thrusts or areas of emphasis: keyboarding (manipulative skill development), formatting (arrangement, placement, and spacing of documents), and document processing (skilled production of letters, reports, tables, and other communication forms). *Century 21* develops each of these skill components in a timely, educationally sound way.

Keyboarding

Keyboarding is the manipulative skill required and used in completing a task on a keyboard. It is also an essential prerequisite for the development of document formatting and processing skills. Thus, keyboarding is not only the first but also a continuing emphasis in the development of document processing competence.

Century 21 has long been the recognized leader in developing keyboarding skill according to widely accepted skill-building principles which are supported by a strong research base. This new edition is no exception.

The major change in initial keyboarding skill development in this new edition is the presentation of only two new keys in each lesson to provide more intensive and comprehensive practice on new learnings before other new learnings are presented. In addition, more review/reinforcement lessons are provided to assure keyboard mastery. Both changes resulted from learner verification revision (LVR) feedback from users of the previous edition.

Phase 1 (the first 25 lessons) is devoted almost exclusively to alphabetic keyboarding skill development. Thereafter, emphasis on keyboarding skill is provided primarily in periodic units of intensive practice. Again, LVR feedback led to the removal of much of the keyboarding skill activity from formatting and document processing units and to the placing of such material in separate units. Doing so focuses the attention and effort of teachers and students on one major goal at a time.

Keyboarding on the top row is delayed until correct technique has been developed on the alphabetic keyboard and an essential level of keyboarding skill has been demonstrated. LVR feedback supports this widely tested plan.

This new edition places first emphasis on technique of keyboard operation (*without* time pressure) and second emphasis on speed of manipulative performance (*with* strategic timed writings). Then, when appropriate, it emphasizes accuracy of copy produced (*with* restricted-speed paced practice). Practice copy is displayed and counted in a variety of ways to accommodate the varied practice goals. This plan of emphasis is in harmony with generally accepted principles of skill learning and with a large body of keyboarding research. Supporting the structure of the skill-building materials are two other important learning principles: work from the known to the unknown; and progress from the simple to the more complex.

Formatting

Formatting includes arranging, spacing, and placing copy according to accepted conventions for specific documents (letters, reports, tables, forms, and so on). It involves learning and following efficient, orderly steps for making machine adjustments, for making within-document decisions, and for evaluating final format acceptability.

Whether one learns to format on a type-writer, computer, or word processor, the concepts and principles are the same. What does differ are the machine-specific procedural steps for accomplishing the task. Because some of the newer document processing devices are limited in formatting capability, certain conventions of spacing and placing documents have had to be changed slightly so that those who learn to format on a typewriter can transfer more readily to personal computers and other electronic devices.

Century 21 begins format learning with the simplest formats in the first cycle. For example, only block letters, unbound reports with internal (textual) citations, and simple tables with blocked columnar headings are presented in the first 75 lessons. Further, each format presented is taught as a basic format that applies equally to personal, professional, and business situations.

Cycle 2 (the next 75 lessons) begins with a review/reinforcement of what is learned in Cycle 1. This serves as a springboard for the new, expanded learning to come. Modified block letters, unbound and leftbound reports with footnotes, more complex formats for tables, and commonly used business forms are presented in Cycle 2.

The formal program of language skills begun in Cycle 1 is continued in intensified form in Cycle 2.

Special drills are provided on those parts of documents that emphasize the format features (opening and closing lines of a letter, for example).

Students work first from model type-script, then from semiarranged print, and later from handwritten and rough-draft copy. Each progression in difficulty of format features and copy source leads the learner increasingly nearer the actual conditions of final performance.

This plan of presentation (simple-to-complex) and periodic review and expansion has received the endorsement of users for almost forty years.

Document Processing

Document processing is the culmination of keyboarding and formatting training. It brings together in a series of related documents the application of all learnings so far presented: keyboarding, formatting, language skills application, ability to follow directions, error detection and correction, and the ability to be self-directive and self-evaluative.

Century 21, Book 1, teaches all these skills in the process of developing keyboarding and formatting ability. Then in specific office job simulations it integrates them in real-life settings.

In these and other ways *Century 21 Keyboarding, Formatting, and Document Processing, Book 1,* Fourth Edition, prepares students for the modern workplace.

CONTENTS

■ **ELECTRIC**

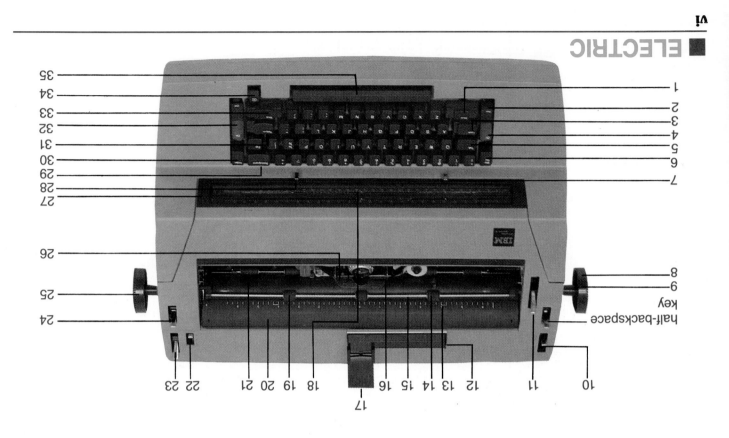

35
34
33
32
31
30
29
28
27

26

25

24

1
2
3
4
5
6
7

8
9
half-backspace key

23 22
21 20 19 18 16 15 14 13 12 11 10
17

■ **MANUAL**

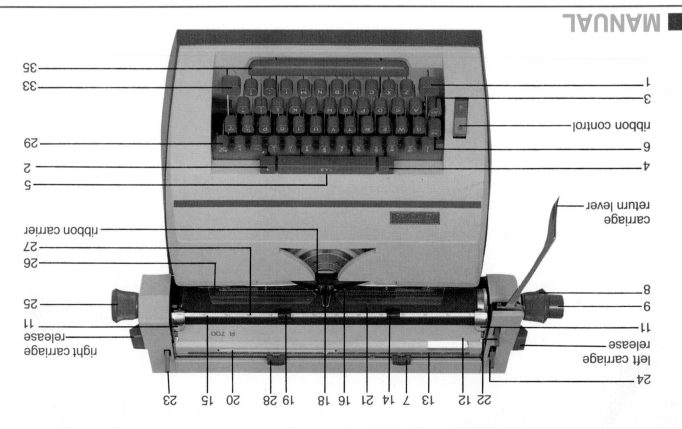

35
33

29

2
5

ribbon carrier
27
26

25
11
right carriage release

1
3

ribbon control
6

4

carriage return lever

8
9
11
left carriage release
24

23 15 20 28 19 18 16 21 14 7 13 12 22

R 700

KNOW YOUR TYPEWRITER

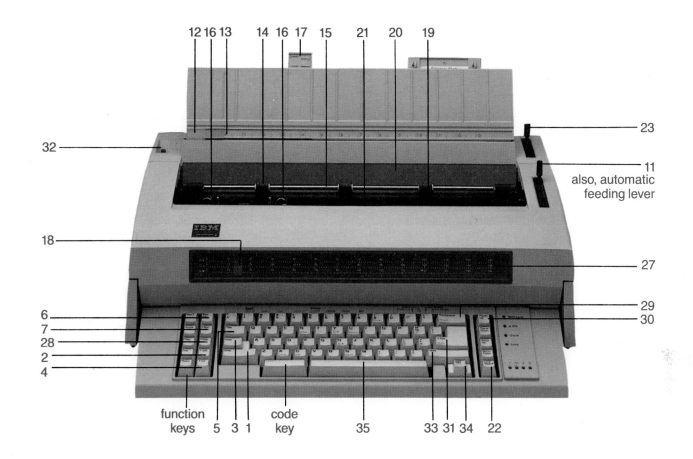

Labels on diagram: 12 16 13, 14 16 17 15, 21 20 19, 23, 11 also, automatic feeding lever, 32, 18, 27, 29, 30, 6, 7, 28, 2, 4, function keys 5 3 1 code key 35, 33 31 34 22

■ ELECTRONIC

The diagram above shows the parts of an electronic typewriter; the diagrams on page vi show the parts of a manual typewriter and an electric typewriter.

Since all typewriters have similar parts, you will probably be able to locate the parts on your typewriter from one of these diagrams. However, if you have the instructional booklet that comes with your machine, use it to identify the exact location of each operative part, including special parts that may be on one machine but not on another.

Illustrated on page viii is an array of microcomputers to which your keyboarding skills will transfer.

1. Left shift key: used to type capitals of letter keys controlled by right hand

2. Tab set: used to set tabulator stops

3. Shift lock: used to lock shift mechanism so that all letters are capitalized

4. Tab clear: used to clear tab stops

5. Tabulator: used to move carriage (carrier) to tab stops

6. Margin release key: used to move carriage (carrier) beyond margin stops

7. Left margin set: used to set left margin stop

8. Left platen knob: used to activate variable line spacer (not on some electronic models)

9. Variable line spacer: used to change writing line setting permanently (not on electronic machines)

10. Pitch selector: used to select 10-pitch (pica), 12-pitch (elite), or 15-pitch spacing (on some electronics, pitch changes automatically when you change daisy wheels; not on manual machines)

11. Paper bail lever: used to pull paper bail away from platen

12. Paper guide: used to position paper for insertion

13. Paper guide scale: used to set paper guide at desired position

14/19. Paper bail rolls: used to hold paper against platen

15. Paper bail: used to hold paper against platen

16. Card/envelope holders: used to hold cards, labels, and envelopes against platen

17. Page end indicator: used to check distance from typing line to lower edge of paper (not on manual machines)

18. Printing point indicator: used to position carriage (or element carrier) at desired point

19. (See 14)

20. Paper table: supports paper when it is in typewriter

21. Platen (cylinder): provides a hard surface against which type element or bars strike

22. Line-space selector: sets machine to advance the paper 1, 2, or 3 lines for single, double, or triple spacing when return lever or key is used

23. Paper release lever: used to allow paper to be removed or aligned

24. Automatic line finder: used to change line spacing temporarily, then refind the line (not on electronic machines)

25. Right platen knob: used to turn platen as paper is being inserted (not on some electronic machines)

26. Aligning scale: used to align copy that has been reinserted (not shown on electronic machine)

27. Line-of-writing (margin) scale: used when setting margin and tab stops and in horizontal centering

28. Right margin set: used to set right margin stop

29. Backspace key: used to move printing point to left one space at a time

30. Index key: used to advance paper one line at a time without returning to left margin (called "paper up" on some electronic machines; not on manual machines)

31. Carriage (carrier) return key: used to return carriage (carrier) to left margin and to move paper up (carriage return lever serves same function on manual)

32. ON/OFF control: used to turn electric-powered machines on or off

33. Right shift key: used to type capitals of letter keys controlled by left hand

34. Correcting key: used to erase a character (not on manual machines)

35. Space bar: used to move printing point to right one space at a time

Know Your Typewriter

KNOW YOUR COMPUTER

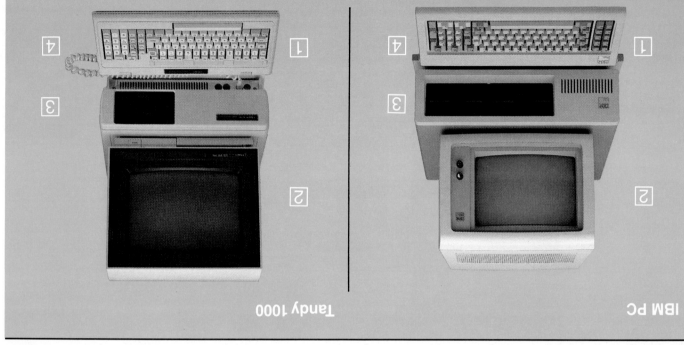

IBM PC

Tandy 1000

Typical components of a microcomputer are:

1. Alpha-numeric keyboard   3. Disk drive(s)
2. Display screen   4. Numeric keypad

Often a printer is attached to the computer so that a "hard" or printed copy of stored information or documents can be made.

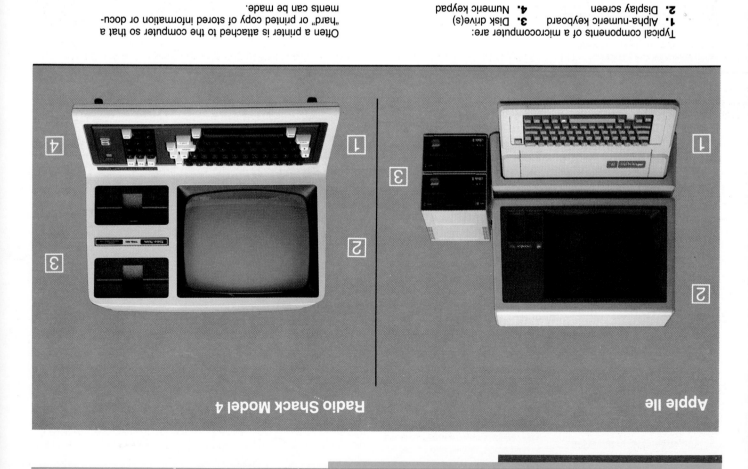

Apple IIe

Radio Shack Model 4

GET READY TO KEYBOARD

Operators of computers should learn from the Operator's Manual for specific machines how to power up the equipment and how to set margins and spacing. The procedures vary from brand to brand.

The procedures for making machine adjustments and getting ready to keyboard given here are primarily for the use of operators of typewriters.

1 Adjust paper guide

Move **paper guide (12)** left or right so that it lines up with 0 (zero) on the **paper guide scale (13)** or the **line-of-writing** or **margin scale (27)**.

2 Insert paper

Take a sheet of paper in your left hand and follow the directions and illustrations below.

1. Pull **paper bail (15)** forward (or up on some machines).

2. Place paper against **paper guide (12)**, behind the **platen (21)**.

3. Turn paper into machine, using **right platen knob (25)** or **index key (30)**.

4. Stop when paper is about 1½ inches above **aligning scale (26)**.

5. If paper is not straight, pull **paper release lever (23)** forward.

6. Straighten paper, then push paper release lever back.

7. Push paper bail back so that it holds paper against platen.

8. Slide **paper bail rolls (14/19)** into position, dividing paper into fourths.

3 Set line-space selector

Many machines offer 3 choices for line spacing -- 1, 1½, and 2 indicated by bars or numbers on the **line-space selector (22)**.

Set the line-space selector on (–) or 1 to single-space (SS) or on (=) or 2 to double-space (DS) as directed for lines in Phase 1. To quadruple-space, set line-space selector on (=) or 2 to double-space, then operate return twice.

```
1  Lines 1 and 2 are single-spaced (SS).
2  A double space (DS) separates lines 2 and 4.
3                 1 blank line space
4  A triple space (TS) separates lines 4 and 7.
5
6                 2 blank line spaces
7  Set the selector on "1" for single spacing.
```

4 Plan margin settings

A machine may have pica type (10-pitch type -- 10 spaces to a horizontal inch) or may have elite type (12-pitch type -- 12 spaces to a horizontal inch).

Machines have at least one **line-of-writing scale (27)** that reads from 0 to *at least* 110 for machines with *elite* type, from 0 to *at least* 90 for machines with *pica* type.

When 8½- by 11-inch paper is inserted into the machine (short side at top) with left edge of paper at 0 on the line-of-writing scale, the exact center point is 51 for elite, 42½ for pica machines. Use 51 for elite center, 42 for pica center.

To center typed lines, set left and right margin stops the same number of spaces left and right from center point. Diagrams at the right show margin settings for 50-, 60-, and 70-space lines. When you begin to use the warning bell, 5 or 6 spaces may be added to the right margin.

Set left margin stop for a 50-space line for each lesson in Phase 1; set right margin stop at right end of line-of-writing scale.

Elite center

Pica center

Pica, 10 per inch.
Elite, 12 per inch.

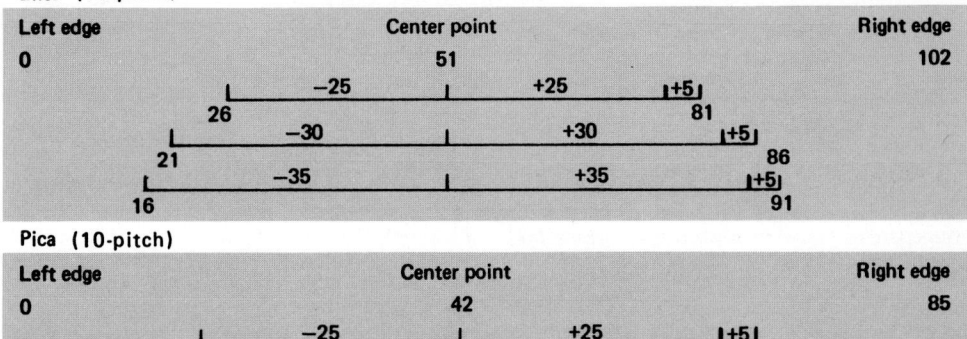
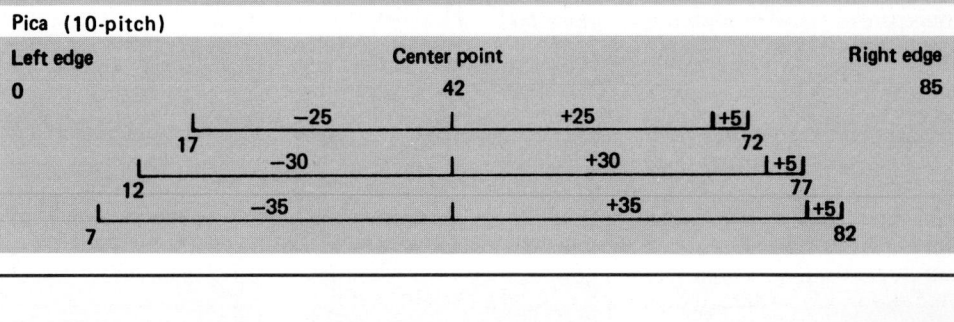

5 Set margin stops

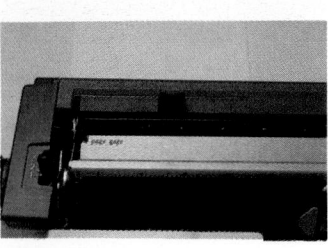

Type A
Push-button set

Adler, Olympia, Remington, Royal, and Smith-Corona manuals

1. Press down on the left margin set button.

2. Slide it to desired position on the line-of-writing (margin) scale.

3. Release the margin set button.

4. Using the right margin set button, set the right margin stop in the same way.

Type B
Push-lever set

Single element typewriters, such as Adler, Olivetti, Remington Rand, Royal, Selectric

1. Push in on the left margin set lever.

2. Slide it to desired position on the line-of-writing (margin) scale.

3. Release the margin set lever.

4. Using the right margin set lever, set the right margin stop in the same way.

Type C
Key set

IBM typebar, Olivetti electric

1. Move carriage to the left margin stop by depressing the return key.

2. Depress and hold down the margin set (IBM reset) key as you move carriage to desired left margin stop position.

3. Release the margin set (IBM reset) key.

4. Move carriage to the right margin stop.

5. Depress and hold down the margin set (IBM reset) key as you move carriage to desired right margin stop position.

6. Release the margin set (IBM reset) key.

Type D
Electronic set

To set margins on some electronic machines, such as Xerox and Silver-Reed, space to the desired margin position and strike the appropriate (left or right) margin key.

On other machines, such as some models of IBM, space to the desired margin position and strike the CODE key and the appropriate (left or right) margin key *at the same time.*

> General information for setting margin stops is given here. If you have the manufacturer's booklet for your typewriter, however, use it; the procedure for your particular model may be slightly different.

GLOSSARY

Defined below are some special terms you may encounter as you complete the activities in this textbook on a typewriter, computer, or word processor. These are terms you need to learn as you prepare yourself for the world of tomorrow.

ACCURACY degree of freedom from errors (mistakes) measured from zero -- usually expressed as 1 error, 2 errors, etc.; sometimes as *errors a minute (eam)* or *percent of error*.

BACKSPACE to move printing or enter point (element, daisy wheel, or cursor) to the left one space at a time by striking the backspace or *back arrow* key once for each character or space.

CPU (central processing unit) the internal operating unit or "brains" of an electronic computer system; *also* "the little black box."

CRT (cathode-ray tube) *see* VDT.

CONTROL the power to cause the hands and fingers to make correct motions; *also* the ability to hold keystroking speed down so that errors (mistakes) are kept to an expected or acceptable number.

CONTROL KEY (CTRL) a special key that is pressed at the same time another key is struck, causing that key to perform a special function.

CURSOR a dot, line, or square of light that shows the point on a display screen where the next letter, number, symbol, or space can be entered.

DAISY WHEEL a printing wheel shaped like a daisy used on some typewriters and printers.

DELETE to remove from text a segment of copy (a character, a word, a phrase, a line, a sentence, a page).

DISK (DISKETTE) DRIVE the unit into which a diskette is inserted to be read or written by the CPU (central processing unit).

DISKETTE (DISK) a magnetic, Mylar-coated record-like disk (encased in a square protective envelope) used for recording, reading, and writing by the CPU (central processing unit).

DISPLAY SCREEN *see* VDT.

DOUBLE-SPACE (DS) to use vertical line spacing which leaves one blank line space between displayed or printed lines of text (copy).

EDIT to rearrange, change, and correct existing text; editing includes proofreading but is not limited to it.

ELEMENT a ball-shaped printing device on many electric and electronic typewriters.

ENTER to input keystrokes; *see* KEY.

ENTER KEY *see* RETURN KEY.

ERROR any misstroke of a key; *also* any variation between source copy and displayed or printed copy; departure from acceptable format (arrangement, placement, and spacing).

ESCAPE KEY (ESC) a key on some computers which lets the user leave one segment of a program and go to another.

FORMAT the style (arrangement, placement, and spacing) of a document.

FORMATTING the process of arranging a document in proper form.

FUNCTION KEYS special keys on typewriters, computers, and word processors that when used alone or in combination with other keys perform special functions such as setting margins, centering copy, and so on.

GLOBAL SEARCH AND REPLACE to direct a computer or word processor to find a repeated series of characters and replace it with a different series of characters automatically throughout a document (for example, find and replace Co. with Company).

GWAM (gross words a minute) a measure of the rate of keyboarding speed; GWAM = total standard 5-stroke words keyed divided by the time required to key or type those words.

HARDWARE the physical equipment that makes up a computer or word processing system.

INDENT to set in from the margin, as the first line of a paragraph.

INFORMATION PROCESSING the job of putting text and data into usable form (documents).

INPUT text and data that enter an information system; the process of entering text and data.

INSERT (INSERTION) new text that is added to existing text; *also* the process of adding new text to existing text.

KEY to strike keys to record or display text and data; *also called* enter, key in, keyboard, input, and type.

Circuit board (including the CPU)

Cursor

Daisy wheel

Disk drive and diskette

GLOSSARY, continued

KEYBOARD an arrangement of keys on a "board" that is attached to or apart from a machine such as a typewriter, computer, or word processor; *also the act of keyboard-ing or typing.*

MEMORY storage location in a computer, word processor, or electronic typewriter.

MENU a list of options from which a key-board operator may (or must) choose when using a word or data processing machine.

MERGE to assemble new documents from stored text such as to form paragraphs; to combine stored text such as a form letter with newly keyboarded text (names, addresses, inserts).

MICROCOMPUTER a small-sized computer with a keyboard, screen, and auxiliary storage; its central processor is usually a single CPU chip; *also* "computer on a chip."

MONITOR *see* VDT.

MOVE to reposition a heading or text up or down the video screen; when a block of copy (paragraph) is moved, it is a "block move."

OUTPUT useful information that leaves an information system, usually presented to the user as a screen display or a printout.

PRINT to produce, using a printer, a paper copy of information displayed on a screen or stored in computer or word processor memory.

PRINTER a unit attached to a computer or a word processor that produces on paper.

PRINTOUT the printed paper output of a computer, word processor, or electronic typewriter.

PROMPT a message displayed in the window of an electronic typewriter or on the screen of a computer or word processor telling the user that the machine is awaiting a specific response.

PROOFREAD to read copy on a display screen or on a printout against the original or source copy and to correct errors (or mark them for correction); *also* one of the steps in editing text.

QUADRUPLE-SPACE (QS) to use vertical line spacing which leaves 3 blank line spaces between displayed or printed lines of text (copy); equals 4 single spaces, 2 double spaces.

RATE the speed of doing a task, as key-boarding or *typing rate* -- usually expressed in words a minute or lines per hour.

RETRIEVE to make stored information available when needed.

RETURN to strike the RETURN or ENTER key to cause the cursor (or enter point) to move to the left margin and down to the next line.

RETURN KEY a key that when struck causes the cursor (or enter point) to move to the left margin and down to the next line; *also* ENTER KEY.

SEARCH to locate an editing or correcting point within a document by matching a series of characters or words.

SHIFT KEY a key used to make capital letters and certain symbols when struck at the same time as another key.

SHIFT LOCK (CAPS Lock) a key that when depressed causes all letters to be capitalized (ALL-CAPPED).

SINGLE-SPACE (SS) to use vertical line spacing which leaves no blank space between printed or displayed lines of text.

SOFTWARE instructions, or programs, that tell a computer or word processor what to do.

SOURCE DOCUMENTS forms on which raw text or data are written and from which a machine operator keys and formats.

SPACE BAR a long bar at the bottom of a keyboard used to move the cursor (enter point) to the right one space at a time.

STORE to save information on magnetic media so that it may be used later.

TAB KEY a key that when struck causes the cursor (enter point) to skip to a preset position, as in indenting paragraphs.

TECHNIQUE the degree of expertness with which a task is performed; *also* good form, style.

TEXT (DATA) ENTRY the process of getting text and data from the writer's mind or from a written or voice-recorded document into the computer or word processing system.

VDT (video display terminal) a TV-like picture tube used to display text, data, and graphic images; *also called* CRT, display screen, and monitor.

WORD PROCESSING the writing and storing of letters, reports, and other documents on a computer, electronic typewriter, or word processor; may also include print-ing of the final document.

Video display terminal (VDT)

Computer printer

Microcomputer

Detached keyboard

PHASE 1

Learn Alphabetic Keyboarding Technique

A typewriter-like keyboard is the modern means of entering data, retrieving information, and communicating facts and ideas. To be a successful participant in the business and professional world of today and tomorrow, you must be able to use a keyboard -- on a typewriter, on a computer, and on a word processor or text-editor.

The letter keyboards on these kinds of machines are quite similar. Therefore, if you learn to operate the keyboard on one kind of machine, you can readily transfer your skill to other keyboarding machines.

Your goal during the next few weeks is to learn to operate a letter keyboard with good technique and reasonable speed.

The 25 lessons of Phase 1 are designed to help you learn:

1. To adjust your machine for correct margins and spacing.

2. To operate the letter keyboard by touch (without looking).

3. To use the basic parts of your machine with skill: space bar, shift keys, the return, and the tabulator.

4. To key words, sentences, and paragraphs without time-wasting pauses and with good keyboarding technique.

5. To apply capitalization guides correctly as you key.

all letters used | A | 1.5 si | 5.7 awl | 80% hfw

gwam 3' | 5'

	4		8		12			

A perfect employee is hard to describe, but most people would agree — 4 | 3 | 67

that one necessary quality for an excellent employee to possess is a good — 9 | 6 | 70

attitude. With a positive attitude, one can attain heights that would — 14 | 8 | 73

not be possible to attain otherwise. On the other hand, a bad attitude — 19 | 11 | 75

will certainly keep a person from reaching goals that are important for — 24 | 14 | 78

success and for the company. — 26 | 15 | 79

A positive work attitude may be exhibited in many ways. One way — 30 | 18 | 82

is through enthusiasm for the job. Employees with positive attitudes — 35 | 21 | 85

believe their jobs are very critical to the success of the company and — 39 | 24 | 88

try to do a good job. They are eager to learn and utilize a new con- — 44 | 26 | 90

cept in order to improve their job performance and make them a more — 48 | 29 | 93

valuable asset to the company. They are always cooperative. — 52 | 31 | 96

Other good work attitudes include the desire to be a productive — 57 | 34 | 98

team member and the willingness to accept criticism in order to improve — 62 | 37 | 101

job performance. An employee is only one part of the entire firm, but — 66 | 40 | 104

a very important part when it comes to the accomplishment of a firm's — 71 | 43 | 107

goals. A good employee has a very cheerful and pleasant attitude to- — 76 | 45 | 109

ward the job and other workers of the company. — 79 | 47 | 111

Another major element of a good attitude is the ability to inte- — 83 | 50 | 114

grate good human relation skills into all aspects of a job. In its — 87 | 52 | 117

simplest form, human relations means dealing with other people the way — 92 | 55 | 119

that you would like to be dealt with if the situation were to be re- — 97 | 58 | 122

versed. Very often good human relation skills provide the channel — 101 | 61 | 125

through which goals are reached. Employees with these attitudes are — 105 | 63 | 128

in high demand. — 107 | 64 | 128

gwam 3'	1	2	3	4	5
5'	1		2		3

Learning Goals

1. To learn to operate letter keys and punctuation by touch.

2. To learn to operate basic service keys (space bar, shift keys, return, shift lock, and tab key) by touch.

3. To build correct techniques.

4. To learn to type (key) sentences and paragraphs with good technique and speed.

Machine Adjustments

1. Paper guide at *0*.

2. Ribbon control to use top half of ribbon.

3. Margin sets: left margin (center - 25); right margin (move to right end of scale).

4. Line-space selector set to single-space (SS) drills.

5. Line-space selector set to double-space (DS) paragraphs.

Lesson 1	Home Keys (ASDF JKL;)	Line length: 50 spaces Spacing: single-space (SS)

1a ▶
Get Ready to Keyboard

1. Arrange your work area as illustrated at the right:

● front frame of machine even with front edge of desk

● book at right of machine, top raised for easy reading

● paper, if needed, at left of machine

● unneeded books and other materials stored or placed out of the way

2. Get to know your machine by studying pages vi-viii.

3. Make needed machine adjustments and insert paper (if necessary) as directed on pages ix-x.

4. Take keyboarding position as illustrated at the right:

● fingers curved and upright

● wrists low, but not touching frame of machine

● forearms parallel to slant of keyboard

● sit back in chair; body erect

● feet on floor for balance

Position at computer

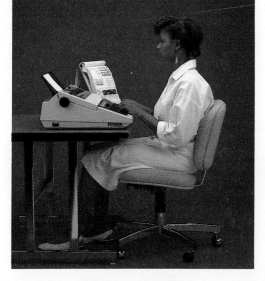

Position at typewriter

Improve Keyboarding Skill:
Guided Writing 3

all letters used | A | 1.5 si | 5.7 awl | 80% hfw

gwam 3' | | 5'

People who are successful utilize their time; those who are not, | 4 | 3 | 67

let their time utilize them. Maybe you have heard people talk about | 9 | 5 | 69

time management. They are talking about the wise use of time in order | 14 | 8 | 72

to achieve professional and personal goals that are desirable. By | 18 | 11 | 75

considering a few of the suggestions listed in the next few paragraphs, | 23 | 14 | 78

you, too, can become a wise manager of your time. | 28 | 16 | 80

Procrastination is one of the key enemies of time. Socializing with | 31 | 18 | 83

friends, postponing the unpleasant, dreaming during the day, and watching | 36 | 21 | 86

television are all forms of procrastination. Being aware of how you | 40 | 24 | 88

currently use your time can assist you in making better use of your time | 45 | 27 | 91

in the future. During the next few days, mentally take inventory of how | 50 | 30 | 94

you use your time and how you could make wiser use of it. | 54 | 32 | 96

If you want to be an effective time manager, you will determine | 58 | 35 | 99

what it is that you really desire or need to accomplish by setting | 63 | 38 | 102

goals. These goals should be formalized in writing so that you can | 67 | 40 | 104

evaluate your progress towards these goals periodically. Once you have | 72 | 43 | 107

listed your goals, the next step is to prioritize the goals in the order | 77 | 46 | 110

that you believe they need to be accomplished. | 80 | 48 | 112

Once the priority of goals to be accomplished has been outlined, | 84 | 50 | 115

you should analyze each individual goal to determine the sequence of | 89 | 53 | 117

steps necessary to assure successful completion of the goal. After you | 94 | 56 | 120

have listed each individual step, you should put a date by it to show | 98 | 60 | 123

when it needs to be completed in order to accomplish the goal on time. | 103 | 62 | 126

Try to meet each deadline you have outlined for yourself. | 107 | 64 | 128

gwam 3' | 1 | 2 | 3 | 4 | 5
5' | 1 | 2 | 3

Enrichment Timed Writings

1b ▶
Place Your Fingers in Home-Key Position

1. Locate on the chart **a s d f** (home keys for left hand) and **j k l ;** (home keys for right hand).

2. Locate the home keys on your keyboard. Place fingers of your left hand on **a s d f** and of your right hand on **j k l ;** *with your fingers well curved and upright (not slanting).*

3. Remove your fingers from the keyboard; then place them in home-key position again, curving and holding them *lightly* on the keys.

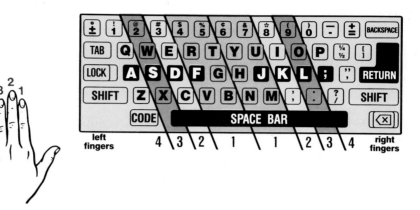

1c ▶
Learn How to Strike Home Keys

1. Study the keystroking illustrations at the right.

2. Place your fingers in home-key position as directed above.

3. Strike each of the following keys once:

fdsajkl;

Strike the key with a quick, sharp finger stroke; snap the finger slightly toward the palm of the hand as the keystroke is made.

If you are using an electric or electronic machine, strike each key with a light tap with the tip of the finger; otherwise, keystroking technique is the same as for a manual typewriter.

1d ▶
Learn How to Return at Line Endings

To return the printing point of a typewriter or the cursor of a computer to the left margin and move down to the next line:

● strike return key (31) on electric and electronic typewriters
● strike RETURN or ENTER key on computers
● operate return lever on manual typewriters

Study the illustrations at the right; and **return** 3 times (triple-space) below the line you completed in 1c above.

Electric typewriter return
Reach with the little finger of the right hand to the return key, tap the key, and return the finger quickly to its typing position.

Microcomputer return
Reach with the little finger of the right hand to the RETURN or ENTER key, tap the key, and return the finger quickly to home-key position.

Manual typewriter return
Move left hand, fingers braced, to return lever; return carriage with quick inward flick-of-the-hand motion. Drop hand quickly to typing position; do not let it follow the carriage across.

1e ▶
Learn How to Space Between Letters

1. Study the spacing illustrations at the right.

2. As you type (key) the following letters, strike the space bar once after each letter:

f d s a j k l ;

Strike the space bar with the right thumb; use a quick down-and-in motion (toward palm). Avoid pauses before or after spacing.

Improve Keyboarding Skill:
Guided Writing 2

all letters used | A | 1.5 si | 5.7 awl | 80% hfw

The use of the computer is becoming very universal. It is next to ... 4 | 3 | 64

impossible to make it through the day without being directly or indi- ... 9 | 5 | 67

rectly affected by some aspect of the computer. The computer will play ... 14 | 8 | 70

an even greater part in your life in future years. This is due in large ... 19 | 11 | 73

part to the fact that with each passing year the computer is becoming ... 23 | 14 | 75

less expensive, has more applications, and is more user friendly. ... 28 | 17 | 78

If you wrote a check or cashed a check today, the computer would ... 32 | 19 | 80

be involved in the processing of that check. A bank can utilize the ... 37 | 22 | 83

computer in many ways. Banks may use it to process bank statements, to ... 41 | 25 | 85

figure interest, to determine mortgage rates, or to figure annuities. ... 46 | 28 | 89

A bank may also use an automatic teller machine to replace the human ... 51 | 30 | 92

teller that it now employs. ... 53 | 32 | 93

The computer is now a part of the field of medicine. Medical cen- ... 57 | 34 | 95

ters are making use of the computer to aid in the handling of their ... 61 | 37 | 98

patient files, to find out if a body part is available for transplant, ... 66 | 40 | 101

and for medical inquiry. A doctor can use an imaging system for patient ... 71 | 43 | 104

diagnosis. The computer is also given partial credit for the longer ... 76 | 45 | 107

life expectancy of people. ... 77 | 46 | 108

The office is another place that is being changed by the computer. ... 82 | 49 | 110

New data entry units, ink-jet printers, and shared logic systems are all ... 87 | 52 | 113

a part of this change. Through electronic creation, storage, and re- ... 91 | 55 | 116

trieval of data, the office of today has been able to assist the execu- ... 96 | 58 | 119

tive in the decision-making process at a pace that was not possible for ... 101 | 61 | 122

prior office help. ... 102 | 61 | 123

gwam 3' | 1 | 2 | 3 | 4 | 5
5' | 1 | 2 | 3

1f ▶
Practice
Home-Key Letters

1. Place your hands in home-key position (left fingers on **asdf** and right fingers on **jkl;**).

2. Type (key) the lines as shown: single-spaced (SS) with a double space (DS) between pairs of lines.

Do not type (key) the line numbers.

Spacing hint
With the **line-space selector (22)** set for single spacing, return twice at the end of the line to double-space.

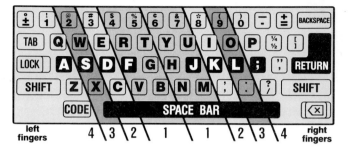

left fingers   4 \3 \2 \ 1   1 \ 2 \3 \4   right fingers

Fingers curved and upright

Strike space bar once to space

```
1  f ff j jj d dd k kk s ss l ll a aa ; ;; fdsa jkl;
2  f ff j jj d dd k kk s ss l ll a aa ; ;; fdsa jkl;
                                                    DS
3  a aa ; ;; s ss l ll d dd k kk f ff j jj fjdk sla;
4  a aa ; ;; s ss l ll d dd k kk f ff j jj fjdk sla;
                                                    DS
5  a;a sls dkd fjf ;a; lsl kdk jfj asdf jkl; a;sl fj
6  a;a sls dkd fjf ;a; lsl kdk jfj asdf jkl; a;sl fj
                                    Return 3 times to triple-space (TS)
```

1g ▶
Type (Key) Letters, Words, and Phrases

Type (key) the lines as shown; return twice to double-space (DS) between lines. If time permits, repeat the drill.

Down-and-in spacing motion

```
1  f f ff j j jj d d dd k k kk s s ss l l ll a a aa;
                                    Return twice to double-space (DS)
2  fj dk sl a; jf kd ls ;a ds kl df kj sd lk sa ;l j
                                                    DS
3  sa as ld dl af fa ls sl fl lf al la ja aj sk ks a
                                                    DS
4  a a as as ad ad ask ask lad lad fad fad jak jak j
                                                    DS
5  all all fad fad jak jak add add ask ask ads ads a
                                                    DS
6  a jak; as all; ask dad; all ads; ask all; a lass;
                           At end of drill, return 3 times to triple-space (TS)
```

1h ▶ End of Lesson: Typewriter

1. Raise **paper bail (15)** or pull it toward you. Pull **paper release lever (23)** toward you.

2. Remove paper with your left hand. Push paper release lever back to its normal position.

3. On movable carriage typewriters, depress **right carriage release;** hold **right platen knob (25)** firmly and center the carriage.

4. Turn electric-powered machines OFF.

The paragraphs on pages 281-284 may be used as 1- and 3-minute writings for building keyboarding speed and accuracy. They may also be used for 5-minute writings to measure the skill you have developed.

Each writing includes at least one use of every letter of the alphabet. Each paragraph is of average difficulty in terms of syllable intensity, average word length, and percent of high frequency words.

Improve Keyboarding Skill: Guided Writing 1

The timed writings are counted with superior dots and figures so that each paragraph can be used for 1-minute guided writings. Use the table below to note the quarter-minute checkpoints for your goal speed.

The same superior word count can be used for 1-minute unguided timed writings on each paragraph.

The word counts at the right of the writings can be used to find *gwam* on 3- and 5-minute writings on the three paragraphs combined.

Quarter-Minute Checkpoints

gwam	1/4'	1/2'	3/4'	1'
32	8	16	24	32
36	9	18	27	36
40	10	20	31	40
44	11	22	33	44
48	12	24	36	48
52	13	26	39	52
56	14	28	42	56
60	15	30	45	60
64	16	32	48	64
68	17	34	51	68
72	18	36	54	72
76	19	38	57	76
80	20	40	60	80

all letters used | A | 1.5 si | 5.7 awl | 80% hfw

	gwam 3'	5'

Our news media and editorial writers have made this idea well known: | 5 | 3 | 47 |

A high school education is not only important -- it is almost essential. | 9 | 6 | 50 |

Most jobs now go to those men and women with the skills needed to run our | 14 | 9 | 53 |

electronic world of today, skills that almost always must be acquired in | 19 | 12 | 55 |

high school or college. Jobs for the unskilled dropout are dying out. | 24 | 14 | 58 |

Very few persons are in the position of not having to earn a living | 29 | 17 | 61 |

for themselves and their families. Moreover, many men and women who have | 34 | 20 | 64 |

enough sources of income prefer to engage in a job of some kind. Your | 38 | 23 | 67 |

primary goal, therefore, should be to learn the skills necessary for a | 43 | 26 | 70 |

career that you would find both pleasant and profitable. | 47 | 28 | 72 |

We need to emphasize the merit of making our next goal that of | 51 | 31 | 75 |

learning how to be complete and fulfilled as a person. Students who | 56 | 33 | 77 |

make a concentrated effort can, by wisely and sensibly using their time, | 60 | 36 | 80 |

take not only technical classes but courses that will help them to think, | 65 | 39 | 83 |

reason, inquire, evaluate, and enjoy. Indeed, not only their business | 70 | 42 | 86 |

life but also their social life can be enriched. | 73 | 44 | 88 |

gwam 3' | 1 | 2 | 3 | 4 | 5 |
5' | 1 | 2 | 3 |

R1a ▶
Get Ready to Keyboard

1. Arrange your work area (see page 2).

2. Get to know your machine (see pages vi-viii).

3. Make needed machine adjustments and insert paper if necessary (see pages ix-x).

4. Take keyboarding position (see page 2).

Margin settings for a 50-space line (paper guide at *0*):

pica, 42 − 25 = 17
elite, 51 − 25 = 26

Move right margin stop to the right end of the margin scale.

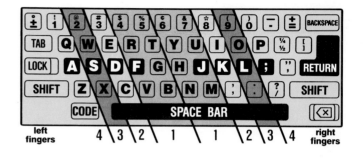

left fingers   4   3   2   1   1   2   3   4   right fingers

R1b ▶ Review Keystroking, Spacing, and Return Technique

Keystroke
Curve fingers of your left hand and place them over **a s d f** keys. Curve fingers of your right hand and place them over **j k l ;** keys. Strike each key with a quick-snap stroke; release key quickly.

Space
To space after letters, words, and punctuation marks, strike the space bar with a quick down-and-in motion of the right thumb. Do not pause before or after spacing stroke.

Typewriter return
Electric: Reach the little finger to RETURN key, strike the key, and release it quickly.

Manual: Reach to lever and return the carriage with a quick flick-of-the-hand motion.

Microcomputer return
Reach the little finger of the right hand to RETURN or ENTER key, strike the key, and release it quickly.

Type (key) the lines once as shown. Do not type the line numbers.

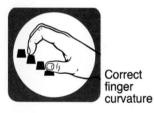

Correct finger curvature

Space once

1 ff jj ff jj aa ;; aa ;; dd kk dd kk ss ll ss ll a;
2 ff jj ff jj aa ;; aa ;; dd kk dd kk ss ll ss ll a;
                  Return twice to double-space (DS)

3 a aa ; ;; s ss l ll d dd k kk f ff j jj fj dk sl a
4 a aa ; ;; s ss l ll d dd k kk f ff j jj fj dk sl a
                  DS

5 f j fj d k dk s l sl a ; a; fj dk sl a; fj dk sl a
6 f j fj d k dk s l sl a ; a; fj dk sl a; fj dk sl a
           Return 3 times to triple-space (TS)

R1c ▶
Improve Home-Key Stroking

Type (key) the lines once as shown.

Goals
- curved, upright fingers
- quick-snap keystrokes
- down-and-in spacing

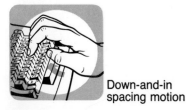

Down-and-in spacing motion

1 fj fj dk dk sl sl a; a; jf jf kd kd ls ls ;a ;a fj
2 fj fj dk dk sl sl a; a; jf jf kd kd ls ls ;a ;a fj
                Return twice to double-space (DS)

3 a al ak aj s sl sk sj d dl dk dj f fl fk fj a; fj;
4 a al ak aj s sl sk sj d dl dk dj f fl fk fj a; fj;
                DS

5 j ja js jd jf k ka ks kd kf l la ls ld lf a; fj a;
6 j ja js jd jf k ka ks kd kf l la ls ld lf a; fj a;
                DS

7 fdsa jkl; asdf ;lkj a;sldkfj fjdksla; fdsa jkl; a;
8 fdsa jkl; asdf ;lkj a;sldkfj fjdksla; fdsa jkl; a;
              Return 3 times to triple-space (TS)

Letter-Combination Drills

Drill 1
Adjacent-Key Reaches

Lines 1-14 twice (slowly, then faster); next, three 1-minute writings on line 15 and line 16 to increase speed. Find *gwam* on each writing.

Adjacent-key reaches (curved, upright fingers)

a/s	1	as say base aspen savor master assign aspirin samples measure asterisk
	2	same aspect|as assembled|biased reason|easy assignment|safe assumption
e/w	3	ewe weak crew were fewer weird western answers welcome steward wealthy
	4	few|wed|weight lifter|we went|the wealth|the weekly news|their welfare
e/r	5	are error there query green really removes certain listener procedures
	6	power mower|either letter|three reasons|offered credit|newer recording
i/o	7	coin boil union spoil motion loiter serious station location questions
	8	superior voice|senior division|additional noise|questionable operation
i/u	9	suit quit build guide liquid equity helium inquired fruitful ingenuity
	10	ruined equipment|quickly acquired|required quizzes|quite distinguished
l/k	11	walk silk polka chalk sickly pickles chuckle Oakland Oklahoma folklore
	12	ankle tackle|belt buckles|bulky milkman|walkie-talkies|talking quickly
o/p	13	poor opera drops proper oppose optimum important impossible optimistic
	14	open optimism|opposite opinion|important apologies|improper opposition
sentences	15	We stopped asking the questions and quietly assisted the poor teacher.
	16	As sad as it may be, we were open for suit when he stated his opinion.

| 1 | 2 | 3 | 4 | 5 | 6 | 7 | 8 | 9 | 10 | 11 | 12 | 13 | 14 |

Long direct reaches (quiet hands)

Drill 2
Long Direct Reaches

Lines 17-30 twice (slowly, then faster); next, three 1-minute writings on line 31 and line 32 to increase speed. Find *gwam* on each writing.

Follow-up Practice

If your *gwam* on lines 15 and 16 or on lines 31 and 32 is more than 2 or 3 *gwam* below your usual 1-minute *gwam*, practice the drills again.

b/t	17	debt doubt obtuse obtund obtain debtor subtract obtrusive subterranean
	18	doubting debtor|obtrusive debts|subtle subterfuge|subterranean redoubt
m/u	19	muse number lumber muffin umpired rummage umbrella cucumbers emulation
	20	humility|the umbrella|mutually humored|emulate the muse|mull the music
m/y	21	my hymn myth foamy balmy myself hymnal symphony mysterious symptomatic
	22	myself|their myths|my mystique|mainly mythical|mysterious but symbolic
n/u	23	sun nut fun numb gunny funny nugget nuzzle number hundreds unpopulated
	24	under the gun|fun in the sun|a number of nuggets|unprecedented numbers
n/y	25	any many tiny lynx rainy sunny penny nylon synod synagogue synchronize
	26	many lynx|tiny bunny|any syncopation|sunny synagogues|synthetic nylons
r/b	27	curb brow herb verb blurb brain brush brass adverbs embraced brunettes
	28	brown bread|brass broiler|brimmed derby|brief embraces|bronze bracelet
r/v	29	larva curve nerve swerve marvel survey carved service vervain survival
	30	a subservient|swerve a curve|serve hors d'oeuvre|marvelous surveillance
sentences	31	Under an umbrella, Harvey nuzzled up to the brunette who embraced him.
	32	Since the sun was bright, the umpire did not notice the runner swerve.

| 1 | 2 | 3 | 4 | 5 | 6 | 7 | 8 | 9 | 10 | 11 | 12 | 13 | 14 |

Skill-Enrichment Drills

R1d ▶
Type (Key)
Home-Key Words

each line twice single-spaced (SS); DS between 2-line groups

Goals

- space quickly between letters and words
- return without spacing at line endings
- begin the new line quickly after return

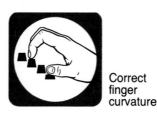
Correct finger curvature

Correct finger alignment

```
1 l la lad j ja jak f fa fad s sa sad f fa fall fall
                                        Return twice to DS
2 a a as as ask ask a a ad ad lad lad all all ad ads
                                        DS
3 a a ad ad as as lad lad all all ask ask fall falls
                                        DS
4 as as jak jak ads ads lass lass fall fall add adds
                                        DS
5 ad ad fad fad jak jak all all fall fall as as asks
                                        DS
6 a as ask asks a ad lad lads a ad add adds all fall
                                        Return 3 times to TS
```

R1e ▶
Type (Key)
Home-Key Phrases

each line twice single-spaced (SS); DS between 2-line groups

Goals

- curved, upright fingers
- eyes on copy in book
- quick-snap keystrokes
- steady pace

Space with right thumb

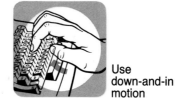
Use down-and-in motion

```
1 a jak; a jak; ask dad; ask dad; as all; as all ads
                                        Return twice to DS
2 a fad; a fad; as a lad; as a lad; all ads; all ads
                                        DS
3 as a fad; as a fad; a sad lass; a sad lass; a fall
                                        DS
4 ask a lad; ask a lad; all jaks fall; all jaks fall
                                        DS
5 a sad fall; a sad fall; all fall ads; all fall ads
                                        DS
6 add a jak; a lad asks a lass; as a jak ad all fall
                                        Return 3 times to TS
```

R1f ▶ End of Lesson: Typewriter

1. Raise **paper bail (15)** or pull it toward you. Pull **paper release lever (23)** toward you.

2. Remove paper with your left hand. Push paper release lever back to its normal position.

3. On movable carriage typewriters, depress **right carriage release**; hold **right platen knob (25)** firmly and center the carriage.

4. Turn electric-powered machines OFF.

Response-Pattern Drills

Drill 1
One-Hand Words

Lines 1-6 twice (slowly, then faster); next, three 1-minute writings on line 5 and line 6 to increase speed. Find *gwam* on each writing.

One-hand words (stroke response)

words

1 my gaze look after dress estate awards minimum created opinion million
2 joy ink oil junk moon milk straw state drawer average address reserves

phrases

3 only you | fazed him | my opinion | you exceeded | after you see | bet a million
4 in effect | water polo | free access | in Honolulu | affected him | better water

sentences

5 Afterwards, Jill Edwards, in fact, referred to him as a great dresser.
6 After you saw him, Dave gave Kimmy a phony street address in Honolulu.

| 1 | 2 | 3 | 4 | 5 | 6 | 7 | 8 | 9 | 10 | 11 | 12 | 13 | 14 |

Drill 2
Balanced-Hand Words

Lines 7-12 twice (first, at an easy unhurried pace, then at top speed); next, three 1-minute writings on line 11 and line 12 to increase speed. Find *gwam* on each writing.

Balanced-hand words (word-recognition response)

words

7 man the may six make town when keys burn eight fight title girls forms
8 cycle eighty profit visitor penalty problem signals neighbor amendment

phrases

9 to do | the key | to blame | did rush | they may go | is a problem | make a profit
10 visit me | blame them | key element | make a wish | big penalty | their neighbor

sentences

11 Diane's neighbor also owns the land to the right of the field of corn.
12 The big problem with the fuel amendment is the title of the amendment.

| 1 | 2 | 3 | 4 | 5 | 6 | 7 | 8 | 9 | 10 | 11 | 12 | 13 | 14 |

Drill 3
Combination Words

Lines 13-18 twice (first, at an easy unhurried pace, then at a faster pace); next, three 1-minute writings on line 17 and line 18 to increase speed. Find *gwam* on each writing.

Combination of balanced- and one-hand words (variable rhythm)

words

13 box end bus junk milk aisle avert whale feasts access bushels federate
14 air tax gaze clay dear maps jumpy visit panels greater opinion element

phrases

15 may see | burlap bag | eighty feet | few bushels | greater than | on the edge of
16 dead end | they are | extra key | they gave | they only paid | for their opinion

sentences

17 Nancie was formal as she addressed the dreaded panels after the feast.
18 The only man awarded the extra six acres may look for reserves of oil.

| 1 | 2 | 3 | 4 | 5 | 6 | 7 | 8 | 9 | 10 | 11 | 12 | 13 | 14 |

Drill 4
Double-Letter Words

Lines 19-24 twice (first, at an easy unhurried pace, then at a faster pace); next, three 1-minute writings on line 23 and line 24 to increase speed. Find *gwam* on each writing.

Follow-up Practice

Practice several times the sentences on which you made less than your top *gwam*.

Double-letter words (uniform keystroking)

words

19 off jazz books apple muggy battle follow misspell occurred Mississippi
20 stuff calls dazzle pepper whittle business immortal Illinois innocence

phrases

21 less effort | poor beggar | good football | business office | efficient manner
22 better see | bigger room | needless error | between innings | crossword puzzle

sentences

23 Colleen took an excellent bookkeeping course at Jefferson High School.
24 The crisscross football patterns were called three times by Tennessee.

| 1 | 2 | 3 | 4 | 5 | 6 | 7 | 8 | 9 | 10 | 11 | 12 | 13 | 14 |

Read Before Beginning
Lesson 2

DO at the beginning of each practice session:

Arrange your work area as directed and illustrated on page 2. Keeping your work area clear of everything except your textbook, paper, and machine will make your practice more efficient and productive.

Adjust the paper guide (if the machine has one) so that it lines up with 0 (zero) on the paper-bail scale or the line-of-writing or margin scale. Doing this will help you in setting margin stops. See page ix.

Adjust the ribbon control (if the machine has one) to use the top half of the ribbon. Ask your teacher to show you how.

Insert paper with short edge at top (long edge against the paper guide) unless your machine has a display screen. See page ix.

Set line-space selector (if your machine has one) to single-space (SS) your practice lines. Move lever opposite 1 or − for single spacing, opposite 2 or = for double spacing. See page ix.

Set margin stops for a 50-space line: left stop = center − 25; right stop at right end of the scale. Since pica center is 42, 25 left of center is 17. Since elite center is 51, 25 left of center is 26. See page x.

Standard Plan for Learning New Keys

All keys except the *home keys* (ASDF JKL;) require the fingers to reach in order to strike them. Follow these steps in learning the reach-stroke for each new key:

1. Find the new key on the keyboard chart given with the new key introduction.
2. *Look* at your own keyboard and find the new key on it.
3. Study the reach-technique drawing at the left of the practice lines for the new key. (See page 8 for illustrations.) Read the printed instructions in it.

4. Identify the finger to be used to strike the new key.
5. Curve your fingers; place them in home-key position (over ASDF JKL;).
6. *Watch* your finger as you reach it to the new key and back to home position a few times (keep it curved).
7. Practice twice SS each of the 3 lines at the right of the reach-technique drawing:
   slowly, to learn the new reach;
   faster, to get a quick-snap stroke.

Technique Emphasis During Practice

Of all the factors of proper position at the keyboard, the position of the hands and fingers is most important because they do the work.

Position the body in front of the keyboard so that you can place the fingers in a vertical (upright) position over the home keys with the fingertips just touching the face of the keys. Move your chair forward or backward or your elbows in or out a bit to place your fingers in this upright position. Do not let your fingers lean over onto one another toward the little fingers.

Curve the fingers so that there is about a 90-degree angle at the second joint of the index fingers. In this position, the fingers can make quick, direct reaches to the keys and snap toward the palm as reaches are completed. A quick-snap stroke is essential for proper keystroking.

Place the thumbs *lightly* on the space bar, the tip of the right thumb pointing toward the *n* key; tuck the tip of the left thumb slightly into the palm to keep it out of the way. Strike the space bar with a quick down-and-in motion of the right thumb.

Body properly positioned

Fingers properly upright

Fingers properly curved

Thumb properly positioned

SOUTH-WESTERN
PUBLISHING CO.

Enrichment Activities

The enrichment drills provided on pages 278-280 are designed to help you build additional keyboarding skill. The drills can be used to force speed, to improve technique patterns, and to build accuracy.

The drills may be used in a variety of ways. They may be used independently for untimed and self-timed practice, or they may be practiced under teacher guidance. Improved technique is the basis for improved speed and accuracy.

Skill-Enrichment Drills

Line length: 70 spaces
Spacing: single-space (SS)

Letter-Concentration Sentences

Each sentence emphasizes the reach to the letter key shown in color at the left.

Select from the sentences those that emphasize the letters on which you frequently make errors. Practice each selected line several times to regain control of the reaches and letter sequences.

The sentences may also be used to improve overall keyboarding skill. For this purpose, practice them in the order given (3 or 4 sentences daily). Key each one three times: first, slowly; next, at a faster pace; and, finally, at top speed.

a The manager was amazed that Alan had sold so many almanacs in January.
b Bob Benz was an unbelievable baseball player before becoming a barber.
c To acquire access to the accounting documents, contact our accountant.
d Do the outdated directions to the advertised land include the address?

e Here are the three gentlemen who desire to speak with the electrician.
f Jeff had won five fights before finishing off the fighter from France.
g The eight giggling girls playing games in the large gym ignored Gregg.
h He was happy to have the chance to exhibit his art at the high school.

i Cecilia, the girl with a big imagination, is from Illinois or Indiana.
j John Jones joined a judge in adjuring a jury to be objective and just.
k Karla and Erika kept Kevin's workbook and keys locked in their locker.
l Lloyd's landlord found him sleepwalking in the lane by the lilac bush.

m Mary's money was managed by a money management firm to maximize gains.
n On Monday evening, it rained more than one inch in less than one hour.
o A two-bedroom home on the north end of town is in very good condition.
p The pickup Paul helped Peter purchase happened to be in tip-top shape.

q To acquire qualification, Quinn quickly acquiesced to a required quiz.
r Our firm provides travel to and from the airport as part of the price.
s His Paris press secretary met with the class for six special sessions.
t Students who typed their tests on electronic typewriters did the best.

u You four guys can put the aluminum gutters around the ugly blue house.
v Vivian gave an overview of their investment in the vaudeville venture.
w Their wigwams were covered with snow from two weeks of winter weather.
x Tax experts expect next year's taxes to exceed the prior year's taxes.

y Your yearly toy and cycle sales may yield plenty of money for charity.
z Zachry Zeltze, a wizard with puzzles, zipped through the prize puzzle.

| 1 | 2 | 3 | 4 | 5 | 6 | 7 | 8 | 9 | 10 | 11 | 12 | 13 | 14 |

2a ▶
Get Ready to Keyboard

1. Arrange your work area as directed on page 7.

2. Make needed machine adjustments as directed on page 7.

3. Insert paper (if necessary) as directed on page 7.

Your teacher may guide you through the steps appropriate for your machine.

2b ▶
Review Home Keys

each line twice single-spaced (SS): once slowly; again, at a faster pace; double-space (DS) between 2-line groups

all keystrokes learned

1 al ks ja fl ds lk fa ll sk as sl da lf sa ff aj ss
2 ad ad as as jak jak fad fad all all fall fall lass
3 ask dad; ask dad; flak falls; flak falls; as a jak

Return 3 times to leave a triple space (TS) between lesson parts.

2c ▶ Learn E and H

For each key to be learned in this lesson and lessons that follow, use the Standard Plan for Learning New Keys given on page 7.

Study the plan now, relating each step to the illustrations and copy at right and below. Your teacher may guide you in these early lessons.

Reach technique for e

Reach technique for h

Do not attempt to type the color verticals separating word groups in Line 7.

Learn e

1 d e ed ed el el led led eel eel lee lee ed el de d
2 ed ed el el led led eel eel fed fed lee lee eke ed
3 a lake; a jade; a jade sale; a desk sale; as a fee

Return twice to double-space (DS) after you complete the set of 3 lines.

Learn h

4 j h hj hj ha ha ah ah had had has has hj hj ha had
5 hj hj ah ah ha ha has has had had ash ash had hash
6 ah ha; has had; had ash; has half; has had a flash

Combine e and h

7 he he he|she she she|shed shed|held held|heed heed
8 a shed; a lash; he held; has jade; she held a sash
9 she has jell; he held a jade; she had a shelf sale

Return 3 times to leave a triple space (TS) between lesson parts.

Job 14
Simplified Memo

Jack Rodriguez, Personnel Director, has prepared a memo restating McGee Enterprises' policy regarding employee use or possession of intoxicating beverages, drugs, or narcotics on company property. He is concerned about possible violation of this policy, so he wants all company personnel to receive a copy of the memo to remind them of the company policy. Provide an appropriate subject line and date the memo May 15.

(¶) McGee Enterprises has always had a policy forbidding use or possession of intoxicating beverages, drugs, or narcotics by employees on company property. There is some evidence that the company policy is being violated. As we have on occasion in the past, we want to make certain all employees, those presently employed as well as all new employees being hired, are aware of the consequences of violating this policy.

(¶) The company policy is very clear. "Reporting for work under the influence of intoxicating beverages, drugs, or narcotics, or the use or possession of intoxicating beverages, drugs, or narcotics on company property (including parking lots) at any time may be just cause for dismissal."

(¶) DON'T JEOPARDIZE YOUR JOB BY VIOLATING THIS POLICY!

Job 15
Simplified Memo

Mrs. Hilda Chou, Director of Industrial Relations, has prepared a memo which is to be attached to the ergonomics report (Job 5). The memo is to be addressed to all union officials and top management personnel. Provide an appropriate subject line and date the memo May 17.

(¶) In preparation for an upcoming meeting between union and management regarding various ergonomic issues, the attached report was compiled by the Personnel Department to provide you with some insights into the factors that will be discussed at the meeting.

(¶) I welcome your observations and comments.

Attachment

2d ▶
Improve Keyboarding Technique

each pair of lines twice SS (slowly, then faster); DS between 4-line groups; if time permits, retype the drill.

Do not attempt to type the line identifications, the line numbers, or the color verticals separating word groups.

> Space once after ; used as punctuation.

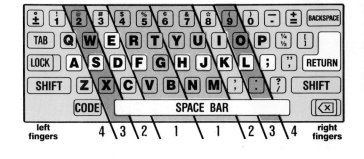

Fingers curved

Fingers upright

home row	1	lad lad|ask ask|jak jak|has has|all all|fall falls
	2	a lad; a lass; a jak; had all; all fall; has a jak
e	3	he he he|el el|led led|elf elf|self self|jell jell
	4	she led; he fell; she had; a jade ad; a desk shelf
all keys learned	5	she she|elf elf|all all|ask ask|led led|hall halls
	6	she had a flask; he had a jell sale; he asked half
all keys learned	7	he fell; a lad fell; she has a desk; he has a sled
	8	he asked a lass; she led all fall; he had a jak ad

Lesson 3   O and R

Line length: 50 spaces
Spacing: single-space (SS)

Time schedule

A time schedule for the parts of this lesson and lessons that follow is given as a guide for your minimum practice. The figure following the triangle in the lesson part heading indicates the number of minutes suggested for the activity. If time permits, however, retype selected lines from the various drills of the lessons.

3a ▶ 5
Get Ready to Keyboard
Follow the steps on page 7.

3b ▶ 7
Conditioning Practice
each line twice SS;
DS between 2-line groups

Goals

First time: Slow, easy pace, but strike and release each key quickly.

Second time: Faster pace; move from key to key quickly; keep element, carriage, or cursor moving steadily.

Technique hints

1. Keep fingers upright and well curved.

2. Try to make each key reach without moving hand or other fingers forward or downward.

home row	1	ah ah|jak jak|has has|lad lad|ask ask|all all|fad;
e/h	2	he he he|ah ah ah|el el el|she she she|elf elf elf
all keys learned	3	all ask; a jade sale; he had half; she has a lead;

Return 3 times to leave a triple space (TS) between lesson parts.

Ms. Beetle gives you a page from their keyboarding/formatting procedures manual that must be updated as indicated. The manual is bound on the left. Correct any unmarked errors you find.

line 6 [PAGE 43
<DS

(ALL CAP & center)

Travel Approval Request)
<QS *form*   *utilized*

A travel aproval request (Tar) is to be used when requesting
#
approval for any travel on company business, whether is is company
t
and reimbursed by the company
paid or paid by the individual. Any travel over 300 miles one way
.   ^
long distance
requires an out-of-state travel from completed and attached to the
follows:
tar form. A tar form should be ocmpleded as indicated below.
e

1. Date Prepared: Enter the data on which you prepared the form.
                               e

2. Traveler's Name: The name of the individual doing *the* traveling.
                                                      ^

3. Department: Name of the Department in which the traveler
works o (*example: Marketing*).

4. Destination: the name of the area (t) which the individual is
traveling o (*example: Philadelphia, PA*).

6. Estimated Cost s, *to include the following:*

--Public Transportation: Estimate the cost of travel if giong
by plane, train, bus, etc.

--Company car: If the individual is using a company car, just
                      CC
enter the initials ca.

--Personal car: If the individual is using her/his own car,
           number of   .225
estimate total miles to be travled and multiply by .025 cents.
Enter   *dg*
--Lodging: The cost of hotel per night. Loing costs are
         ^   ^
per person
limited to $50.00, plus tax, per night.
        price   *each* *per person*   *is*
--Meals: The allowance for meals while traveling are indicated
       ^   ^
as follows: (*including gratuity*)
                              8.00
Breakfast--$6.50
                              12.00
Lunch--$10.00
                              22.50
Dinner--$20.00

center each line, DS

SS each item, but DS above and below each item.

Indent items 4 spaces from left margin.

276   McGee Enterprises (An Information Processing Simulation)

3c ▶ 18 Learn O and R

each line twice SS (slowly, then faster); DS between 2-line groups; if time permits, key each line once more

Follow Standard Plan for Learning New Keys, page 7.

Goals
- curved, upright fingers
- finger-action keystrokes
- quick return, your eyes on textbook copy

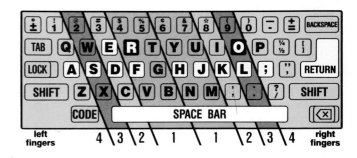

left fingers 4 \3 \2 \ 1 \ \ 1 \ 2 \3 \4 right fingers

Reach technique for o

Reach *up* with *right third* finger.

Reach technique for r

Reach *up* with *left first* finger.

Learn O ▼

1 l o ol ol lo lo so so of of do do old old foe foes
2 ol ol so so old old doe doe foe foe oak oak of off
3 do so; a doe; of old; of oak; old foe; of old oak;

Learn r ▼

4 f r rf rf fr fr jar jar her her ark ark lark larks
5 rf rf fr fr her her rah rah jar jar jerk jerk rake
6 a lark; a rake; a jerk; has a jar; had a jell jar;

Combine O and r

7 or or or|for for for|fork fork|door door|food food
8 a rod; a roll; a door; he rode; for her; he or she
9 for her; he has oak; she sold jade; she had a rose

Triple-space (TS) between lesson parts.

3d ▶ 20 Improve Keyboarding Technique

each pair of lines twice SS (slowly, then faster); DS between 4-line groups; if time permits, key selected lines again

Goals
- curved, upright fingers
- finger-action keystrokes
- down-and-in spacing
- quick return, your eyes on textbook copy

reach review

1 hj ed ol rf hj de lo fr hj ed ol rf jh de lo fr hj
2 ah ah el el or or he he she she for for hold holds

e/h

3 he he he|she she she|eel eel|elf elf|her her|shell
4 he had a sled; she has jak jell; she held a shell;

o/r

5 or or or|for for|rod rod|fork fork|rode rode|doors
6 for food; her fork; oak door; her doll; ash or oak

all keys learned

7 ask for; ask for her; sold a jar; has jak for sale
8 she had hash for food; so he asked her for a fork;

all keys learned

9 of old jade; half a loaf; has a rash; old oak keel
10 she asked for a jar of jell; he had asked for hash

10

Lesson 3 (O and R) | Unit 1, Learn Letter-Key Operation

Job 11
Program for a Seminar

Mr. McGee has just finished the program for the Office Systems Seminar. Format the program for duplication. You will need to make 5 copies. Center the program horizontally and vertically on a full sheet. DS between items.

OFFICE SYSTEMS SEMINAR
JUNE 15, 8:00 - 4:30
CONFERENCE ROOM -- HOTEL McGEE

8:00-8:30	Refreshments, Opening Remarks
8:30-10:00	Defining System Needs and Measuring Productivity
	Mr. Thomas Clark, Elgin Office Systems
10:00-10:15	Break
10:15-11:45	Linking Business Goals with Systems Plans
	Mr. Carl Williams, VDT Corporation
12:00-1:00	Lunch (provided)
1:15-2:45	The Optimal Integrated Office Automation System
	Ms. Nancy Dittman, Ranel Business Systems
2:45-3:00	Break
3:00-4:30	Human Factors in Implementing an Office System
	Ms. Patricia Bayne, Mona Life Insurance Co.

Job 12
Simplified Memos

Attached to the program you were given in Job 11 is copy for a memo to be prepared and sent with the finished program. Provide an appropriate subject line. Date the memo April 30. You will need 5 original copies -- one for each of the following people and one copy for the files.

Adam Smith, Purchasing
Sally Lynn, Finance
LeRoy Jones, Marketing
Lydia Melendez, Legal

The sender of the memo is John McGee.

¶ McGee Enterprises has always been on the "cutting edge" of new and emerging technologies. In order to keep abreast of the information processing explosion, I have scheduled a one-day seminar for all administrative personnel on the topic of OFFICE SYSTEMS.

¶ The attached agenda provides you with the specifics of the seminar. I know you won't want to miss this important and exciting one-day event.

4a ▶ 26
Review What You Have Learned

1. Review the steps for arranging your work area (see page 2).

2. Review the steps required to ready your machine for keyboarding (see pages ix-x for typewriters; see the appropriate User's Guide for computers).

3. Review the steps for inserting paper into a typewriter (see page ix).

4. Take good keyboarding position:

- fingers curved and upright
- wrists low, but not touching frame of machine
- forearms parallel to slant of keyboard
- sit back in chair; body erect
- feet on the floor for balance

5. Type (key) each line twice SS: first, slowly; again, at a faster speed. DS between 2-line groups.

Fingers curved

Fingers upright

Home-row emphasis (Keep unused fingers on home keys.)

```
1 a;sldkfj a;sldkfj fjdksla; fjdksla; fj dk sl a; fj
2 a ah as ha ad all ask jak lad had fad has sad fall
3 ask a lass; had a fall; all had hash; a jak salad;
4 a fall ad; has a sash; a jak falls; had a sad fall
```
TS

Third-row emphasis (*Reach* up without moving the hands.)

```
5 ed ol rf de lo fr ded lol frf ed ol rf de lo fr hj
6 he or of so do for she off doe foe led odd she rod
7 he led her; a jade jar; ask for her; a jar of jell
8 for a hero; hoe for her; off her desk; a fake jade
```
TS

All keystrokes learned (Curved, upright fingers; steady pace.)

```
9 a la do ha so ah of he or el as fa jak sod foe for
10 lo old she off jar her led roe rod ark doe eke elk
11 held flak half hero desk road jerk load lead shelf
12 ask her for a jade jar; he sold oak desks for half
```
TS

Job 10
Letters from Form
Paragraphs (Boilerplate)
(LM pp. 157-160)

Ms. Beetle hands you addresses and variables which are to be formatted into letters using the standard paragraphs given at the right. The addresses are listed below; the variables are indicated in the paragraphs and are listed below. Supply an appropriate salutation with each letter; date the letters April 30. The letters will be signed by John L. McGee, President.

Note: As in Job 4, you will have to key each letter if you are using an electric or manual typewriter. If, however, you are using a word processor or computer, you can store the form paragraphs in memory and call them up as needed, inserting the addresses and variables as you format each letter. Consult your equipment manual for specific and additional information.

V = Variable
¶s = Paragraphs

Two paragraphs suitable for opening paragraph of letters.

(¶1) Thank you for agreeing to participate in our Office Systems Seminar to be held in the Conference Room of the Hotel McGee in Bloomsburg, PA on June 15.

(¶2) Thank you for working into your busy schedule the Office Systems Seminar at the Hotel McGee on June 15.

Three paragraphs suitable for main messages.

(¶3) The title of your topic is {V2} scheduled from {V3}. The duration of your presentation should be approximately 90 minutes. Also, it would be my pleasure to have you join the group for lunch. An honorarium of {V4} plus travel expenses will be provided. The necessary forms are enclosed with this letter.

(¶4) Your presentation, {V2}, is scheduled from {V3}. An honorarium of {V4} will be provided. Any expenses you incur in making this presentation should be forwarded to my attention. I hope your plans enable you to join the group for lunch.

(¶5) Details regarding the seminar have been finalized. You are scheduled to talk on the topic {V2} from {V3}. As I stated, an honorarium of {V4} will be provided along with any travel expenses you may incur. A fantastic lunch has been planned, so I hope you will be able to join the group.

Two short paragraphs suitable for letter closing.

(¶6) I look forward to your participation in this program. Enclosed is a map of the area. If you have any questions or need additional information, please contact me.

(¶7) I feel confident your comments will be well received by the group, and I look forward to your presentation. See you at the seminar.

Address List

V1	V2	V3	V4	¶s
Mr. Thomas Clark Elgin Office Systems 27 Long Ridge Road Stamford, CT 06905-8325	"Defining System Needs and Measuring Productivity"	8:30-10:00	$150	1, 4, 7
Mr. Carl Williams VDT Corporation 900 King Street Rye, NY 10580-2483	"Linking Business Goals with Systems Plans"	10:15-11:45	$100	2, 5, 6

4b ▶ 8
Build Keystroking Speed by Repeating Words

Each word in each line is shown twice. Practice a word the first time at an easy speed; repeat it at a faster speed.

1. Type (key) each line once SS; DS when you finish the drill. Use the plan suggested above.

2. Type (key) each line again. Try to keep the printing point or cursor moving at a steady speed. TS at the end of the drill.

Technique hint
Think and say the word; key it with quick-snap strokes using the fingertips.

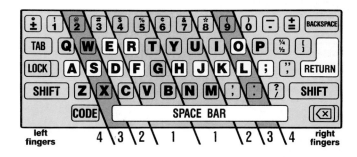

left fingers   4 \ 3 \ 2 \   1   \   1   \ 2 \ 3 \ 4   right fingers

GOAL: To speed up the combining of letters

```
1  do do|so so|sod sod|or or|of of|for for|fork forks
2  of of|off off|or or|rod rod|re re|ore ore|are hare
3  ad ad|had had|he he|she she|as as|has has|jak jaks
4  ha ha|has has|el el|eel eel|lo lo|old old|ark arks
```
TS

4c ▶ 8
Build Keystroking Speed by Repeating Phrases

1. Type (key) each line once SS. Speed up the second try on each phrase. DS when you finish the lines.

2. Type (key) the lines once more to improve your speed. TS when you finish.

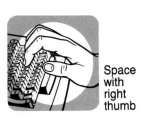
Space with right thumb

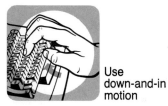
Use down-and-in motion

GOAL: To speed up spacing between words

```
1  do a|do a|do so|do so|or as|or as|as he|as he fell
2  ah so|ah so|ah ha|ah ha|a jar|a jar|or all|or fall
3  as he|as he|a jak|a jak|a rod|a rod|as old|as sold
4  he held|he held|she rode|she rode|for all|for fall
```
TS

4d ▶ 8
Build Keystroking Speed by Striking Keys at a Steady Pace

1. Type (key) each line DS. Try to keep the printing point or cursor moving steadily.

2. Type (key) each line again. Try to finish each line without slowing down or stopping.

Curved, upright fingers

Finger-action keystroking

GOAL: To keep printing point or cursor moving steadily

```
1  he had a fall jade sale; she asked for a jade doll
2  she held a jar of salad; she asked for half a jar;
3  she has a sales lead; her dad had a lead all fall;
4  he has a sled load of leeks for her fall lake sale
```

McGee Enterprises
P.O. Box 705 Bloomsburg, PA 17815-0705
(717) 389-4510

PURCHASE ORDER

WORLD GLOBAL SUPPLIES CO
45 ROCKLAND ROAD
DEPT 53
WHITE PLAINS NY 10604-3793

Purchase Order No.: P3204-705
Date: April 28, 19--
Terms: 2/10, n/30
Shipped Via: Parcel Post

Quantity	Description/Stock Number	Price	Per	Total
5 boxes	8-Inch Floppy Diskettes (D1732)	35 20	bx	
7 boxes	Lume M/S Film Ribbon (C2391)	48 10	bx	
7 cases	8½" x 11" White Paper (E4580)	68 50	cs	
3	CRT Shuttle Modules (C6226)	225 00	ea	

By Rhonda Barnett

Job 9
Format an Invoice
(LM p. 155)
Mr. Jones, Operations' Manager of the Carpet Division, needs this invoice processed so that a customer can be billed. Complete all mathematical calculations.

McGee Enterprises
P.O. Box 705 Bloomsburg, PA 17815-0705
(717) 389-4510

INVOICE

NATIONAL MOTORS
FLINT PLANT #325
GRAND BOULEVARD
FLINT MI 48505-5272

Date: April 28, 19--
Customer Order No.: CV4892

Terms	Shipped Via	Our Order No.	Date Shipped
2/10, n/25	Highland Express	M3054	5/4/--

Quantity	Description/Stock No.	(Unit Price)	(Amount)
275 yds	Model 3467 Carpet Backing (7896)	4 00	
275	Model 4562 Carpet Adhesive Strips (7824)	2 83	
275 yds	Style 732 Molded Carpet (54110)	13 25	

5a ▶ 8
Conditioning Practice

each line twice SS (first, slowly; again, at a faster speed); DS between 2-line groups

In this lesson and remaining lessons in this unit, the time for the Conditioning Practice is changed to 8 minutes. In this time you are to arrange your work area, ready your machine for keyboarding, and practice the lines of the Conditioning Practice.

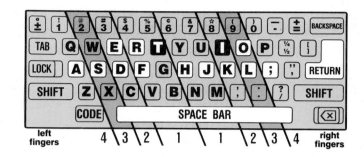

left fingers   4 \3 \2 \ 1 \ 1 \2 \3 \4   right fingers

1 as has ask jak rod led off she had elf oak for her
2 do so|so he|ask her|led off|had roe|has oak|of all
3 he had roe; for a jar; she led off; ask for a fork
TS

5b ▶ 18 Learn I and T

each line twice SS (slowly, then faster); DS between 2-line groups; if time permits, key lines 7-9 again

Follow the Standard Plan for Learning New Keys outlined on page 7.

Reach technique for i

Reach *up* with *right second* finger.

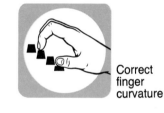

Correct finger curvature

Correct finger alignment

Learn i   ▼

1 k i ik ik is is if if fir fir die die did did side
2 i ik ik ki ki if if is is kid kid ski ski hid hide
3 a ski; a kid; a fir; he is; if she is; he did ride
TS

Reach technique for t

Reach *up* with *left first* finger.

Learn t   ▼

4 f t tf tf to to at at the the toe toe dot dot loft
5 t tf tf to to tot tot dot dot the the too too toot
6 to do; to the; to dot; the toe; to toss; to do the
TS

Combine i and t

7 i t it it fit fit sit sit tie tie hit hit kit kite
8 if it is; it is his; dot the i; if the tie is his;
9 she is fit; if the toe; the hat fits; it is a jet;
TS

Job 6
Announcement

In an effort to get top management to utilize the information processing center, Ms. Beetle hands you an announcement that will be placed in the pay envelopes of all top management personnel. She asks you to center, DS, and key the announcement vertically and horizontally on a full sheet of paper. Consult your equipment manual for automatic centering if you are using automated equipment.

Save Time
and
Increase Your Productivity
Use the
Information Processing Center
Call Susan Posey
Extension 4106
For More Details

(ALL CAP the announcement)

Job 7
Table

Ms. Beetle gives you the tentative holiday schedule which should be centered vertically and horizontally on a full sheet of paper. As a secondary heading use the current year and the next year. DS body; decide intercolumn spacing.

Fall - Winter
~~tentative~~ holiday schedule) ALL CAP and center

19--/19-) center

Division	November		December			January
	27	28	24	25	31	1
Automotive Carpets	NS	NS	NS	NS	S	NS
Customer Service	S	NS	NS	NS	S	NS
Warehouse	S	NS	NS	NS	S	NS
Corporate Offices	S	NS	S	NS	S	NS
Radio Station Switchboard	S	NS	S	NS	S	NS
Hospitality Switchboard	S	S	S	S	S	S

(3 spaces) } SS

S - Scheduled to work.

NS - Not scheduled to work.

~~For those~~ salaried employees who must work on # any of the above holidays, ~~they make~~ may take time off at a later date. SS

(DS between notes)

5c ▶ 24 Improve Keyboarding Technique

each line twice SS (slowly, then faster); DS between 2-line groups; if time permits, key the lines again

Fingers properly curved

Fingers properly aligned

Home-row emphasis *(Keep unused fingers on home keys.)*

1 a add lad had all as ask jak ha has jaks asks lads
2 a fall hall dash sash half flash shall salad salsa
3 a lad; a fall; a dash; a jak salad; has a fall ad;
TS

Third-row emphasis *(Reach up without moving hands.)*

4 ed led ol old rf for ik kid tf fit it or he so off
5 so do of or is it if to he she the toe fit sir for
6 of it; if it is; he or she; it is she; for the jet
TS

All keystrokes learned *(Strike keys at a steady, brisk pace.)*

7 he said it is her jade jar; he also has a jade jar
8 she took a jet to the lake; he is to see her there
9 she asked if all the jade is at this old lake fort
TS

Space-bar emphasis *(Space quickly between words and phrases.)*

10 it so if do he to of as oh or ha is re ah at id hi
11 if it|to do|he is|of it|do so|or if|ah so|to do it
12 he is to do it for a fee; the jet took to the air;

| Lesson 6 | **Left Shift and . (period)** | Line length: 50 spaces
Spacing: single-space (SS) |

6a ▶ 8 Conditioning Practice

each line twice SS (first, slowly; again, at a faster speed); DS between 2-line groups

> **Recall**
> Space once after ; used as punctuation except at line endings. Do not space at the end of *any* line. Instead, return and start the new line.

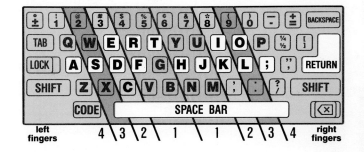

> **Technique hint**
> Eyes on copy in book; look at keyboard only when lost.

1 hj ed ol rf ik tf jh de lo fr ki ft hj ed ol rf ik
2 a kid led fir for dot fit held sift half loft jerk
3 she took the oak oars; she has a skiff at the lake
TS

Remedies [DS]

Since VDT operators have a high incidence of some type of health complaints, the following remedies may be helpful in resolving these problems complaints:

1. Have workers take frequent rest breaks from the VDT by performing other types of tasks such as copying or filing. This will help reduce eye strain.

2. Install task-ambient lighting instead of overhead fluorescent. This will greatly reduce screen glare.

3. Acquire proper support furniture, chairs and desks, which will accommodate individual body structures.

4. Install acoustical panels and ceiling tiles to absorb distracting sounds.

Summary [DS]

Computerized technology has the capability to greatly enhance the jobs of office workers by reducing undesirable, repetitive work tasks that require little thought and increasing the content of jobs by providing greater task variety and meaning. However, this technology also has the opposite capability; that is, to reduce office jobs to assembly-line systems in which job meaning is lost. In order to protect the health of the office worker affected by computerized technology, union and management must begin to work together to provide an adequate office environment.

Alphabetize for Reference List

Indent 2d line of each entry 5 spaces from left margin.

McQuade, Walter. "Easing Tensions Between Man and Machine." Fortune, March 19, 1984, pp. 58-66.

Chol, Warren E. "The Role of Ergonomics in Aiding Productivity." The Office, March 1985, pp. 16-20.

Grunning, Carl F. "VDTs and Vision--New Problems for the '80s." The Office, February 1985, pp. 19-22, 34.

Arndt, Robert. "What is Ergonomics?" Prompts, March 1985, pp. 7-9.

6b ▶ 20 Learn
Left Shift and . (Period)

each line twice SS (slowly, then faster); DS between 2-line groups; if time permits, repeat each line

Follow the Standard Plan for Learning New Keys outlined on page 7.

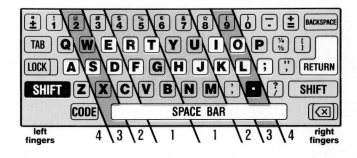

| left fingers | 4 | 3 | 2 | 1 | | 1 | 2 | 3 | 4 | right fingers |

Control of left shift key

Reach *down* with *left little* finger; shift, type, release.

Reach technique for . (period)

Reach *down* with *right third* finger; space twice after . at end of sentence.

Learn **Left Shift Key**   (Shift, strike key, release both.)

1 Ja Ja Ha Ha Ka Ka La La Hal Hal Kae Kae Jae Jae Jo

2 Ida fell; Jae did it; Hal has jade; Kae had a fall

3 I see that Jake is to aid Kae at the Oak Lake sale
TS

Learn **.** (Period)

4 l . . .l .l ed. ed. fl. fl. rd. rd. ft. ft. asstd.

5 . .l .l ed. ed. fl. fl. off. off. ord. ord. dissd.

6 fl. ed. rd. hr. ft. rt. ord. fed. off. alt. theol.
TS

Combine **Left Shift** and **.**

7 I do. Jo is. I did. Ola is ill. I shall do it.

8 Hal did it. Jae said so. Jake has left the lake.

9 I shall ask Kae if she left her skis at Oats Lake.
TS

6c ▶ 22 Improve
Keyboarding Technique

each pair of lines twice SS (slowly, then faster); DS between 4-line groups; if time permits, practice selected lines again

Spacing hints

Space *once* after ; and after . used with abbreviations and initials.

Space *twice* after . at the end of a sentence except at line endings. There, return without spacing.

3d row emphasis

1 Jo is to ask at the old store for a kite for Kier.
2 Ike said he is to take the old road to Lake Heidi.

abbrev./ initials

3 He said ft. for feet; rd. for road; fl. for floor.
4 Lt. Oats let O. J. take the old skiff to Lake Ord.

key words

5 a or he to if ha of do it so is as led jet old for
6 ah off the aid dot ask jar she fit oak are had rod

key phrases

7 it is|to do|if so|if it|do so|he is|is so|to do it
8 to the|do the|is the|if the|for it|for the|ask for

all keys learned

9 J. L. said he took fish; Karla said she had salad.
10 Jake is to fish at the lake if Odie is also there.

Job 5
Unbound Report with Textual Citations and Reference List
Ms. Beetle gives you a rough-draft copy of a report and asks you to format it in unbound style and to place the reference list on a separate page. Correct any errors Ms. Beetle may have overlooked.

ergonomics - *all cap and center* [QS]

Introduction - *center* [DS]

    The desire to increase *office* productivity has accounted for much of *top* management's commitment to embrace office automation here at McGee Enterprises. *However research studies indicate that* The worker's physical, social, and psychological needs must be met before automation can have the desired effect on productivity.

    Ergonomics, or Human factors engineering *views* the relationships between workers and their environment (Arndt, 1985, 6). It focuses on the aspects of the study of, and planning of, the work place and the workplace environment in order to adept them as much as possible to the physical and mental needs of the workers. It has become *an essential* component of office automation. *In simplest terms, ergonomics translates to compatibility.*

The VDT Problem - *center* [DS]

    There is a body of *evidence* that indicates working with VDTs can produce a variety of health *problems* including *visual fatigue, aches and pains, stress,* and job dissatisfaction (McQuade, 1984, 59). *A study conducted by* The National Institute of Occupational Safety and Health (NIOSH) linked VDTs to a decrease in output as a result of these health *complaints.* NIOSH also concluded that productivity could be enhanced 50% by solving posutral and visual problems associated with VDTs and their furniture (Chol, 1985, 17).

    With the growing number of office workers now coming in contact with VDTs--it is estimated that by 1987, 41 million VDTs will be in use and by 1990, over 60 million desk top computers will be employed (Grunning, 1985, 19)--management and unions must begin to deal with the ergonomics issues related to the modern office environment.

(Job 5 is continued on next page.)

7a ▶ 8
Conditioning Practice
each line twice SS (first, slowly;
then faster); DS between 2-line
groups

```
1 ik rf ol ed hj tf .l ki fr lo de jh ft l. La. Ltd.
2 he to jet ash rid she jot fled jerk half tore fork
3 Karla has the first slot; Jeff is to ride for her.
                                                   TS
```

7b ▶ 18
Learn U and C
each line twice SS (slowly,
then faster); DS between 2-line
groups; if time permits, repeat
selected lines

Reach technique for u

Reach **up** with
right first finger.

Reach technique for c

Reach *down* with
left second finger.

Follow the Standard Plan for
Learning New Keys outlined on
page 7.

left
fingers   4 \3 \2 \ 1   1 \2 \3 \4   right
fingers

Learn U   ▼

```
1 j u u uj uj us us jut jut due due sue sue fur furs
2 u uj uj ju ju us us jut jut hue hue fur fur us use
3 a jut; is due; sue us; due us; is rude; it is just
                                                   TS
```

Learn C   ▼

```
4 d cd cd dc dc cod cod; ice ice cot cots code codes
5 cd cd dc dc cod cod cot cot tic tic dock dock kick
6 a cod; a cot; a code; to dock; to cite; for a code
                                                   TS
```

Combine U and C

```
7 c u cud cud cue cue cut cut cur cur cure cure duck
8 a cud; a cur; to cut; the cue; the cure; for luck;
9 of the cue; use the clue; cut the cake; a fur coat
                                                   TS
```

7c ▶ 4 Review
Spacing with Punctuation

No space   One space

Spacing hint
Do not space after an internal
period in an abbreviation.

```
1 Use i.e. for that is; ck. for check; cs. for case.
2 Lt. Houck said to use fl. for fluid; hr. for hour.
3 K. J. Loft has used ed. for editor; Ir. for Irish.
                                                   TS
```

Ms. Beetle gives you two file cards and a message, a copy of which is to be sent to the address on each card.

She asks you to prepare the letters, supplying an appropriate salutation for each. Date each letter April 25. You are also to supply appropriate closing lines. The letters will be signed by Mr. Jeffrey Lewis, who is the Quality Control Manager of McGee Enterprises.

NOTE: If you are using an electric or manual typewriter, the form letter will have to be typed for each individual to whom it is addressed. If a word processor or computer is available, you need to key the letter only once, store it in memory, and insert only the variables (addresses and salutations) for each succeeding letter. Consult your equipment manual for specific instructions and additional information.

```
Norton Rubber Products, Inc.

Mr. Bruce Thompson, President
Norton Rubber Products, Inc.
157 South Wyoming Avenue
Kingston, PA   19345-0157
```

```
Beacon Container Company

Ms. Janice Keil
Production Manager
Beacon Container Company
326 Maple Avenue
Magnolia, NJ   08049-3206
```

(¶) The future of McGee Carpet Division depends on the quality carpets we produce and our performance. McGee Carpet Division is known as a quality source throughout the automotive industry, and it is vital to our survival that we maintain this reputation.

(¶) Our primary buyer has established a quality and performance rating system. The MCN (Materials Complaint Notice) is the format used for this system which notifies McGee (the source) that discrepant materials have been received by National Motors (the buyer). McGee has been issued 12 MCN's thus far this year.

(¶) As suppliers of materials for our carpets, you can easily understand our position. We must eliminate the MCN's and strive together for the highest ratings. We know we can do it; but it requires that everyone, including our suppliers, help us achieve this goal. Our future, and possibly yours, depends on it.

(¶) Please call my office to schedule an appointment so that we can discuss this issue in detail and pinpoint problem areas.

7d ▶ 20
Improve Keyboarding Technique

each pair of lines twice SS (slowly, then faster); DS between 4-line groups; if time permits, practice selected lines again

Goals
- reach *up* without moving hands away from you
- reach *down* without moving hands toward your body
- quick-snap keystrokes

3d/1st rows	1 cod fir cot for ice led cut sit due call rule duel
	2 for sure; cash is due; off the cuff; just her luck
abbrev./ initials	3 He used Ut. for Utah; Oh. for Ohio; Id. for Idaho.
	4 Lori Koch had a lot of luck as she led J. O. Hull.
key words	5 led cue for jut hut kid fit old ice just half coed
	6 us cut due such rich fuss lack juke dock turf coil
key phrases	7 to use|to cut|for us|is due|use it|cut off|call us
	8 such a|is sure|like to|just as|curl it|lot of luck
all keys learned	9 Lisa said it is a just cause; Katie is sure of it.
	10 Jack said he is sure he left for the lake at four.

Lesson 8 | Review

8a ▶ 8
Conditioning Practice

each line twice SS (slowly, then faster); DS between 2-line groups; if time permits, practice each line again

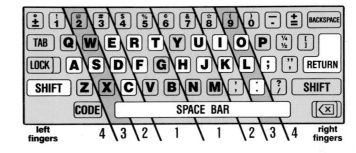

1 u uj ed ik rf ol ed hj tf cd .l; do us if ah or it
2 a for did sit due toe cut just such tusk half fuel
3 Jud is sure to share the cash if he cuts the lead.
                                                   TS

8b ▶ 8
Improve Return Technique

each pair of lines once as shown (SS); DS between pairs

Return hint
Keep up your pace to the end of the line; return immediately; start the new line without pausing.

Eyes on copy as you return

1 Ora asked us to take her;
2 I had a ski race set for four.

3 Jacki left a file at the desk
4 for us to use at the old lake dock.

5 Hal asked her to talk to all of us
6 to see if there is just cause for a cut.

7 Lora said that she has a hut at the old
8 lake site for the use of all the late skiers.
                                                   TS

Job 3 (LM p. 147)
Letter from Rough Draft
Ms. Beetle, head of the information processing center, hands you a letter drafted by Mr. McGee. You are to prepare it in final form for his signature.

Mr. McGee prefers his letters formatted in block style with open punctuation. He also prefers his title placed on the line beneath his typed name. Date the letter April 24.

Mr. Stanley ^W. Kobel

osha representative--~~Southern~~ *Eastern* Region

~~123 White Horse Pike~~ *285 Lincoln Drive*

Philadelphia, PA ~~18123-7132~~ *19144-3922*

Dear Mr. Kobel

I write this letter to request you^r presence at an upcoming ~~union/management meeting.~~ A meeting between McGee Enterprises

and local 485 of the service employees international union

(seiu), *which* has been set for June 10, at ~~8:00~~ *9:30* a.m., in the conference *room*

of our office building. The ~~main item~~ *purpose* of this meeting will

focus on the problems associated with ~~CRT~~ *VDT* usage. More specifi-

cally, the following ~~two components:~~ *issues will be addressed:*

1. Right-to-know laws.

2. Issues that are related to ~~CRT~~ *VDT* usage. *at # VDT*
   a. Number of hours a person should work ~~on~~ a ~~CRT~~ with out
      a rest break. *transfer to*
   b. The right of women to jobs that do not require the
      use of ~~CRTs~~ *VDTs* during pregnancy. *, Director of Labor Relations*

¶Representing the company will be Mr. Richard Keyser and myself.

Union representatives will be Ms. Susan Posey, President, and Mr.
~~James Kincaid~~ *Edward Blair*, Business Manager.

¶~~I look forward to~~ your assistance in answering specific questions

regarding health and safety factors as related to ~~CRT~~ *VDT* usage. *will be extremely beneficial to this meeting*

Please contact me *at 717-389-4510* by May 15 to confirm. I look forward to hear-

ing from you.

c. The use of nonglare screens and other ergonomic factors.

Sincerely

John L. McGee

president

8c ▶ 10
Build Keyboarding Skill: Space Bar/ Shift Key

each line twice SS; DS after each 2-line group

Goals
- to reduce the pause between words
- to reduce the time taken to shift/type/release when making capital letters

Down-and-in spacing

Out-and-down shifting

Space bar (Space *immediately* after each word.)

1 if he is to do so or us if ah of ha it el id la ti
2 if he|he is|is to|to do|do so|so it|it is|is to us
3 if he is|is to do|to do so|so it is to|it is to us

Left shift key (Shift; strike key; release both quickly.)

4 Lt. Ho said she left the skiff at Ute Lake for us.
5 Jae or Hal is to hike to Oak Lake to see Kate Orr.
6 He is to call for J. O. Hess at Luft Hall at four.

TS

8d ▶ 24
Improve Keystroking Skill

each line twice SS (slowly, then faster); DS after each 2-line group

Correct finger curvature

Correct finger alignment

Direct downward stroke

Quick-snap release of key

Third/bottom rows (Reach with *fingers*; not the hands.)

1 us she cut for due ode use tic dot oak fit cue sit
2 coal tick lock cite said coat sock cuff sick thick
3 code jack luck jute suit duet soft froth etc. Ltd.

Key words (*Think, say*, and *key* the words.)

4 as the did oak she for off tie cut has led jar all
5 re ore air cue her his aid rid sit had fir ask jet
6 talk side fold just fled call stir fork hurt route

Key phrases (*Think, say*, and *key* the phrases.)

7 to do|it is|of us|if he|is to|or us|to it|if he is
8 if she|for us|he did|of the|to all|aid us|is a fur
9 he or she|if she did|is to aid|to cut it|is to ask

Easy sentences (Strike keys at a brisk, steady pace.)

10 Jo said she left her old fur coat at the ski lake.
11 Jack asked us for a list of all the furs she sold.
12 Joel said he did code four tests left at his desk.

At the beginning of each
work session, warm up
and check to see that
your machine is in good
working order by keying
each line twice.

alphabet	1	Janice V. Deck exports quality white azalea bushes to foreign markets.
figures	2	The 14 VDTs acquired 3/26 and 5/7 have 29 lines of 80 characters each.
fig/sym	3	This CompuCenter (phone: 718-233-9446) lists 50% off on all software.
speed	4	The lame neighbor may wish a field hand to dig for worms in the field.

| 1 | 2 | 3 | 4 | 5 | 6 | 7 | 8 | 9 | 10 | 11 | 12 | 13 | 14 |

Job Application Activities

**Job 1
Complete an Application
Form** (LM p. 145)

**Job 2
Take a Keyboarding
Test**

As a final step in your
job application, take a 5'
timed writing and record
your *gwam* and number
of errors for use by the
personnel department.

You have written an application letter and submitted a data sheet to McGee Enterprises.

After the job interview, you are asked to complete a formal application blank for the personnel file.

You are given an application blank (LM p. 145) and told to fill in your own information at a keyboard.

all letters used | A | 1.5 si | 5.7 awl | 80% hfw

gwam 3' | 5'

Personal computers (PCs) are smart enough to play games, help teach   5 | 3 | 46

students, and solve problems that would take a person hours or even   9 | 5 | 49

years to solve. But inside, PCs are really quite simpleminded. When   14 | 8 | 52

you come right down to it, they can comprehend only two things: on and   19 | 11 | 55

off. A PC makes up for its limited vocabulary by being very, very fast.   24 | 14 | 58

For example, in the time it takes you to read this paragraph, a PC can   28 | 17 | 60

verify the spelling of every word, provide an analysis, and sometimes   33 | 20 | 63

even indicate other possible word choices.   36 | 22 | 65

The idea for the PC was born when people began to find that infor-   40 | 24 | 68

mation could be represented by the presence or absence of electric cur-   45 | 27 | 70

rent by means of electrical circuits now called chips. With the growth   50 | 30 | 73

of technology, PCs have become much faster, smaller, cheaper, and more   55 | 33 | 76

reliable. The PCs of today can fit on a desk top, cost much less than   59 | 36 | 79

a car, and are many times more powerful than the first room-size com-   64 | 38 | 82

puter built years ago. Today, many business organizations make use of   69 | 41 | 85

the personal computer to process job-based information.   72 | 43 | 87

gwam 3' | 1 | 2 | 3 | 4 | 5 |
5' | 1 | 2 | 3 |

9a ▶ 8
Conditioning Practice

each line twice SS (first, slowly; again, at a faster speed); DS between 2-line groups; if time permits, repeat selected lines

Curved, upright fingers

Finger-action keystroking

All keys learned

1 ed uj rf ik tf ol cd hj rt hu do if so us or it he
2 a risk; a cook; is just; to take; if this; of that
3 Lt. Li has just sold us four fish to cook at dusk.

TS

9b ▶ 20
Learn N and W

each line twice SS (slowly, then faster); DS between 2-line groups; if time permits, repeat each line

Follow the Standard Plan for Learning New Keys outlined on page 7.

left fingers   4 \3 \2 \ 1 \ 1 \2 \3 \4   right fingers

Reach technique for n

Reach *down* with *right first* finger.

Learn n

1 j n nj nj an an and and ant ant end end land lands
2 n nj nj an an en en in in on on and and hand hands
3 an oak; an ant; an end; and so; the end; she is in

Reach technique for w

Reach *up* with *left third* finger.

Learn w

4 s w ws ws sw sw ow ow wow wow sow sow cow cow owes
5 w ws ws ow ow low low owe owe how how sow sow sows
6 so low; we sow; to owe; is how; too low; is to row

Combine n and w

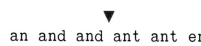

7 n w own own win win won won now now when when news
8 to win; to own; is low; of now; she won; to own it
9 Lou owns an inn in the town; she won it on a show.

TS

Simulation

Learning Goals

1. To become familiar with the keyboarding, formatting, and document processing tasks in a diversified corporation.

2. To improve your ability to work from different kinds of copy sources.

3. To sharpen your skill at detecting/correcting errors that have not been marked in source documents.

Machine Adjustments

1. Paper guide at *0*.

2. Margins: 70-space line for drills and paragraphs; as appropriate for documents.

3. Spacing: SS drills; DS paragraphs; space documents as directed or appropriate.

OFFICE JOB SIMULATION

Before you begin the jobs in this simulation, read carefully the information at the right. Make notes of any standard procedures that you think will save you time during the completion of the document production activities.

WORK ASSIGNMENT

Welcome to McGee Enterprises, a diversified corporation which consists of three major divisions -- McGee Carpets, McGee Hospitality, and McGee Radio. The corporate offices of McGee Enterprises are located at 703 East Fifth Street in Bloomsburg, PA. The mailing address is P.O. Box 705, Bloomsburg, PA 17815-0705. Each division of the enterprise operates independently of the other divisions. All major correspondence, however, is processed through the information processing center located in the corporate office building.

You will begin your career at McGee Enterprises as an entry-level information processing operator. Your work assignments, from various members of the staff, will be made by the head of the information processing center, Ms. Tina Beetle. The training coordinator (your teacher) will supervise your work and evaluate your performance.

EXCERPTS FROM THE KEYBOARDING/ FORMATTING PROCEDURES MANUAL

McGee Enterprises has based its keyboarding/formatting procedures manual on CENTURY 21 KEYBOARDING, FORMATTING, AND DOCUMENT PROCESSING, so use the reference guide and index of this book to look up matters of style and placement when in doubt. The following brief summary of formatting guides may be used for quick reference.

Letters: All letters are formatted in block style with open punctuation. A standard 60-space line is used, regardless of letter length.

Envelopes: An envelope is formatted in USPS style for each letter prepared.

Reports: Report manuscripts are prepared in unbound format unless another style is specified. Formal reports use textual citation/reference list documentation.

Memos: Memos are formatted in simplified style (without printed headings).

Forms: Standard format and copy placement are used for purchase orders/invoices.

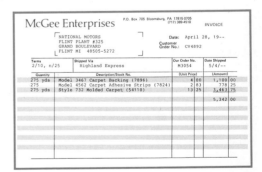

Purchase Order

Invoice

When you successfully complete your training/probation period, you will be eligible for promotion to other positions within the company. Again, welcome to McGee Enterprises. Good luck to you in this first phase of your employment.

9c ▶ 22

Improve Keyboarding Technique

each line twice SS (slowly, then faster); DS between 2-line groups; if time permits, practice selected lines again

Down-and-in spacing

Out-and-down shifting

Reach-out-and-tap returning

New-key emphasis (*Think, say,* and *key* the letters.)

1 is we on ow no an jaw own and owl end now win down

2 we do|an end|to owe|an owl|and won|was due|the new

3 I now know that a new skill takes the will to win.

Shift-key emphasis (Shift; strike key; release quickly.)

4 Nan or Jena; Jan. or Oct.; Lew and I are in Haiti.

5 Nell and Hew; see Lt. Lowe; Jan asked to see N. K.

6 Newt and Lana can work for the new chef at Hainan.

Key words (*Think, say,* and *key* the words.)

7 a an is do if to el or the cut own and she due jak

8 we ran owe one win den sow new won nor tin awl sun

9 wish then work corn jack down land lend thus cloth

All letters learned (Strike keys at a steady, brisk pace.)

10 Janis had won just one set of three when luck hit.

11 Les can do the work if he will just use his skill.

12 Jacki knew she owned the land where oil was found.

Lesson 10 | **G and Right Shift Key** | Line length: 50 spaces
Spacing: single-space (SS)

10a ▶ 8

Conditioning Practice

each line twice SS (first, slowly; again, at a faster speed); DS between 2-line groups; if time permits, practice selected lines again

Goals

● quick-snap keystrokes
● brisk, steady pace
● down-and-in spacing

All keystrokes learned

1 nj ws hj rf ol tf ik ed uj cd; I now know I own it.

2 if we|so as|is in|as is|he saw|an art|is nul|we cut

3 Kirt had just taken the race of the week at school.

TS

An increasing number of people are giving attention to the importance of 615
physical health to their productivity and goal achievements. They realize 630
that being physically fit enables them to function more effectively in today's 646
dynamic world. Many companies are beginning to implement physical fit- 660
ness programs within their companies, since they, too, realize the impor- 674
tance of their employees' physical health to their job productivity. The 689
primary areas that individuals and companies should examine if they wish 704
to influence physical fitness are proper diet, exercise, and sufficient rest. 720

On the other hand, mental health may be influenced by such things as 733
living in the present and maintaining balance in our lives. Living in the past 749
is unrealistic, and living in the future may mean looking forward to things 765
that will never happen. The people who constantly say, "Someday, I'll…" 780
will probably never do the many things that they had intended to do. Setting 796
realistic daily or weekly goals will help people achieve the more dramatic 811
and greater goals in life. Equally important is to maintain an appropriate 826
balance between work and play. Whatever people's hobbies or forms of en- 840
tertainment, it is important that a certain amount of time be given to these 856
"play" activities. It is important to give the mind a rest from daily work 871
routines. 873

Identifying and Eliminating Sources of Stress
891

Many of life's events can be controlled by people, but many others are 905
outside the realm of control. To aid in preventing stress, people should peri- 921
odically analyze and evaluate the stress-producing events in their lives. If 937
the number is high, people should strive to eliminate the stress-producing 952
events that they can. By eliminating stress-causing events wherever possible, 967
people can deal more effectively with those events beyond their control. 982

The first step in the evaluation process is to identify the sources of stress 998
because only after identification can action be taken. Several aids are avail- 1013
able in literature and from professionals which will aid in the detection of 1029
specific sources of stress. Questionnaire-type forms may be helpful in deter- 1044
mining what particular aspects of a job or an organization may be causing 1059
stress to employees. For example, people may feel stress about their job 1074
positions because their roles at work are ambiguous or because there is 1088
some conflict concerning their roles. Or stress may be caused by the lack 1103
of opportunity for career development. Additional causes of job stress may 1118
be related to the climate or structure of the organization. Responses to spe- 1134
cially designed questionnaires help to determine the specific problems that 1149
cause stress and if they can be eliminated. 1158

Recognizing Alternatives
1168

All too often stress is compounded if people feel trapped in a situation. 1183
Sometimes people feel helpless to change a situation. It is a great relief, 1198
though, to realize that alternatives are often available. If one cannot elimi- 1214
nate a stress-producing event, it is important to look for alternative ways 1229
of dealing with the event or alternative ways of transforming a situation 1244
so that it will be less stressful. Options are usually available; one just has 1260
to determine what they are and to assume responsibility for the alternatives 1275
they elect. 1277

10b ▶ 20
Learn G and Right Shift Key

each line twice SS (slowly, then faster); DS between 2-line groups; if time permits, practice selected lines again

Follow the Standard Plan for Learning New Keys outlined on page 7.

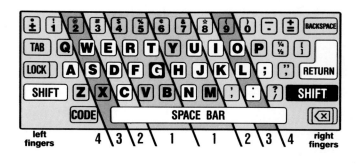

left fingers   4 \ 3 \ 2 \ 1 \ 1 \ 2 \ 3 \ 4   right fingers

Reach technique for g

Reach to *right* with *left first* finger.

Control of right shift key

Reach *down* with *right little* finger; shift, type, release.

Technique hint
Shift, strike key, and release both in a quick 1-2-3 count.

Learn **g** ▼

1 f g g gf gf go go fog fog fig fig got got jog jogs
2 g gf gf go go got got jog jog fig fig log log golf
3 to go; he got; to jog; to jig; the fog; he is gone

Learn **Right Shift** ▼

4 A; A; Al Al; Cal Cal; Ali or Flo; Di and Sol left.
5 Dale lost to Wes; Elsa lost to Cal; I lost to Del.
6 Tish has left for Tulsa; Rich is to see her there.

Combine **g** and **Right Shift**

7 Gig has gone to Rio on a golf tour with Gene Soto.
8 Golda got an A for her win; Rog got a C for fifth.
9 Gilda is to sign for Reggie; I can sign for Signe.
                                                    TS

10c ▶ 22
Improve Keyboarding Technique

each pair of lines twice SS (slowly, then faster); DS between 4-line groups; if time permits, practice selected lines again

Goals
- Reach *up* without moving hands away from you
- Reach *down* without moving hands toward your body
- quick-snap keystrokes

3d row emphasis

1 or sow got for due the sit low dot rug owe fir law
2 he is; to go; of us; is low; he got it; if we owe;

1st row emphasis

3 an can nag and cash land call hand dank lack slack
4 a fan; a can; a nag; an ad; an ash; a call; a jack

key words

5 if all rug her cot and dig fur the cut own jet ask
6 us an this wore disk that cook just lend sign work

key phrases

7 to go|a foot|an inch|to sign|at work|is just|a dog
8 to ask|the jet|the lawn|her disk|and sign|too high

all keys learned

9 Jan and Chris are here; Di and Rick are also here.
10 Doug walked two hours in the fog to get to Newton.

150c ▶ 37
Evaluate Document Processing
Skill: Reports

JOB STRESS

Coping with Stress

Time Schedule

Plan and prepare	4'
Document processing	25'
Proofread and correct errors	6'
Compute *n-pram*	2'

Problem 1
Unbound Report
Format and key the first page of the report at right in unbound report style.

Problem 2
Leftbound Report
Beginning with page 2, continue the report at right in leftbound style.

Bonus
1. At the conclusion of the 25' production time, you will have 6' to proofread again, correct any errors you find, or rekey if errors cannot be corrected. This step must be completed accurately before credit for bonus problem may be earned.
2. If time remains, rekey Problem 1 in leftbound style.

The rapid rate of change in the business environment leads to the potential for increased levels of job stress. This potential becomes a reality, though, only if office personnel allow it to do so. People who have learned to cope effectively with situations that could increase stress to unproductive levels are the people who can function most successfully in today's business world. 20 35 51 67 82 84

People vary greatly in their abilities to cope with stress. Some people seem to accept change and undesirable problems that may arise with little noticeable effect on their ability to perform on the job. At the other extreme are those whose job performance seems to suffer by even the most insignificant events. Fortunately, people can raise their tolerance for stress if they wish to do so. By gaining a proper perspective toward problems and by keeping physically and mentally healthy, it is much easier to cope with stress. In addition, by eliminating sources of stress that can be eliminated and by recognizing that often alternatives to problems exist, we can learn to have some control over stress-producing situations. 98 113 128 142 158 173 188 204 219 230

Gaining a Proper Perspective
241

Some people seem to look upon almost all of life's events with a negative viewpoint. Even when something good happens, their most immediate thoughts are pessimistic. They worry about how the good event may be taken away from them or how it will probably lead to some other undesirable occurrence. On the other hand, some people find good in almost any situation. These people have a unique talent for "turning lemons into lemonade." They look at a negative situation and realize that the situation could be worse. Further, they immediately look for ways to solve a problem. By using energy to eliminate a bad situation instead of wasting energy worrying or being negative, positive people often turn a problem into an opportunity. 256 270 284 299 313 328 343 358 374 389

Further, Dr. Denis E. Whitley indicates that there is a causal relationship between people's perspectives and what actually occurs in people's lives. He suggests that people move toward their currently dominant thoughts. Thus, those with negative thoughts move in a negative direction; those with positive thoughts move in a direction that leads to the achievement of their goals. In other words, people's perspectives are a great determining factor of their futures. 404 419 434 449 464 480 484

In conclusion, individuals must realize that only they can control their own minds, and a problem is only a problem if they perceive it to be one. If people refuse to regard a situation as a problem, it ceases to be one. 498 514 528

Keeping Physically and Mentally Healthy
544

Both physical and mental health influence people's ability to cope with stress. In addition, physical and mental health are interrelated. Physically healthy people are more likely to be mentally healthy; likewise, mentally healthy people are more likely to be physically healthy. 558 574 589 601

(continued on next page)

Lesson 11 B and P

Line length: 50 spaces
Spacing: single-space (SS)

11a ▶ 8
Conditioning Practice
each line twice SS (first, slowly; again, at a faster speed); DS between 2-line groups; if time permits, practice selected lines again

Finger-action keystroking

Down-and-in thumb motion

All letters learned

1 go as of or to and cut jot irk the own for cog all
2 of it|go for it|jot it down|take a cut|she will go
3 A kid had a jag of fruit on his cart in New Delhi.
TS

11b ▶ 20
Learn B and P
each line twice SS (slowly, then faster); DS between 2-line groups; if time permits, practice selected lines again

Reach technique for b

Reach *down* with *left first* finger.

Reach technique for p

Reach *up* with *right little* finger.

Follow the Standard Plan for Learning New Keys outlined on page 7.

Learn b

1 f b b bf bf fb fib fib rib rib big big rob rob but
2 bf bf fib fib fob fob but but lob lob bib bib ribs
3 a bud; to fib; but us; lob it; too big; to buff it

Learn p

4 ; p p p; p; pa pa; up up; apt apt pen pen nap naps
5 p p; p; pa pa paw paw pan pan lap lap pen pen kept
6 apt to keep; pick it up; take a nap; pack the pans

Combine b and p

7 b p up but put bit pit rib rip bid dip pub sup sub
8 a bus; a pan; to dip; to pit; the bid; put both up
9 Peg put both pans in a bin at the back of the pub.
TS

22   Lesson 11 (B and P) | Unit 1, Learn Letter-Key Operation

149c (continued)

Problem 3

half sheet, short edge at top; SS body; 4 spaces between columns

SALES REPORT

(Quarter Ending June 19--)

Office	Sales Volume	Increase/ Decrease	
			3
			8
			10
			21
Atlanta	$ 64,186	up	25
Dallas	87,241	up	29
Kansas City	26,424	down	33
Little Rock	14,861	down	38
New Orleans	56,743	up	43
Omaha	12,166	down	46
Santa Fe	26,841	up	50
Springfield	48,236	up	54
Tulsa	33,885	up	61
Total	$370,583	up	64

Problem 4

full sheet; DS body; decide spacing between columns

Bonus

1. At the conclusion of the 25′ production time, you will have 6′ to proofread again, correct any errors you find, or rekey if errors cannot be corrected. This step must be completed accurately before credit for bonus problem may be earned.

2. If time remains, rekey Problem 2 on a full sheet, DS, decide spacing between columns.

BUSINESS DEPARTMENT COURSE OFFERINGS

Spring 1987

Course Name	No. of Sections	Total Enrollment	
			7
			10
			14
Accounting	9	224	26
Computer Literacy	6	136	29
Computer Programming	3	77	34
Economics	5	133	39
Information/Word Processing	6	118	43
Keyboarding/Typewriting	12	335	49
Office Practice	2	47	56
		2,070	61
Total	43	2,200	64

Lesson 150 — Evaluation: Keyboarding/Report Skills

150a ▶ 5
Conditioning Practice

each line twice SS (slowly, then faster); DS between 2-line groups; if time permits, repeat selected lines

alphabet	1	The new professor gave six quizzes in math by the second week of July.
figures	2	Our 1987 inventory lists 362 diskettes, 40 computers, and 15 printers.
fig/sym	3	If the cost is $3,548.19 (less 20%), I can save $709.64 by buying now.
speed	4	An auditor may sign the forms to pay for half of the eight oak panels.

| 1 | 2 | 3 | 4 | 5 | 6 | 7 | 8 | 9 | 10 | 11 | 12 | 13 | 14 |

150b ▶ 8
Check Straight-Copy Skill

1. Take a 5′ writing on 148b, page 260.

2. Find *gwam* and number of errors.

3. Record score. Compare score with 148b and 149b.

11c ▶ 22
Improve Keyboarding Technique

each pair of lines twice SS (slowly, then faster); DS between 4-line groups; if time permits, practice selected lines again

Goals
- Reach *up* without moving hands away from you
- Reach *down* without moving hands toward your body
- quick-snap keystrokes

reach review

1 cd nj ws uj ed ol gf ik bf hj rf .l tf ce un rb p;
2 jut led gift cold turf lows bike herb pace Bif Jan

1st/3rd rows

3 an win cut fan bus pad new cog hen cub tan cup pen
4 curt plan want curb wisp torn pick cost high clips

key words

5 go bid can jet pen rub pep own for nap his irk all
6 lend pack high wish club jest gold silk fold court

key phrases

7 to put|an old|of use|is all|go for|to irk|the jets
8 a wire|to know|on land|big bus|the cord|a new chip

all keys learned

9 Peg can take a bus at one; Cal gets a jet at four.
10 Chloe used to work for a big pet shop in San Juan.

Lesson 12   Review

Line length: 50 spaces
Spacing: single-space (SS)

12a ▶ 8
Conditioning Practice

each line twice SS (slowly, then faster); DS between 2-line groups; if time permits, practice each line again

Goals
- curved, upright fingers
- quiet hands and arms
- steady keystroking pace

All keys learned

1 we up as in be on re ok no us if la do ah go C. J.
2 up to us; get a cup; the bid is; in a jet; to work
3 Fran now knows it is her job to take the gold cup.
                                                    TS

12b ▶ 12
Improve Return Technique

1. Key each 2-line sentence once as teacher calls "Return" each 30 seconds (30").

Goal: To reach the end of each line just as the 30" guide ("Return") is called.

2. Repeat the drill.

Note: The 30" *gwam* scale at right shows gross words a minute if you reach the end of each line as the 30" guide is called.

Eyes on copy as you return

		gwam 30"	20"
1	Deb wants to see the old globe	12	18
2	that he has to sell this fall.	12	18
3	Jack will take the first train into	14	21
4	town to see the big car show there.	14	21
5	Keisha will ask her to talk with all the	16	24
6	workers who are here for the first week.	16	24
7	Peg will add to her skill when she learns not	18	27
8	to look up or pause at the ends of the lines.	18	27

TS

149a ▶ 5
Conditioning Practice

each line twice SS (slowly, then faster); DS between 2-line groups; if time permits, repeat selected lines

alphabet 1 Not to be jeopardized, Max moved quickly away from the burning bushes.

figures 2 Flight 798 with 16 to 20 irate hostages was due to arrive at 3:45 p.m.

fig/sym 3 Please add a tax of 5% to Sales Slip #3479 to make a total of $268.10.

speed 4 The girls got a big quantity of the profit of the firm for their work.

| 1 | 2 | 3 | 4 | 5 | 6 | 7 | 8 | 9 | 10 | 11 | 12 | 13 | 14 |

149b ▶ 8
Check Straight-Copy Skill

1. Take a 5' writing on 148b, page 260.

2. Find *gwam* and number of errors.

3. Record score. Compare score with 148b.

149c ▶ 37
Evaluate Document Processing Skill: Tables

Time Schedule
Plan and prepare .... 4'
Document processing .... 25'
Proofread and correct errors ... 6'
Compute *n-pram* .... 2'

Problem 1

full sheet; DS body; 8 spaces between columns

			words
EQUIPMENT INVENTORY			4
Maintenance Department			9
		Estimated	11
Item	Quantity	Value	19
Electric Rotary Mower	1	$150	25
Commercial-Duty Mower	3	700	30
Lawn Thatcher	1	80	34
Lawn Sweeper	2	220	38
Lawn Roller	2	180	41
Electric Weedwhacker	2	75	46
Electric Blower	1	55	51
Edger-Trimmer	2	120	54

Problem 2

half sheet, long edge at top; SS body; 8 spaces between columns

				words
LONG DISTANCE PRICING SCHEDULE				6
Rate per Minute				9
			Night/	11
Mileage	Day	Evening	Weekend	21
1-50	0.2037	0.1368	0.0912	26
51-124	0.3510	0.2268	0.1512	32
125-292	0.3618	0.2268	0.1512	38
293-430	0.4400	0.2310	0.1540	43
431-1910	0.4920	0.3129	0.2090	49
1911-3000	0.5831	0.3465	0.2371	55
3001-4250	0.6035	0.3560	0.2478	61
4251-5750	0.6212	0.3759	0.2573	67

(Problem 3 is on next page.)

12c ▶ 10
Build Keyboarding Skill: Space Bar/ Shift Keys

each line twice SS; DS between 2-line groups

Goals
- to reduce the time used between words
- to reduce the time taken to shift/ type/release when making capital letters

Down-and-in spacing

Out-and-down shifting

Space bar (Space *immediately* after each word.)

1 Pat saw an old gold urn she wants for the new den.
2 Cleo is to go to work as a clerk at the town hall.
3 I know she is to be here soon to talk to the club.

Shift keys (Shift; strike key; release both quickly.)

4 Janet Pell left the file on the desk for Lana Orr.
5 Rod and Coila went to the lake with Sig and Bodie.
6 Nita Salas and Luis Rios work for us in Los Gatos.

TS

12d ▶ 10
Improve Keystroking Skill

each line twice SS (slowly, then faster); DS after each 2-line group

Goals
- quick-snap keystrokes
- quick joining of letters to form words
- quick joining of words to form phrases

Key words and phrases (*Think, say,* and *key* words and phrases.)

1 ah cub pan dog all jak got rid the off sit own irk
2 of us|do the|to rub|all of|he got|for the|to do it
3 if we do|is to be|as it is|in all the|if we own it

All letters learned (Strike keys at a brisk, steady pace.)

4 Prudence just left for work up at the big ski tow.
5 Jacob said that all of us can pick the right work.
6 June had gone for the big ice show at Lake Placid.

TS

12e ▶ 10
Check Keyboarding Skill

1. Take a 20-second (20″) timed writing on each line. Your rate in gross words a minute (*gwam*) is shown word for word above the lines.

2. Take another 20″ writing on each line. Try to increase your keystroking speed.

Goal

At least 15 *gwam.*

20″ gwam

	3	6	9	12	15	18	21	24	27	30

1 Al is to go with us.
2 Jan is to be at the lake.
3 Cal said he will take his dog.
4 Olga sold an old pair of ski boots.
5 She told us to set a goal and go for it.
6 It is now up to us to see how high we can go.
7 Jake is to go to town to work with the rich girls.

148c ▶ 37
Evaluate Document Processing
Skill: Letters

Time Schedule

Plan and prepare .... 4'
Document processing .... 25'
Proofread and correct errors ... 6'
Compute *n-pram* .... 2'

1 cc; correct errors; address envelopes

Problem 1
(LM p. 127)

block format; open punctuation

Problem 2
(LM p. 129)

modified block format; blocked ¶s; open punctuation

Problem 3
(LM p. 131)

modified block format; indented ¶s; open punctuation

Problem 4
(LM p. 133)

modified block format; blocked ¶s; open punctuation

Repeat Problem 2 with these changes:

Holt & Holt
Attention Office Systems Manager
P.O. Box 1847
Montclair, NJ 07042-2199
(words including envelope count: 183)

Bonus

1. At the conclusion of the 25' processing time, you will have 6' to proofread again, correct any errors you find, or rekey if errors cannot be corrected. This step must be completed accurately before credit for the bonus problem may be earned.

2. If time remains, rekey Problem 1 in modified block format, blocked ¶s, and mixed punctuation, on plain paper.

words

Problem 1

May 3, 19-- Mr. Clark M. Pruett Pruett, Inc. P.O. Box 3033 Bend, OR 97702-9322 Dear Mr. Pruett Subject: Publication Committee Audit

(¶ 1) The three copies of the audit requested by the Board of Trustees concerning the activities of the Publication Committee are enclosed. I have sent one copy to Leigh Cozier and would like for you to make any other distributions that you consider appropriate.

(¶ 2) On the morning of May 22, I will report directly to the Board to discuss this audit in detail. Since you were instrumental in preparing this year's audit, could you also plan to attend the meeting. We will meet at 10:30 a.m. in Room 203.

(¶ 3) If you cannot attend the meeting, will you please let me know as soon as possible so that I can reschedule it.

Sincerely HTM ASSOCIATES Ronald D. Martin, Vice President xx Enclosures pc John T. Baker, President There will be a luncheon at Nobel's directly following the meeting, and you are cordially invited to join us.

| | 14 |
| 27 |
| 40 |
| 55 |
| 70 |
| 78 |
| 93 |
| 108 |
| 124 |
| 127 |
| 141 |
| 149 |
| 162 |
| 176 |
| 191 |
| 205 |

Problem 2

June 25, 19-- Office Systems Manager Energy Alternatives, Inc. 13186 North Sunset Boulevard Renton, WA 98056-8871 Dear Sir or Madam

(¶ 1) Many office systems managers are beginning to realize that the dependability of their office copiers significantly affects their productivity. They recognize that frequent breakdowns are causing bottlenecks and worker frustration.

(¶ 2) For this reason, many progressive offices have switched to the new LAN copier. The LAN 650 is reliable and produces high-quality copies. Each document to be copied is read electronically and adjustments are made automatically to ensure a clear, clean copy every time.

(¶ 3) May we have our representative call you to set up a demonstration and explain how you can get better copies at a lower cost.

Cordially LAIR OFFICE MACHINES Ms. Dana R. Lipke Sales Manager xx

Problem 3

July 3, 19-- REGISTERED Ms. Roberta Sanchez 488 North Murray Avenue Anderson, SC 29621-7722 Dear Ms. Sanchez

(¶ 1) The agreement between you and Forrest W. Wilcox has been prepared according to our understanding of your instructions of last Tuesday. You will notice that Mr. Wilcox has signed each of the three enclosed copies.

(¶ 2) If you agree with all of the terms set forth in this document, would you please sign the three copies enclosed and return two of them to me by registered mail. One copy is for your files.

(¶ 3) If there are any points that you question, would you please call me as soon as possible for clarification. We would appreciate hearing from you immediately because Mr. Wilcox is eager to complete this agreement.

Sincerely yours Susan Yamada Attorney-at-Law xx Enclosures

M and X

13a ▶ 8
Conditioning Practice
each line twice SS (slowly, then faster); DS between 2-line groups; if time permits, practice each line again

1 bf nj cd ik ws ol rf p; tf hj gf an be up we on of
2 up cup but own can sub pep ran tic bit owe run ice
3 Bick will win a gold if he just runs at top speed.
                                                    TS

13b ▶ 18
Learn M and X
each line twice SS (slowly, then faster); DS between 2-line groups; if time permits, practice selected lines again

Follow the Standard Plan for Learning New Keys outlined on page 7.

Reach technique for m

Reach *down* with *right first* finger.

Reach technique for x

Reach *down* with *left third* finger.

Learn **m**

1 j m m mj mj me me am am ma ma jam jam ham ham make
2 m mj mj am am jam jam ham ham dam dam map map same
3 to me; am to; a ham; a man; a map; an amp; has jam

Learn **X**

4 s x x xs xs sx ox ox ax ax six six fix fix fox fox
5 xs xs sx sx ox ox fix fix nix nix fox fox lax flax
6 a fox; an ox; to fix; is lax; at six; to fix an ax

Combine **m** and **X**

7 m x mx am ox me ax jam six ham fox men lax fix mix
8 a fox; a jam; a mix; am lax; six men; to me at six
9 Pam can mix a ham salad; Max can fix soup for six.
                                                    TS

13c ▶ 4
Review Spacing with Punctuation
each line once DS

▽ Do not space after an internal period in an abbreviation.

1 Mae has a Ph.D. from Miami; Dex will get his Ed.D.
2 J. D. Marx will go to St. Croix in March with Lex.
3 Ms. Fox is to send to me this week six maps c.o.d.
                                                    TS

SOUTH-WESTERN
PUBLISHING CO.

Unit 31 Lessons 148-150

Measurement Goals
1. To evaluate straight-copy speed and control.
2. To evaluate document processing skill.

Documents Processed
1. Letters
2. Tables
3. Reports

Lesson 148 — Evaluation: Keyboarding/Letter Skills

**148a ▶ 5
Conditioning
Practice**

each line twice SS
(slowly, then faster);
DS between 2-line
groups; if time permits,
repeat selected lines

alphabet	1	Jackie Dexter gave his music classes a pop quiz while Faye was absent.
figures	2	In 1987, we bought 46 textbooks, 20 workbooks, and 35 placement tests.
fig/sym	3	Al's stores (1987 data) hired 1,623 clerks at a minimum rate of $4.50.
speed	4	They wish to make six big signs to make the title visible to the town.

| 1 | 2 | 3 | 4 | 5 | 6 | 7 | 8 | 9 | 10 | 11 | 12 | 13 | 14 |

**148b ▶ 8
Check Straight-
Copy Skill**

1. A 5' writing on all ¶s.
2. Find *gwam* and number of errors.

all letters used | A | 1.5 si | 5.7 awl | 80% hfw

	gwam 3'		5'
The technology used in most business organizations today makes it	4	3	45
quite needless to rekey a document. Also, there is no economic justi-	9	5	48
fication for ever recording a letter, for example, more than one time.	14	8	51
This is possible, of course, only if the person who first writes the	18	11	54
letter, as well as any other person who may edit or revise it, has	23	14	56
keyboarding skill. It is plain to see that one who is not able to	27	16	59
keyboard by touch is handicapped in her or his ability to communicate	32	19	62
efficiently, and this creates a business problem.	35	21	64
If the communication system of a business firm does not run effi-	40	24	66
ciently and smoothly, the flow of information is hampered. If the flow	44	26	69
of information lags, executives and others who make dozens of critical	49	29	72
decisions each day may not have the information that they require in	54	32	75
order to do their jobs well. In some cases, getting this information	58	35	78
a day late or maybe just an hour late can cause serious problems and	63	38	80
can be costly. An efficient and effective flow of information is crit-	68	41	83
ical in a complex and competitive business world.	71	43	85

gwam 3'	1	2	3	4	5
5'	1		2		3

13d ▶ 20
Improve Keyboarding Technique

each pair of lines twice SS (slowly, then faster); DS between 4-line groups; if time permits, practice selected lines again

Goals
- reach *up* without moving hands away from you
- reach *down* without moving hands toward your body
- quick-snap keystrokes

3d/1st rows

1 ox me ax ma be fix can box map but six man hex hem
2 am nix cut bomb name fans came gnat plan form comb

space bar

3 am to an is of me us do if ma or en em bun sum gem
4 an and lob hem din fob sum fun rob man cab fan lab

key words

5 us do if an me big cut sow pep has jam oak rub lax
6 just work name form born flax curl high dope rough

key phrases

7 is big|to jam|if she|for me|an end|or lap|is to be
8 to cut|and fix|the call|for work|and such|big firm

all keys learned

9 Bix left for camp last week; Judith is to go soon.
10 Jamie knew he could fix an old speed bike for Peg.

Lesson 14   Y and Z

Line length: 50 spaces
Spacing: single-space (SS)

14a ▶ 8
Conditioning Practice

each line twice SS (slowly, then faster); DS between 2-line groups; if time permits, practice each line again

Goals
- curved, upright fingers
- quiet hands and arms
- steady keystroking pace

All letters learned

1 if do us pa go me an is to he am or in we no be ax
2 of lace|so when|or just|of work|to sign|is to form
3 Herb Roe can win a gold cup for the six ski jumps.
TS

14b ▶ 6
Improve Return Technique

Each 2-line sentence once as "Return" is called each 30 seconds (30").

Goal: To reach the end of each line just as the 30" guide ("Return") is called.

Note: The 30" gwam scale shows gross words a minute if you reach the end of each line as the 30" guide is called.

Eyes on copy as you return

	gwam 30"	20"
1 Amber was to pick a slow pace	12	18
2 and then work up to top speed.	12	18
3 Alex has worked for her as a sales	14	21
4 clerk in the shop since last March.	14	21
5 Mae sang a solo at the last music show;	16	24
6 Cam joins her in a duet in the next one.	16	24
7 Bo is to work for a big auto firm this fall;	18	27
8 his job is to check cars coming off the line.	18	27

TS

147c ▶ 10
Check Straight-Copy Skill

1. A 5' writing on all ¶s.
2. Find *gwam* and number of errors.

all letters used | A | 1.5 si | 5.7 awl | 80% hfw

gwam 3' | 5'

Choosing a career is not an easy task, but it is a significant 4 | 2
decision that requires careful consideration. It is important to think 9 | 5
about the education that you will need in order to attain expertise in 13 | 8
the exact field that may interest you. Also, you should consider 18 | 11
the income you will realize after you have finished your schooling. You 23 | 14
may wish to ask yourself if the rewards will exceed the amount of energy 28 | 17
and time that will be required in the process of getting prepared for 33 | 20
a chosen career. Furthermore, you should consider if you are suited to 37 | 22
the career chosen. If you wished to be a teacher, for example, you 42 | 25
might contemplate the points below. 44 | 27

There are some traits that are desirable in a teacher, and one 48 | 29
should possess many of them before entering the profession. For example, 53 | 32
excellent teachers should be interested in the exact needs of each indi- 58 | 35
vidual student as well as the needs of a class as a whole. The quiet 63 | 38
student in the back row should be given as much attention as the rowdy 67 | 41
student in the front row. An expert teacher will be capable of recog- 72 | 43
nizing the unique qualities possessed by each student and helping each 77 | 46
student to develop important traits. 80 | 48

An adept teacher must have many insights into the learning process. 84 | 50
Even if we do not know all of the cause and effect relationships, we do 89 | 53
know that students learn more if they are treated in certain ways. For 94 | 56
example, we recognize that learners react to praise better than reproof. 99 | 59
Also, there is no question that learners who do a job well initially 103 | 62
will do even better when confronted with another task. Further, learners 108 | 65
who are given feedback about the accuracy of their work do better than 113 | 68
if they are given little or no feedback. 116 | 69

Gathering information about the skills that are required in a 120 | 72
designated field before you make a career choice is very important. 124 | 75
Also, spending the time initially looking into various aspects of a 129 | 77
career that may interest you will reap rewards in the long run. In 133 | 80
addition, it will allow you to make the right choice. 137 | 82

gwam 3' | 1 | 2 | 3 | 4 | 5
5' | 1 | 2 | 3

14c ▶ 18
Learn Y and Z

each line twice SS (slowly, then faster); DS between 2-line groups; if time permits, practice selected lines again

Follow the Standard Plan for Learning New Keys outlined on page 7.

Reach technique for y

Reach *up* with *right first* finger.

Reach technique for z

Reach *down* with *left little* finger.

Learn y ▼

1 j y y yj yj jy jay jay lay lay hay hay day day may
2 y yj yj ja jay jay eye eye yes yes yet yet dye dye
3 a jay; an eye; to pay; he may; you say; you may be

Learn z ▼

4 a z z za za zoo zoo zap zap oz. oz. zone zone maze
5 z z za za zap zap zoo zoo zed zed zag zag zip zips
6 an adz; to zap; zip it; the zoo; zap it; eight oz.

Combine y and z

7 y z zy jay zap eye zoo yes zip boy zag you adz yet
8 to zip; an eye; an adz; to you; the boy; by a zoo;
9 Liz likes a hazy day for a lazy trip to buy pizza.
TS

14d ▶ 18
Improve Keyboarding Technique

each pair of lines twice SS (slowly, then faster); DS between 4-line groups; if time permits, practice selected lines again

Goals
- Reach *up* without moving hands away from you
- Reach *down* without moving hands toward your body
- use quick-snap keystrokes

1st/3d rows

1 ox an oz. mix net may cut buy zoo ten icy win size
2 Roz and Pixie may catch a bus; you can go by bike.

space bar

3 an by ran buy dim any sky form sign corn many from
4 Ann is to jog with me to the city park by the zoo.

key words

5 an the for own six you led zoo but jam cup got irk
6 city firm next zone both land work turn pick eight

key phrases

7 to be|is dim|to zip|fix it|of coal|if both|to lend
8 is to pay|buy the lamp|owns the land|does the work

all letters learned

9 Doug will pack sixty pints of prize jams for Beth.
10 Makuzi has sixty jobs he can get done for low pay.

147b (continued)

Problem 3
Leftbound Report
Format and key page 1 of the report at the right as a left-bound report.

Problem 4
Unbound Report
Beginning where you stopped at the end of Problem 3, format and key the remainder of the copy as page 2 of an unbound report.

Bonus

1. At the conclusion of the 25′ production time, you will have 6′ to proofread again, correct any errors you find, or rekey if errors cannot be corrected. This step must be completed accurately before credit for the bonus problem may be earned.

2. If time remains, rekey Problem 1 in modified block style, blocked ¶s, and open punctuation.

AN INFORMATION SYSTEM

Common Elements

For information processing to occur, an information system must be developed. The essential elements of such a system are the people, procedures, equipment, and data.

People

An information system is developed as a tool or a support for the individuals who will use it. Users give an information system a purpose, and most people associated with an information system will be users. Other people associated with an information system are those who develop the hardware and software and those people who specialize in systems design and programming.

Procedures

Procedures consist of instructions and directions. Instructions tell the computer what to do to achieve the desired results, and directions tell users how to accomplish the desired results with the hardware and software being used. Instructions are given in the form of computer programs, and directions are written in the form of procedures manuals.

Computer programs. Programs are the instructions that are written in English-like statements to control the processing done by the machine. They must be written in a specific format to be read by the computer and translated into machine language (through a different program that is a part of the operating system) before processing can occur.

Procedures manuals. For people to use programs successfully, they must be guided through appropriate steps to make the program work. This is accomplished through a manual that gives directions for preparing input data, for setting up the computer to run or process the data, and for setting up the computer for output data.

Equipment

Equipment consists of the computer and what is known as peripherals. Peripherals are devices such as keyboards, VDTs,* disk or tape drives, and printers and other output devices.

Data

The very reason for the existence of an information system is to handle data. Data must be controlled in such a way to assure that it is accurate, safe, and secure. The control system provides a means of checking output data periodically to verify its quality. In addition, stored files must be protected from disasters such as fires, floods, and tornadoes as well as theft.

Finally, an appropriate environment, sometimes with special air conditioning, must be provided to assure proper operation of equipment and to save and protect data media.

*VDT stands for video display terminal.

	words
	4
	8
	22
	37
	42
	44
	60
	74
	89
	102
	117
	120
	124
	139
	154
	169
	187
	195
	212
	226
	241
	256
	267
	285
	300
	314
	330
	336
	340
	354
	369
	376
	378
	394
	410
	424
	440
	454
	469
	483
	488
	492
	500

15a ▶ 8
Conditioning Practice

each line twice SS (slowly, then faster); DS between 2-line groups; if time permits, practice each line again

All letters learned

1 ox had zoo but jam ski got for men pay low sic you
2 by the oz.; pay the zoo; buy the adz; the hazy day
3 Marj had kept a sly tab on cut wages of six zones.

TS

15b ▶ 18
Learn Q and ,

each line twice SS (slowly, then faster); DS between 2-line groups; if time permits, practice selected lines again

> Follow the Standard Plan for Learning New Keys outlined on page 7.

Reach technique for q

Reach *up* with *left little* finger.

Reach technique for , (comma)

Reach *down* with *right second* finger; space once after , used as punctuation.

Learn Q ▼

1 a q q qa qa aq quo quo qt. qt. quit quit quay quay
2 q q qa qa qw quo quo quit quit aqua aqua quiz quiz
3 a qt.; a quiz; to quit; pro quo; the quay; to quiz

Learn , (comma) ▼

4 k , , ,k ,k kit, kit; Jan, Kit, or I will go, too.
5 a ski, a ski; a kit, a kit; a bike, a bike; to ski
6 Ike, go to work with Shep; Sue, stay here with me.

Combine Q and ,

7 Key in the words quo, quit, quiz, quay, and quite.
8 I quit the quiz show, Quen. Jaques has quit, too.
9 Quig, Raquel, and Quincy will quit the squad soon.

TS

15c ▶ 4
Review Spacing with Punctuation

each line once DS

▽ Space once after comma used as punctuation.

▽ ▽

1 Aqua means water, Rico; it is a unique blue, also.

2 R. J. used oz. for ounce and qt. for quart, I see.

3 Send the books c.o.d. to Dr. Su at the Quinta Inn.

TS

146d ▶ 5
Check Language Skills: Verb Agreement

half sheet; 60-space line; SS
Key the sentences at the right (including number) selecting the correct word choice from the words in parentheses. Use the dictionary if necessary.

1. I have (swam, swum) three laps every day this week.
2. I (saw, seen) in the paper that you have (wrote, written) a book.
3. Mike (drank, drunk) two cokes while Amy (eat, ate) her lunch.
4. Jan has (spoke, spoken) of the beauty of the (froze, frozen) lake.
5. Betty has (went, gone) to check on the (broke, broken) window.
6. The data that you submitted (is, are) not accurate.
7. Either Susan or her friend (is, are) here.
8. The number of people requesting information (is, are) small.
9. Neither Doris nor Richard (is, are) willing to accept credit.
10. A number of people (is, are) expected to attend the game.

Lesson 147 | Prepare for Evaluation: Sustained Production

147a ▶ 5
Conditioning Practice

each line twice SS (slowly, then faster); DS between 2-line groups; if time permits, repeat selected lines

alphabet 1 Jackie Quatman will realize her big desire to pole-vault by next fall.

figures 2 Kathrine had swum 26 laps by 12:39 p.m. today and 78 laps by 4:05 p.m.

symbols 3 Is the high-priced suit (the blue one -- not the red one) Vi's favorite?

speed 4 The orient is a rich land of enchantment, and a visit is Nancy's goal.

| 1 | 2 | 3 | 4 | 5 | 6 | 7 | 8 | 9 | 10 | 11 | 12 | 13 | 14 |

147b ▶ 35
Build Sustained Document Processing Skill: Letter, Table, Report

Timed Schedule

Plan and prepare	3'
Timed production	25'
Proofread and correct errors	5'
Compute n-pram	2'

plain paper; correct errors

Problem 1
Letter

block style; open punctuation

Supply current date, salutation, subject line (**office space**), complimentary close, enclosure notation, and carbon copy notation to Mr. Tom Blake. (Words supplied by student are included in word count.)

Problem 2
Table

Full sheet; make all other decisions.

words

State Board of Engineers Attention Ms. Tracy Lambert, President P.O. — 17
Box 1999 Athens, GA 30603-7731 — 34
(¶ 1) The State Board of Designers has decided to decline your proposal — 48
to share our office space, although the decision was a difficult one. — 62
The arrangement would have provided us with several benefits; however, — 76
we anticipate that our office activity will continue to increase and — 96
we will have a shortage of office space. — 98
(¶ 2) The enclosed brochure is for an office locator service. They have — 112
a good reputation for assisting organizations such as yours. — 124
Lee K. Kirk postscript Please let us know your new address when it is — 140
available. — 147

NATIONAL ASSOCIATION FOR BUSINESS TEACHER EDUCATION			10
Past Presidents			14

Years Served	Name	State	
1985-87	Thomas B. Duff	Minnesota	29
1983-68	Paul H. Steagall, Jr.	Virginia	37
1979-83	Lloyd W. Bartholeme	Utah	43
1977-79	Harry H. Jasinski	South Dakota	51
1975-77	Mearl R. Guthrie	Ohio	57
1973-75	Z. S. Dickerson, Jr.	Virginia	65
1971-73	Lawrence W. Erickson	California	73
1969-71	T. Jaems Crawford	Indiana	80

15d ▶ 20
Improve Keyboarding Technique

each pair of lines twice SS (slowly, then faster); DS between 4-line groups; if time permits, practice selected lines again

Goals
- keep fingers curved, upright
- reach the third and fourth fingers without twisting the wrists outward
- use quick down-and-in spacing

1st/2d fingers	1 fit her met dim bin tic but bug yet city kick rich
	2 if he|in it|my fur|the jet|met her|cut him|but get
3d/4th fingers	3 ap. aq. oz. ox as lox pal was zap paw all low also
	4 a zoo; a paw; lax law; all saw; so slow; was also;
key phrases	5 of us|of all|is to go|if he is|it is due|to pay us
	6 if we did|up to you|if we aid|is of age|she saw me
space bar	7 Al is to go to the firm for the pay due the clerk.
	8 Jan is to go by bus to the town to audit the firm.
all letters learned	9 Zampf did log quick trips by jet to the six towns.
	10 Jantz will fix my pool deck if the big rain quits.

Lesson 16 — Review

Line length: 50 spaces
Spacing: single-space (SS)

16a ▶ 8
Conditioning Practice

each line twice SS (slowly, then faster); DS between 2-line groups; if time permits, practice each line again

Goals
- curved, upright fingers
- quiet hands and arms
- steady keystroking pace

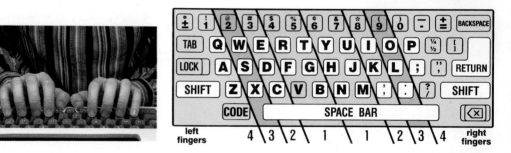

all letters learned	1 Jorgie plans to find that mosque by six with Zack.
shift keys	2 Maria Paso had a tea for Dr. and Mrs. Ruiz in Rio.
easy sentence	3 He is to work with us if he is right for the work.
5-stroke words	| 1 | 2 | 3 | 4 | 5 | 6 | 7 | 8 | 9 | 10 |

TS

16b ▶ 10 Type (Key) Block Paragraphs

each paragraph (¶) once SS as shown; DS between ¶s; at your teacher's direction, take a 1-minute (1′) writing on each ¶; find your rate in *gwam*

> To determine your speed in *gwam* (gross words a minute):
> **1.** Note the figure at the end of your last complete line.
> **2.** Note from the scale under the ¶s the figure below where you stopped in a partial line.
> **3.** Add the two figures; the resulting number is your *gwam*.

Paragraph 1

gwam 1′

Do not stop at the end of the line before you make 10
a return. Keep up your pace at the end of a line, 20
and return quickly after you strike the final key. 30

DS

Paragraph 2

Make the return with a quick motion, and begin the 10
next line with almost no pause. Keep your eyes on 20
your copy as you return to cut time between lines. 30

gwam 1′ \| 1 \| 2 \| 3 \| 4 \| 5 \| 6 \| 7 \| 8 \| 9 \| 10 \|

146b ▶ 20
Build Straight-Copy Skill

1. A 3′ writing on all ¶s combined to establish base rate. Find *gwam*.

2. Add 4-6 words to base rate to establish goal rate. Note quarter-minute checkpoints in ¶ 1.

3. Two 1′ writings on ¶ 1 trying to match or exceed goal rate.

4. Repeat Steps 2 and 3 for ¶s 2, 3, and 4.

5. A 3′ writing on all ¶s combined. Compare with *gwam* achieved in Step 1.

Quarter-Minute Checkpoints

gwam	¼′	½′	¾′	1′
24	6	12	18	24
28	7	14	21	28
32	8	16	24	32
36	9	18	27	36
40	10	20	30	40
44	11	22	33	44
48	12	24	36	48
52	13	26	39	52
56	14	28	42	56
60	15	30	45	60
64	16	32	48	64
68	17	34	51	68
72	18	36	54	72
76	19	38	57	76
80	20	40	60	80

146c ▶ 20
Build Document Processing Skill: Report

plain paper; proofread and circle errors

1. Process the copy at the right as a leftbound report. Insert headings listed below.

Main heading: HUMAN NEEDS IN DESIGN

Side heading: (above ¶ 2): Social Needs

Paragraph heading (¶ 2): Determining by questionnaire.

Paragraph heading (¶ 3): Determining by resident participation.

Side heading (above ¶ 4): Psychological Needs

---

all letters used | A | 1.5 si | 5.7 awl | 80% hfw

gwam 3′

Quite often the major stress in landscape and site plans is on only 4

the natural forces with all too much being assumed as to the needs of 9

people. One must realize that dozens of complex social and psychological 14

factors are known about our human needs. These factors should be given 19

much thought in the designing of houses, of recreation space, and of 24

other use areas in order to provide a more conflict-free setting. 28

Even though much is known about our social needs in general, it is 32

essential for a designer to recognize the wants of the region where 37

a job is to be done. Much data may be gained by using a questionnaire 42

to survey attitudes, facts, and opinions. However, in the end, judgment 47

must be based on these results along with some direct observation, as 51

people do not always express honest answers. 54

There is one other way by which design form can be matched with 58

the needs and desires of the people of an area. With this plan residents 63

build their own environments, parks, playgrounds, and even housing or 68

at least participate in these projects. Because the quality of the concept 73

is limited by the experiences of the people, the role of the designer is 78

to present options and to help analyze them. 81

In addition to social wants, we realize that we have psychological 85

needs that differ from time to time. We have some needs some of the 90

time and other needs at other times; so we must beware of the danger of 95

quickly developing an exact design form just to satisfy or fulfill tempo- 100

rary wants. The design process should identify some of the fundamental 104

demands to be satisfied and should make sure that the design does so. 109

gwam 3′ | 1 | 2 | 3 | 4 | 5 |

16c ▶ 12
Build Keyboarding Skill: Space Bar/ Shift Keys

each line twice SS; DS between 2-line groups

Goals
- to reduce the time used between words
- to reduce the time taken to shift/ type/release when making capital letters

Down-and-in spacing

Out-and-down shifting

Space bar (Space *immediately* after each word.)

1 of an if us to me is am so pan urn may own buy jam
2 am to pay│he may own│for a day│is to buy│a new law
3 I may go to the city to pay the firm for the sign.

Shift keys (Shift; strike key; release both quickly.)

4 Cory and Lara went with Jose and Rosa to San Juan.
5 Maria Eppel is at school in Miami with Susie Quan.
6 Max, Raul, and I may see Aida or Luis in San Jose.

TS

16d ▶ 10
Improve Keystroking Skill

each line twice SS (slowly, then faster); DS after each 2-line group

Goals
- quick-snap keystrokes
- quick joining of letters to form words
- quick joining of words to form phrases

Key words and phrases (*Think, say,* and *key* words and phrases.)

1 them with they make than such when both then their
2 to risk│both of│sign it│but then│and when│too busy
3 an oak box│for the city│such a risk│six of the men

All letters learned (Strike keys at a brisk, steady pace.)

4 size next help jack went same form quit body signs
5 Gus Zia packed the box with quail and jam for you.
6 Quig can ski with Lex Zemp but just for four days.

TS

16e ▶ 10
Check Keyboarding Skill

1. Take a 30-second (30″) timed writing on each line. Your rate in gross words a minute (*gwam*) is shown word for word above the lines.

2. If time permits, take another 30″ writing on each line. Try to increase your keyboarding speed.

Goal
At least 18 gwam.

30″ gwam

    2   4   6   8   10   12   14   16   18   20   22

1 I paid for the rich lake land.
2 Dana is to go to work for them now.
3 Zoe is to pay half price for an old urn.
4 Jack docks his boat next to ours at the quay.
5 You must keep up the good work if you want to win.
6 Size up a job and work at it with all the zeal you can.

    2│   4│   6│   8│ 10│ 12│ 14│ 16│ 18│ 20│ 22

If you finish a line before time is called and start over, your *gwam* is the figure at the end of the line PLUS the figure above or below the point at which you stopped.

Build Document Processing Skill: Tables

Review table formatting guides on pages 177-178, if necessary.

plain paper; proofread and circle errors; center by longest item, whether column entry or column heading.

Drill 1: Center columns; leave 6 spaces between columns.

Drill 2: Center columns; leave 8 spaces between columns.

Drill 1

Movie	Stars	Name of Director
Airplane II The Sequel	Robert Hays, Julie Hagerty	Ken Finklemen

Drill 2

Year	Prize Winner	Country
1982	Kenneth G. Wilson	U.S.

Drill 3: Center on half sheet, long edge at top; decide intercolumn spacing; SS body.

Drill 4: Center on full sheet; 8 spaces between columns; DS body.

Drill 5: Center on half sheet, short edge at top; 4 spaces between columns; DS body.

Drills 3, 4, 5

REGIONAL SALES
(In Millions)

Region	Sales This Year	Sales Last Year
Southwestern	# 1.6	# 1.4
Southeastern	1.8	1.8
Northwestern	2.1	2.0
Northeastern	.6	.5
Central	3.0	2.8
Total	# 9.1	# 8.5

Lesson 146 — Prepare for Evaluation: Reports

146a ► 5

Conditioning Practice

each line twice SS (slowly, then faster); DS between 2-line groups; if time permits, repeat selected lines

alphabet 1 Exemplary jobs quite often have been done by a caring, zealous worker.

figures 2 In 1987, Al took 20 courses and made the grade point average of 3.645.

symbols 3 "Joel!" she exclaimed, "where is your brother's new three-piece suit?"

speed 4 Their problem is to make the girls sign the forms or pay for the work.

| 1 | 2 | 3 | 4 | 5 | 6 | 7 | 8 | 9 | 10 | 11 | 12 | 13 | 14 |

17a ▶ 8
Conditioning Practice

1. Each line twice SS (slowly; then faster); DS between 2-line groups.

2. If time permits, take three 1' writings on line 3; find *gwam* (total 5-stroke words typed or keyed): words in complete line PLUS words in a partial line.

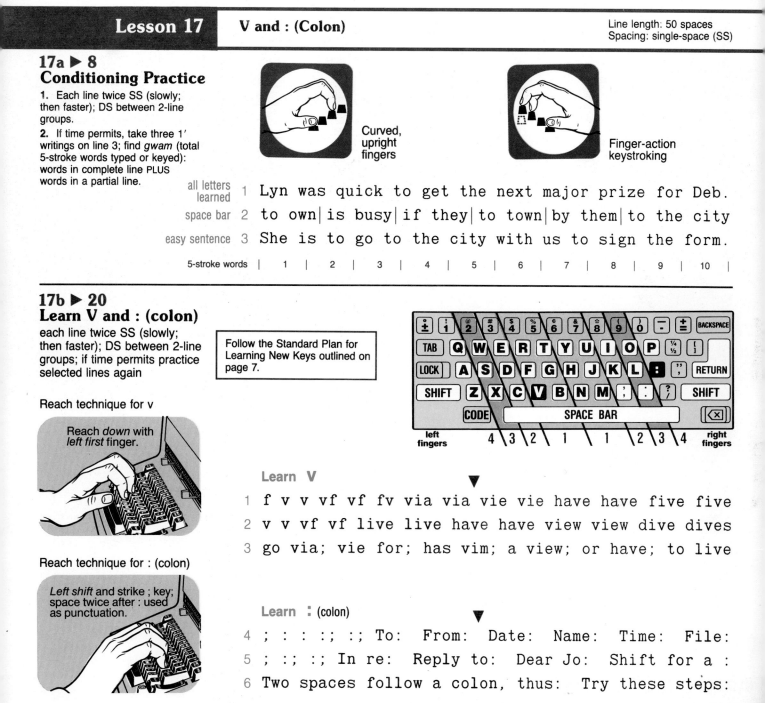

Curved, upright fingers

Finger-action keystroking

all letters learned	1	Lyn was quick to get the next major prize for Deb.
space bar	2	to own| is busy| if they| to town| by them| to the city
easy sentence	3	She is to go to the city with us to sign the form.

5-stroke words | 1 | 2 | 3 | 4 | 5 | 6 | 7 | 8 | 9 | 10 |

17b ▶ 20
Learn V and : (colon)

each line twice SS (slowly; then faster); DS between 2-line groups; if time permits practice selected lines again

Follow the Standard Plan for Learning New Keys outlined on page 7.

Reach technique for v

Reach *down* with *left first* finger.

Reach technique for : (colon)

Left shift and strike ; key; space twice after : used as punctuation.

Learn V

1 f v v vf vf fv via via vie vie have have five five
2 v v vf vf live live have have view view dive dives
3 go via; vie for; has vim; a view; or have; to live

Learn : (colon)

4 ; : : :; :; To: From: Date: Name: Time: File:
5 ; :; :; In re: Reply to: Dear Jo: Shift for a :
6 Two spaces follow a colon, thus: Try these steps:

Language Skills Notes

● Space twice after : used as punctuation.

● Capitalize the first word of a complete sentence following a colon.

Combine V and :

7 Vic: Enter via, view, and have five times for me.
8 Marv read: Shift to enter : and then space twice.
9 Vi, key the right word: let or leave; then go on.
10 Vida has a micro with the : where the ; should be.

145b ▶ 5
Check Language Skills: Homonyms

half sheet; 60-space line; SS
Key the sentences at the right (including number) selecting the correct word choice from the words in parentheses. Use the dictionary if necessary.

1. Susan gave Nancy a box of (stationary, stationery) for Christmas.
2. (Their, There) are several good reasons for the delay.
3. The (due, dew) made the grass quite wet.
4. I love you, (deer, dear), for your kindness during my illness.
5. Some people seem to have lost (sight, site) of the value of time.
6. Did you (lose, loose) $5 or $10 yesterday?
7. The (principle, principal) reason for the loss is obvious.
8. Jim ran much (further, farther) than Paul in the race.
9. Do you know (weather, whether) Jane will be here soon?
10. I would like to go, (two, to, too), if you don't mind.
11. How did you (advice, advise) the students about going to college?
12. The wind (blew, blue) fiercely last evening.

145c ▶ 15
Improve Skill on Statistical Copy

1. Take a 3' writing on all 3 ¶s to establish a base rate. Find *gwam.*

2. Take two 1' writings on each ¶ trying to improve rate with each timing.

3. Take another 3' writing on all 3 ¶s and compare *gwam* with the first 3' writing.

all letters used | A | 1.5 si | 5.7 awl | 80% hfw

	gwam 1'	3'
The Grand Canyon National Park, which is located in Arizona, was	13	4
established as a national park on February 26, 1919. However, additional	28	9
land was absorbed by the park as late as 1975, making a total acreage	42	14
of just over 1.2 million. This unique exposure of rock is 217 miles long	57	19
and from 4 to 18 miles wide. During recent years, it has been seen by	71	24
about 2,840,000 people each year.	78	26
Another beautiful national park is the Great Smoky Mountains Na-	13	30
tional Park. It has an acreage of about 273,550 in North Carolina and	27	35
about 241,206 in Tennessee, for a total of over 500,000. It was ap-	41	39
proved on May 22, 1926, and established for full development in 1934.	55	44
The diverse plant life is quite beautiful and is seen by over 11 million	69	49
persons each year.	73	50
Fascinating in even a different way and older and larger than any	13	55
of the other national parks, Yellowstone was established in 1872. Its	27	59
more than 2,219,000 acres cover parts of three states. It has over	41	64
10,000 geysers, dozens of majestic falls, canyons, and quiet wildlife	55	69
areas. People from all over the world come to it in numbers that exceed	70	73
2,487,000 each year.	74	75

gwam 1' | 1 | 2 | 3 | 4 | 5 | 6 | 7 | 8 | 9 | 10 | 11 | 12 | 13 | 14 |
3' | 1 | | 2 | | 3 | | 4 | | 5 |

17c ▶ 22
Improve Keyboarding Technique

each pair of lines twice SS (slowly; then faster); DS between 4-line groups; if time permits, practice selected lines again

q/v
1 via qua vow quo have quit move quiz vote aqua live
2 Viva has quit the squad to move to Quebec to live.

y/x
3 by ox you fix yes mix any six try fox say lax boys
4 Xica, you and the boys are to fix my mixer by six.

key words
5 by bid map key bit fix die end tie apt ivy ale wig
6 paid fuel maps soap born laid rush duty pens chair

key phrases
7 key it|apt to|lay it|to fix|an end|to tie|due them
8 she got it|key the name|fix the sign|boot the disk

easy sentences
9 He is to pay the man for the work and sign a form.
10 Lana is due by six and may go to the city with us.

all letters
11 am quo box can via jar zoo sip owl the dug oak fly
12 Glenda saw a quick red fox jump over the lazy cub.

Lesson 18	**SHIFT LOCK and ? (Question Mark)**	Line length: 50 spaces Spacing: single-space (SS)

18a ▶ 8
Conditioning Practice

each line twice SS (slowly; then faster); DS between 2-line groups; if time permits, practice selected lines again

all letters 1 Bev aims next to play a quick game with Jud Fritz.
v and : 2 To: Miss Val Devlin; From: Dr. Silvia J. Vicars.
easy sentence 3 He is to go to the town and to do the work for me.

18b ▶ 5
Type (Key) Block Paragraphs

each paragraph (¶) once SS as shown; DS between ¶s; if time permits, practice ¶ 1 again

If you take a 1' timed writing, see 16b, page 29, for the steps to find *gwam*.

Paragraph 1   *gwam 1'*

You know all the letters now, so keep up the good   10
work. Just pick a new goal each day, and work in   20
the correct way to gain it. Good form is the way.   30

Paragraph 2

First, set a goal that is easy to gain; next, try   10
one that will push you a bit to reach. Speed can   20
grow only if you force the rate and use good form.   30

gwam 1' | 1 | 2 | 3 | 4 | 5 | 6 | 7 | 8 | 9 | 10 |

Build Document Processing
Skill: Letters

plain full sheets; 1cc; correct errors

Take a 20' timing on the problems below. Determine number of problems completed and number of uncorrected errors.

Problem 1
block format; open punctuation

Problem 2
modified block format; indented ¶s; mixed punctuation

Letter address:
Ms. Dana Forman
Vice President of Finance
E & M Production, Inc.
6501 West Sunset Boulevard
Los Angeles, CA 90028-7711

Subject line:
Overdue Account with Station Video, Inc.

Amount: $1,864.25
(total words: 199)

Problem 3
block format; open punctuation

Repeat Problem 1 substituting the information below.

Letter address:
Mr. Berl M. Rebenar, President
Otto Home Improvements
2109 East Russell Street
Covington, KY 41014-8882

Subject line:
Overdue Account with Cam Outdoor Lighting

Amount: $895.00
(total words: 200)

	words
Current date │CERTIFIED MAIL │Mr. Frederick Mayo, President│	12
Reinier Scientific Enterprises │ 45 South Penn Street │	22
Allentown, PA 18105-2295 │Dear Mr. Mayo │Subject:	32
Overdue Account with Franklin Chemical Company │	42
(¶1) This letter represents our final attempt to collect	52
your overdue account with Franklin Chemical Company.	63
Unless your remittance is received within five days	73
from receipt of this letter, we shall have no alternative	85
but to place your account with an attorney for collection.	97
(¶2) The files of the Credit Bureau are available to banks	108
and other financial institutions throughout the United	119
States. To keep your record with the Bureau as favorable	130
as possible, please send a check for $2,856.44 in full	141
payment of your account. You will find an itemized	152
statement enclosed. │Sincerely yours │ELLIS CREDIT BUREAU│	163
Ms. Maria Duvall │Manager of Collections │xx│ Enclosure│	173
cc Franklin Chemical Company │ If you have sent your	184
check, please verify with us that we have received	194
it in order to protect your credit.	201

Lesson 145   Prepare for Evaluation: Tables

145a ▶ 5
Conditioning Practice

each line twice SS (slowly, then faster); DS between 2-line groups; if time permits, repeat selected lines

alphabet 1 Your math quiz was given on Monday to all future juniors except Becky.

figures 2 Flight 374 will be arriving at either Gate 28 or Gate 29 at 10:56 p.m.

fig/sym 3 B & C's has 20# paper for $3.58 and 16# paper for $2.74 (a 9% saving).

speed 4 When the eight towns amend the six bills, then their problems may end.

| 1 | 2 | 3 | 4 | 5 | 6 | 7 | 8 | 9 | 10 | 11 | 12 | 13 | 14 |

18c ▶ 15
Learn SHIFT LOCK and ? (question)

each line twice SS (slowly; then faster); DS between 2-line groups; if time permits, practice each line again

Follow the Standard Plan for Learning New Keys outlined on page 7.

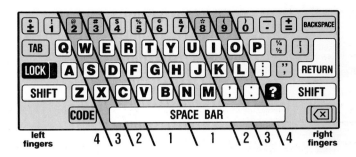

Reach technique for shift lock

Reach *left* with *left little* finger.

Reach technique for ? (question)

Left shift; reach *down* with *right little* finger; space twice after ? at end of sentence.

Learn SHIFT LOCK

1 The CPA firm said we should explore IRA and Keogh.
2 Jo Ann is sure the VDT showed UPS instead of USPS.
3 Oki joined FBLA when her sister joined PBL at MSU.

Learn ? (question)

Space twice

4 ; ?; ?; Who? Who is? Who is it? Did she not go?
5 Why not? Was it he? Shall we go? Are they here?
6 Is it up to me? Do you have it? Can you do this?

18d ▶ 22
Improving Keyboarding Technique

1. Each pair of lines twice SS (slowly; then faster); DS between 4-line groups.

2. As time permits, take two or three 1' timed writings on line 12; find *gwam*.

Goals
- reach *up* without moving hands away from you
- reach *down* without moving hands toward your body
- use SHIFT LOCK to make ALL CAPS; strike either shift key to release lock.

LOCK and ?	1 Did she join AMS? Did she also join OEA and DECA? 2 Do you know the ARMA rules? Are they used by TVA?
v and :	3 Harv, look up these words: vex, vial, shiv, cove. 4 Show state names with ZIP Codes thus: VA, WV, VT.
q and ,	5 I missed the words quay, aqua, mosque, and quince. 6 Quentin, Quig, and Jacques passed the quiz, I see.
key words	7 pick they next just bone more wove quiz code flags 8 flax plug quit name wore jack zinc busy vine third
key phrases	9 to aid us|is to pay|or to cut|to fix it|apt to own 10 if we did|to be fit|is on the|to my pay|due at six
all letters	11 Bix Glanz packed my bag with five quarts of juice.
easy sentence	12 He or she is to go to the lake to do the map work.

5-stroke words | 1 | 2 | 3 | 4 | 5 | 6 | 7 | 8 | 9 | 10 |

To find 1' *gwam*: Add 10 for each line you completed to the scale figure beneath the point at which you stopped in a partial line. The total is your 1' *gwam*.

Unit 30　Lessons 144-147

Learning Goals

1. To improve straight-copy skill.
2. To review and improve skill on letters, tables, and reports.
3. To improve language skills.

Machine Adjustments

1. Paper guide at *0*.
2. Paper bail rolls at even intervals across page.
3. Margins: 70-space line for drill lines and timed paragraphs; as needed or directed for other problems.
4. Spacing: SS for drill lines and letters. DS for timed paragraphs and reports.

Lesson 144　Prepare for Evaluation: Letters

144a ▶ 5
Conditioning Practice

each line twice SS (slowly, then faster); DS between 2-line groups; if time permits, repeat selected lines

alphabet　1　Jack quickly opened the exits when the fire alarm gave a warning buzz.

figures　2　The population was 6,453 in 1987, which was an increase of 20 percent.

fig/sym　3　If we pay by May 7, we can save $659.48 with their terms (2/10, n/30).

speed　4　Their amendment will aid the panel of men and the auditor of the firm.

| 1 | 2 | 3 | 4 | 5 | 6 | 7 | 8 | 9 | 10 | 11 | 12 | 13 | 14 |

144b ▶ 20
Build Speed: Letters

plain paper; modified block format; blocked ¶s; open punctuation

1. A 5' writing on the letter to establish a base rate. If you finish before time is called, start over.

2. Find *gwam*. Use this rate as your goal rate. Turn to page 242 to find quarter-minute checkpoints if necessary; note these figures in opening lines through ¶ 1.

3. Take three 1' guided writings on the opening lines through ¶ 1. Leave proper spacing between letter parts.

4. Repeat Steps 2 and 3, but begin with ¶ 3 and continue through closing lines.

5. Take another 5' writing on the letter. Try to maintain your new goal rate.

gwam 5'

May 28, 19--　SPECIAL DELIVERY　Department of Office Administration　3｜36

Attention　Dr. Milton Baker　Ohio Valley College　800 Noel Drive　Spring-　5｜38

field, OH　45506-3312　Ladies and Gentlemen　Subject: Summer Conference　8｜41

(¶ 1) Participating in your summer conference last week was an educational　11｜44

and enjoyable experience for me.　The program was well-planned, and your　14｜47

faculty extended a special welcome to me.　16｜49

(¶ 2) As you requested, I am sending brochures related to our records　18｜51

management software.　These are being sent by special delivery in hopes　21｜54

that you will have time to consider them for your summer session.　24｜57

(¶ 3) I look forward to working with you again as you plan future pro-　26｜59

fessional programs.　Sincerely　B & C OFFICE TECHNOLOGY　Mrs. Jan S.　29｜62

Holton　Vice President　xx　Enclosures　pc Dr. Ray Camp, Dean　Postscript　31｜64

Receipts for my expenses are also enclosed.　33｜66

19a ▶ 8
Conditioning Practice

each line twice SS (slowly; then faster); DS between 2-line groups; if time permits, practice the lines again

Spacing summary

Space once after , and ; and once after . at end of an abbreviation or following an initial. Space twice after . and ? at end of sentence. *Do not* space after any punctuation mark that ends a line.

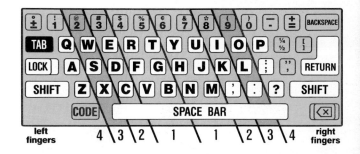

left fingers 4 \ 3 \ 2 \ 1 \ 1 \ 2 \ 3 \ 4 right fingers

alphabet	1	Buck Zahn will vex the judge if he quits my group.
space bar	2	than busy them city then many sign duty when proxy
easy sentence	3	I am to go to the dock, and he is to work with me.

5-stroke words | 1 · | 2 | 3 | 4 | 5 | 6 | 7 | 8 | 9 | 10 |

19b ▶ 12
Learn Tabulator

To clear electric/manual tabs

1. Move carrier to extreme *right* (or carriage to extreme *left*).

2. Hold **clear key (4)** down as you return carrier to extreme *left* (or carriage to extreme *right*) to remove all tab stops.

To clear electronic tabs

1. Depress tab key to move carrier to the tab stop to be cleared.

2. Depress tab clear key to clear the stop.

3. To clear all stops, depress tab clear key, then the repeat key.

To set tabs (all machines)

1. Move carrier (carriage) to desired tab position by striking space bar or backspace key.

2. Depress **tab set key (2)**. Repeat this procedure for each stop needed.

Tabulating procedure

Strike the **tab key (5)** with the nearer little finger or the **tab bar (5)** with the right index finger; release it quickly and return the finger to home-key position.

Drill procedure

1. Clear all tab stops, as directed above.

2. Set a tab stop 5 spaces to the right of left margin stop.

3. Set the **line-space selector (22)** on "2" for DS (double spacing).

4. Type (key) the paragraphs once DS as shown, indenting the first line of each paragraph.

Tab ⟶ To indent the first line of a block of copy, use the tab key or bar.

Tab ⟶ On electrics, just strike the key or bar and release it at once.

Tab ⟶ On some manuals, though, you must strike and hold down the key or bar.

<u>Guest</u> talent show. Our guests started this function five years ago, and we have continued to do it by popular demand. The ~~show~~ repertoire usually consists of various musical songs with dance routines; however, short skits or a play is sometimes opted for by our guests. The "stars" perform on Saturday evenings.

<u>Daily Activities</u>

For those who like to throw away the watch during vacation time, most of the daily activities can be selected without notice.

"<u>Nature activities</u>." Field trips, nature walks, lectures, films, and other "nature activities" are scheduled several times a week. Watch the bulletin board in the lobby for specific information because the schedule may be changed as the weather changes. In addition, we have designed nature trails that are accessible by foot or bicycle. You will find maps for our various trails in the lobby; or if you are adventurous, take an uncharted hike through the woods.

<u>Beaches</u>. the beach on the north side of the lake has been designated the quiet area. It is reserved for those who like to read, write, paint, or just day dream in tranquility while enjoying the sun. If you like action, the south beach is for you. Three volleyball nets are in place, and you can check out volleyballs from the health club and spa. Paddle boats and row boats are available to rent for a nominal fee. Radios or other distractions are not permitted on the north side of the lake.

<u>Pools</u>. The out door pool is for general use during the summer months, while the indoor pool is reserved for planned activities such as swimming lessons and water exercise sports. Let us know if you or family members are interested in swimming lessons so that we can make the necessary arrangements.

<u>Health club and spa</u>. Visit this area early in the week to see the many activities offered at the club and spa; they are too numerous to describe here. We have to mention, though, the installation of whirlpool baths and a new exercise room {with the latest body-building equipment}.

If all of this is not enough, just tell us what is missing and we will do our best to provide it.

19c ▶ 12
Improve Keyboarding Technique

each pair of lines twice SS; DS between 4-line groups

Lines 1-2

Clear tab stops; beginning at left margin, set a tab stop every 9 spaces until you have set 5 tab stops. Type (key) the first word in Column 1; tab to Column 2 and type the first word in that column; and so on. There will be 5 blank spaces between the columns.

tabulator
```
1  pair   Tab  auto   Tab  kept   Tab  goal   Tab  worn   Tab  their
2  body        fuel        sick        born        soap        risks
```

space bar
```
3  go am he me so do an us if by or it is of fur keys
4  an we me as am re us my if on by pi he no the join
```

shift keys
```
5  The winners are:  Elena and Juan; Masami and Bing.
6  Did Miss Quadnau send us the report of Dr. Lamont?
```

shift lock
```
7  The FHA meeting is on Monday; the FFA, on Tuesday.
8  Luis watched the game on HBO; Nana saw it on WKRC.
```

19d ▶ 18
Build Keyboarding Speed

Lines 1-4

each line twice SS; DS between 2-line groups; speed up the second attempt at the line

Key words and phrases   (*Think, say,* and *key* words and phrases.)
```
1  in we on be as no at up ad my are you was him gets
2  my ad|at no|as we|be in|we are|was him|you get set
3  turn rush duty girl maps rich laid down held spend
4  to rush|if they|by them|the duty|she kept|and paid
```

Lines 5-8

a 1′ timed writing on each line; find *gwam* on each writing (see bottom of page 33)

Goal: *At least 21 gwam*

Easy sentences   (Key the words at a brisk, steady pace.)
```
5  Did they go by bus to visit six of the lake towns?
6  To do the work right is the duty of the six of us.
7  He is to do all the field forms for the usual pay.
8  She did lend all the audit forms to the six girls.
```

```
5-stroke words  |  1  |  2  |  3  |  4  |  5  |  6  |  7  |  8  |  9  |  10  |
```

Easy paragraph

1. Type (key) the paragraph once DS as shown.
2. Two 1′ timed writings on the paragraph; find *gwam* on each writing.

Goal: *At least 19 gwam*

Alphabetic paragraph   (all letters used)
```
            .    2    .    4    .    6    .    8    .
Tab    In just a few weeks, you have found the keys
       10   .    12   .    14   .    16   .    18   .
to a top job.  You know you need good form in the
     20   .    22   .    24   .    26   .    28
next plan for a high speed.  Be quick to prize it.
```

I have edited this information to be given to guests when they register at the lodge. Would you please check to make sure I have not overlooked any errors; then, process this material in unbound report format.
r.c.

center ─ WOLF CREEK LODGE ACTIVITIES

To ~~aid~~ *help* you ~~with~~ *plan* your vacation so that you can have a fun-filled week let me review the many options available to you. If we fail to mention something you had in mind, please tell us so *that* we can as*s*ist in making this your most memorable vacation ever.

Weekly Scheduled Activities

Y*o*u will want to decide soon which of thes*e* activiti*es* you wish to participate in, since some *of* them require reservations.

Get-acquainted brunch. You should not miss *this opportunity* ~~the chance~~ to get to know our *o*ther guests before you *begin* ~~start~~ the week. On sunday from 11 a.m. to 2 p.m., you may attend a free buf*f*et brunch. This buffet will introduce you to the excellant cuisine you can expect to enjoy for the week and will give you the opportunity to meet other guests and sign up for *several* exciting events occuring d*r*uing the week.

Dinner show. A flyer announcing the dinner show for the week is in your room. This is an event you won't *want* to miss!

Overnight camp-out. For those who enjoy sleeping under the stars, we hav*e* a camp-out in the mountains on wednesday evnings--again, weather permitting. We will cook our "catch"; but just in case the big one gets away, we will take along adequate provisions. Fishing lisense will be provided by the lodge. Call the main desk *(ext. 613)* if you wish to register.

Outdoor barbe*c*que. Each tuesday evening at 6 p.m. {weather permitting}, we have an old-fashioned barbecue in the pavilion by the lake. A *western* band accompanies the festivities; and after a*p*petites have been satiated, we clear the deck for dancing until 11:30 p.m. The cost is $18 for adults and $7 for children under 12; *we need reservations by noon on Monday.*

20a ▶ 8
Conditioning Practice

1. Each line twice SS (slowly; then faster); DS between 2-line groups.

2. If time permits, take three 1' writings on line 3; find *gwam* (total 5-stroke words typed or keyed): words in complete line(s) PLUS words in a partial line.

Finger-action keystroking

Down-and-in spacing

alphabet	1	Jo Fox made five quick plays to win the big prize.
space bar	2	a of to is it or if an do so he go she the and for
easy sentence	3	Pay them for the sign work they do if it is right.

5-stroke words | 1 | 2 | 3 | 4 | 5 | 6 | 7 | 8 | 9 | 10 |

20b ▶ 22
Check Keystroking Technique

each set of lines twice SS; DS between 6-line groups; on the second attempt, try to increase your speed

Ask your teacher to check your keystroking technique as you type (key) the following lines.

left fingers 4 3 2 1 1 2 3 4 **right fingers**

Fingers upright

Fingers curved

Rows (Reach *up*, reach *down* without moving the hands.)

home/3d	1	pay got law jar lap rod dug sit hue risk four aqua
home/1st	2	an ax jab can zag ham van cash lack hand flax glad
3d/1st	3	Beryl is apt to win the gold cup in the next race.

Fingers (Keep on home row the fingers not used for reaching.)

1st/2d	4	it dig cut run den net fur yet vie jet fib rub the
3d/4th	5	so pal zoo lax low zap sow sap also slaw laws wasp
all	6	A judge will next read the laws to the open court.

One-hand words (*Think, say,* and *key* words at a steady pace.)

words	7	pi as on at in we on re oh are oil was ink gas nil
words	8	ax up ad no be you saw him get ilk tax mop bad pun
sentence	9	As you see, we aced a pop test on a poll tax case.

Balanced-hand words (*Think, say,* and *key* the words as *words.*)

words	10	am us own bus lay fix but key big pay due cut half
phrases	11	to pay half|if the city|of the maps|is to pay them
sentence	12	Aisha did fix the dock sign; the city paid for it.

5-stroke words | 1 | 2 | 3 | 4 | 5 | 6 | 7 | 8 | 9 | 10 |

Job 6
Table
(full sheet)

> Please prepare this list to send to Betsy Barnes, Director of Youth Activities. Alphabetize the list by surnames and check for errors I may have overlooked.
>
> r.c.

LIST OF TEENAGERS

June 15-~~22~~ 21

Name	Hometown	Age
Karla Zorba	Albuquerque, NM	16
Jeffrey Grimsley	Kansas City, KS	13
Neal Butler	Omaha, NE	17
Janet Brewer	Tulse, OK	14
Brian Manzer	Denver, CO	~~17~~ 18
Tien Su	~~Moab, UT~~ Houstan, TX	19
Chriss Porter	Tompeka, KS	17
Nicole Jordan	Minneaspolis, ~~MP~~ MN	15
Don ~~Reeder~~ Rentear	Peublo, CO	16
Teresa Weaver	Santa Fe, NM	14
Victor Lopez	Austin, TX	15
~~Lynn~~ Ann Hoyer	~~Pullman, WV~~ Seatle, WA	~~23~~ 13

Job 7
Simplified Memo
(LM p. 125)

> Please prepare this memo to Betsy Barnes, Director of Youth Activities, to accompany the list of teenagers you just prepared. Let me sign the memo when you have finished. Use today's date: June 2.
>
> r.c.

LIST OF TEENAGERS FOR WEEK OF JUNE 15-21

At the suggestion of Paul Skidmore, I have prepared a list of the presently registered teenagers who will be here during the week of June 15-21. We thought that it might be helpful for you to have this information in advance, along with ages and hometowns, so that you can plan activities for the week.

As soon as you have finalized your list of activities, could you please send me a copy.

Attachment

20c ▶ 10
Check/Improve Keyboarding Speed

1. Take a 30-second (30″) timed writing on each line. Your rate in *gwam* is shown word for word above the lines.

2. If time permits, take another 30″ writing on each line. Try to increase your keyboarding speed.

Goal

At least 22 gwam.

30″ gwam

| | 2 | 4 | 6 | 8 | 10 | 12 | 14 | 16 | 18 | 20 | 22 |

1 Aida is to fix their gold urn.
2 Jay is to pay all six for the work.
3 Did the queen also visit the lake towns?
4 The theme for the panel is world fuel profit.
5 Buzz works for the big map firm for the usual pay.
6 Elena is to fix the sign then go to the lake with Rick.

| | 2| | 4| | 6| | 8| | 10| | 12| | 14! | 16| | 18| | 20| | 22| |

If you finish a line before time is called and start over, your *gwam* is the figure at the end of the line PLUS the figure above or below the point at which you stopped.

20d ▶ 10
Check/Improve Keyboarding Speed

1. A 1′ writing on each ¶; find *gwam* on each writing.

2. Using your better *gwam* as a base rate, select a *goal rate* and take two 1′ guided writings on each ¶ as directed at the bottom of the page.

Copy used to measure skill is triple-controlled for difficulty:
E = easy   HA = high average
LA = low average   D = difficult
A = average

Difficulty index (shown above copy)
↓

E	1.0 si	4.4 awl	95% hfw
1	**2**	**3**	
Syllable intensity	Average word length	High-frequency words	

Difficulty index

all letters used	E	1.0 si	4.4 awl	95% hfw

gwam 2′

. 2 . 4 . 6 . 8 .

¶ 1   Good form means to move with speed and quiet   5
10 . 12 . 14 . 16 . 18 .
control. My next step will be to size up the job   10
20 . 22 . 24 . 26 . 28 .
and to do the work in the right way each day.   14

. 2 . 4 . 6 . 8 .
¶ 2   To reach my goal of top speed, I have to try   19
10 . 12 . 14 . 16 . 18 .
to build good form. I will try for the right key   24
20 . 22 . 24 . 26 . 28 .
each time, but I must do so in the right way.   28

gwam 2′ | 1 | 2 | 3 | 4 | 5 |

Guided (Paced) Writing Procedure

Select a practice goal:

1. Take a 1′ writing on ¶ 1 of a set of ¶s that contain superior figures for guided writings, as in 20d above.

2. Using the *gwam* as a base, add 4 *gwam* to determine your goal rate.

3. Choose from Column 1 of the table at the right the speed nearest your goal rate. At the right of that speed, note the ¼′ points in the copy you must reach to maintain your goal rate.

Quarter-minute checkpoints

gwam	¼′	½′	¾′	Time
16	4	8	12	16
20	5	10	15	20
24	6	12	18	24
28	7	14	21	28
32	8	16	24	32
36	9	18	27	36
40	10	20	30	40

4. Note from the word-count dots and figures above the lines in ¶ 1 the checkpoint for each quarter minute. (Example: Checkpoints for 24 *gwam* are 6, 12, 18, and 24.)

Practice procedure

1. Take two 1′ writings on ¶ 1 at your goal rate guided by the quarter-minute calls (¼, ½, ¾, time).

Goal: To reach each of your checkpoints just as the guide is called.

2. Take two 1′ writings on ¶ 2 of a set of ¶s in the same way.

3. If time permits, take a 2′ writing on the set of ¶s combined, without the guides.

Speed level of practice

When the purpose of practice is to reach out into new speed areas, use the *speed* level. Take the brakes off your fingers and experiment with new stroking patterns and new speeds. Do this by:

1. Reading 2 or 3 letters ahead of your typing to foresee stroking patterns.

2. Getting the fingers ready for the combinations of letters to be typed.

3. Keeping your eyes on the copy in the book.

Here is a rough draft of the menu we need for 6/17. I've marked changes and errors, but you may find additional errors that I've overlooked. Please prepare a final copy to photocopy and enclose with letters I will be sending to guests.

r.c.

GARDEN RESTURANT

June 17, 19--
6 - 10 p.m.

THE BEGINNING

To tanelize your taste buds - a petite assortment of canpes, cheeses, and reslishes

Plus your choice of:
Spinach and Bacon Salad
Fresh Fruit Salad
*Gazpacho

ENTREES

*Chicken Orental - served in a sauce of mushroms and a special blend of herbs and spices, over a bed of white rice, with stir-fried vegetables.

*Beef Pot Roast (au jus) - served with twice-baked potato and asparagus tips in cheese sauce.

*Golden Glazed Ham - served with orange slices and garnish, fresh green beans, and parsley new potatoes.

THE FINALE

*Fresh Blueberries With Whipped Cream
Cheese Cake with or without Cherry Topping
German Chocolate Cake

Beverages — All CAP
Coffee (Regular or Expresso)
Tee (Iced or Hot)
Milk

Bread and Butter — ALL CAP
Bread Basket of asorted fresh baked rolls and breads

CHILDREN'S Menu (Under 12)

Western Burger - a juicy, old-fashioned hamburger served with country fries, choice of dessert and beverage.

Fried Chicken - a drum tick and wing browed to perfection, mashed potatoes, gravy, green beans, and beverage.

*House specialties

Unit 2 Lessons 21-25

Learning Goals
1. To improve keyboarding techniques.
2. To improve speed on sentence and paragraph copy.
3. To review and improve language skills: capitalization.

Machine Adjustments
1. Paper guide at *0*.
2. Ribbon control to use top half of ribbon.
3. Margin sets: left margin (center - 25); right margin (move to right end of scale).
4. Line-space selector set to single-space (SS) drills.
5. Line-space selector set to double-space (DS) ¶s.

Lesson 21	Basic/Language Skills	Line length: 50 spaces Spacing: single-space (SS)

21a ▶ 6
Conditioning Practice
1. Each line twice SS.
2. A 1′ writing on line 3; find *gwam*.

alphabet 1 Jewel amazed Vic by escaping quickly from the box.

punctuation 2 Have we used these words: view, vote, five, gave?

easy sentence 3 He is to do social work for the city if they wish.

5-stroke words | 1 | 2 | 3 | 4 | 5 | 6 | 7 | 8 | 9 | 10 |

21b ▶ 22
Improve Keyboarding Technique
each set of lines twice SS (slowly; then faster); DS between 4-line groups; if time permits, practice selected lines again

Fingers curved

Reach review (Keep hands and arms quiet, almost motionless.)

ol/lo
1 old lot lox loan told long hold local whole school
2 Lou told me that her local school loans old books.

za/az
3 zap maze lazy jazz hazy zany raze haze amaze crazy
4 A jazz band played with pizzazz at my pizza stand.

ik/ki
5 kite bike kind like kilt kick pike kiwi hike skill
6 The striking pink kite skimmed over the ski trail.

ed/de
7 led side heed used made need wide idea guide delay
8 Ned said the guide used a slide film for her talk.

ws/sw
9 was saw laws rows swan swam sway flaws shows swing
10 Wes said the first two rows saw flaws in the show.

ft/ju
11 oft jug sift just left jury lift judge often juice
12 Jud left fifty jugs of juice on a raft for a gift.

(¶7) Last, we haven't forgotten that teenagers require their "special" brand of entertainment. That is why we have hired Betsy Barnes, a full-time youth director, who is responsible for keeping teenagers happy. From rowboating to horseback riding to backpacking hikes, Betsy has planned a wide variety of activities. And, judging from the volume of fan mail that Betsy has received this past year, I would say that she has made quite a hit with teenagers. Another benefit from the teenage program is the lasting friendships that continue long after the vacation at Wolf Creek is over.

(¶8) We hope these details are helpful to you as you continue to plan your vacation. If we can answer questions or be of assistance in any way, do let us know. You can reach us at 1-800-227-8800.

(¶9) We are eager to have you (and your children) (and your son--use name) (and your daughter--use name) as our guest(s). Do let us know if we can be of assistance in any way.

Job 4
Dinner Show Announcement
(plain sheet)

Please prepare this announcement to photocopy for enclosure in the letters you have just completed. Align items in second column at the left. Thanks.
r.c.

THE RIVERSIDE ROOM
Dinner Show
For the Week of
June 15 - 21

Dinner Music	Lou Springer
Master of Ceremonies	Eric Sampson
Hula Dancing	The Polynesian Dancers
	Fort Lewis College
	Durango, CO
Music and Humor	The Gold Rushers
Comedian	Steven Baird
Dance Band	The Gold Rushers

Adults: $18*
Children under 12: $10*

Dinner: 6:30 - 8 p.m.
Show Time: 8 - 10 p.m.
Dancing: 10:30-midnight

*Price includes Hawaiian Buffet and show, including tax. Gratuities are not included.

21c ▶ 12
Check/Improve Keyboarding Speed

1. Take one 1′ timed writing and two 1′ *guided* writings on ¶ 1 as directed on page 37.

2. Take one 1′ timed writing and two 1′ *guided* writings on ¶ 2 in the same way.

3. As time permits, take one or two 2′ timed writings on ¶s 1 and 2 combined *without* the call of the guide; find *gwam*.

1′ Gwam Goals

▽ 17 = acceptable
☐ 21 = average
○ 25 = good
◇ 29 = excellent

all letters used | E | 1.2 si | 5.0 awl | 95% hfw |

gwam 2′

```
         .         2         .         4         .         6         .         8         .
    It is important for me to learn to force two        4
    10    .    12         .    14         .    16    ▽    18    .
to four letters close together in time.  If I can        9
    20    ⊡    22         .    24    ⊙    26         .    28    ◇
cut the time between them, my skill will increase.       14
         .         2         .         4         .         6         .         8         .
    The size of the word and the sequence of its        19
    10    .    12         .    14         .    16    ▽    18    .
letters may determine just how fast I can move to       24
    20    ⊡    22         .    24    ⊙    26         .    28    ◇
handle it.  To cut time should get next attention.      29
```

gwam 2′ | 1 | 2 | 3 | 4 | 5 |

21d ▶ 10 Improve Language Skills: Capitalization

1. Read the first rule highlighted in color at the right.

2. Type (key) the *Learn* sentence below it, noting how the rule has been applied.

3. Type (key) the *Apply* sentence, supplying the needed capital letters.

4. Read and practice the other rules in the same way.

5. If time permits, type (key) the three *Apply* sentences again to increase decision-making speed.

> Capitalize the first word in a sentence.

Learn 1 You left your book here. Shall I bring it to you?
Apply 2 do you plan to go? the bus will get here at noon.

> Capitalize personal titles and names of people.

Learn 3 Did Mrs. Hickman say that Mr. Mazla would take us?
Apply 4 ask if alma and suzan took the trip with ms. diaz.

> Capitalize names of cities, states, and other important places.

Learn 5 While in New York, they saw the Statue of Liberty.
Apply 6 she will visit the white house in washington, d.c.

Lesson 22 | Basic/Language Skills

Line length: 50 spaces
Spacing: single-space (SS)

22a ▶ 6
Conditioning Practice

1. Each line twice SS.
2. A 1′ writing on line 3; find *gwam*.

alphabet 1 Have my long quiz boxed when Jack stops by for it.
space bar 2 to do it|go to the|and to do|if she is|he may work
easy 3 He may do all the work if he works with good form.

5-stroke words | 1 | 2 | 3 | 4 | 5 | 6 | 7 | 8 | 9 | 10 |

22b ▶ 12
Check/Improve Keyboarding Speed

1. Take one 1′ timed writing and two 1′ *guided* writings on ¶ 1 of 21c, above, as directed at the bottom of page 37.

2. Type (key) ¶ 2 of 21c, above, in the same way.
Goal: To increase speed.

3. As time permits, take one or two 2′ timed writings on ¶s 1 and 2 combined; find *gwam*.

139b-143b (continued)

Job 3
Form Letters
(LM pp. 117-124)

Please prepare letters and envelopes for Mr. Paul R. Skidmore, Lodge Director, to be sent to the families for whom you just prepared index cards. Use today's date (June 1, 19—) for each letter.

Use the form paragraphs listed beside each name. In some cases, you will need to select the appropriate phrase from those suggested in parentheses.

GOMEZ -- 2, 3, 7, 9
MUNSON -- 3, 5, 9
GUINN -- 1, 3, 4, 5, 6, 8
PEREZ -- 1, 4, 5, 6, 7, 8

Use personal titles and last names in the salutation except for the Munsons. Use their first names, i.e., Dear Gene and Lois.

List appropriate items in an enclosure notation if enclosures are to accompany the letter. For example:

Enclosures: 2 Brochures
              Sample Menu

The longer letters may need to be processed as two-page letters. Use plain full sheets for second page of letter. Thanks.

r.c.

(¶1) Your vacation at Wolf Creek Lodge will be one that you _(and your family) (and your son) (and your daughter)_ will recall as one of the most enjoyable vacations you have ever taken. How can I make this statement with such confidence? It is because people like you have been sharing their vacations with us for the past 30 years, and they tell us repeatedly that their memories of Wolf Creek Lodge linger long after they have returned home. In fact, they tell us that their enjoyable memories of Wolf Creek are frequently the subject of "Remember the time when . . ." stories.

(¶2) WELCOME BACK TO WOLF CREEK LODGE!

(¶3) Looking forward to a vacation and planning that vacation are almost as much fun as the vacation itself. So let us help you with the planning by describing what your fun-filled vacation will be like this summer at Wolf Creek Lodge. We've retained the most popular "old" events--our "get-acquainted" party soon after you arrive, the guest talent show, and the "Back to Nature" lectures and field trips, and much more. In addition, we've expanded our offerings to include an overnight camp-out in the mountains, a fabulous dinner show, and an old-fashioned barbecue with entertainment by a western band.

(¶4) The two enclosed brochures describe in detail the wide variety of services and activities at the lodge and in the surrounding community. Whether you are looking for fun and action or peace and tranquillity, you will find it at Wolf Creek. The lodge is surrounded by acres of woods which are accessible by foot or bicycle; and, on the north side of our lake, you will find the seclusion you are longing for.

(¶5) Naturally, an important part of every successful vacation is good, nutritional food offered at affordable prices. We have enclosed a sample menu (for the Garden Restaurant), which will give you an idea of the tasty, nutritional meals we offer at the lodge. You will notice, also, that we have not forgotten appetizers in planning the menu! Meal tickets for any of our three restaurants may be purchased at a 10 percent discount if purchased at least one week in advance. Also, tickets for our dinner show may be purchased at a discount when you register (see enclosed announcement for details of discount and description of the show). Although we welcome you to dine at any of our restaurants, every unit is equipped with a complete kitchenette if you prefer the casual meal at home.

(¶6) As a parent of _(a young child) (young children)_, you may be interested in our child-care services. From 1 to 5 each afternoon, the lodge provides for "parents' time out." Our playground is equipped to entertain children from 1 to 12 years of age, and our experienced staff is committed to seeing that children enjoy their vacation too. In addition, we maintain a staff of qualified individuals who thoroughly enjoy entertaining children. Each person on staff was carefully screened because we realize how important quality child care is to parents.

(continued on page 247)

22c ▶ 20
Improve Keyboarding Technique: Response Patterns

1. Each pair of lines twice SS; DS between 4-line groups.

2. A 1' writing on line 11 and then on line 12 to increase speed; find *gwam* on each.

Practice hints

One-hand lines:
Think, *say*, and *key* the words by letter response at a steady but unhurried pace.

Balanced-hand lines:
Think, *say*, and *key* the words by word response at a fast pace.

> **Letter response**
> Many one-hand words (as in lines 1-2) are not easy to key. Such words may be keyed *letter by letter* with continuity (steadily, without pauses).

> **Word response**
> Short, balanced-hand words (as in lines 3-4) are so easy to key they can be keyed as words. Think and key them at your top speed.

	one-hand words	
1	at up as in we on be no ax oh ex my pi are you was	
2	ad him get ink few pin tax pop set ilk far pup car	

	balanced-hand words	
3	us do if an so am go he to me or is of ah it by ox	
4	el the and for may but pay due own men did box map	

	one-hand phrases	
5	as in|at no|be up|as my|be in|at my|we hum|see you	
6	get set|get him|you are|pop art|red ink|my oil tax	

	balanced-hand phrases	
7	of us|if he|do so|it is|to us|or by|an ox|to do it	
8	he did|the map|and for|she may|the six|got the bus	

	one-hand sentences	
9	You set my tax only after I gave you my wage data.	
10	As you saw up at my mill, my rate was up on water.	

	balanced-hand sentences	
11	He is to go to the city and to do the work for me.	
12	I am to pay the six men if they do the work right.	

5-stroke words | 1 | 2 | 3 | 4 | 5 | 6 | 7 | 8 | 9 | 10 |

22d ▶ 12
Improve Language Skills: Capitalization

1. Read each rule and type (key) the Learn and Apply sentences beneath it.

2. If time permits, practice the Apply lines again to increase decision-making speed.

> Capitalize the days of the week.

Learn 1 Are you sure the FBLA contest is to be on Tuesday?
Apply 2 the joggers meet on monday, wednesday, and friday.

> Capitalize the months of the year.

Learn 3 April was quite chilly, but May has been pleasant.
Apply 4 from june to september seems like a long vacation.

> Capitalize names of holidays.

Learn 5 We usually picnic in the park on Independence Day.
Apply 6 bev plans to visit her family on thanksgiving day.

> Capitalize the names of historic periods and events and special events.

Learn 7 Bastille Day is in honor of the French Revolution.
Apply 8 the fourth of july honors the american revolution.

Here is a list of names and addresses of guests who made reservations today. Prepare index cards for our information file. See the attached card for format.

r.c.

```
MERCER, CARY AND CRYSTAL (MR. AND MRS.)

Mr. and Mrs. Cary Mercer
2643 West Quail Avenue
Phoenix, AZ   85027-9977

Home:   (602) 499-4577
Office:  (602) 466-2016

Children:  Bob 7; Karen 5; Previous Guest:
No; Week:  June 8-15
```

Dr. Jack R. Gomez 920 Harmon Street Birmingham, MI 48009-4320   Home: (313) 440-8124   Office: (313) 447-9967   Child: John 16 Previous Guest: 7 consecutive years   Week: July 13-20

Mr. and Mrs. Gene Munson (Lois) 1486 West Catalpa Drive Baton Rouge, LA 70815-4733 Home: (504) 887-2114 Office: (504) 886-2338 Children: None Previous Guest: 4 times   Week: June 22-29

Mr. and Mrs. Roger Guinn (Cindy) 1486 East Cornell Avenue Englewood, CO 80110-6255 Home: (303) 462-8841 Office: (303) 899-6521 Children: Rob 4, Elizabeth 2 Previous Guest: No Week: June 15-22

Ms. Ada Perez 1741 North First Street Fort Smith, AR 72901-7312 Home: (501) 772-4118 Office: (501) 772-6403 Children: Marcus 14, Paula 7 Previous Guest: No Week: July 17-August 3

23a ▶ 6
Conditioning Practice
1. Each line twice SS.
2. A 1' writing on line 3; find *gwam*.

alphabet 1 Aquela Javicz kept the new forms by the tax guide.

shift lock 2 Did you OK this show for ABC, for NBC, or for CBS?

easy 3 They may cut the fish down by the end of the dock.

5-stroke words | 1 | 2 | 3 | 4 | 5 | 6 | 7 | 8 | 9 | 10 |

23b ▶ 20 Improve Keyboarding Technique: Response Patterns
1. Each set of lines twice SS (slowly; then faster); DS between 6-line groups.
2. A 1' writing on line 10, next on line 11, then on line 12; find *gwam* on each; compare rates.

letter response

1 as no we in be you far him few oil get pin age kin

2 you set|oil car|see him|few kin|bad pun|set my tax

3 As you were in a tax case, we set up rates on gas.

word response

4 is to if am ox own and but did she may air end big

5 if so|to own|if she|of six|did own|but she|the air

6 Vi is to go with them to the quay by the big lake.

Combination response

Normal copy (as in lines 7-9) includes both word- and letter-response sequences. *Use top speed for easy words, lower speed for more difficult ones.*

combination response

7 if on so as or we of no us up go my to be am at by

8 is in|go on|if no|to be|is up|so as|is my|am up to

9 If we are to be in the city, she may see him then.

letter 10 You gave only a few facts in my case on oil taxes.

word 11 Dick is to make a visit to the eight island towns.

combination 12 Daq may be paid extra if he works on my big barge.

5-stroke words | 1 | 2 | 3 | 4 | 5 | 6 | 7 | 8 | 9 | 10 |

23c ▶ 12
Improve Language Skills: Capitalization
1. Read each rule and type (key) the Learn and Apply sentences beneath it.
2. If time permits, practice the Apply lines again to increase decision-making speed.

Capitalize names of clubs, organizations, and companies.

Learn 1 The Beaux Arts Club did a show at Jewish Hospital.

Apply 2 apex corp. aids our chapter of junior achievement.

Capitalize geographic names, regions, and locations.

Learn 3 Texas and Mexico share the Rio Grande as a border.

Apply 4 i viewed the grand canyon as we flew over arizona.

Capitalize names of streets, avenues, and buildings.

Learn 5 Suzi Quan has moved to Croix Towers on Park Place.

Apply 6 their office is in gulf plaza on san pedro avenue.

139a-143a ▶ 5 (daily)

Each day before you begin work on the problems (139b-143b), check your equipment to see that it is in good working order by typing the paragraph at the right at least twice (first slowly, then faster).

Val's keyboarding speed is quite high now. She increased from 60 gwam to 85 gwam (a gain of 29.41%) in just 37 days. Her extra practice has "paid off," as her employer recognizes her exceptional level of skill. She keys with proficiency all of the rush work of the eight officials.

| 1 | 2 | 3 | 4 | 5 | 6 | 7 | 8 | 9 | 10 | 11 | 12 | 13 | 14 |

139b-143b ▶ 45 (daily)
Work Assignments

Job 1
Employee Record Forms
(LM p. 113)

Obtain information from the application forms and complete Employee Record Forms for three new employees. You will need the following additional information:

OWENS: employed 6/1/19--
Notify: Mr. or Mrs.
   Ralph Owens
   (303) 422-8640

WILLIAMS: employed
5/20/19--
Notify: Mrs. Mary Jane Williams
(303) 390-6897

LIN: employed 5/25/19--
Notify: Mr. Thomas Ryan
(303) 921-8847

Thanks. Roberta Callahan

APPLICATION FOR EMPLOYMENT

PLEASE PRINT WITH BLACK INK OR USE TYPEWRITER   *AN EQUAL OPPORTUNITY EMPLOYER*

NAME (LAST, FIRST, MIDDLE INITIAL)	SOCIAL SECURITY NUMBER	CURRENT DATE
Owens, Sarah J.	440-85-8840	March 3, 19--

ADDRESS (NUMBER, STREET, CITY, STATE, ZIP CODE)	HOME PHONE NO.
P.O. Box 322, Monte Vista, CO 81144-7321	(303) 422-8640

REACH PHONE NO.	U.S. CITIZEN?	DATE YOU CAN START
	X YES NO	May 28, 19--

ARE YOU EMPLOYED NOW?   IF SO, MAY WE INQUIRE OF YOUR PRESENT EMPLOYER?

APPLICATION FOR EMPLOYMENT

PLEASE PRINT WITH BLACK INK OR USE TYPEWRITER   *AN EQUAL OPPORTUNITY EMPLOYER*

NAME (LAST, FIRST, MIDDLE INITIAL)	SOCIAL SECURITY NUMBER	CURRENT DATE
Williams, Rex J.	522-86-4968	May 1, 19--

ADDRESS (NUMBER, STREET, CITY, STATE, ZIP CODE)	HOME PHONE NO.
386 West First Street, South Fork, CO 81154-8820	(303) 390-6897

REACH PHONE NO.	U.S. CITIZEN?	DATE YOU CAN START
	X YES NO	May 15, 19--

ARE YOU EMPLOYED NOW?   IF SO, MAY WE INQUIRE OF YOUR PRESENT EMPLOYER?

APPLICATION FOR EMPLOYMENT

PLEASE PRINT WITH BLACK INK OR USE TYPEWRITER   *AN EQUAL OPPORTUNITY EMPLOYER*

NAME (LAST, FIRST, MIDDLE INITIAL)	SOCIAL SECURITY NUMBER	CURRENT DATE
Lin, Yang	522-80-3854	April 2, 19--

ADDRESS (NUMBER, STREET, CITY, STATE, ZIP CODE)	HOME PHONE NO.
975 West 18 Avenue, Pagosa Springs, CO 81147-6311	(303) 447-8028

REACH PHONE NO.	U.S. CITIZEN?	DATE YOU CAN START
	X YES NO	May 15, 19--

ARE YOU EMPLOYED NOW?   IF SO, MAY WE INQUIRE OF YOUR PRESENT EMPLOYER?

23d ▶ 12
Check/Improve Keyboarding Speed

1. Take one 1' timed writing and two 1' *guided* writings on ¶ 1 as directed on page 37.

2. Take one 1' timed writing and two 1' *guided* writings on ¶ 2 in the same way.

3. As time permits, take one or two 2' timed writings on ¶s 1 and 2 combined *without* the call of the guide; find *gwam*.

1' Gwam Goals

▽ 19 = acceptable
□ 23 = average
○ 27 = good
◇ 31 = excellent

all letters used | E | 1.2 si | 4.5 awl | 91% hfw

gwam 2'

¶ 1   Now it is up to me to build a major skill to   4
prize. I will develop my speed if I will key the   9
copy in the right way. To reach the next goal, I   14
must move quickly from one letter to another.   19

¶ 2   A step to which I must give attention in the   23
days just ahead is reading. The size of the word   28
can limit how I read and key it. I must focus on   33
a short, easy word and then key it as a unit.   38

gwam 2' | 1 | 2 | 3 | 4 | 5 |

Lesson 24 — Basic/Language Skills

Line length: 50 spaces
Spacing: single-space (SS)

24a ▶ 6
Conditioning Practice

1. Each line twice SS.
2. A 1' writing on line 3; find *gwam*.

alphabet 1 By solving the tax quiz, Jud Mack won first prize.
? 2 Where is Yuri? Who can say? Is he to go with us?
easy 3 Title to all of the lake land is held by the city.

5-stroke words | 1 | 2 | 3 | 4 | 5 | 6 | 7 | 8 | 9 | 10 |

24b ▶ 12
Improve Language Skills: Capitalization

1. Read each rule and type (key) the Learn and Apply sentences beneath it.

2. If time permits, practice the Apply lines again to increase decision-making speed.

> Capitalize an official title when it precedes a name, and elsewhere if it is a title of high distinction.

Learn 1 Our company president spoke with President Reagan.
Learn 2 The Vice President asked to speak with the doctor.
Apply 3 in what year did juan carlos become king of spain?
Apply 4 masami chou, our class president, made the awards.

> Capitalize initials; also letters in abbreviations if the letters would be capitalized when the words were spelled out.

Learn 5 We have a report from Ms. R. J. Buckley of London.
Learn 6 M.D. means Doctor of Medicine, not medical doctor.
Apply 7 does dr. j. t. Peterson have a ph.d., or an ed.d.?
Apply 8 he said that UPS stands for united parcel service.

24c ▶ 12
Check/Improve Keyboarding Speed

Using the directions of 23d, practice ¶s at top of page.

Goal: An increase of *at least* 2 gwam.

Learning Goals
To integrate the knowledge and skills acquired in Cycle 2 in:
1. processing documents.
2. detecting and correcting errors.
3. applying language skills.
4. making decisions.

Documents Processed
1. Memorandums and letters (one- and two-page)
2. Report
3. Table
4. Special documents: index cards, ruled form, menu, and announcement

WOLF CREEK LODGE: AN OFFICE JOB SIMULATION

Second Page of Letter with Blocked Second-Page Heading

John Smith	Vocalist
Maxine Freeland . .	Pianist

Aligned Leaders Between Columns

Work Assignment
Wolf Creek Lodge is a large vacation resort located in a scenic area near Pagosa Springs, Colorado. It offers a wide variety of activities, facilities, and services for single and family vacations. Although the lodge rents units on a single-night basis, most of their summer business results from guests who stay at least a week.

You have been hired to work as an office assistant for Wolf Creek Lodge. As such, you will work directly under the supervision of Ms. Roberta Callahan, Office Manager, who will assign to you various keyboarding tasks. You will prepare an assortment of documents (letters, memos, tables, menus, and announcements) for Ms. Callahan and other individuals at the lodge. You are expected to correct any undetected errors (whether in spelling, punctuation, and/or capitalization) which Ms. Callahan or others at the lodge have overlooked. Also, the finished document must be technically correct with all typographical errors neatly corrected.

Before beginning your first assignment, Ms. Callahan asks you to read "Excerpts from the Office Procedures Manual."

Excerpts from the Office Procedures Manual
While Wolf Creek Lodge uses a standard format for letters and memos (see below), most other formatting decisions are made by office personnel. You are expected to use good judgment in attractively arranging such documents as menus, tables, and announcements.

Letters and memorandums. Most letters are signed by Mr. Skidmore, Lodge Director. Memos, however, may be prepared for the signature of several different lodge employees. Use your reference initials and an enclosure notation, if needed, when preparing letters and memos. Use block format and open punctuation for all letters; use simplified memo format for all memos. Prepare one cc and company envelope unless otherwise directed.

Second page of letter. When keying two-page letters, use block format for second-page headings. Begin heading on line 6, flush with the left margin; supply receiver's name, page number, and date (see illustration at left).

Form letters. Wolf Creek Lodge often uses form letters to correspond with potential guests, since they have such a large mailing list. Stock paragraphs (standardized text known as boilerplate) will be written, and the keyboard operator will be instructed as to which appropriate paragraphs are needed for a particular letter. In some cases, you will be instructed to select an appropriate phrase from those suggested to adapt your letter to the receiver of a letter.

If you are using a manual, electric, or an electronic typewriter, key subsequent letters from the letter you have just prepared if the same paragraphs are used. This way you can proofread the previous letter while keying. All materials should be proofread twice to make sure the material is error free. If, on the other hand, you are using a word processor, and if the copy has been stored correctly, then you have to proofread only the variable material to make certain that it is error free.

Leaders. At times, documents need leaders to help the reader's eyes horizontally align material presented in columns (see example at left). Leaders are made by alternating periods and spaces between columns.

When keying leaders, space once after the first item in the first column. Then alternate periods and spaces to a point 2 or 3 spaces before beginning of second column. To help align periods, note on the line-of-writing scale whether the first period is keyed on an odd or even number, and then place all subsequent periods accordingly.

24d ▶ 20
Improve Keyboarding Technique

1. Each set of lines twice SS (slowly; then faster); DS between 8-line groups.

2. Note the lines that caused you difficulty; practice them again to develop a steady pace (no pauses between letters).

Adjacent (side-by-side) keys (as in lines 1-4) can cause many errors unless the fingers are kept in an upright position and precise motions are used.

Long direct reaches (as in lines 5-8) reduce speed unless they are made without moving the hands forward and downward.

Reaches with the outside fingers (as in lines 9-12) are troublesome unless made without twisting the hands in and out at the wrist.

Adjacent-key letter combinations

ew/we	1	The news is that we may view a new film next week.
ui/iu	2	The genius quickly drank fruit juice after a quiz.
er/re	3	The terms of her sale are there on the other side.
oi/io	4	Eloise may join the oil firm; she has that option.

Long direct reaches with same finger

un/nu	5	Our unit may not have its annual bonus until June.
ec/ce	6	Once we receive the pacer, you may expect a check.
um/mu	7	I must assume that sales volume is our mutual aim.
ny/yn	8	Lyn says a smile turns a rainy day sunny for many.

Reaches with 3d and 4th fingers

op/po	9	The poet will opt for a top spot in our port town.
as/sa	10	Sam said the cash price for gas went up last week.
az/za	11	Zane played a zany tune that amazed the jazz band.
q/a	12	My squad set a quarter quota to equal our request.

Lesson 25 | Basic/Language Skills

Line length: 50 spaces
Spacing: single-space (SS)

25a ▶ 6
Conditioning Practice

1. Each line twice SS.
2. A 1' writing on line 3; find *gwam*.

alphabet	1	Virgil Quin has packed twenty boxes of prize jams.
capitalization	2	Rule: When : precedes a sentence, cap first word.
easy	3	When she got such a profit, she paid for the land.

| 5-stroke words | | 1 | | 2 | | 3 | | 4 | | 5 | | 6 | | 7 | | 8 | | 9 | | 10 | |

25b ▶ 14
Improve Keyboarding Response Patterns

1. Each set of lines twice SS; DS between 6-line groups.

2. A 1' writing on line 10, next on line 11, then on line 12 to increase speed; find *gwam* on each.

Goal: *At least 24 gwam on line 12.*

letter response	1	were only date upon rate join gave milk gets jumps
	2	my tax| saw him| bad oil| raw milk| you beat| get a fee
	3	Zac gave only a few facts in a case on wage taxes.
word response	4	goal town iris pens turn risk coal fuel auto elbow
	5	the risk| pay them| for both| six girls| but rush them
	6	They did lend the formal gowns to the eight girls.
combination response	7	so ink she are for him own far tie mop apt war and
	8	for him| due you| did zag| may set| and get| she saw me
	9	You may join their union only if you pay the fees.
letter	10	You served poppy seed bread as a sweet noon treat.
combination	11	Vi read a theory on the state of art in the world.
word	12	The firm also owns the big sign by the town field.

| 5-stroke words | | 1 | | 2 | | 3 | | 4 | | 5 | | 6 | | 7 | | 8 | | 9 | | 10 | |

ENRICHMENT ACTIVITY: Skill-Building Drill and Timed Writings

The two sets of paragraphs on this page are counted internally for 1' guided and unguided writings. In addition, the paragraphs at the bottom of the page are counted for 3' and 5' timed writings. They may be used at any time additional drills and/or timed writings are desired.

Straight-Copy Drill

1. A 1' writing on the ¶ at the top to establish a base rate.

2. Add 4-8 words to base rate to set goal rate. Note quarter-minute checkpoints.

3. Three 1' writings on the ¶, trying to achieve goal rate each quarter minute as guides are called. Set goal rate higher each time the goal is achieved.

4. Note quarter-minute checkpoints for base rate established in Step 1 above.

5. Three 1' writings at reduced speed for control.

Goal: Not more than one error a minute. Reduce speed if necessary.

Quarter-Minute Checkpoints

gwam	¼'	½'	¾'	Time
16	4	8	12	16
20	5	10	15	20
24	6	12	18	24
28	7	14	21	28
32	8	16	24	32
36	9	18	27	36
40	10	20	30	40
44	11	22	33	44
48	12	24	36	48
52	13	26	39	52
56	14	28	42	56
60	15	30	45	60

Timed Writings

Two 3' or 5' writings on the ¶s at the right. Find *gwam* and errors. Record the better of the 3' and 5' writings. Compare 5' score with score of 129b, page 225.

all letters used | A | 1.5 si | 5.7 awl | 80% hfw

It is well-known that computer systems are now widely accepted as tools that organizations use to run and manage office affairs. As a tool, the system must be maintained just as the tools of a builder, for example, must be maintained. A wide variety of technical people is needed to establish and support a system; this need has created a demand for a number of different kinds of specialists. Some of these specialists are needed to design and care for the hardware or equipment; others are needed to develop and maintain software or programs.

all letters used | A | 1.5 si | 5.7 awl | 80% hfw

	gwam 3'	5'

The experts who design, build, and modify computer equipment are [4 | 3 | 48] known to us as computer engineers. An advanced mastery of both the areas [9 | 6 | 51] of electronics and mechanics is needed by these people if they are to do [14 | 8 | 54] their jobs properly. From the first day a system is installed, a busi- [19 | 11 | 57] ness must begin to upgrade the new system; the new system must be adapted [24 | 14 | 60] to the needs of each individual business, and continuous improvements [28 | 17 | 63] must be made if optimum results are to be realized. Thus, a computer [33 | 20 | 65] engineer's job does not end once the system is installed, and her or his [38 | 23 | 68] expertise is important if the system is going to work. [42 | 25 | 70]

There are two kinds of software experts. The ones who deal with the [46 | 28 | 73] programs that control only the operation of the computer are the computer [51 | 31 | 76] scientists; also, they set up the programs that make sure that the equip- [56 | 34 | 79] ment gives valid results. Those who develop the programs to process the [61 | 37 | 82] data are the application programmers; they also write the codes that [65 | 39 | 85] instruct a computer to perform the given tasks and solve the various [70 | 42 | 88] problems. The skills of both kinds of experts are needed to make sure [74 | 45 | 90] the system works. [76 | 46 | 91]

gwam 3' | 1 | 2 | 3 | 4 | 5
5' | 1 | 2 | 3

25c ▶ 20
Check/Improve Keyboarding Speed

1. A 1' writing on each ¶; find *gwam* on each; record the best *gwam*.

2. A 2' writing on ¶s 1-3 combined; find *gwam*.

3. Using your best *gwam* in Step 1 as a base rate, take a 1' *guided* writing on ¶ 1 as directed on page 37.

4. Take a 1' writing on ¶ 2 and on ¶ 3 in the same way.

5. If time permits, take another 2' writing on ¶s 1-3 combined; find *gwam*.

1' Goal: At least 22 *gwam*
2' Goal: At least 20 *gwam*

all letters used | E | 1.2 si | 4.9 awl | 92% hfw | *gwam 2'*

As you key copy, read it with care. Do more than that, though; think each word, too. You can key the word as a unit if you think it and say it.

You must realize that some words have letter sequences that are hard to type. These are often traps for a new person who does not yet know them.

Your major purpose now should be to learn to key the easy words quickly and to drop your speed for hard ones. Learn next to vary the speed rate.

25d ▶ 10
Check Language Skills: Capitalization

1. Type (key) each sentence once, capitalizing words according to the rules you have learned in this unit.

2. Check with your teacher the accuracy of your application of the rules.

3. As time permits, do again the lines in which you made errors in capitalization.

The references refer to previous lesson parts containing capitalization rules.

all letters used

Reference

21d   1   is this your coat? it was left here this morning.

21d   2   is enrique going with mrs. dover to the book sale?

21d, 23c   3   did you tour the black hills when in south dakota?

21d, 24b   4   alice has gone to work for nasa in houston, texas.

22d   5   all term reports are due the last friday in april.

22d   6   labor day is always the first monday in september.

22d, 24b   7   l. k. syke may go to the hula bowl game this year.

23c   8   do you know if the zorn building is on oak street?

23c, 24b   9   does fbla mean future business leaders of america?

24b   10   tomas garcia is an m.d.; joann markham is a d.d.s.

24b   11   ms. lincoln is a manager in our office in phoenix.

24b   12   was margaret thatcher a prime minister of england?

APPLICATION FOR EMPLOYMENT

PLEASE PRINT WITH BLACK INK OR USE TYPEWRITER

AN EQUAL OPPORTUNITY EMPLOYER

NAME (LAST, FIRST, MIDDLE INITIAL)	SOCIAL SECURITY NUMBER	CURRENT DATE
Espino, Margarita	448-38-5940	May 18, 1987

ADDRESS (NUMBER, STREET, CITY, STATE, ZIP CODE)	HOME PHONE NO.
385 West Grant Street, Pauls Valley, OK 73075-2277	(405) 273-3591

REACH PHONE NO.	U.S. CITIZEN?	DATE YOU CAN START
	X YES NO	May 25, 1987

ARE YOU EMPLOYED NOW?	IF SO, MAY WE INQUIRE OF YOUR PRESENT EMPLOYER?
Yes	Yes

TYPE OF WORK DESIRED	REFERRED BY	SALARY DESIRED
Office Assistant	Mr. Samuel Crampton	$ open

IF RELATED TO ANYONE IN OUR EMPLOY, STATE NAME AND POSITION

	YES	NO	IF YES, EXPLAIN
DO YOU HAVE ANY PHYSICAL CONDITION THAT MAY PREVENT YOU FROM PERFORMING CERTAIN KINDS OF WORK?		X	
HAVE YOU EVER BEEN CONVICTED OF A FELONY?		X	

E D U C A T I O N	EDUCATIONAL INSTITUTION	LOCATION (CITY, STATE)	DATES ATTENDED FROM MO. YR.	DATES ATTENDED TO MO. YR.	DIPLOMA, DEGREE, OR CREDITS EARNED	CLASS STANDING (CHK QUARTER) 1	2	3	4	MAJOR SUBJECTS STUDIED
	COLLEGE									
	HIGH SCHOOL									
	Pauls Valley High	Pauls Valley, OK	9 83	5 87	Diploma	X				Bus./Eng.
	GRADE SCHOOL									
	OTHER									

LIST BELOW THE POSITIONS THAT YOU HAVE HELD (LAST POSITION FIRST)

1. NAME AND ADDRESS OF FIRM	DESCRIBE POSITION RESPONSIBILITIES
Pauls Valley High School P.O. Box 874 Pauls Valley, OK 73075-2278	Kept attendance reports, typed corres- pondence, and helped with bookkeeping
NAME OF SUPERVISOR Dr. M. J. Alexander, Principal	for athletic programs.
EMPLOYED (MO-YR) FROM: 8/86 TO: 5/87	REASON FOR LEAVING Graduation

2. NAME AND ADDRESS OF FIRM	DESCRIBE POSITION RESPONSIBILITIES
	Solicited customers, scheduled work,
Directed my own lawn mowing service.	purchased and maintained equipment,
NAME OF SUPERVISOR	mowed lawns, and hired assistants.
EMPLOYED (MO-YR) FROM: 4/84 TO: present	REASON FOR LEAVING Continues to operate on limited basis.

3. NAME AND ADDRESS OF FIRM	DESCRIBE POSITION RESPONSIBILITIES
NAME OF SUPERVISOR	
EMPLOYED (MO-YR) FROM: TO:	REASON FOR LEAVING

I UNDERSTAND THAT I SHALL NOT BECOME AN EMPLOYEE UNTIL I HAVE SIGNED AN EMPLOYMENT AGREEMENT WITH THE FINAL APPROVAL OF THE EMPLOYER AND THAT SUCH EMPLOYMENT WILL BE SUBJECT TO VERIFICATION OF PREVIOUS EMPLOYMENT, DATA PROVIDED IN THIS APPLICATION, ANY RELATED DOCUMENTS, OR RESUME. I KNOW THAT A REPORT MAY BE MADE THAT WILL INCLUDE INFORMATION

CONCERNING ANY FACTOR THE EMPLOYER MIGHT FIND RELEVANT TO THE POSITION FOR WHICH I AM APPLYING, AND THAT I CAN MAKE A WRITTEN REQUEST FOR ADDITIONAL INFORMATION AS TO THE NATURE AND SCOPE OF THE REPORT IF ONE IS MADE.

Margarita Espino
SIGNATURE OF APPLICANT

Application for Employment Form

Learn Numeric Keyboarding Technique and Correspondence Formatting

In the 25 lessons of this phase, you will:

1. Learn to type (key) figures and basic symbols by touch and with good technique.

2. Improve speed/control on straight copy, script (handwritten) copy, rough-draft (corrected) copy, and statistical copy (copy containing figures and some symbols).

3. Review/improve language skills.

4. Apply your keyboarding skill in preparing simple personal and business papers.

The copy from which you have typed (keyed) up to now has been shown in pica (10-pitch) typewriter type. In Phase 2 much of the copy is shown in large easy-to-read printer's type.

All drill lines are written to an exact 60-space line to simplify checking. Some paragraphs and problem activities, however, contain lines of variable length. Continue to key them line for line as shown until you are directed to do otherwise.

137a ▶ 5
Conditioning Practice

each line twice SS (slowly, then faster); DS between 2-line groups; if time permits, repeat selected lines

alphabet 1 Lucy scored very high on every major botany quiz taken except for two.

figures 2 Ki passed out 43,570 pamphlets at 26 meetings in 19 towns in 8 months.

direct reach 3 Greg's voice echoed in the museum after he became unnecessarily angry.

speed 4 Lana may work and fight with vigor to handle a giant fish in the lake.

| 1 | 2 | 3 | 4 | 5 | 6 | 7 | 8 | 9 | 10 | 11 | 12 | 13 | 14 |

137b ▶ 45
Prepare Application Forms

(LM p. 109-112)

Problem 1

Format and key the application form on p. 241, being especially careful in proofreading and correcting errors.

Problem 2

Study the headings and questions on the application form. Make notations to complete an application form if you were applying for the job you wrote about in 136b, Problem 2, p. 239. Then prepare a final application form with your own data as if you were applying for the position. Use the extra form on LM p. 111.

138a ▶ 5
Conditioning Practice

each line twice SS (slowly, then faster); DS between 2-line groups; if time permits, repeat selected lines

alphabet 1 Zed Loy was exceedingly jovial at making his quota before his partner.

figures 2 The group ate 259 hot dogs, 186 hamburgers, 370 colas, and 42 pickles.

space bar 3 Al and his son may try to tell us why they have not yet cut your bush.

speed 4 The goal of both of the panels is to halt all of their civic problems.

| 1 | 2 | 3 | 4 | 5 | 6 | 7 | 8 | 9 | 10 | 11 | 12 | 13 | 14 |

138b ▶ 45
Prepare Follow-Up Letters

plain full sheets; 1 cc; modified block format; blocked paragraphs; open punctuation; proofread and correct errors

Problem 1

Format and key the follow-up letter at the right. It is to Mr. Goodwin from Margarita Espino (see 135b, Problem 1, and 136b, Problem 1). Use current date and supply missing letter parts.

Problem 2

Study the guidelines for follow-up letters on p. 237. Assume that you interviewed for the job you applied for in 136b, Problem 2. Compose your follow-up letter; edit and prepare final copy.

words

opening lines 35

(¶ 1) Thank you, Mr. Goodwin, for the opportunity to discuss with you your 49 needs for an office assistant and my qualifications for that position. I ap- 64 preciate your thorough explanation of the objectives of your firm, and Ms. 79 Benson was especially helpful in outlining the details of the job. 93

(¶ 2) After visiting with you and Ms. Benson, meeting your office staff, and 107 seeing your facilities, I am even more enthusiastic about joining your firm. 123 I believe that my education, experiences, and ability to learn quickly qualify 138 me for this position; and I think working under Ms. Benson's supervision 153 would be a pleasure. Furthermore, I look upon your organization as one 167 which will provide me with an opportunity for career growth; and that is 182 important to me. 186

(¶ 3) I look forward, Mr. Goodwin, to becoming a part of your office team. 200

closing lines 206

Unit 3   Lessons 26-30

Learning Goals
1. To learn the location of each figure key.
2. To learn how to strike each figure key properly with the correct finger.
3. To build keyboarding speed and technique on copy containing figures.
4. To improve keyboarding speed and technique on alphabetic copy.

Machine Adjustments
1. Paper guide at 0.
2. Ribbon control to use top half of ribbon.
3. Margin sets: left margin (center - 30); right margin (move to right end of scale).
4. Line-space selector set to single-space (SS) drills.
5. Line-space selector set to double-space (DS) paragraphs.

| **Lesson 26** | **1 and 7** | Line length: 60 spaces |
| | | Spacing: single-space (SS) |

26a ▶ 6
Conditioning Practice
1. Each line twice SS.
2. A 1' writing on line 3; find *gwam* (total 5-stroke words completed).

alphabet	1	Vida was quick to get the next bus to Juarez to play for me.
space bar	2	to row|is to row|is to|is to fix|to the|to the lake|the sign
easy	3	Keith is to row with us to the lake to fix six of the signs.

5-stroke words | 1 | 2 | 3 | 4 | 5 | 6 | 7 | 8 | 9 | 10 | 11 | 12 |

26b ▶ 18
Learn 1 and 7
each line twice SS (slowly, then faster); DS between 2-line groups; if time permits, practice each line again

Reach technique for 1

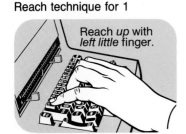

Reach *up* with *left little* finger.

Reach technique for 7

Reach *up* with *right first* finger.

Follow the Standard Plan for Learning New Keys outlined on page 7.

Learn figure 1

1 a 1 a 1 aa 11 aa 11 a1a a1a 11a Reach up for 1, 11, and 111.
2 Key the figures 1, 11, and 111. Please study pages 1 to 11.

Learn 7

3 j 7 j 7 jj 77 jj 77 j7j j7j 77j Reach up for 7, 77, and 777.
4 Add the figures 7, 77, and 777. Have just 7 of 77 finished?

Combine 1 and 7

5 Key 11, 17, 71, and 77. Only 11 of the 17 joggers are here.
6 Do you want a size 7 or 11? I have 17 of each one in stock.
7 The stock person counted 11 coats, 17 slacks, and 77 shirts.

Lesson 135 — Personal Data Sheet/Composing

135a ▶ 5
Conditioning Practice

each line twice SS (slowly, then faster); DS between 2-line groups; if time permits, repeat selected lines

alphabet 1 Jan's views quickly became fogged and hazy during the perplexing exam.

figures 2 Terry bought 293 rings, 485 watches, 601 bracelets, and 749 necklaces.

3d row 3 The trusted reporter tried quietly to wire her top story to our paper.

speed 4 If they sign the forms, any proficient auditor can handle the problem.

| 1 | 2 | 3 | 4 | 5 | 6 | 7 | 8 | 9 | 10 | 11 | 12 | 13 | 14 |

135b ▶ 45
Prepare Data Sheets

plain paper; 1" side margins

Problem 1
Format and key the data sheet shown on page 238.

Problem 2
Compose at the machine a rough-draft data sheet for yourself using the one on page 238 as a model

(also, see guidelines on page 237, if necessary). Edit; then make a final copy.

Lesson 136 — Application Letter/Composing

136a ▶ 5
Conditioning Practice

each line twice SS (slowly, then faster); DS between 2-line groups; if time permits, repeat selected lines

alphabet 1 Galena may have to think hard about just a few complex quiz questions.

figures 2 Our last order, dated May 30, was for Part No. 2974 and Part No. 1586.

adjacent key 3 Ophelia's and Polonius' performances in a serious rendition were good.

speed 4 If Shana pays for fuel for the auto, then she may go to town to visit.

| 1 | 2 | 3 | 4 | 5 | 6 | 7 | 8 | 9 | 10 | 11 | 12 | 13 | 14 |

136b ▶ 45
Prepare Application Letters

plain full sheets; 1 cc; modified block format; blocked ¶s; mixed punctuation; proofread and correct errors

Problem 1
Format and key the application letter for Ms. Margarita Espino. Study the guidelines and model illustration (p. 237); use personal-business letter format and begin return address on line 11. (See data sheet, p. 238, for Ms. Espino's return address.)
(words in return address: 10)

Problem 2
Compose at the keyboard a rough-draft letter applying for a job that you have seen advertised in the newspaper or one you have actually heard about and would like to do. In the latter case, include a short description of the job and how you learned about it. Edit your letter; then process it in final form.

words

Current date | Mr. Clarence J. Goodwin | Attorney-at-Law | 384 East Pine 24
Street | Pauls Valley, OK 73075-2200 | Dear Mr. Goodwin: 35

(¶ 1) Thank you, Mr. Goodwin, for giving me the opportunity to discuss on 49
the phone last week your needs for an office assistant. Your description of 64
the job matches well my qualifications, and your expectations from office 79
personnel are consistent with my own. I should like very much to be a part 94
of a professionally managed office such as yours; therefore, I wish to be 109
considered for the position of office assistant. 119

(¶ 2) I have acquired many office skills which I believe will be useful in this 133
position. I can keyboard at 65 words a minute; and, in addition to operating 149
standard office equipment, I am proficient at operating most office com- 164
puters. I have mastered software for word processing and editing, spread 178
sheet, payroll, and records management. Further, I have taken several 193
writing courses in honors English class, which I feel will be useful in a 207
law office. 210

(¶ 3) As indicated on the enclosed data sheet, I have spent the past year 224
working as an office assistant for Dr. Maria Alexander, our high school prin- 239
cipal. Much of the work required accurate, precise, detailed reporting simi- 254
lar to what will be necessary in your office. I believe that Dr. Alexander 269
feels that I am able to perform this kind of task well, and she has indicated 285
that she would be glad to talk to you about my performance if you wish. 299

(¶ 4) May I please have an interview to discuss further the possibility of join- 314
ing your office staff. I am free after 3 p.m. each afternoon. 327

Sincerely, | Ms. Margarita Espino | xx | Enclosure 335

26c ▶ 14
Improve Keyboarding Technique

1. Each pair of lines (1-6) twice SS (slowly, then faster); DS between 4-line groups.

2. A 1' writing on line 7, then on line 8; find *gwam* on each writing.

Technique hints
- Make *upward* reaches without moving the hand forward.
- Make *downward* reaches without twisting the wrists or moving the elbows in or out.

Row emphasis

home/3d
1 just try| will keep| they quit| you would| play golf| did ship it
2 Pat always tries to keep her eyes off the keys as she works.

home/1st
3 can call| hand ax| can land| lava gas| small flag| jazz band ball
4 Hannah had a small van all fall. Max has a small jazz band.

figures
5 Just 17 of the 71 boys got 77 of the 117 quiz answers right.
6 The test on the 17th will cover pages 11 to 17 and 71 to 77.

easy
7 Alan may make a bid on the ivory forks they got in the city.
8 Tien may fix the bus panel for the city if the pay is right.

5-stroke words | 1 | 2 | 3 | 4 | 5 | 6 | 7 | 8 | 9 | 10 | 11 | 12 |

26d ▶ 12 Improve Keyboarding Speed: Guided Writing

1. A 1' writing on each ¶; find *gwam* on each writing.

2. Using your better *gwam* as a base rate, select a *goal rate* 2-4 *gwam* higher than your base rate, and take three 1' writings on each ¶ with the call of the quarter-minute guide (see p. 37 for routine).

Quarter-minute checkpoints

gwam	¼'	½'	¾'	Time
16	4	8	12	16
20	5	10	15	20
24	6	12	18	24
28	7	14	21	28
32	8	16	24	32
36	9	18	27	36
40	10	20	30	40

all letters used | E | 1.2 si | 4.8 awl | 90% hfw | *gwam 2'*

I am now trying to learn to vary my keying rate to fit   5
the job of keying the words. When I learn to speed up more   11
of the easy words, I can take time to break the longer ones   17
into small parts and handle them quickly.   22

With a bit more practice, I shall be able to handle by   27
word response more of the shorter ones that just now I must   33
analyze and key letter by letter. As I learn to do more of   39
these words as units, I shall become more expert.   44

gwam 2' | 1 | 2 | 3 | 4 | 5 | 6 |

| **Lesson 27** | **4 and 8** | Line length: 60 spaces
Spacing: single-space (SS) |

27a ▶ 6
Conditioning Practice

1. Each line twice SS.

2. A 1' writing on line 3; find *gwam* (total 5-stroke words completed).

alphabet 1 Marv wanted a quiet place, but Felix kept playing show jazz.
figure 2 Please review Figure 11 on page 17 and Figure 17 on page 77.
easy 3 Iris is to go to the lake towns to do the map work for them.

5-stroke words | 1 | 2 | 3 | 4 | 5 | 6 | 7 | 8 | 9 | 10 | 11 | 12 |

27b ▶ 12 Improve Keyboarding Speed: Guided Writing

Practice again the 2 ¶s above, using the directions in 26d.

Goal: To improve your speed by at least 2-4 *gwam*.

47

```
                    MARGARITA ESPINO
                   385 West Grant Street
                 Pauls Valley, OK  73075-2277
                      (405) 273-3591
                        Date          QS
```

EDUCATION

    Senior at Pauls Valley High School
    High School Diploma, pending graduation
    Majors: Business and English
    Grade Average: 3.48; upper 15% of class

SCHOOL ACTIVITIES

    Student Council President, senior year; member for 3 years

    Member of National Honor Society, junior and senior years

    Pen and Quill Secretary (literary writing club), senior year;
    member for 2 years

    Junior Class Treasurer (handled budgeting, bookkeeping, and
    bills for junior-senior banquet and prom)

WORK EXPERIENCE

    Office assistant to high school principal 24 hours a week during
    senior year; kept attendance reports, typed correspondence,
    filed, and helped with bookkeeping for athletic programs.

    Director of own lawn mowing service for three years; solicited
    customers, scheduled work, purchased and maintained equipment,
    mowed lawns, and hired assistants.

REFERENCES (by permission)

    Ms. Betty Jo Markley, Computer Instructor, Pauls Valley High
    School, P.O. Box 874, Pauls Valley, OK 73075-2278

    Mr. Franklin J. Reeves, Loan Officer, First National Bank, 416
    North Main Street, Pauls Valley, OK 73075-2309

    Dr. M. J. Alexander, Principal, Pauls Valley High School, P.O.
    Box 874, Pauls Valley, OK 73075-2278

Data Sheet

27c ▶ 18
Learn 4 and 8

each line twice SS (slowly, then faster); DS between 2-line groups; if time permits, practice each line again

Follow the Standard Plan for Learning New Keys outlined on page 7.

Reach technique for 4

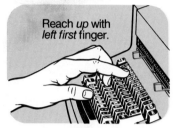
Reach *up* with *left first* finger.

Reach technique for 8

Reach *up* with *right second* finger.

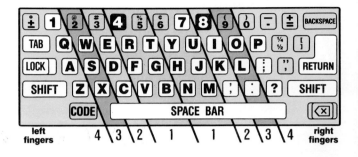

left fingers   4 3 2 1   1 2 3 4   right fingers

Learn 4
1 f 4 f 4 ff 44 ff 44 f4f f4f 44f Reach up for 4, 44, and 444.
2 Key the figures 4, 44, and 444. Please study pages 4 to 44.

Learn 8
3 k 8 k 8 kk 88 kk 88 k8k k8k 88k Reach up for 8, 88, and 888.
4 Add the figures 8, 88, and 888. Have just 8 of 88 finished?

Combine 4 and 8
5 Key 44, 48, 84, and 88. Just 48 of the 88 skiers have come.
6 Reach with the fingers to key 48 and 488 as well as 4 and 8.
7 On October 8, the 4 hikers left on a long hike of 448 miles.

27d ▶ 14
Improve Keyboarding Technique

1. Each of lines 1-6 twice SS (slowly, then faster); DS between 2-line groups.
2. Two 1′ writings on the ¶ which contains all the letters; find *gwam* on each writing.
Goal: *At least 22 gwam.*

Fingers upright

Figure sentences
1 Key 1 and 7 and 4 and 8. Add 4, 11, 17, 44, 48, 78, and 88.
2 I based my April 4 report on pages 447 to 488 of Chapter 17.
3 Just 17 of the boys and 18 of the girls passed all 47 tests.

Alphabetic sentences
4 Elena may have Jack rekey parts two and six of the big quiz.
5 Vic Kibold may win quite a just prize for his next pop song.
6 Peg can have a jeweler size my antique ring to fit Burk Dix.

Alphabetic paragraph | E | 1.1 si | 4.9 awl | 92% hfw

```
        2       4       6       8       10
    Seize the chance to build your speed to the quite high
  12      14      16      18      20      22
level you want.  If you will just try harder for a new high
  24      26      28      30      32      34
speed each week, you can gain in speed more than you expect.
```

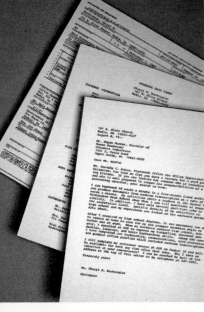

Learning Goals

1. To learn guidelines for preparing a data sheet, application letter, application form, and follow-up letter.

2. To apply guidelines for preparing employment documents.

3. To compose and process personal employment documents.

4. To improve language skills through composing activities.

Machine Adjustments

1. Paper guide at *0*.

2. Paper bail rolls at even intervals across page.

3. Margins: 70-space line (drill lines) or as directed.

4. Spacing: as directed.

FORMATTING GUIDES: DATA SHEET, APPLICATION LETTER, APPLICATION FORM, AND FOLLOW-UP LETTER

Application Letter

Special care should be given to the preparation of all employment documents. Such documents will most likely be the first impression you make on a prospective employer; they may also determine whether an interview will be granted to you. Thus, it is important to use extra care in preparing these documents.

Make sure that each document you prepare is neat in appearance, is correct grammatically, and presents both accurate and appropriate information. It is also important to follow exactly the specific directions that are given and to answer all relevant questions.

Prepare application documents on a keyboard with the possible exception of the application form. You may be asked to complete the application form at the time of the interview, in which case it may be prepared with a pen. Always use high-quality paper when preparing your data sheet and application letter.

Data Sheet

In most cases, a data sheet should be limited to one page. The information presented usually covers five major areas: personal information (*your name, address and telephone number*), education, school activities, work experience, and references. It may also include a section listing community activities and hobbies and/or special interests.

Top, bottom, and side margins may vary depending on the length of the data sheet. The specific format may also vary with personal preference. In general, the most important information is presented first, which means that a person who has been out of school for several years and has considerable work experience may place that information before educational background information. References, however, are usually the last item on the page.

Always get permission from the people on your reference list before using their names. Also, keep them informed about the jobs that you apply for and the specific skills that are important in qualifying you for each job.

Application Letter

An application letter is a personal business letter and includes the sender's return address, as shown in the model at the left. The letter should be limited to one page.

The first paragraph of an application letter contains a "you" message. It may point out something positive that the sender knows about the company or someone who works for the company. Worked into this paragraph may be information about how you learned of the opening. Conclude the paragraph with a statement indicating the specific position for which you are applying (or the kind of position you desire if you are sending a letter to determine if an opening is available in your area).

The next one or two paragraphs are "I" paragraphs. They should state how you are uniquely qualified for the job in question and why you should be hired. You may elaborate on the information on your data sheet -- mentioning that the data sheet is enclosed -- and explain how the experiences listed there qualify you for the job. This information, though, must go beyond just repeating what is on the data sheet. It explains the significance of your activities and experiences for the position you are seeking.

The final paragraph is a "request for action." It specifically asks for an interview and tells when you are available for an interview.

Follow-Up Letter

The follow-up letter is a thank you for being given an interview. If you can honestly do so, give positive impressions of the company and the people you met. Indicate that you would like an offer and provide a courteous ending to the letter.

28a ▶ 6
Conditioning Practice

1. Each line twice SS.

2. A 1' writing on line 3; find *gwam* (total 5-stroke words completed).

alphabet   1   Gavin made a quick fall trip by jet to Zurich six weeks ago.

figure   2   Today we sold 18 pairs of gloves, 4 coats, and 17 knit caps.

easy   3   The man is to fix the big sign by the field for a city firm.

5-stroke words | 1 | 2 | 3 | 4 | 5 | 6 | 7 | 8 | 9 | 10 | 11 | 12 |

28b ▶ 18
Learn 5 and 9

each line twice SS (slowly, then faster); DS between 2-line groups; if time permits, practice each line again

Follow the Standard Plan for Learning New Keys outlined on page 7.

Reach technique for 5

Reach *up* with *left first* finger.

Reach technique for 9

Reach *up* with *right third* finger.

Learn 5

1   f 5 f 5 ff 55 ff 55 f5f f5f 55f Reach up for 5, 55, and 555.

2   Key the figures 5, 55, and 555. Please study pages 5 to 55.

Learn 9

use the letter "l"

3   l 9 l 9 ll 99 ll 99 l9l l9l 99l Reach up for 9, 99, and 999.

4   Add the figures 9, 99, and 999. Have just 9 of 99 finished?

Combine 5 and 9

5   Key 55, 59, 95, and 99. Only 59 of the 99 flags are flying.

6   Reach with the fingers to key 59 and 599 as well as 5 and 9.

7   My goal is to sell 55 tacos, 59 pizzas, and 5 cases of cola.

28c ▶ 12
Improve Keyboarding Technique: Numbers

each line twice SS; DS between 2-line groups

Language skills notes
1. No space is left before or after : when used with figures to express time.
2. Most nouns before numbers are capitalized; exceptions include page and line.

No space

1   She should be on Jetair Flight 1749 at 5:58 p.m. at Gate 48.

2   I used Chapter 18, pages 419 to 457, for my April 19 report.

3   The club meeting will be held in Room 1748 at 59 Park Place.

4   Can you meet me at 1849 Marsh Street at 7:45 a.m. August 11?

5   Of the 79 students, 18 keyed at least 45 w.a.m. on March 19.

6   They had 145 workers in 1987 and expect to have 195 by 1999.

134c ▶ 35
Measure Document Processing: Forms/Special Documents

Time Schedule

Plan and prepare	3'
Timed production	25'
Proofread and correct errors ...	5'
Compute *n-pram*	2'

1 cc for forms; proofread and correct errors

Problem 1
Purchase Order
(LM p. 95)

Use the information at the right to prepare a purchase order.

Problem 2
Invoice
(LM p. 97)

Use the information at the right to prepare an invoice. Add 6% sales tax ($28.29) to total.
(total words: 79)

Problem 3
Formal Memorandum
(LM p. 99)

Key a formal memorandum from the information at the right and the information listed below.

To: The Council on Education
From: Karen Rosenfeld, Director of Education
Date: Current
Subject: Continuing Education Proposal

Problem 4
Simplified Memorandum
(LM p. 101)

Using the information supplied above, rekey Problem 3 as a simplified memo.

Problem 1

HIGH-TECH INC
1408 WASHINGTON BOULEVARD
DETROIT MI 48226-9433

			words
Purchase Order No.:	**TEL-468201**		2
Date:	**May 2, 19--**		8
Terms:	**2/10, n/30**		15
Shipped Via:	**Main Express**		22

Quantity	Description/Stock No.	Price	Total	
3	Automatic Memory Dialer -- #32-289	57.75/ea	173.25	33
2	Pocket Tone Dialer -- #32-132	54.95/ea	109.90	42
4	Phone Amplifier -- #32-274	47.50/ea	190.00	51
2	Tone Dialer with Memory -- #32-134	34.95/ea	69.90	61
3	Amplified Headset -- #32-289	33.75/ea	101.25	70
1	Office Monitor -- #32-146	189.95/ea	189.95	78
	Prepared by: **Carl Quintana**		834.25	85

Problem 2

BAKER AUDIO SYSTEMS
1401 SOUTH HAVANA STREET
AURORA CO 88012-7712

		words
Date:	**May 4, 19--**	2
Cust. Order No.:	**361482**	8
Terms:	**2/10, n/30**	15
Shipped Via:	**Bear Express**	22
Our Order No.:	**HG-46184**	24
Date Shipped:	**4/24/--**	26

Quantity	Description/Stock No.	Price	Total	
2	Surface Mount Speaker -- #16-1741	58.95	117.90	35
3	6" × 9" 3-Way Speaker -- #42-1241	25.95	77.85	44
1	Graphic Stereo Equalizer -- #16-1756	89.95	89.95	54
4	AM/FM Stereo Antenna -- #16-1284	8.99	35.96	63
3	AM/FM Radio -- #16-1664	49.95	149.85	70
			471.51	75

Problem 3

words in heading 22

(¶ 1) A new copy of the Continuing Education Proposal is enclosed. You will 36 notice that a few minor changes have been made, among them being the 50 addition of a table of contents for easy reference. 60

(¶ 2) Ed has reviewed the proposal and has suggested that it be divided into 75 two parts -- one that describes in detail the changes we are proposing in the 90 program and one that describes the new budget we will be establishing. 104

(¶ 3) Since I anticipate that you will have other changes you wish to incorpo- 118 rate in the proposal, I shall wait to hear from you and then make all of the 134 changes at one time. May I have your comments within the next two weeks. 149
xx | Enclosure 151

28d ▶ 14

Improve Keyboarding Technique: Response Patterns

1. Each pair of lines twice SS (slowly, then faster); DS between 4-line groups.

2. A 1' writing on line 2, then on line 4; find *gwam* on each writing.

letter response	1	face jump area only ever upon save milk safe pump vast onion
	2	As you are aware, only we look upon him as a great pop star.
word response	3	disk envy alto down hang corn hand body worn lend quay shale
	4	He is to pay them for the social work they did for the city.
combination response	5	wish upon|they save|then jump|kept safe|half join|quay trade
	6	It was then up to him to pay the duty they set on the ivory.

5-stroke words | 1 | 2 | 3 | 4 | 5 | 6 | 7 | 8 | 9 | 10 | 11 | 12 |

Lesson 29   3 and 0

Line length: 60 spaces
Spacing: single-space (SS)

29a ▶ 6

Conditioning Practice

1. Each line twice SS.

2. A 1' writing on line 3; find *gwam* (total 5-stroke words completed).

alphabet	1	Mazy helped Jared quickly fix the big wood stove in the den.
figure	2	Key 1 and 8 and 4 and 9 and 5 and 7 and 194 and 718 and 584.
easy	3	Alfie is to go to work for the city to fix eighty bus signs.

5-stroke words | 1 | 2 | 3 | 4 | 5 | 6 | 7 | 8 | 9 | 10 | 11 | 12 |

29b ▶ 18

Learn 3 and 0

each line twice SS (slowly, then faster); DS between 2-line groups; if time permits practice each line again

> Follow the Standard Plan for Learning New Keys outlined on page 7.

Reach technique for 3

Reach *up* with *left second* finger.

Reach technique for 0

Reach *up* with *right little* finger.

Learn 3

1   d 3 d 3 dd 33 dd 33 d3d d3d 33d Reach up for 3, 33, and 333.

2   Key the figures 3, 33, and 333. Please check Rooms 3 to 33.

Learn 0 (zero)

3   ; 0 ; 0 ;; 00 ;; 00 ;0; ;0; 00; Reach up for 0, 00, and 000.

4   Snap the finger off the 0. Do you want 0, 00, or 000 paper?

Combine 3 and 0

5   Key in the figures 0, 3, and 30; then try 300, 303, and 330.

6   Did they key at the rate of 30, or was it 33 words a minute?

7   Of 33 members, 3 were 30 minutes late for 3 of the meetings.

133a ▶ 5
Conditioning Practice

each line twice SS (slowly, then faster); DS between 2-line groups; if time permits, repeat selected lines

alphabet	1	At Jaxton Zoo, they may hear ducks quack, wolves bark, and pigs fight.
figures	2	I planted 138 rose bushes, 57 crape myrtles, 40 lilacs, and 269 bulbs.
fig/sym	3	Styles #70-A and #93-C (see page 24 of the catalog) cost $186.50 each.
speed	4	Lem is the name visible on the visor of the big cycle, for he owns it.

| 1 | 2 | 3 | 4 | 5 | 6 | 7 | 8 | 9 | 10 | 11 | 12 | 13 | 14 |

133b ▶ 10
Improve Basic Skill: Speed-Forcing Drill

1. Repeat 130b, p. 228, Steps 1-5.

2. Take a 1' writing on line 24.

3. Compare with rate in Lessons 130 and 131.

133c ▶ 35
Build Sustained Document Processing: Forms and Special Documents

(LM p. 85)
(LM pp. 89-94)

company envelopes for formal memos; correct errors

Time Schedule

Plan and prepare	3'
Timed production	25'
Proofread and correct errors	5'
Compute *n-pram*	2'

1. Make a list of problems to be processed:

page 229, 130c, Problem 1
page 229, 130c, Problem 2
page 230, 130c, Problem 3
page 231, 131c, Problem 2
page 232, 131c, Problem 3

2. Arrange forms, supplies, and correction materials for easy access. Process as many problems as you can in 25'. Proofread and correct errors before removing problems from machine.

3. Compute *n-pram* for problems completed. Turn in work, arranged in order listed in Step 1.

Net production rate a minute **(n-pram) = (total words keyed − penalty*) ÷ time**
*Penalty is 15 words for each uncorrected error.

134a ▶ 5
Conditioning Practice

each line twice SS (slowly, then faster); DS between 2-line groups; if time permits, repeat selected lines

alphabet	1	Buz will make a quick trip next Monday to judge five recipes for fish.
figures	2	Dale drove 376 miles on 18 gallons of gas and 459 miles on 20 gallons.
fig/sym	3	The 326 numbers in the table add up to $190.87 (45% of overall total).
speed	4	The city may cut their payment to an endowment, and a fight may ensue.

| 1 | 2 | 3 | 4 | 5 | 6 | 7 | 8 | 9 | 10 | 11 | 12 | 13 | 14 |

134b ▶ 10
Figure and Tab-Key Drill

three 1' writings and two 2' writings; 65-space line; set tab stops and 10-space intervals

Concentrate on figure locations; quiet hands; quick tab spacing.

							words
3601	5702	4803	7904	5704	9506	4607	7
6208	7909	9401	6911	8512	6813	8914	14
9015	5716	8617	6818	4719	8520	9621	21
9722	4823	6924	8725	9426	8627	7528	28
5029	5730	8531	6132	7033	2734	4735	35
6936	9637	1838	5839	6540	7341	7842	42
1	2	3	4	5	6	7	

29c ▶ 12
Improve Keyboarding Technique: Numbers

each line twice SS (slowly, then faster); DS between 2-line groups; if time permits, practice each line again

1/7	1	Kyle will be 17 on Tuesday, October 7; he weighs 177 pounds.
4/8	2	The exam on the 4th is to be over pages 4 to 8 and 48 to 88.
5/9	3	For the answer to Problem 59, see Unit 9, page 595, line 59.
3/0	4	The meeting is to be held June 30 at 3:30 p.m. in Suite 300.
all figures learned	5	Key these figures as units: 30, 40, 50, 91, 85, 73, and 49.
	6	Our group sold 850 chili dogs, 497 sandwiches, and 301 pies.

29d ▶ 14
Improve Keyboarding Technique: Service Keys

1. Clear all tab stops; then, starting at left margin, set 2 tab stops 25 spaces apart.
2. Key the drill once as shown.
3. Rekey the drill at a faster speed.

space bar	1	I am|go by|he may|she can|if they|for them|the city|may form
	2	They may make their goals if they work with the usual vigor.
shift keys and lock	3	Sachi Kato of Japan won the finals from Lydia Diaz of Spain.
	4	Yuan used a quote from FAMILIAR QUOTATIONS by John Bartlett.
tabulator and return	5	she did -------- tab --------→ and the -------- tab --------→ pay for
	6	work with ... they paid ... make them
	7	busy towns ... worn panel ... work goals

Lesson 30	**2 and 6**	Line length: 60 spaces Spacing: single-space (SS)

30a ▶ 6
Conditioning Practice

1. Each line twice SS.
2. A 1' writing on line 3; find *gwam* (total 5-stroke words completed).

alphabet	1	Gwen asked me to have Buzz cap the six jars of quince jelly.
figure	2	Mandy lives at 1748 Elm Street; Gordy, at 3059 Jayson Drive.
easy	3	Tisha is to go to the lake with us if she is to do the work.

5-stroke words | 1 | 2 | 3 | 4 | 5 | 6 | 7 | 8 | 9 | 10 | 11 | 12 |

30b ▶ 14
Check Keyboarding Technique

1. Key lines 1-10 twice each, SS, as your teacher checks your keyboarding technique.
2. If time permits, take a 1' writing on line 11, then on line 12. Find *gwam* on each writing.

quiet hands and arms	1	Pam wants the quartz box for Belle and a jade ring for Vick.
	2	Zip, can you have this quaint jug fixed for Ms. Lock by two?
quick-snap keystrokes	3	Rick paid for both the visual aid and the sign for the firm.
	4	Did the bugle corps toot with the usual vigor for the queen?
down-and-in spacing	5	Nan is to go to the city hall to sign the land forms for us.
	6	Ty is to pay for the eight pens she laid by the audit forms.
out-and-down shifting	7	Julia and Leon will visit Yang and Chin on their China trip.
	8	Are you going in May, or in June? Willa is leaving in July.
finger reaches to top row	9	or 94|if 85|am 17|do 39;|tug 575|lap 910|fork 4948|kept 8305
	10	We moved from 3947 Brook Road to 1750 Aspen Place on May 18.
easy sentences	11	Glena kept all the work forms on the shelf by the big chair.
	12	Ella may go to the soap firm for title to all the lake land.

5-stroke words | 1 | 2 | 3 | 4 | 5 | 6 | 7 | 8 | 9 | 10 | 11 | 12 |

132d (continued)

Problem 2
Activity Log
(LM p. 83)

Prepare an activity log from the handwritten copy at the right. Fill in the time elapsed column in minutes. Correct errors.

ACTIVITY LOG

Date _____ 5-18 _____   Name _Margaret Roderick_____

Code	Started	Finished	Elapsed	Remarks
P	7:35	8:05		
A	8:05	8:30		Talked w/6 people
V	8:35	8:50		Tod Miller
T	8:50	9:15		Returned 5 calls
V	9:15	9:25		Michelle Kopecky
C	9:30	10:30		Productivity
RM	10:35	11:05		
AM	11:10	11:55		8 letters
O	12:00	1:25		Lunch--Dick Martin

A   Assigning tasks to subordinates   T   Telephone
R   Reading professional journals   V   Visitor
RM   Reading mail   P   Planning
AM   Answering mail   O   Other
C   Committee meetings/conferences

Problem 3
Formal Memorandum
(LM p. 85)

Format and key the memo to Kevyn Slovak from Chris L. Hoy. Use current date. Supply an appropriate subject line.
(words in heading lines: 13)

	words
At your convenience, Kevyn, I would like to visit with you	25
about a research project that I believe we should consider	37
for next year. It would involve a number of people from	48
your area; therefore, your input is essential. Please call	60
me as soon as you can.	66

Problem 4
Purchase Order
(LM p. 87)

1 cc; correct errors; complete total column

To: TGC PLAY EQUIPMENT
     14106 FIVE POINTS ROAD
     CLEVELAND OH 44181-7771
Order No.: PE-47804
Date: Current
Terms: Net/30
Ship Via: Vey Lines
(total words: 62)

Quantity	Descriptions/Stock Nos.	Price
2	Big "T" Gym Set--#74568N	219.99
3	4-Activity Swing Set--#78421N	289.98
1	Big Slider--#76218N	159.99
1	Crazy Slide--#75248N	125.00

Jack Benson, Purchasing Agent

30c ▶ 18
Learn 2 and 6
each line twice SS (slowly, then faster); DS between 2-line groups; if time permits, practice each line again

Follow the Standard Plan for Learning New Keys outlined on page 7.

Reach technique for 2

Reach *up* with *left third* finger.

Reach technique for 6

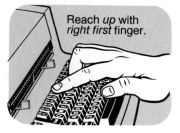
Reach *up* with *right first* finger.

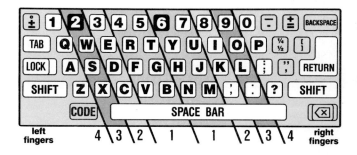

left fingers   4 3 2 1   1 2 3 4   right fingers

Learn 2 ▼
1 s 2 s 2 ss 22 ss 22 s2s s2s 22s Reach up for 2, 22, and 222.
2 Key the figures 2, 22, and 222. Review pages 2 to 22 today.

Learn 6 ▼
3 j 6 j 6 jj 66 jj 66 j6j j6j 66j Reach up for 6, 66, and 666.
4 Add the figures 6, 66, and 666. Have only 6 of 66 finished?

Combine 2, 6, and other figures
5 Key 22, 26, 62, and 66. Just 22 of the 66 skaters are here.
6 Reach with the fingers to key 26 and 262 as well as 2 and 6.
7 Key the figures as units: 26, 59, 17, 30, 46, 162, and 268.
8 The letter dated June 26, 1987, was vital in Case No. 30564.

30d ▶ 12
Check Keyboarding Speed

1. A 1′ writing on ¶ 1, then on ¶ 2; find *gwam* on each.

2. Two 2′ writings on ¶s 1 and 2 combined; find *gwam* on each writing.

3. A 3′ writing on ¶s 1 and 2 combined (or if your teacher prefers, an additional 1′ writing on each ¶).

1′ Gwam Goals
▽ 21 = acceptable
□ 25 = average
○ 29 = good
◇ 33 = excellent

all letters used	E	1.2 si	5.1 awl	90% hfw			gwam 2′	3′

You now know not just where each letter and figure key   5   4
is located but also how to strike it quickly in the correct   11   8
way. With additional practice of the right kind, you could   17   12
build your skills to the level of the expert.   22   15

Your skill in using a keyboard of an office machine is   27   18
a major one you will prize throughout your life. It should   33   22
open many doors to work of real worth. Build it high right   39   26
now in order to have many a future job offer.   44   29

gwam 2′ | 1 | 2 | 3 | 4 | 5 | 6 |
     3′ | 1 | 2 | 3 | 4 |

132b ▶ 10
Language Skills: Learn Commonly Misspelled Words

70-space line; SS

1. Key the first word as shown in the example. Capital letters show the portion commonly misspelled.

2. Repeat Step 1 for each of the other words in the list.

3. From dictation, key each word 3 times in lowercase letters with the book closed.

(This procedure is recommended for any words you may have trouble spelling.)

Example

amONg amONg amONg among among among

amONg	elIgIble
calendAr	grAtEful
coMMiTment	pErcEIve
defInIte	precEDe
desirAble	simIlar

132c ▶ 10
Preapplication Drill: Key on Ruled Paper

(plain full sheet)

1. Use the underline key to key a line 4 inches long (40 pica spaces; 48 elite spaces).

2. Center and key your full name on the line.

3. Study the proximity of the letters in your name to the underline. Only a slight space should separate the letters from the underline. Downstem letters (p, y, q, g, etc.) may touch the line.

4. Remove paper from machine.

5. With a pencil and ruler (or other straight edge), draw 3 horizontal lines 4″ long and 1/2″ apart.

6. Insert the paper and use the variable line spacer to align for keying the copy shown below. You may check the alignment by setting the ribbon control in stencil position and keying a downstem letter. This letter should be near or barely touch the line.

If it does not, make needed adjustments in the position of the paper.

7. Key the information below on lines, leaving 15 spaces between columns.

Mary Hargrove _____   Muncie _____

Mark Hauser _____   Gary _____

Terry Sumpter _____   Kokomo _____

132d ▶ 25
Keyboard on Ruled and Unruled Forms

Problem 1
Index Cards
(LM p. 81)

Key an index card from the model at right using same format as shown. Key 2 more index cards from information provided below.

Mr. Juan Guazero, President
Highland Industries, Inc.
200 Boyce Road
New Orleans, LA 70121-8809
(504) 932-1000

HOME BEAUTIFUL MAGAZINE
Attention Joanne Langley
90 Connally Avenue
Jacksonville, FL 32209-5530
(904) 655-2290

MILLER, JANE (DR.)

Dr. Jane Miller
200 Watson Road
Jackson, MS   39212-1110

(601) 439-2210

Learning Goals

1. To improve alphabetic keyboarding speed and technique.
2. To improve number keyboarding speed and control.
3. To review/improve language skills: number expression.
4. To extend skill on longer paragraph writings.

Machine Adjustments

1. Paper guide at 0.
2. Ribbon control to use top half of ribbon.
3. Margin sets: left margin (center - 30); right margin (move to right end of scale).
4. Line-space selector set to single-space (SS) drills; to double-space (DS) ¶s.

Lesson 31	**Basic/Language Skills**	Line length: 60 spaces Spacing: single-space (SS)

31a ▶ 6
Conditioning Practice

1. Each line twice SS.
2. A 1' writing on line 3; find *gwam* (total 5-stroke words completed)

alphabet 1 Roz fixed the crisp okra while Jan made a unique beef gravy.

figure 2 I stocked the lake with 628 perch, 759 carp, and 1,340 bass.

easy 3 Six of the big firms may bid for the right to the lake land.

5-stroke words | 1 | 2 | 3 | 4 | 5 | 6 | 7 | 8 | 9 | 10 | 11 | 12 |

31b ▶ 10
Improve Language Skills: Number Expression

1. Read the first rule highlighted in color at the right.
2. Key the *Learn* sentence below it, noting how the rule has been applied. Use the 60-space line for which your machine is set.
3. Key the *Apply* sentence, supplying the appropriate number expression.
4. Practice the other rules in the same way.
5. If time permits, key the three *Apply* sentences again to improve number control.

> Spell a number that begins a sentence even when other numbers in the sentence are shown in figures.

Learn 1 Sixteen of the books are now overdue; 37 have been returned.
Apply 2 30 members of the club have signed up; only 12 have not.

> Use figures for numbers above ten, and for numbers one to ten when they are used with numbers above ten.

Learn 3 He has ordered 10 computers, 20 disk drives, and 5 printers.
Apply 4 Mrs. Cruz said she will need ten to 12 copies of Z64 and Z98.

> Use figures to express dates and times.

Learn 5 I take Wasach Flight 64 at 5:39 p.m. on January 27 to Boise.
Apply 6 At eight ten p.m. on May six, the curtain rises on OUR TOWN.

31c ▶ 18
Improve Keyboarding Technique: Response Patterns

1. Each pair of lines twice SS (slowly, then faster); DS between 4-line groups.
2. Two 1' writings on line 7, then on line 8; find *gwam* on each writing.

letter response 1 oil case|pop star|you face|pin test|pink area|pump data card
2 As you are on my state tax case, get a few tax rates set up.

word response 3 tie with|big name|key firm|but rush|rich soap|make them risk
4 Sign the work form for the six men to do the city dock work.

combination response 5 you held|raw fish|sat down|oil land|safe auto|they draw maps
6 At the start signal, work with great vigor to make the rate.

easy sentences 7 Did they make the right title forms for the eight big firms?
8 The key social work may end if they turn down the usual aid.

| 1 | 2 | 3 | 4 | 5 | 6 | 7 | 8 | 9 | 10 | 11 | 12 |

131c (continued)

Problem 3
Invoice
(LM p. 77)
Key invoice as
shown at right.

Problem 4
Invoice
(LM p. 79)
Repeat Problem 3
changing the
quantities to 6, 10,
6, and 3. Calcu-
late the total col-
umn. Add 6%
sales tax.

Garrison's Office Supplies

300 Circle Drive
Corpus Christi, TX 78412-3101
(512) 893-7216

INVOICE

MATHEWS INTERIORS
284 NORTH MESA STREET
EL PASO TX 79901-2023

Date: May 1, 19--   6
Customer   10
Order No.: N-8838334   17

Terms	Shipped Via	Our Order No.	Date Shipped	
2/10, n/30	Our truck	CG-294889	5/1/--	25

Quantity	Description/Stock No.	(Unit Price)	(Amount)	
10	Chair Arc Lamp--#22 SP 4007	39 99	399 90	33
3	Shell-Style Lamp--#22 SP 4009	29 99	89 97	42
4	Accent Chair--#14 SP 3886	219 99	879 96	51
2	Replacement Seats--#14 SP 2004	19 99	39 98	62
			1409 81	63
	Sales tax		84 59	68
			1494 40	70

131d ▶ 10
Language Skills: Learn Commonly Misspelled Words

70-space line; SS

1. Key the first word as shown in
the example. Capital letters show
the portion commonly misspelled.
2. Repeat Step 1 for each of the
other words in the list.
3. From dictation, key each word
3 times in lowercase letters with
the book closed.
(This procedure is recommended
for any words you may have trouble spelling.)

Example

aCross   aCross   aCross   across   across   across

aCross   noticEable
aLL riGHt   oCCaSion
benEfiTed   pamPHlet
embaRRaSS   recoMMend
juDGment   transfeRRed

Lesson 132	Spelling/Business Forms

132a ▶ 5
Conditioning Practice

each line twice SS
(slowly, then faster);
DS between 2-line
groups; if time permits,
repeat selected lines

alphabet 1 Just after Max passed the quiz on keyboarding, we left for a vacation.

figures 2 On June 30, 1987, shipments of 52 boxes of paper and 64 books arrived.

fig/sym 3 The new contract (#64382) will assure 75% of the workers a $109 raise.

speed 4 The field hand may work to fix the problems with the dock by the lake.

| 1 | 2 | 3 | 4 | 5 | 6 | 7 | 8 | 9 | 10 | 11 | 12 | 13 | 14 |

31d ▶ 16
Improve Keyboarding Skill: Guided Writing

1. Take one 1' timed writing and two 1' *guided* writings on ¶ 1 as directed on page 37.

2. Take one 1' timed writing and two 1' *guided* writings on ¶ 2 in the same way.

3. Take two 2' timed writings on ¶s 1 and 2 combined; find *gwam* on each.

4. Take one 3' writing on ¶s 1 and 2 combined; find *gwam*.

1' Gwam Goals
▽ 23 = acceptable
□ 27 = average
○ 31 = good
◇ 35 = excellent

all letters used	E	1.2 si	5.1 awl	90% hfw		*gwam* 2'	3'

When you aim to do better something that you cannot do | 5 | 4

as well as you wish, you try again. You do not just repeat | 11 | 8

old actions; or if you do, you do not improve. Rather, you | 17 | 12

repeat the general response but with some change in the act. | 23 | 16

The next time you are asked to do the drill again, try | 29 | 19

to use a better method. Try to make quick, precise motions | 35 | 23

and let your mind tell the fingers what to do. Size up the | 41 | 27

problem and learn better ways of increasing your speed. | 46 | 31

gwam 2' | 1 | 2 | 3 | 4 | 5 | 6 |
3' | 1 | 2 | 3 | 4 |

Lesson 32 — Basic/Language Skills

Line length: 60 spaces
Spacing: single-space (SS)

32a ▶ 6
Conditioning Practice

1. Each line twice SS.
2. A 1' writing on line 3; find *gwam*.

alphabet 1 Jacki may have to plan big, unique duets for Zahn next week.

figure 2 Take 485 bags of crab and 630 bags of shrimp to 1792 Market.

easy 3 Nana did sign the usual title forms for the eight box firms.

5-stroke words | 1 | 2 | 3 | 4 | 5 | 6 | 7 | 8 | 9 | 10 | 11 | 12 |

32b ▶ 10
Improve Language Skills: Number Expression

1. Read the first rule highlighted in color at the right.

2. Key the *Learn* sentence below it, noting how the rule has been applied. Use the 60-space line for which your machine is set.

3. Key the *Apply* sentence supplying the appropriate number expression.

4. Practice the other rules in the same way.

5. If time permits, key the three *Apply* sentences again to improve number control.

> Use figures for house numbers except house number *One*.

Learn 1 My office is at One Baker Plaza; my home, at 9 Devon Circle.
Apply 2 The Wilsons moved from 3740 Erie Avenue to 1 Beach Place.

> Use figures to express measures and weights.

Learn 3 Silvia Vallejo is 5 ft. 6 in. tall and weighs 121 lbs. 8 oz.
Apply 4 The package measures one ft. by six in. and weighs four lbs.

> Use figures for numbers following nouns.

Learn 5 Today, review Rules 1 to 12 in Chapter 6, pages 129 and 130.
Apply 6 Case 4657 is reviewed in Volume four, pages seven and eight.

131c ▶ 25
Process Special Forms

Study the Formatting Guides for processing purchase requisitions, purchase orders, and invoices on p. 227.

1 cc; proofread carefully and correct errors.

Problem 1
Purchase Requisition (LM p. 73)
Key purchase requisition as shown at right.

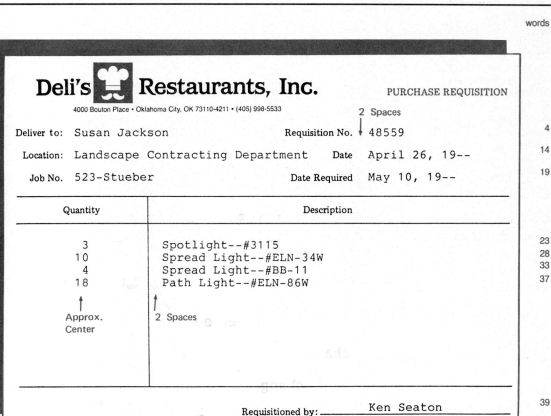

Deli's Restaurants, Inc.   PURCHASE REQUISITION
4000 Bouton Place • Oklahoma City, OK 73110-4211 • (405) 998-5533

	2 Spaces
Deliver to: Susan Jackson	Requisition No. ↓ 48559	4
Location: Landscape Contracting Department	Date April 26, 19--	14
Job No. 523-Stueber	Date Required May 10, 19--	19

Quantity	Description	
3	Spotlight--#3115	23
10	Spread Light--#ELN-34W	28
4	Spread Light--#BB-11	33
18	Path Light--#ELN-86W	37

↑ Approx. Center   ↑ 2 Spaces

Requisitioned by: _____ Ken Seaton _____   39

Problem 2
Purchase Order (LM p. 75)
Key purchase order as shown at right.

Deli's Restaurants, Inc.   PURCHASE ORDER
4000 Bouton Place • Oklahoma City, OK 73110-4211 • (405) 998-5533

	2 Spaces	
	Purchase Order No.: ↓ LC-385793	2 / 6
KEN LIGHTING COMPANY	Date: April 26, 19--	14
384 ADMIRAL BOULEVARD	Terms: 2/10, n/30	20
TULSA OK 74120-5549	Shipped Via: Sun Express	22

Quantity	Description/Stock Number	Price		Per	Total		
3	Spotlight--#3115	52	85	ea	158	55	30
10	Spread Light--#ELN-34W	31	45	ea	314	50	38
4	Spread Light--#BB-11	15	75	ea	63	00	46
18	Path Light--#ELN-86W	27	50	ea	495	00	55
					1031	05	57

↑ Approx. Center   ↑ 2 Spaces

By _____ Ken Seaton _____   59

32c ▶ 10
Improve Keyboarding Technique

1. Each pair of lines once SS as shown; DS between pairs.

2. Two 1' writings on line 6, then on line 8; find *gwam* on each writing.

adjacent reaches

1 a safe|a coin|a tree|to buy|the ads|to stop|is here|the silk
2 Reba has tried various copiers to buy one to suit her needs.

long, direct reaches

3 a peck|a myth|a brim|an ace|to pace|he must|of many|the sums
4 Myra must decide if curved fingers help when keying numbers.

one-hand words

5 at no|we are|no act|my art|set up|saw him|as you see|in case
6 You acted on my tax case only after you saw my estate cards.

balanced-hand words

7 of the|she pays|big risk|but wish|cut work|key city|due them
8 He may profit by good form and a firm wish to make the goal.

5-stroke words | 1 | 2 | 3 | 4 | 5 | 6 | 7 | 8 | 9 | 10 | 11 | 12 |

32d ▶ 12
Check/Improve Keyboarding Speed

1. Two 1' writings on each ¶; find *gwam* on each writing.

2. A 2' writing on ¶s 1 and 2 combined; find *gwam*.

3. A 3' writing on ¶s 1 and 2 combined; find *gwam*.

Goals

1': At least 24 *gwam*
2': At least 23 *gwam*
3': At least 22 *gwam*

all letters used | E | 1.2 si | 5.2 awl | 90% hfw | *gwam* 2' | 3'

| | | 2 | | 4 | | 6 | | 8 | | 10 | |
Just how well do you adjust to change? Recognize that   5 | 4

| | 12 | | 14 | | 16 | | 18 | | 20 | | 22 |
change is as certain to come as death or taxes. You cannot   11 | 8

| | 24 | | 26 | | 28 | | 30 | | 32 | | 34 |
avoid change, but you can adjust to it. How quickly you do   17 | 12

| | 36 | | 38 | | 40 | | 42 | | 44 | | 46 |
this is one index of your likely success in the world ahead.   23 | 16

| | | 2 | | 4 | | 6 | | 8 | | 10 | |
As well as acts of nature, people cause change to take   29 | 19

| | 12 | | 14 | | 16 | | 18 | | 20 | | 22 |
place. Growth in use of computers in homes and business is   35 | 23

| | 24 | | 26 | | 28 | | 30 | | 32 | | 34 |
an example of change caused by people. Will you be able to   41 | 27

| | 36 | | 38 | | 40 | | 42 | | 44 | | 46 |
handle the many changes the computer may bring to your life?   47 | 31

gwam 2' | 1 | 2 | 3 | 4 | 5 | 6 |
3' | 1 | 2 | 3 | 4 |

32e ▶ 12
Learn to Proofread Your Copy

1. Note the kinds of errors marked in the typed ¶ at right.

2. Note how the proofreader's marks above the copy are used to mark corrections in the ¶.

3. Using the copy you keyed in the 3' writing above, proofread and mark for correction each error you made.

Goal: To learn the first step in finding and correcting your errors.

\# = space   ∧ = insert   ◡ = close up   ℓ = delete   ∩ = transpose (tr)

Just howwell do you ajust to change? Recognize that
change is certain to come as death or taxes. /You cannot
avoid change, but your can adjust to it. How quickly you do
do this is one index of likely success inthe world ahead.

Line 1	Line 2	Line 3	Line 4
1 Failure to space	1 Omitted word	1 Misstroke	1 Repeated word
2 Omitted letter	2 Added letter	2 Added letter	2 Omitted word
3 Faulty spacing	3 Incorrect spacing	3 Transposition	3 Failure to space

130c (continued)

words

Problem 3
Simplified Memorandum
(plain full sheet)

Format and key the memorandum at the right as a simplified memo. Proofread and circle errors.

Problem 4
Formal Memorandum
(LM p. 71)

Repeat Problem 3 as a formal memorandum. Prepare a company envelope (address to Marketing Department).
(total words: 287)

April 25, 19--   3
QS

Tony Mendez, Marketing Manager   9
DS

CONDUCTING POSITIVE PERFORMANCE APPRAISALS   18
DS

It is almost time again for annual performance reviews, a process that you,   33
like many of our other managers, may not anticipate eagerly. So often   47
employees and managers look upon these conferences as a time to discuss   62
all the things employees have done wrong during the past year. With this   76
approach to performance reviews, tension is high; and neither the managers   91
nor the employees feel good at the completion of the reviews. Further, the   107
overall productivity of the company seems to suffer, at least for a few weeks.   123

Our Executive Board recognizes that improvements need to be made in our   137
performance appraisal procedures, and they have asked me to arrange for   151
two half-day programs on this topic. The programs will involve a small   166
amount of lecture, videotapes illustrating positive and negative performance   181
appraisals, discussion of problems encountered in performance appraisals,   196
and videotaped role playing to be critiqued and discussed.   208

If you would like to participate in this program, please send me a list of half   224
days when you can attend during the month of May. I have enclosed a form   239
that you may use to indicate if you are interested in the program and, if so,   255
to mark the times and dates you can attend.   264
QS

Terry Austin, Director of Human Resources   272
DS

xx   273
DS

Enclosure   274

Lesson 131 | Keyboarding Skills/Business Forms

131a ▶ 5
Conditioning Practice

each line twice SS (slowly, then faster); DS between 2-line groups; if time permits, repeat selected lines

alphabet 1 Zack quit going fox hunting, so we can provide him with a job all day.

figures 2 The 24 students lost 13 of the 97 textbooks and 85 of the 460 pencils.

fig/sym 3 Mark's car insurance (effective 6/21/87) went from $335.50 to $409.75.

speed 4 Name an auditor to handle the problems and pay the city for this work.

| 1 | 2 | 3 | 4 | 5 | 6 | 7 | 8 | 9 | 10 | 11 | 12 | 13 | 14 |

131b ▶ 10
Improve Basic Skill: Speed-Forcing Drill

1. Repeat 130b, p. 228, Steps 1-5.

2. Take a 1' writing on line 23; compare with rate in Lesson 130.

3. Record score on your paper to compare in Lesson 133.

Unit 5 Lessons 33-38

Learning Goals

1. To learn the location of basic symbol keys.
2. To learn how to strike the symbol keys properly with the correct fingers.
3. To improve keyboarding speed/technique on alphabetic and statistical copy.
4. To review/improve language skills.

Machine Adjustments

1. Paper guide at *0*.
2. Ribbon control to use top half of ribbon.
3. Margin sets: left margin (center - 30); right margin (move to right end of scale).
4. Line-space selector set to single-space (SS) drills and to double-space (DS) ¶s.

Lesson 33	**/ and $**	Line length: 60 spaces Spacing: single-space (SS)

33a ▶ 6
Conditioning Practice

1. Each line twice SS.
2. A 1' writing on line 3; find *gwam*.

alphabet 1 Quent was just amazed by five great tackles Alex put on him.

figure 2 Our group planted 284 cedar, 375 elm, and 1,690 maple trees.

easy 3 It is their wish to pay for land maps of eight island towns.

| 1 | 2 | 3 | 4 | 5 | 6 | 7 | 8 | 9 | 10 | 11 | 12 |

33b ▶ 18
Learn / and $

each line twice SS (slowly, then faster); DS between 4-line groups; if time permits, practice the lines again

/ = diagonal
$ = dollar(s)

Do not space between a figure and the **/** or the **$** sign.

Reach technique for /

Reach *down* to / with *right little* finger.

Reach technique for $

Shift; then reach *up* to $ with *left first* finger.

Learn / (diagonal)

1 ; / ; / /; /; ?/; ?/; 2/3 4/5 and/or Key 1/2, 3/4, and 5/16.

2 Space between a whole number and a fraction: 7 2/3, 18 3/4.

Learn $ (dollar sign)

3 f $ f $ $f $f f$f f$f $4 $4 for $4 Shift for $ then key $44.

4 A period separates dollars and cents: $4.50, $6.25, $19.50.

Combine / and $

5 I must shift for $ but not for /: Order 10 gal. at $16/gal.

6 Do not space on either side of /: 1/6, 3/10, 9 5/8, 4 7/12.

7 We sent 5 boxes of No. 6 3/4 envelopes at $11/box on June 2.

8 We can get 2 sets of disks at $49.85/set, 10 sets at $39.85.

130c ▶ 35
Format Documents: Interoffice Memorandums

Study the Formatting Guides for interoffice memorandums and company envelopes on p. 227.

Problem 1
Formal Memorandum
(LM p. 67)

Format and key the memorandum from the model copy below. Proofread and circle errors. Prepare a company envelope to:
Ms. Patricia Hamilton
Sales Representative
Sales Department

words

SALT LAKE
SUPPLY COMPANY   Interoffice Communication

		words
TO:	Patricia Hamilton, Sales Representative	8
FROM:	Albert C. Chung	11
DATE:	April 25, 19--	14
SUBJECT:	Sales Presentation for Product X-38	21

We have had several requests for a session on how to present Product X-38 successfully to our clients. Since your sales of this product have been unusually high, would you be in charge of a two-hour program on this topic at our regional sales conference next month. — 35 49 61 75

You may have complete freedom, Pat, on how to conduct the program. Just let me know what equipment and/or assistance you need, and we will be glad to help. — 89 102 105

xx — 107 **121**

Problem 2
Formal Memorandum
(LM p. 69)

Format and key the memo to Joe R. Marshall, Administrative Assistant, from Beverly K. Hesser, Executive Vice President. Use current date. Supply an appropriate subject line. Add your reference initials and send one cc to Denise Mendez. Prepare a company envelope (address to Personnel Department). Proofread and correct errors.
(words in heading lines: 27)
(total words: 172/**187**)

(¶1) As you know, one of the major company objectives this year is — 40
to evaluate the productivity of our office in order to determine — 53
if and how our productivity may be improved. To address — 64
this objective, we have decided to appoint a committee — 75
consisting of members from each department as well as — 86
members from the various organizational levels. — 95
(¶2) I believe that your input as a member of this com- — 105
mittee will be very valuable since you have demonstrated — 117
considerable creativity in solving problems in the past. This — 129
committee needs people who are visionary and unafraid — 140
of change, and you fit that description. — 149
(¶3) Are you willing to serve on this important committee? — 159
Please let me know as soon as possible. — 167

33c ▶ 10
Check Language Skills: Number Expression

1. Read each handwritten (script) line, noting mentally where changes are needed in spacing and number expression.

2. Key each line, making needed changes; then check accuracy of work against rules on pages listed at left of sentences.

3. If time permits, key each line again at a faster speed.

Ref.		
p. 53	1	20 players are in the locker room; twelve are on the field.
p. 53	2	Of the 15 art entries, only two made it to the final judging.
p. 53	3	The tipoff is at eight thirty p.m. on Saturday, December two.
p. 54	4	The wedding is at Four Jay Lane; the reception, at 1 Del Mar.
p. 54	5	Use three oz. steak sauce, 1 bay leaf, and two tsp. mixed herbs.
p. 54	6	You will find it in Volume Two, Section One, pages ten and 11.

33d ▶ 16
Improve Keyboarding Technique

1. Key each 2-line group (lines 1-12) twice SS; DS between 4-line groups. For lines 7-8, set 7 tab stops 8 spaces apart, beginning at left margin.

2. Take a 1' writing on line 13, then on line 14; find *gwam* on each writing.

space bar	1	am to|of an|go by|an ant|of oak|to pay|did fit|am to cut oak
	2	I am to pay him for any of the pecan wood you buy from them.
shift keys	3	Clay Epps is in New Haven; Jan Appel has left for Cole Lake.
	4	Mandy Wold works in Towne Hall; Hal Epstein, in Arps Center.
shift lock	5	The musical CATS will be shown live on HBO at 8 p.m., May 3.
	6	OLIVER, the play, is based on the classic book OLIVER TWIST.
tab	7	he tab 63 tab or tab 94 tab is tab 82 tab the tab 563
	8	as 12 up 70 we 23 opt 905
adjacent keys	9	news quiz|last trip|safe view|same suit|over part|true power
	10	Sam Quincy read a short poem about a trip on the Milk River.
long, direct reaches	11	to run|a unit|an echo|so many|an herb|the curb|a bonus check
	12	I found that many bonus checks are expected for top service.
alphabet	13	Janet will quickly explain what Dave Gibson made for prizes.
easy	14	I did rush the die to shape the auto panels to the big firm.

| 1 | 2 | 3 | 4 | 5 | 6 | 7 | 8 | 9 | 10 | 11 | 12 |

Lesson 34

% and -

Line length: 60 spaces
Spacing: single-space (SS)

34a ▶ 6
Conditioning Practice

1. Each line twice SS.

2. A 1' writing on line 3; find *gwam*.

alphabet	1	Zoe will buy six unique jackets from Davis for a high price.
figure	2	Order 10 boxes of Disk No. 847 and 25 boxes of Disk No. 639.
easy	3	Eight of them did go to the social held by the big box firm.

| 1 | 2 | 3 | 4 | 5 | 6 | 7 | 8 | 9 | 10 | 11 | 12 |

34b ▶ 16
Improve Keyboarding Technique

1. Key lines 1-12 of 33d, above, twice each.

2. Take a 1' writing on line 13, then on line 14 of 33d.

Goals: To refine technique. To increase speed.

130a ▶ 5
Conditioning Practice

each line twice SS (slowly, then faster); DS between 2-line groups; if time permits, repeat selected lines

alphabet	1	As Gay kept varied time for him on the drums, Jacques blew a jazz sax.
figures	2	I shall buy 230 dresses, 197 suits, 185 hats, and 364 pants at market.
fig/sym	3	The dress is $238.46, and the coat is $598.70 (includes 15% discount).
speed	4	If they keep the busybody busy with the work, then my problem may end.

| 1 | 2 | 3 | 4 | 5 | 6 | 7 | 8 | 9 | 10 | 11 | 12 | 13 | 14 |

130b ▶ 10
Improve Basic Skill: Speed-Forcing Drill

The columns at the right of the sentences show the rate at which you are keying if you complete each sentence the number of times indicated at the top.

1. From lines 1-12, select a speed-goal rate from the columns at the right.

2. Using the sentence at the left of that speed rate, take a 1' writing, trying to complete the sentence the number of times indicated at the top of the column.

3. If in the first writing you reach your speed goal, select the next higher speed rate from the columns. Take additional 1' writings until you reach the new goal rate. Continue to increase your goal with each new achievement.

4. From lines 13-21, select a goal rate equal to your highest rate on lines 1-12.

5. Repeat Steps 2-4 above.

6. Take a 1' writing on line 22; record your rate to compare in Lessons 131 and 133.

Balanced hand

		times per minute to type sentence 4	6	8
1	Sue also works for an auditor. *gwam*	24	36	48
2	The robot turns right to do work.	26	40	53
3	Ana may go to the big lake to fish.	28	42	56
4	Pay the city for the visual aid I got.	30	46	61
5	The haughty man paid a buck for the pen.	32	48	64
6	The visit by the chap got rid of a problem.	34	52	69
7	The eye may focus to the right of the chapel.	36	54	72
8	A widow may sign both of the audit forms in pen.	38	58	77
9	An amendment may entitle me to pay for their fuel.	40	60	80
10	Make their oak shelf and hang it by their oak mantle.	42	64	85
11	Make idle chaps of the city do their work to keep busy.	44	66	88
12	The goal is to make a big profit so we may keep the land.	46	68	91

Combination

13	I saw the eight autos go downtown after he left.	38	58	77
14	The wild deer and turkey on the land are so plump.	40	60	80
15	We paid high duty on the case of food we sent by air.	42	64	85
16	My social sorority had their rituals in an aged chapel.	44	66	88
17	The beggar greeted him as he passed the field by the city.	46	70	93
18	If you have a cataract on the eye, it may impair your sight.	48	72	96
19	The fable was of a cat with a beard and a big dog with red fur.	50	76	101
20	Bob agrees that we may make a great profit if we handle the deal.	52	78	104
21	If you do withdraw the endowment, we may have to end a good program.	54	82	109
22	The sun on an area of icy trees seems to create a land of enchantment.	56	84	112
23	The agreement on exactly what was to be in the chapter was news to us.	56	84	112
24	The defacement of authentic artwork adds to our problems as officials.	56	84	112

| 1 | 2 | 3 | 4 | 5 | 6 | 7 | 8 | 9 | 10 | 11 | 12 | 13 | 14 |

34c ▶ 18
Learn % and -

each line twice SS (slowly, then faster); DS between 4-line groups; if time permits, practice the lines again

% = percent
- = hyphen

Do not space between a figure and %, nor before or after - or -- (dash) used as punctuation.

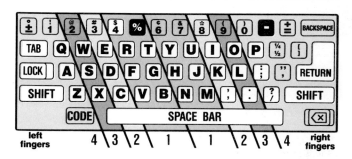

left fingers 4 \ 3 \ 2 \ 1 \ 1 \ 2 \ 3 \ 4 right fingers

Reach technique for %

Shift; then reach *up* to % with *left first* finger.

Reach technique for -

Reach *up* to - with *right little* finger.

Learn % (percent)

1 f % f % %f %f f%f f%f 5% 5% Shift for % as you key 5% or 4%.
2 Do not space between a number and %: 5%, 75%, 85%, and 95%.

Learn - (hyphen)

3 ; - ; --; -; ;-; ;-; 4-ply I use a 4-ply tire on the mower.
4 I gave each film a 1-star, 2-star, 3-star, or 4-star rating.

Combine % and -

5 You can send the parcel by first-class mail at a 50% saving.
6 A dash is two unspaced hyphens -- no space before or after it.
7 The new prime rate is 12% -- but you have no interest in that.
8 You need 60 signatures -- 51% of the members -- on the petition.

34d ▶ 10
Build Keyboarding Skill Transfer

1. Take a 1' writing on ¶ 1; find *gwam*.

2. Take a 1' writing on ¶ 2, then on ¶ 3; find *gwam* on each writing.

3. Compare rates. On which ¶ did you have the highest *gwam*?

4. Take two 1' writings on each of the slower ¶s, trying to equal your highest *gwam* of the first 3 writings.

Note: Most students key straight copy at the highest *gwam*; script (handwritten) copy at the next highest; and statistical copy at the lowest *gwam*.

| E | 1.2 si | 5.1 awl | 90% hfw |

Figures and words share a lot in common as far as ease of keying is concerned. A balanced-hand word or number may be keyed more easily than a one-hand one. Through practice you learn to speed up easy ones and to slow down for others.

Two-digit numbers like 16, 37, 49, and 85 that you key with both hands are easy. Longer ones like 142 and 790 are harder since each one is handled by only one of your hands.

Copy that is written by hand, called script, is not as easy to key as copy shown in type. Writing is less easy to read than type is; as a result, the keying speed is reduced.

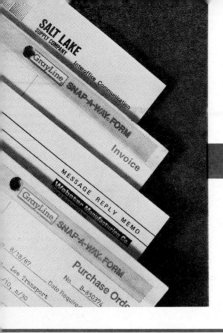

Learning Goals

1. Improve stroking rate.
2. Format and process formal and simplified memorandums.
3. Format and process special forms.
4. Improve language skills.
5. Format and process documents on lined forms.

Machine Adjustments

1. Paper guide at 0.
2. Margins: 70-space line for drills; as directed for problems.
3. Spacing: as directed.

FORMATTING GUIDES: FORMS AND SPECIAL DOCUMENTS

Formal Memo and Company Envelope

Simplified Memo

Interoffice Memorandums

Communications within an organization are often formatted as memorandums rather than as letters. Two styles of the interoffice memorandum are commonly used. The *formal memorandum* is processed on a form having special printed headings. The *simplified memorandum* is prepared on plain paper without headings.

Formatting guides for the interoffice memo are listed below.

1. Use either a half or full sheet.
2. Use block style.
3. Use approximately 1″ side and bottom margins.
4. Omit personal titles (Miss, Mr., Ms., Dr., etc.) on memo, but include them on the company envelope.
5. Omit salutation and complimentary close.
6. SS the body, but DS between ¶s.
7. Use special colored envelopes. If unavailable, use plain envelope with COMPANY MAIL printed in the usual stamp position. Include on the envelope the receiver's personal title, name, and business title; also, include receiver's department (see illustration at left).

Formal memorandum. Begin heading information 2 spaces to the right of printed headings (as shown on page 229). Note that headings are printed in the 1-inch left margin so that the lines of the heading data and the message can begin at the 1″ left margin setting. A memo may be sent to more than one individual; if so, each name is included on the same line as the "To:" heading. DS between all parts of the formal memorandum.

Simplified memorandum. Begin the date on line 6 for a half sheet and line 10 for a full sheet. DS between all parts of the simplified memo, *except* below date and the last ¶ of the body. Quadruple-space (QS) below the dateline and last ¶ of body.

Special Forms (See models on pp. 231-232.)

Purchase requisitions, purchase orders, invoices, and other similar documents are prepared on printed forms. Although forms vary from company to company, well-designed forms allow the keyboard operator to follow the general guidelines listed below.

1. Set left margin stop so that items are approximately centered in the Quantity column of purchase requisitions, purchase orders, and invoices. (This stop is also used to begin the *Deliver to* block of Purchase Requisitions.)
2. Set a tab stop to begin the Description items of Purchase Requisitions and to begin the address and Description items of Purchase Orders and Invoices. (The address must be placed so that all of it shows through the window of a window envelope; items in the Description column should begin 1 or 2 spaces to the right of the vertical rule.)
3. Set a tab stop for keying information in the upper right-hand area of the form (1 or 2 spaces to the right of printed items). This stop may also be used to key items in the Price column, or an additional stop may be set for that purpose.
4. Set additional tab stops for aligning and keying items in remaining column(s).
5. SS column entries, beginning on the first or second space below the horizontal rule under the column headings.
6. If the form lists prices and totals, position monetary amounts so that cent figures fall to the right of the vertical rules. Use of commas to indicate thousands in figure columns is optional.
7. Underline the last figure in the Total column; then, DS before keying the total amount.
8. Tabulate and key across the form rather than keying all items column by column.

35a ▶ 6
Conditioning Practice

1. Each line twice SS.
2. A 1' writing on line 3; find *gwam*.

alphabet	1	Grayson was amazed at just how quickly Pavan fixed the bike.
figure	2	Speed up easy pairs of figures: 10, 26, 37, 48, 59, and 61.
easy	3	Diana is to handle all title forms for the eight auto firms.

| 1 | 2 | 3 | 4 | 5 | 6 | 7 | 8 | 9 | 10 | 11 | 12 |

35b ▶ 10
Check Language Skills: Capitalization

1. Read and key each line, making needed changes in capitalization.
2. Check accuracy of work against rules on pages listed; rekey any line that contains errors in capitalization.

Ref.		
39, 40	1	did you read Chapter 3 for monday? i will read it saturday.
39	2	ask if miss alvarez excused anita and keith xica from class.
39	3	jacques said that he will attend mexicana college next year.
39	4	the golden gate bridge connects san francisco and sausalito.
40, 41	5	ayres gives the first monday in september off for labor day.
41	6	citizens bank is located at walnut street and dayton avenue.
39, 42	7	gloria ryan, the club secretary, wrote to president markham.
39, 41, 42	8	dr. h. j. lindon has a ph.d. from brown, an m.d. from emory.

35c ▶ 18
Learn # and &

each set of lines twice SS (slowly, then faster); DS between groups; if time permits, practice the lines again

= number/pounds
& = ampersand (and)

Do not space between # and a figure; space once before and after & used to join names.

Reach technique for #

Shift; then reach *up* to # with *left second* finger.

Reach technique for &

Shift; then reach *up* to & with *right first* finger.

Learn # (number/pounds)

1 d # d # #d #d d#d d#d 3# 3# Shift for # as you key 3# or #3.

2 Do not space between a number and #:   3# of #33 at $10.35/#.

Learn & (ampersand)

3 j & j & &j &j j&j j&j 7& 7& Have you written to Parks & Lim?

4 Do not space before or after & in initials; as in CG&E, B&O.

Combine # and **&**

5 Shift for # and &. Recall: # stands for number and pounds.
6 Names joined by & require spaces; a # sign alone does, also.
7 Letters joined by & are keyed solid: List Stock #3 as C&NW.
8 I bought 10# of #830 grass seed from Locke & Uhl on March 3.

Evaluate Document Processing:
Letters with Special Features

Time Schedule

Plan and prepare	3′
Timed Production	25′
Proofread and correct errors ...	7′

LM pp. 61-66; supply current date, salutation, complimentary close, and special features as directed; proofread and correct errors

Problem 1

modified block format; blocked ¶s; mixed punctuation

Special features:

REGISTERED
Attention Mr. George All
Subject: 401(k) Profit-Sharing Plan
Company name in closing lines:
    FINANCIAL ADVISORS, INC.
Enclosures: 401(k) PLANS/
    ADMINISTERING 401(k) PLANS
pc Mr. Dale Grimes

words in body: 132
total words: 217

Problem 2

block format; open punctuation

Special features:

Attention Human Resources
    Manager
Company name in closing lines:
    BUSINESS NEWSLETTER
    SERVICE
Enclosure: Reservation Card

words in body: 149
total words: 225

Problem 3

Decide letter and punctuation style.

Send letter by SPECIAL DELIVERY to:
    Mr. Kenneth K. Mattison
    Executive Vice President
    Brentwood Inns
    2186 North Main Street
    Santa Ana, CA 92706-6214

words in body: 107
total words: 156

Problem 4

Repeat Problem 1 on plain paper if you finish before time is called.

Mueller, Huddleston, Osberghaus, Schroeder, and Triplett | 586 Riverside Avenue | Jacksonville, FL 32202-8301

(¶ 1) Companies like yours are always looking for ways to offer greater benefits to their employees, and one that I recommend for your consideration is the 401(k) Profit-Sharing Plan. This plan is practical for large organizations such as yours, and many Fortune 500 companies are already offering it to their employees as a type of retirement plan.

(¶ 2) The 401(k) offers several advantages over an IRA. They are explained in the enclosed booklet entitled 401(k) PLANS. The second enclosure explains the requirements of the employer in administering the plan.

(¶ 3) If you have questions about this plan, call me; and we can set a time to get together for a discussion.

Mrs. Carry Lorenzo, President | postscript If you wish, I can provide a list of local firms that offer 401(k)'s.

Oki & Fong Office Systems | 486 South Second Street | Macon, GA 31201-4910
Subject: Winning at Organizational Politics

(¶ 1) Office politics are a part of every organization; and as much as you might like to ignore them, it would not be wise to do so. Perhaps you wish that the employees in your company could concentrate solely on doing their jobs; however, you are well aware that hard work alone cannot protect your workers from various kinds of political hazards.

(¶ 2) Our monthly newsletter entitled WINNING AT ORGANIZATIONAL POLITICS provides an effective educational program. It creates an awareness of the various aspects of office politics and suggests how to deal with them in a manner that will result in a win-win situation.

(¶ 3) Return the enclosed reservation card and start distributing ten copies of WINNING AT ORGANIZATIONAL POLITICS to your employees each month.

Miss Elaine McLaurin, President postscript If you are not completely satisfied, you may cancel within three months for a total refund.

Subject: Portfolio of Designs

(¶ 1) A portfolio of my work will be sent to you under separate cover by priority mail. It will be marked for special delivery, so I believe it will arrive by the date that you requested.

(¶ 2) Since I am sending several pieces of original work, I would like to have the portfolio returned after you have completed your review.

(¶ 3) I shall be pleased to submit a proposal for your project and can begin the work within the month. I am looking forward to hearing from you after you have received and reviewed my portfolio.

Cordially yours | OFFICE DESIGNS, INC. | Mrs. Jessica Martinez

35d ▶ 16
Improve Keyboarding Skill Transfer

1. Take a 1' writing on ¶ 1; find *gwam.*

2. Take a 1' writing on ¶ 2; find *gwam.*

3. Take two more 1' writings on the slower ¶.

4. Take a 2' writing on ¶ 1, then on ¶ 2; find *gwam* on each writing; 1' *gwam* ÷ 2.

5. Take 2 more 2' writings on the slower ¶.

Goal: To transfer at least 75% of your straight-copy speed to statistical copy.

To determine % of transfer:

¶ 2 *gwam* ÷ ¶ 1 *gwam*

all letters/figures used | LA | 1.4 si | 5.4 awl | 85% hfw

One good way to build speed is called mental practice. When not at a machine, just make believe your hands rest on a keyboard. Next, as you mentally say words like if, also, they, city, and dizzy to yourself, quickly move the fingers through the stroking motions. Doing so can add to speed.

Learn to read and key figures in groups. For example, read 165 as one sixty-five and key it that way. Tackle the longer sequences in like manner. Read 1078 as ten seventy-eight and handle it as 2 units. Try this for 2493, also.

Lesson 36   (and)

Line length: 60 spaces
Spacing: single-space (SS)

36a ▶ 6
Conditioning Practice

1. Each line twice SS.

2. A 1' writing on line 3; find *gwam.*

alphabet 1   Juan Lopez knew our squad could slip by the next five games.

figure 2   Key these figures with quiet hands: 105, 281, 364, and 947.

easy 3   Dixie may amend the six audit forms if it is right to do so.

| 1 | 2 | 3 | 4 | 5 | 6 | 7 | 8 | 9 | 10 | 11 | 12 |

36b ▶ 12
Recall/Improve Language Skills: Capitalization and Numbers

1. Read the first rule highlighted in color.

2. Key the *Learn* sentence below it, noting how the rule has been applied.

3. Key the *Apply* sentence, supplying the appropriate capitalization (and/or number expression).

4. Practice the other rules in the same way.

5. If time permits, key the four *Apply* lines again to improve decision-making speed.

Capitalize nouns preceding numbers (except page and line).

Learn 1   See Rule 12 in Chapter 3, page 34, lines 24 and 25.
Apply 2   Check volume 10, section 29, page 364, lines 75-82.

Spell (capitalized) names of small-numbered streets and avenues (ten and under).

Learn 3   We walked several blocks along Fifth Avenue to 65th Street.
Apply 4   At 4th Street he took a taxi to his home on 32d Avenue.

Use figures for a series of fractions, but spell isolated fractions and indefinite numbers.

Learn 5   Carl has a 1/4 interest in Parcel A, 1/2 in B, and 2/3 in C.
Learn 6   Nearly twenty-five members voted; that is almost two thirds.

Apply 7   Guide calls: one fourth, 1/2, 3/4, and one -- each 15 seconds.
Apply 8   About 60 students passed the test; that is over 1/2.

128c ▶ 35
**Build Sustained Document
Processing: Letters with
Special Features**

plain paper; proofread; correct
errors

Time Schedule
Plan and prepare .... 3′
Timed production .... 25′
Proofread and correct errors ... 7′

1. Make a list of problems to be
processed:
page 222, 126b, Problem 2
page 223, 127b, Problem 2
page 223, 127b, Problem 3
page 223, 127b, Problem 4
Bonus: page 224, 127c

2. Arrange paper and correction
materials for easy access. Process
as many letters as you can in 25′.
Proofread and correct errors before removing letters from machine.
3. After 25′ timing, proofread
again and correct errors or rekey.

If time remains after correcting/
rekeying, process the bonus letter.
4. Determine number of problems
and number of errors; turn in work,
arranged in order listed in Step 1.

Lesson 129 | Letters with Special Features

129a ▶ 5
**Conditioning
Practice**

each line twice SS
(slowly, then faster);
DS between 2-line
groups; if time permits,
repeat selected lines

alphabet	1	Zack expressed some vague ideas on equality while a few jested boldly.
symbols	2	Iba & Kane Co. (located on Elm Street) sells hunting/fishing licenses.
direct reach	3	Annually, Myra goes to a ceremony to celebrate many of these advances.
speed	4	Jane's big wish is to sit in a chair on the dock by the lake and fish.

| 1 | 2 | 3 | 4 | 5 | 6 | 7 | 8 | 9 | 10 | 11 | 12 | 13 | 14 |

129b ▶ 10
**Evaluate Straight-Copy
Skill**

1. A 5′ writing on both ¶s.
2. Find *gwam* and number of errors.
3. Compare to score in
Lesson 123d, page 214.
4. Record on LM p. 3.

all letters used | A | 1.5 si | 5.7 awl | 80% hfw |

	gwam 1′		5′
Many firms feel that their employees are their most valuable re-	13	3	45
sources. Excellent companies realize that people working toward common	27	5	48
goals influence the success of the business. They are also aware of the	42	8	51
need to hire qualified people and then to create a work environment to	56	11	54
allow the people to perform at their highest potential. Firms which	70	14	56
believe that the main job of managers is to remove obstacles that get	84	17	59
in the way of the output of the workers are the firms that do, in fact,	98	20	62
achieve their goals.	102	20	63
Not only do executives and managers in the most successful firms	13	23	65
admit to themselves the value of their employees, but they also reveal	27	26	68
this feeling to their workers. They know that most people enjoy being	41	29	71
given credit for their unique qualities. They also know that any action	56	32	74
on their part that aids the workers in realizing their own self-worth	70	34	77
will lead to a higher return for the firm, since such people are self-	84	37	80
motivated. When leaders do not have to be occupied with employee moti-	98	40	82
vation, they can devote their energy to other vital tasks.	110	42	85

gwam 1′	1	2	3	4	5	6	7	8	9	10	11	12	13	14
5′		1				2				3				

36c ▶ 18
Learn (and)

each set of lines twice SS (slowly, then faster); DS between groups; if time permits, practice the lines again

(= left parenthesis
) = right parenthesis

> Do not space between ( ) and the copy they enclose.

Reach technique for (

Shift; then reach *up* to (with *right third* finger.

Reach technique for)

Shift; then reach *up* to) with *right little* finger

use the letter "l"

Learn ((left parenthesis)

1 l (l ((l (l l(l l(l 9(9(Shift for (as you key (9 or (l.
2 As (is the shift of 9, use the l finger to key 9, (, or (9.

Learn) (right parenthesis)

3 ;) ;));); ;); ;); 0) 0) Shift for) as you key 0) or l).
4 As) is the shift of 0, use the ; finger to key 0,), or 0).

Combine (and **)**

5 Hints: (1) depress shift; (2) strike key; (3) release both.
6 Tab steps: (1) clear tabs, (2) set stops, and (3) tabulate.
7 Her new account (#495-3078) draws annual interest at 6 1/2%.

36d ▶ 14
Improve Keyboarding Technique

1. Clear all tab stops.
2. Set 5 tab stops 11 spaces apart, beginning at left margin.
3. Key each set of lines once SS as shown.
4. Take two 1' writings on line 15, then on line 16; find *gwam* on each writing.

fig/sym

1 $44 tab 50% tab #39 tab 1/3 tab (1) tab 2-day
2 $84 tab 18% tab 70# tab 3/4 tab (9) tab 6-ply

adjacent-key reaches

3 new are here try dirt say last pot rope buy yule lions coins
4 The trip guide let the pony rest before the last open trail.

long, direct reaches

5 any sync deck once sum mug sun nut nerve debts curbs brought
6 A great many people must make payment at the central branch.

letter response

7 ploy edge join gave pink ever upon save only best pump facts
8 At best, I fear only a few union cases were ever acted upon.

word response

9 their right field world visit chair throw proxy risks eighty
10 The girls did their work then spent their pay for the chair.

combination response

11 maps were hand only sign card pair link also fast paid plump
12 We may amend the rate if the union agrees to the work risks.

alphabetic sentences

13 Jerold quickly coaxed eight avid fans away from Buzz Parker.
14 Having pumped in six quick points, Jaye Wold froze the ball.

easy sentences

15 Do rush the worn panels to the auto firm for them to enamel.
16 The right bid may entitle the girl to the handy ivory forks.

| 1 | 2 | 3 | 4 | 5 | 6 | 7 | 8 | 9 | 10 | 11 | 12 |

127c ▶ 20
Formatting Drill: Letter with Special Features

plain paper; modified block format; open punctuation

1. A 5' writing on the letter to establish a base rate. If you finish before time is called, start over.

2. Find *gwam*. Use this rate as your goal rate. From the table below, find quarter-minute checkpoints; mentally note these figures in opening lines through ¶ 1.

3. Take three 1' guided writings on the opening lines through ¶ 1. Leave proper spacing between letter parts.

4. Repeat Steps 2 and 3, but begin with ¶ 3 and continue through closing lines.

5. Take another 5' writing on the letter. Try to maintain your new goal rate.

Quarter-Minute Checkpoints

gwam	¼'	½'	¾'	1'
24	6	12	18	24
28	7	14	21	28
32	8	16	24	32
36	9	18	27	36
40	10	20	30	40
44	11	22	33	44
48	12	24	36	48
52	13	26	39	52
56	14	28	42	56
60	15	30	45	60
64	16	32	48	64
68	17	34	51	68
72	18	36	54	72
76	19	38	57	76
80	20	40	60	80

gwam 5'

June 3, 19-- SPECIAL DELIVERY C. M. Moore Company Attention Office | 3 | 42
Manager 409 East 14 Street Oakland, CA 94612-4401 Ladies and Gentlemen | 5 | 45
Subject: EDM Copiers | 6 | 46

(¶ 1) It was a pleasure to visit with your associate, Robby Kerr, last | 9 | 48
week at our exhibit at the Office Systems Convention in San Francisco. | 12 | 51
Robby indicated that you are in the process of selecting a new copying | 15 | 54
machine and that two of our models appear to fit your needs -- Models | 17 | 57
1403 and 8645. | 18 | 57

(¶ 2) The enclosed brochure explains in detail the special features of | 20 | 60
both our 1400 series and our 8600 series. Further, the great news is | 23 | 63
that we can offer these copiers at last year's prices for all orders | 26 | 65
received before July 1 (as indicated on the enclosed price list). | 29 | 68

(¶ 3) May we help you make your selection of an EDM Copier. | 31 | 70
Sincerely EDM OFFICE SYSTEMS Bill Newell Vice President xx Enclo- | 34 | 73
sures: Brochure Price List pc Robby Kerr postscript Our representative, | 37 | 76
Kyle Stabler, will call you next week to see how we can be of assistance. | 39 | 79

Lesson 128 — Letters with Special Features/Composing

128a ▶ 5
Conditioning Practice

each line twice SS (slowly, then faster); DS between 2-line groups; if time permits, repeat selected lines

alphabet	1	Jeff seized every chance to make progress to quash unwanted tax bills.
symbols	2	Shelley's article -- her second one -- entitled "Job Interviews" is great.
direct reach	3	After writing many checks, I put a number of them under my brown book.
speed	4	He may wish to aid the sick with their problems if they wish such aid.

| 1 | 2 | 3 | 4 | 5 | 6 | 7 | 8 | 9 | 10 | 11 | 12 | 13 | 14 |

128b ▶ 10
Language Skills: Compose at Keyboard

plain paper; 1" side margins

Repeat 126d, p. 222, but select a different topic from the one you selected earlier or select a topic of your choice to be approved by your teacher.

37a ▶ 6
Conditioning Practice

1. Each line twice SS.
2. A 1' writing on line 3; find *gwam*.

alphabet 1 Maria Bow fixed the prized clock seven judges say is unique.

fig/sym 2 I bought the new CMD #940 for $2,385, a TLC #306 for $1,750.

easy 3 The auto firm owns the big signs by the downtown civic hall.

| 1 | 2 | 3 | 4 | 5 | 6 | 7 | 8 | 9 | 10 | 11 | 12 |

37b ▶ 20
Learn ' and "

' = apostrophe
" = quotation mark

Apostrophe (')

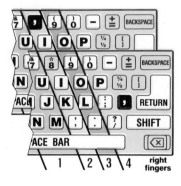

Manual and some computers

Key ' (shift of 8) with the *right second finger*. Reach with the controlling finger. Try to hold the other fingers over the home keys.

Electric and most computers

The ' is to the right of ; and is controlled by the *right little finger*.

Quotation (")

Manual and some computers

Key " (the shift of 2) with the *left third finger*. Reach with the controlling finger. Hold other fingers over home keys.

Electric and most computers

Key " (the shift of ') with the *right little finger*. Don't forget to shift *before* striking the " key.

Learning procedure

1. Locate new key on appropriate chart above (electric or manual); read the reach technique given opposite it.
2. Key twice the appropriate pair of lines given at the right.
3. Repeat steps 1 and 2 for the other new key.
4. Key twice the 4 lines at the bottom of the page.
5. If time permits, key again those lines with which you had difficulty.

Learn ' (apostrophe)

manual

1 k ' k ' ' 'k 'k k'k k'k 8' 8' Is this Rick's? No, it's Ike's.
2 On Lei's machine the ' is on 8; on Dick's, it's in home row.

electric

3 ; ' ; ' '; '; ; '; ; '; 's it's he's I'm I've It's his, I see.
4 If it's his, I'll return it; but I'm not sure it isn't Ed's.

Learn " (quotation mark)

manual

5 s " s " "s "s s"s s"s 2" 2" "Go for the goal," the boy said.
6 I keyed "loss" for "laws" and "sow" for "sew" from the tape.

electric

7 ; " ; " "; "; ; "; ; "; "Keep going," he said, but I had quit.
8 Did you use "there" for "their" and Joe use "two" for "too"?

Combine ' and "

9 "Its" is an adjective; "it's" is the contraction of "it is."
10 Miss Han said, "To make numbers plural, add 's: 8's, 10's."
11 O'Shea said, "Use ' (apostrophe) to shorten phrases: I'll."
12 "If it's Jan's or Al's," she said, "I'll bring it to class."

127b ▶ 25
Improve Formatting Skill: Short Letters with Special Features

plain paper; proofread and circle errors; supply current date, salutation, complimentary close, and special features as directed

Problem 1
modified block format; blocked ¶s; mixed punctuation

Special features:

AIRMAIL

Subject: Moving Arrangements

Enclosures: Transportation Request/Change-of-Address Form

words in body: 94
total words: 144

Problem 2
modified block format; blocked ¶s; mixed punctuation

Special features:

Attention Ms. Vera Patton

Company name in closing lines:
    ELAND MANUFACTURING, INC.

pc Martha Cullen, Senior Vice President

Postscript: Also, please bring your lightest weight portable printer to demonstrate.

words in body: 100
total words: 164

Problem 3
block format; open punctuation

Special features:

Attention Mr. Lyndon Sommer

Subject: Managing Change Seminar

Enclosures: Program Outline/ Registration Forms

Postscript: Note the 10 percent discount if you send three or more participants.

words in body: 91
total words: 161

Problem 4
block format; open punctuation

Special features:

Subject: Meeting Room for May 3, 19--

Company name in closing lines:
    BELMONT HOTELS, INC.

words in body: 57
total words: 104

Dr. Neal Esposito│Isar Strasse 22│D-6082 WALLDORF│GERMANY, FED REP OF

(¶ 1) Your transfer to the Boston Regional Office will be simplified if you will complete the enclosed Transportation Request and Change-of-Address Form that I have enclosed. Please return them to the personnel office within two weeks so we can issue airline tickets for you and your family well in advance of the time of your departure.

(¶ 2) We hope that your experiences during your three years in Walldorf have been rewarding; however, we understand your desire to return home.

Fred R. Stevens│Director of Personnel

Baker and Smith, Inc.│821 West Forbes Avenue│Pittsburgh, PA 15219-5505│

(¶ 1) Thanks for sending the booklets which describe the various brands and models of microcomputers that you sell. We have thoroughly reviewed the material and would like to schedule demonstrations for the Elon 220 and the PEC 8021.

(¶ 2) After checking the schedules of the four employees most interested in seeing the demonstrations, I find that next Thursday afternoon or Friday morning will be the best time for us. Are either of these times convenient for you?

(¶ 3) Please call us to set up an appointment.

Terry Peck, Manager

Southwestern-Continental Airfreight Co., Inc.│486 San Jacinto Street│Houston, TX 77002-1134│

(¶ 1) A detailed outline of our Managing Change Seminar is enclosed to help you determine if this program is appropriate for your middle managers. From our discussion last week, I believe that it is; however, I will be happy to work with you in tailoring an individualized program for your company if you prefer.

(¶ 2) Several registration forms are enclosed and should be returned within the next week if you wish to send participants to our next open seminar.

Alan Conners│Program Director

Mrs. Kim Matsumoto, President / Matsumoto, Inc./586 East Broad Street / Columbus, OH 43215-1913

(¶1) We have reserved the Phoenix Room for your use on the afternoon of May 3. We shall be happy to provide coffee, soft drinks, and refreshments of cheese and fruit. Please have your guests register at the front desk upon their arrival.

(¶2) Thank you for selecting the Belmont once again! Ms. Lara Howard / Conference Director

37c ▶ 10
Improve Language Skills: Capitalization

1. Read the first rule highlighted in color.
2. Key the *Learn* sentences below it, noting how the rule has been applied.
3. Key the *Apply* sentences, supplying the appropriate capitalization.
4. Practice the other rule in the same way.
5. If time permits, key the *Apply* lines again at a faster speed.

> Capitalize the first word of a direct quotation unless the quote is built into the structure of the sentence.

Learn 1 Cissy quoted Pope: "To err is human, to forgive is divine."
Learn 2 I said that "making more errors doesn't make us more human."

Apply 3 The message read: "complete Lesson 38 on text pages 63-64."
Apply 4 Ms. York urged all of us to "Dot the i's and cross the t's."

> Capitalize the first word of the first part of an interrupted quotation, but not the first word of the second part.

Learn 5 "To gain speed," she said, "think the word, not the letter."
Apply 6 "curve the fingers," I said, "and make a quick-snap stroke."

37d ▶ 14
Improve Keyboarding Technique

1. Key each pair of lines once SS as shown.
2. Take two 1' writings on line 11, then on line 12; find *gwam* on each writing.

Technique goals
- curved, upright fingers
- quick-snap keystrokes
- quiet hands and arms

fig/sym sentences
1 I signed a 30-year note--$67,495 (at 12.8%)--with Ott & Jay.
2 Order #26105 reads: "18 sets of Cat. #4716B at $39.25/set."

outside-reach sentences
3 Alex Quails was our prize shortstop for most of last season.
4 Perhaps all will pass a fast quiz on tax laws of past years.

adjacent-key sentences
5 Louisa has opened her radio studio in the new western plaza.
6 Violet reads the meters on the oil heaters in the buildings.

long-reach sentences
7 My group collected a large sum for her musical concert fund.
8 Cecil carved this unique marble lynx for the county exhibit.

alphabetic sentences
9 Marquis has just solved the exciting new puzzle from Byke's.
10 Jack Wilford may have enough cash for six quite big topazes.

easy sentences
11 The signs the six girls wish to hang may handle the problem.
12 He lent the field auditor a hand with the work for the firm.

| 1 | 2 | 3 | 4 | 5 | 6 | 7 | 8 | 9 | 10 | 11 | 12 |

Lesson 38 — ＿ and *

Line length: 60 spaces
Spacing: single-space (SS)

38a ▶ 6
Conditioning Practice

1. Each line twice SS.
2. A 1' writing on line 3; find *gwam*.

alphabet 1 Max Pelz has flown the big jet over the quaint, dark canyon.
fig/sym 2 She asked, "Isn't Order #3046 from C&NW dated May 25, 1987?"
easy 3 The auditor is to aid the six antique firms with their work.

| 1 | 2 | 3 | 4 | 5 | 6 | 7 | 8 | 9 | 10 | 11 | 12 |

38b ▶ 14
Improve Keyboarding Technique

1. Key lines 1-12 of 37d, above, once SS as shown.

2. Take two 1' writings on line 11, then on line 12; find *gwam* on each writing.

Goals: To refine te
To increas

222

Lesson 126 — Letters with Special Features/Composing

126a ▶ 5
Conditioning Practice

each line twice SS (slowly, then faster); DS between 2-line groups; if time permits, repeat selected lines

alphabet	1	Kay revealed her expert qualities as a jazz artist by coming with Fay.
figures	2	In my classes, I have 6 students at 7:30, 52 at 9:30, and 84 at 10:30.
adjacent key	3	As we agreed, the new shop we build will serve the fashionable people.
speed	4	Nancy and Nema may pay the busy auditor a visit to amend a formal bid.

| 1 | 2 | 3 | 4 | 5 | 6 | 7 | 8 | 9 | 10 | 11 | 12 | 13 | 14 |

126b ▶ 25
Format Documents: Letters with Special Features

Review the formatting guides for correspondence with special features on p. 220.

Problem 1 (plain paper)
Format and key the letter on p. 221, giving careful attention to the placement of the special features. Proofread and circle errors. Keep the copy to use as a model in the next lesson.

Problem 2 (plain paper)
If time permits, repeat the letter on p. 221 with the changes listed at the right. Proofread and circle errors.

Addressee: Loper and Martinez, Attorneys-at-Law, Attention Ms. Mary Struble
(same street and city address)
Sender: Mrs. Kaye Payne Attorney-at-Law

126c ▶ 10
Formatting Drill: Letter with Special Features

plain paper

1. Two 1' writings in correct letter format on opening lines (date through ¶ 1) of letter on page 221. Concentrate on correct placement of letter parts.

2. Two 1' writings in correct letter format on closing lines (¶ 3 through postscript). Concentrate on correct placement of letter parts.

3. A 3' writing in correct letter format on the complete letter. Concentrate on correct format.

126d ▶ 10
Language Skills: Compose at Keyboard

plain paper; 1" side margins

1. Compose at the keyboard 1 or 2 paragraphs on one of the topics shown at right. DS paragraph(s); ignore typographical errors. If necessary, x-out copy and continue keying.
2. Edit your copy, marking corrections and changes to improve sentence structure and organization.

Topics:
My Plans Following Graduation
My Ideal Job
My Life Five Years From Now
Why I Need Good Keyboarding Skills
How the Computer Affects My Life
How Composing at the Keyboard Can Save Time

Lesson 127 — Letters with Special Features

127a ▶ 5
Conditioning Practice

each line twice SS (slowly, then faster); DS between 2-line groups; if time permits, repeat selected lines

alphabet	1	Vicki's quick signal was for Perry to come and judge the zany exhibit.
figures	2	Flights 329 and 475 will be replaced by Flights 168 and 420 next week.
adjacent key	3	Oliver hoped to please a few vacationers with a choice mountain guide.
speed	4	Sofia may end the problem if she pays the big penalty and the tax due.

| 1 | 2 | 3 | 4 | 5 | 6 | 7 | 8 | 9 | 10 | 11 | 12 | 13 | 14 |

38c ▶ 18 Learn __ (underline) and * (asterisk)

Underline (__)

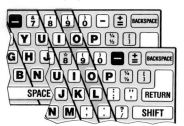

Note: To position the carrier (cursor) to underline a word, strike the backspace key with the right little finger once for each letter in the word.

Learning procedure

1. Locate new key on appropriate chart above (electric or manual); read the reach technique given opposite it.

2. Key twice the appropriate pair of lines given at the right.

3. Repeat steps 1 and 2 for the other new key.

4. Key lines 9-10 three times.

5. If time permits, key again those lines with which you had difficulty.

Manual and some computers

Type __ (shift of **6**) with the *right first finger*. Reach with the finger without letting the hand move forward.

Electric and most computers

Type __ (shift of the - key) with the *right little finger*. Reach with the finger without swinging elbow out.

Asterisk (*)

Manual and some computers

Type * (the shift of -) with the *right fourth (little) finger*.

Electric and most computers

Type * (the shift of **8**) with the *right second finger*.

Learn __ (underline)

manual

1 j _ j _ j j j j 6 j 6 j Underline the words <u>fully</u> and <u>daily</u>.
2 <u>Curve</u> your fingers and keep them <u>upright</u> over the home <u>keys</u>.

electric

3 ; _ ; _ ;; ;; ; _; _; They are to underline <u>stop</u> and <u>gallop</u>.
4 To <u>develop</u>, you should <u>plan</u> the work and then <u>work</u> the plan.

Learn * (asterisk)

manual

5 ; * ; * *; *; ;*; ;*; We may use an * for a single footnote.
6 All special gift items are indicated by an *; as 746*, 936*.

electric

7 k * k * *k *k k*k k*k 8*k 8*k Use * for a table source note.
8 All discounted items show an *, thus: 48K*, 588*, and 618*.

Combine __ and *

9   Use an * to mark often confused words such as <u>then</u> and <u>than</u>.
10 An * after a name identifies an understudy for <u>Wizard of Oz</u>.

38d ▶ 12
Check/Improve Keyboarding Skill

1. A 1′ writing on each ¶; find *gwam* on each.

2. A 2′ writing on ¶s 1-2 combined; find *gwam*.

3. An additional 1′ writing on each ¶; find *gwam*.

4. An additional 2′ writing on ¶s 1-2 combined; find *gwam*.

5. If time permits, take a 3′ writing on ¶s 1-2 combined; find *gwam*.

1′ Gwam Goals

▽ 25 = acceptable
□ 29 = average
○ 33 = good
◇ 37 = excellent

all letters used	E	1.2 si	5.1 awl	90% hfw

gwam 2′ | 3′

You may have noticed that until now the lines you have   5 | 4
keyed have been even at the right as well as at the left if   11 | 8
you keyed them properly. They were written that way to aid   17 | 12
your learning. Next, you will learn to work from materials   23 | 16
in which the lines vary in length by seven or eight letters.   29 | 20

When lines vary in length, they are centered on a page   35 | 23
according to the longest line in the copy. You can quickly   41 | 27
learn how to center copy, a major concern for a keyboarder.   47 | 31
You will then not have to puzzle about how to place letters   53 | 35
and reports on a page so that they will draw the eye.   58 | 39

gwam 2′ | 1 | 2 | 3 | 4 | 5 | 6
3′ | 1 | 2 | 3 | 4

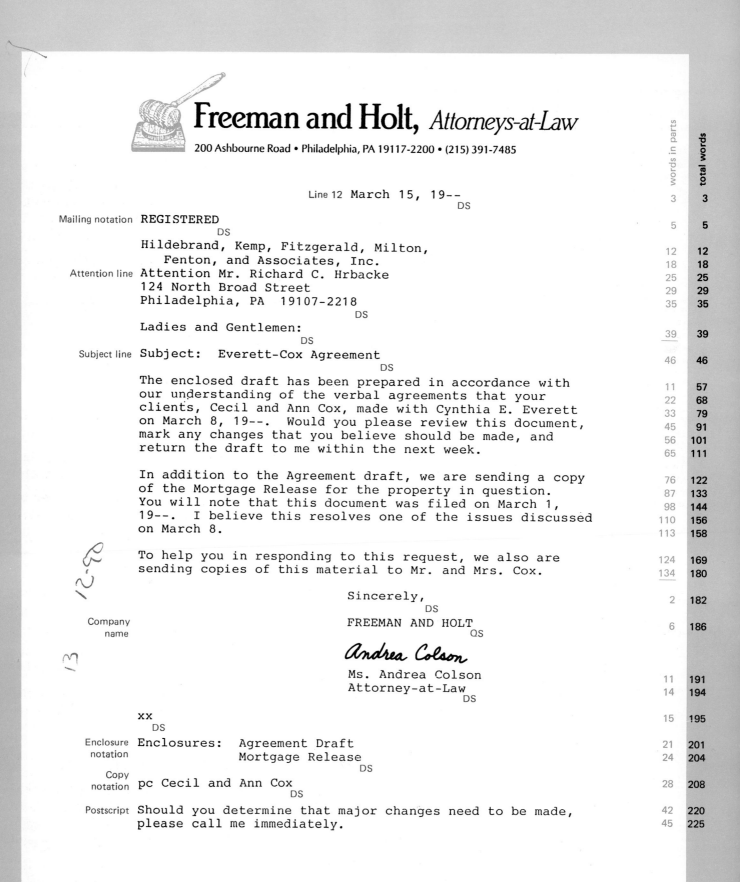

Freeman and Holt, Attorneys-at-Law

200 Ashbourne Road • Philadelphia, PA 19117-2200 • (215) 391-7485

	words in parts	total words

Line 12 March 15, 19--   3   3
DS

Mailing notation REGISTERED   5   5
      DS

Hildebrand, Kemp, Fitzgerald, Milton,   12   12
   Fenton, and Associates, Inc.   18   18
Attention line Attention Mr. Richard C. Hrbacke   25   25
124 North Broad Street   29   29
Philadelphia, PA 19107-2218   35   35
      DS

Ladies and Gentlemen: 39   39
      DS

Subject line Subject: Everett-Cox Agreement   46   46
      DS

The enclosed draft has been prepared in accordance with   11   57
our understanding of the verbal agreements that your   22   68
clients, Cecil and Ann Cox, made with Cynthia E. Everett   33   79
on March 8, 19--. Would you please review this document,   45   91
mark any changes that you believe should be made, and   56   101
return the draft to me within the next week.   65   111

In addition to the Agreement draft, we are sending a copy   76   122
of the Mortgage Release for the property in question.   87   133
You will note that this document was filed on March 1,   98   144
19--. I believe this resolves one of the issues discussed   110   156
on March 8.   113   158

To help you in responding to this request, we also are   124   169
sending copies of this material to Mr. and Mrs. Cox.   134   180

        Sincerely,   2   182
          DS
Company   FREEMAN AND HOLT   6   186
name   QS

Andrea Colson

       Ms. Andrea Colson   11   191
       Attorney-at-Law   14   194
          DS

xx   15   195
  DS

Enclosure Enclosures: Agreement Draft   21   201
notation   Mortgage Release   24   204
          DS

Copy pc Cecil and Ann Cox   28   208
notation   DS

Postscript Should you determine that major changes need to be made,   42   220
please call me immediately.   45   225

Letter with Special Features

Practice Procedure

1. Key each line of a group 3 times: first, to improve keyboarding technique; next, to improve keyboarding speed; then, to build precise control of finger motions.

2. Take several 1' writings on the 2 sentences in each set of lines to measure your skill on each kind of copy.

As time permits, repeat the drills. Keep a record of your speed scores to see how your skill grows.

Each of the 120 *different* words used in the drills is among the 500 most-used words in the English language. In a study of over 2 million words in personal and business communications, these 120 words accounted for over 40 percent of all word occurrences. Thus, they are important to you in perfecting your keyboarding skill. Practice them frequently for both speed and accuracy.

Balanced-Hand Words of 2-5 Letters (use word response)

words

1 of to is it he by or an if us so do me am go the and for but
2 a may she did man own end due pay got big air with they when
3 them than also such make then work both down form city their
4 men they when wish name hand paid held half it's world field

phrases

5 of us |to me |she may |and own |but due |pay the |big man |for them
6 is to make |am to work |a big city |by the name |if they wish to

sentences

7 He is to do the work for both of us, and she is to pay half.
8 She paid the big man for the field work he did for the city.

| 1 | 2 | 3 | 4 | 5 | 6 | 7 | 8 | 9 | 10 | 11 | 12 |

One-Hand Words of 2-5 Letters (use letter response)

words

9   a in be we on as at no up my you was are him get see few set
10 tax war act car were only best date case fact area free rate
11 you act him fact only ever card face after state great water

phrases

12 at no |as my |on you |we are |at best |get set |you were |only date
13 get him in |act on my case |you set a date |get a rate on water

sentences

14 We are free only after we get him set up on a tax rate case.
15 A tax rate was set in my area only after we set a case date.

| 1 | 2 | 3 | 4 | 5 | 6 | 7 | 8 | 9 | 10 | 11 | 12 |

Double-Letter Words of 2-5 Letters (speed up double letters)

words

16 all see too off will been well good need feel look less call
17 too free soon week room took keep book bill tell still small
18 off call been less free look need week soon will offer needs

phrases

19 a room |all week |too soon |see less |call off |need all |will see
20 see a need |took a book |need a bill |all will see |a good offer

sentences

21 It is too soon to tell if we will need that small book room.
22 They still feel a need to offer a good book to all who call.

| 1 | 2 | 3 | 4 | 5 | 6 | 7 | 8 | 9 | 10 | 11 | 12 |

Balanced-Hand, One-Hand, and Double-Letter Words of 2-5 Letters

words

23 of we to in or on is be it as by no if at us up an my he was
24 and all him for see you men too are may get off pay him well
25 such will work best then keep were good been only city needs
26 make soon ever wish tell area name bill face paid tell great

phrases

27 is too great |they will be |she will state |the offer was small
28 if at all |may get all |off the case |to tell him |to keep after

sentences

29 If you wish to get to the rate you set, keep the hand still.
30 All of us do the work well, for only good form will pay off.

| 1 | 2 | 3 | 4 | 5 | 6 | 7 | 8 | 9 | 10 | 11 | 12 |

Learning Goals

1. To learn to format and process letters with special features: mailing notation, attention line, subject line, company name in closing lines, multiple enclosures, copy notations, and postscripts.

2. To learn to format letter addresses with long lines.

3. To improve production speed.

4. To compose and edit paragraphs.

Machine Adjustments

1. Paper guide at *0*.

2. Paper bail rolls at even intervals across page.

3. Margins: 70-space line for drill lines and timed paragraphs; as needed for letters.

4. Spacing: SS for drill lines and letters, unless otherwise directed. DS for timed paragraphs.

FORMATTING GUIDES: CORRESPONDENCE WITH SPECIAL FEATURES

Although not frequently used, several special features may be used in business letters. These features are illustrated in the model letter on page 221. In some cases, alternative formats for special parts are correct (for example, the subject line may be placed in various positions). The simplest and most efficient formats, however, are illustrated in this unit.

Mailing notations (REGISTERED, CERTIFIED, SPECIAL DELIVERY, or AIRMAIL) begin at the left margin in ALL CAPS a double space below the dateline and a double space above the first line of the letter address. (Note: AIRMAIL is used only on foreign mail.)

An *attention line* may be used if the first line of the letter address is a company name. Place the attention line on the second line of the letter address. Some examples are:

Attention Mrs. Susan Jay, Manager
Attention Mr. Edward Jackson
Attention Office Manager

When a letter is addressed to a company, the correct salutation is "Ladies and Gentlemen," even though an attention line may name an individual.

Place the *subject line* a double space below the salutation. If the body paragraphs are blocked, block the subject line at left margin. If the body paragraphs are indented, indent the subject line or center it. The word "Subject" may be used. If used, follow the word "Subject" by a colon and two spaces before completing the subject line.

When used, place *company name* a double space below the complimentary close in ALL CAPS. QS (quadruple-space) to signature line.

Place *enclosure notation* a double space below reference initials. If multiple enclosures are referred to in the letter, follow the word "Enclosures" with a colon and two spaces and list each enclosure.

Enclosures: Order Forms
             Price List

A *photocopy* or *carbon copy* notation indicates that a copy of the letter is being sent to someone other than the addressee. Use "pc" (*photocopy*) or "cc" (*carbon copy*) followed by the name of the person(s) to receive a copy. Place copy notation a double space below Enclosure, if used, or the reference line if there is no enclosure.

pc James C. Smith
   Cynthia J. Maxon
   Julio Sanchez

A *postscript* is an additional paragraph that may be added after a letter has been completed. It is the last item in the letter. Place a double space below the preceding item, and begin at same paragraph point (indented or blocked) as the body paragraphs.

Long lines in the letter address are carried to the next line and indented three spaces.

In both the letter address and closing lines, *professional titles* may be placed on the same line as the name separated by a comma or placed on the following line without a comma.

Ms. Anna Cox, Office Manager
            or
Ms. Anna Cox
Office Manager

Use the form which gives the best balance and attractiveness.

Note. When several special features are used in a letter, the dateline may be raised to present a more attractive appearance on the page. Generally, raise the dateline one line for each two special-feature lines used.

ENRICHMENT ACTIVITY: Timed Writing

The two sets of paragraphs are counted internally for 1' guided and unguided writings; at the side and bottom for 2' and 3' measurement writings. They may be used at any time additional timed writing practice is desired.

1. A 1' writing on ¶ 1; determine *gwam*.

2. Add 4 *gwam* to set a new goal rate.

3. Two 1' writings on ¶ 1, trying to maintain your goal rate each ¼ minute.

4. Key ¶ 2 in the same way.

5. A 2' unguided writing on each ¶. If you complete a ¶ before time is called, begin that ¶ again.

6. A 3' writing on ¶s 1-2 combined; determine *gwam*.

gwam	¼'	½'	¾'	Time
16	4	8	12	16
20	5	10	15	20
24	6	12	18	24
28	7	14	21	28
32	8	16	24	32
36	9	18	27	36
40	10	20	30	40
44	11	22	33	44
48	12	24	36	48

Unit 5 Goals (1')
▽ 25 = acceptable
□ 29 = average
○ 33 = good
◇ 37 = excellent

all letters used | LA | 1.4 si | 5.4 awl | 85% hfw | gwam 2' | 3'

Typewriter spacing is regular; that is, each letter of — 5 | 4
the alphabet uses the same amount of space. Most type used — 11 | 8
by printers, though, varies in space; that is, wide letters — 17 | 12
take more space than narrow ones. Every line of typed copy — 23 | 16
lines up at the left side but usually not at the right. — 29 | 19

Printers can force lines of different lengths to align — 5 | 23
at the right side by adjusting the space between words. As — 11 | 27
you copy from print, then, do not expect every line to stop — 17 | 31
at quite the same point. Many students and more than a few — 23 | 35
teachers are puzzled by this peculiar quality of print. — 29 | 39

gwam 2' 1 2 3 4 5 6
3' 1 2 3 4

all letters used | LA | 1.4 si | 5.4 awl | 85% hfw | gwam 2' | 3'

An excellent performance shows the true concern of the — 5 | 4
performer for the task. It gives one a feeling of personal — 11 | 8
triumph and prompts us as a matter of habit to do our best. — 18 | 12
Really successful men and women take great delight in their — 24 | 16
work and pursue it with a lot of dedication. — 28 | 19

A factor common to all who succeed is the need to have — 5 | 22
a good job recognized by others. If good work goes without — 11 | 26
notice, the desire to excel may be reduced. Lucky, indeed, — 17 | 30
are those who can study their own performance, evaluate its — 23 | 34
quality, and do what must be done to improve. — 28 | 37

gwam 2' 1 2 3 4 5 6
3' 1 2 3 4

PHASE 6

Process Special Documents

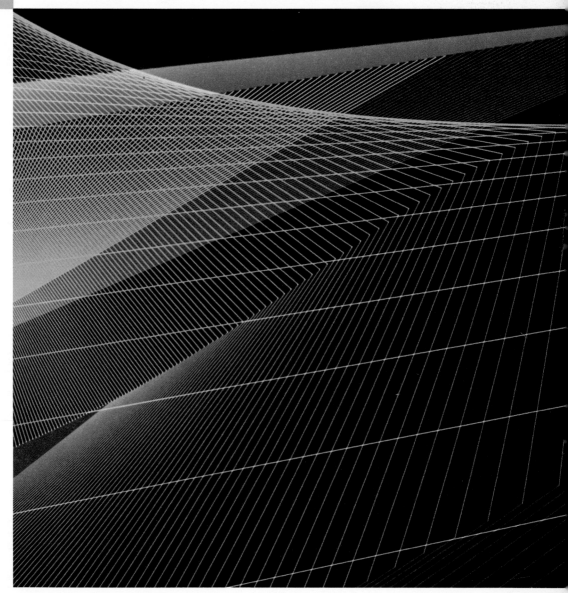

The primary goals of Phase 6 are to continue the development of your skill in processing documents and to integrate the knowledge and skills you acquired in Phases 4 and 5. You will learn to format correspondence with special features, various kinds of forms, and office employment documents. You will compose employment documents for your own personal use.

The specific objectives of Phase 6 are to improve, develop, and/or measure the following competencies:

1. Straight-copy speed and accuracy.

2. Production of documents such as letters with special features, forms, and employment documents.

3. Decision-making skills.

4. Language skills.

Learning Goals

1. To learn how to center lines horizontally (side to side).
2. To learn how to format a numbered list with a centered heading.
3. To learn how to format short personal notes.
4. To learn how to format short simplified memos.

Machine Adjustments

1. Paper guide at *0*.
2. Ribbon control to use top half of ribbon.
3. Margin sets: left margin (center - 30); right margin (move to right end of scale).
4. Line-space selector set to single-space (SS) drills and to double-space (DS) ¶s.

Lesson 39 — Centering Lines

Line length: 60 spaces
Spacing: single-space (SS)

39a ▶ 6
Conditioning Practice

1. Each line twice SS.
2. A 1' writing on line 3; find *gwam*.

alphabet 1 Flo Gomez may have a jinx on our squad, but we kept the cup.

fig/sym 2 Key these data: $40, $84, 95%, #30, 6-point, 1/5, J&W 27's.

speed 3 They risk a big penalty if they throw a fight for the title.

| 1 | 2 | 3 | 4 | 5 | 6 | 7 | 8 | 9 | 10 | 11 | 12 |

39b ▶ 9
Correct Errors as You Keyboard

Errors in the paragraph at the right have been circled.

1. Key the ¶ once DS, correcting the circled errors.

2. Proofread your completed work and mark any errors for correction. (Use proofreader's marks.)

3. Key the ¶ again from your marked copy.

/ Change letter   ⌐# Delete space   ∧ Insert space   ⟋ Delete

⌒ Close up   ℓ∧ Insert letter   ∿ Transpose

(Standerd)-size paper is (81/2) inches wide by 11 inches (long). The (maximun) line length for such (papre) is 102 elite spaces or 85 pica (spaces .) The horizontal (side (toside)) center point (fir) such (pa per) is 51 for elite (tyep) or 42 for pica.   A full sheet has a total of (6 6) vertical line spaces; a half (shet) used (longg) edge up, 33 line (spazes .)

39c ▶ 5
Learn to Use the Backspace Key

1. Read the copy in the block at the right to learn one use of the backspace key.

2. Key each word of each line *exactly* as shown. After you complete a word with a missing letter, backspace and fill in the missing letter **e**.

Backspacer	**Electric/Electronic**	**Manual**
To position the printing point (or cursor) to fill in an omitted letter, depress the backspace key. Locate the key on your machine.	Make a light, quick stroke with the little finger. Release the key quickly to avoid a double backspace. Hold the key down when you want repeat backspacing.	Straighten the little finger slightly and reach it to the backspace key with minimum hand motion. Depress the backspace key firmly; release it quickly.

1 Do try to ke p your ey s on th copy as you key th se lin s.

2 Backspace to th point of an omitt d lett r; k y the l tter.

REFERENCES

Corder, Jim W. Handbook of Current English. 5th ed. Glenview, IL: Scott,
  Foresman and Company, 1978.
Taylor, Karl K. "Teaching Summarization Skills." Journal of Reading,
  February 1984, 390-391.

ENRICHMENT ACTIVITY: Timed Writing

Increase Your Keyboarding Speed and/or Improve Your Control

1. Take a 3' timed writing. Find *gwam*; circle errors.

2. *If you made six or fewer errors* in the Step 1 writing, take a 2' guided writing on each ¶; work for increased speed. **Goal:** To increase your speed 2-4 *gwam*.
  If you made more than 6 errors in the Step 1 writing, follow Step 3.

3. Take a 2' guided writing on each ¶ for improved control. Reduce your Step 1 rate by 4 *gwam*. **Goal:** To keyboard with not over 2 errors a minute.

4. Take five 1' writings on each ¶; *start each new writing at the end of the previous writing.* Try to maintain your rate for either speed or control (according to your needs) for the second and succeeding writings. *Example:* If you keyboarded to the 40-word mark in the first 1' timed writing, you should try to get to the 80 word mark in the second timed writing since you will start it at the 40-word mark, etc.

5. Take a 5' timed writing on both paragraphs. **Goal:** To maintain your Step 4 rate for the 5' writing. Find *gwam*; circle errors.

all letters used | A | 1.5 si | 5.7 awl | 80% hfw

	gwam 3'	5'
Over the years, the eraser has been the principal method or proce-	4 3	51
dure used to correct typewriting errors. The eraser is still used to	9 5	53
a limited extent; however, other ways or methods used to correct errors	14 8	56
are taking its place. For example, in many typewriting classrooms,	18 11	59
correction tape or paper is often used as the chief method to correct	23 14	62
errors. In using the tape, the typist backspaces to the point of the	28 17	65
error. The tape is placed behind the ribbon, and then he or she types	32 19	67
the error again as it was made, with chalk from the tape covering the	37 22	70
error. The tape is then taken out, and the typist backspaces and types	42 25	73
the needed changes.	43 26	74
In the business office, many typewriters now have a special lift-off	48 29	77
tape. When an error is made, a special key is used to backspace to the	53 32	80
point of the error. The incorrect letter or figure is taken off the	57 34	82
paper by again striking that particular letter or figure. The correc-	62 37	85
tion can then be typed immediately. This entire process is simple and	67 40	88
may take just a few seconds. With specialized typing equipment, errors	72 43	91
can be corrected simply by backspacing. Using this procedure, an error	76 46	94
is corrected at once. The procedure is quick and easy.	80 48	96

gwam 3' | 1 | 2 | 3 | 4 | 5
5' | 1 | 2 | 3

39d ▶ 30
Learn to Center Lines Horizontally (Side to Side)

3 half sheets (long edge at top)

1. Insert a half sheet with the long edge at top (short edge against the paper guide).

2. Set line space selector to double-space (DS) the lines.

3. Read the copy in the block at the right.

4. Center horizontally (side to side) each line of Drill 1. Begin the drill on line 14 from the top edge of the half sheet.

5. Key Drills 2 and 3 in the same way.

6. If time permits, key Drill 3 again, substituting your name, *gwam*, and *eam* (errors a minute).

Enrichment problems appear on page 73.

Get ready to center	How to center	
1. Insert paper with left edge at 0.	**1.** Tabulate to center of paper.	**3.** Do not backspace for an odd or leftover stroke at the end of the line.
2. Move left margin stop to 0; move right margin stop to right end of scale.	**2.** From center, backspace *once* for each 2 letters, spaces, figures, or punctuation marks in the line.	**4.** Begin the line where backspacing ends.
3. Clear all tab stops; set a new stop at horizontal center of paper; elite, 51; pica, 42.	Example	• center point

backspace ◀ | 1 | 1 | 1 | 1 | 1 | 1 | 1 | 1 | 1

LE AR NI NG space T O space CE NT ER

Drill 1

WORDS I MISSPELLED
DS
judgment

experience

accommodates

Drill 2

GOALS
DS
Good Technique

High Speed

Low Error Rate

Drill 3

LEE W. TIBBS
DS
Speed: 25 gwam

Error Rate: 2 eam

Time: 3 minutes

Lesson 40	**Formatting Numbered Lists**	Line length: 60 spaces Spacing: single-space (SS)

40a ▶ 6
Conditioning Practice

1. Each line twice SS.
2. A 1' writing on line 3; find *gwam*.

alphabet 1 David Jakes may win the next big prize for our racquet club.

fig/sym 2 Roe & Hahn's note (#8927) for $6,490 at 13% is due August 5.

speed 3 A neighbor paid the girl to fix the turn signal of the auto.

| 1 | 2 | 3 | 4 | 5 | 6 | 7 | 8 | 9 | 10 | 11 | 12 |

40b ▶ 12
Improve Keyboarding Speed: Skill Comparison

1. A 1' writing on each line; find *gwam* on each writing.

2. Compare rates and identify your 3 slowest writings.

3. A 1' writing on each of the 3 slowest lines.

4. As time permits in later lessons, do this drill again to improve speed and control.

balanced-hand 1 When did the field auditor sign the audit form for the city?

combination 2 You may chair my panel if you work on the tax audit for him.

double-letter 3 I need to use a little more effort to boost my keying skill.

outside-reach 4 Sal amazed us all as she won two prizes for six old plaques.

adjacent-key 5 Three bands played as he walked cheerfully up to the podium.

one-hand 6 You deferred my tax case after my union traced my wage card.

figure 7 The number of votes cast was 29,571 in 1980; 35,640 in 1988.

fig/sym 8 Tina asked, "Can't you touch-key 65, 73, $840, and 19 1/2%?"

| 1 | 2 | 3 | 4 | 5 | 6 | 7 | 8 | 9 | 10 | 11 | 12 |

Evaluate Report Formatting Skill

Arrange copy in unbound manuscript form; DS; number second and additional pages in upper right corner; correct errors if so directed.

PREPARING A TERM PAPER

Preparing a term paper for a class requirement can be an ordeal, or it can be an enjoyable learning experience. Here are some suggestions that may make your experience easier and help you produce a winning term paper.

Select a Topic

If a topic for your term paper isn't assigned to you, try to select a topic which may be of interest to you or that will further your knowledge about a particular field. Once you've decided on a topic, read a general overview about it in an encyclopedia or a specialized reference book. This overview should give a history of your topic, acquaint you with many of the definitions relating to your topic, and highlight those aspects you may wish to research further. In addition, it will pinpoint major controversies and problems dealing with your topic and will usually contain references that will give you new leads to follow.

Locate and Summarize Information About Your Topic

Once you have some general knowledge about your topic, you will want to locate and examine more detailed data. Look in books, periodicals, abstracts, newspapers, and government documents. Also, personal interviews with knowledgeable persons may be a rich source of information.

After locating and reading your source material, you will need to take detailed notes on the material. Most persons like to use cards (6″ × 4″ or 8″ × 5″) for their notations and summaries. You may wish to use one set of cards for necessary reference information (author, title, publisher, city, and date of publication) and another for summaries and quotations. When compiling your reference information, be sure to record accurately and completely all needed information.

Good note taking is essential for producing a good research paper. Do not try to write down everything you read but rather select only the key points that you think you might later use. Further, you will not want your paper to be a string of quotations; therefore, learn to paraphrase main ideas from your sources, quoting directly only the information you feel is of major importance. Taylor describes what he found that good summarizers often did:

The successful (summarizers)...(saw) objectively how the pieces were organized -- the introduction, key points, and the conclusion. They knew where to look for meaning.... In addition, the successful summarizers read each article four or five times to make sure they understood what the author had said (1984, 390-391).

Write and Edit Your Paper

The central purpose of a reference paper should be clear in your mind before you have finished investigating all your resources. When you have gathered a sufficient amount of material to put your topic in focus, it is time to formulate a thesis statement. Your thesis statement -- the main idea or statement of purpose -- makes a claim about a topic. Usually this claim will argue a specific position, analyze a problem, or explain a situation.

Organize your reference cards and prepare an outline. Read through your cards so that you will have a working knowledge of the information you have compiled. Sort your cards into piles, using the title headings on each card as a guide. Working from your cards, prepare an outline showing the order in which you wish to present your material. Each point in the outline should contribute in some way to the central idea or thesis.

Prepare a rough draft. Use your notes and your outline to prepare a rough draft. It should include an introductory paragraph (which contains your thesis statement), the body of your paper (substantive content which supports your thesis), and a conclusion. You should also, as Corder suggests, "Make certain that you are thoroughly familiar with your material before you begin to write. You should have the information on your note cards so well in mind that you can write rapidly and with confidence once you start" (1978, 425).

Edit and revise your rough draft and prepare the final copy. Consult a standard English grammar handbook to help you correct any usage errors. You may also want to incorporate into your paper any suggestions made by persons who have read your rough draft. Make other changes which you think will improve your paper. Then, prepare the final draft. A neatly keyboarded double-spaced report is an added plus when you submit your work for evaluation by your teacher. In preparing your final draft, you may wish to incorporate some of the suggestions given in Unit 23, Lessons 111-118, of this book.

After following the above suggestions, you should have a winning term paper!

(Lesson 125 is continued on next page.)

Space down 6 times,
then center the heading

STEPS IN HORIZONTAL CENTERING

QS (quadruple-space);
space down 4 times

2 spaces

1. Check to see that paper is inserted with left edge at 0
    on the line-of-writing scale.
                                    DS
2. Move left margin set to extreme left and right margin set
    to extreme right of line-of-writing scale.
                                    DS
3. Clear all tabulator (tab) stops.
                            DS
4. Set a tabulator stop at horizontal center point of paper.
                                        DS
5. For each line to be centered, tabulate to center point.
                                        DS
6. From center point, backspace once for each two characters
    and spaces in the line as you spell-say them in pairs.
    If an odd or leftover stroke remains at the end of a line,
    do not backspace for it.
                            DS
7. Begin each line where the backspacing for it ends.

Numbered List with Centered Heading

40c ▶ 32
Learn to Format Numbered Lists

2 half sheets, long edge at top; 60-space line; tabs: one 4 spaces from left margin, one at center point

Problem 1

Format and key the list shown above. Use the spacing directions given in color on the model. (SS each numbered item.) When an item has more than 1 line, tab over 4 spaces to begin each line after the first (to align it with first line).

Problem 2

Format and key in the same way the list at the right.

An enrichment problem appears on page 73.

SPACING WITH SYMBOLS

1. Do not space between a figure and $, %, #, and /.

2. Do not space before or after - used to join words or a figure and a word -- nor before or after a dash (2 hyphens).

3. Do not space between ( ) and the copy they enclose. Space once before the opening (and once after the closing) except when) is followed by a quotation or punctuation mark.

4. Do not space between ' and a preceding or following letter.

5. Do not space between opening " and the copy it precedes, nor between closing " and the copy it follows.

6. Do not space between & and the letters it joins; space once before and after & used to join words.

7. Do not space between * and the copy it precedes or follows.

124b (continued)

Problem 2
full sheet; DS data; correct errors

						words
Main heading:	KEYBOARDING TASKS PERFORMED					6
	ACCORDING TO JOB CLASSIFICATIONS					12
Secondary heading:	(Percent of Keyboarding Time)					18
	Typist	Steno.	Secretary	W.P.O.*	Other**	32
Letters	21%	27%	32%	32%	23%	36
Reports	16	20	19	24	21	39
Memos	12	19	22	14	13	42
Forms	29	11	11	7	24	45
Tables	9	13	9	15	8	48
Other	13	10	7	8	11	55
Totals	100%	100%	100%	100%	100%	61

65

*Word Processing Operators. — 70
**Workers with titles other than those listed. — 79

Problem 3
full sheet; DS data; block headings; correct errors

			words
Main heading:	LARGEST PARKS LOCATED WITHIN		6
	THE LIMITS OF AMERICAN CITIES		12
Column headings:	Name of Park / City / Acres		21
	Fairmont Park	Philadelphia	3,845	27
	Griffith Park	Los Angeles	3,761	34
	Pelham Bay Park	New York City	2,117	41
	Rock Creek Park	Washington	1,800	48
	Balboa Park	San Diego	1,400	53
	Forest Park	St. Louis	1,380	59
	Washington Park	Cleveland	1,212	65
	Lincoln Park	Chicago	1,185	71
	Golden Gate Park	San Francisco	1,107	78
	Belle Isle Park	Detroit	985	84

87

If time permits, repeat as many problems as possible for extra credit. Make these changes:
Problem 1, half sheet, short
    edge at top
Problem 2, half sheet, short
    edge at top
Problem 3, half sheet, long
    edge at top, SS data

Source: National Recreation and Parks Association, Washington, DC. — 98 / 101

Lesson 125 | **Evaluate Report Skills**

125a ▶ 5
Conditioning Practice

each line 3 times (slowly, faster, in-between rate); as time permits, repeat selected lines

alphabet	1	Visitors did enjoy the amazing water tricks of six quaint polar bears.
fig/sym	2	Order #3-170 (May 24) from Smith & Co. totals $58.69, less 2/10, n/30.
long words	3	These laboratories specialize in solid-state space propulsion systems.
speed	4	Their men may do the work for us and the city if she pays them for it.

| 1 | 2 | 3 | 4 | 5 | 6 | 7 | 8 | 9 | 10 | 11 | 12 | 13 | 14 |

41a ▶ 6
Conditioning Practice
1. Each line twice SS.
2. A 1' writing on line 3; find *gwam*.

alphabet 1 Gwen Jackson placed the next bid for my prized antique vase.

fig/sym 2 Items marked * are out of stock: #391*, #674A*, and #2850*.

speed 3 The audit by the city signals the end of their profit cycle.

| 1 | 2 | 3 | 4 | 5 | 6 | 7 | 8 | 9 | 10 | 11 | 12 |

41b ▶ 44
Learn to Format Personal Notes

3 half sheets, long edge at top; 60-space line; block format

Problem 1

Format and key the model note shown below. Use the spacing instructions given in color on the model. (Problems 2 and 3 are on page 71.)

Personal notes
Personal notes are messages between two people on topics of mutual interest. Notes consist of a dateline, salutation (greeting), message (body), complimentary close (farewell), and typed or printed name of the writer. They are often prepared on half sheets.

Block format and placement
Because it is easy to arrange, block format is often used for personal notes. In block style all lines begin at the left margin. The dateline is placed on line 6 of a half sheet (long edge at top). Because such notes are short, a 60-space line is commonly used for both 10-pitch (pica) and 12-pitch (elite) machines.

Spacing of parts
A quadruple space (4 line spaces) separates the dateline and the salutation as well as the complimentary close and the typed or printed name. A double space is left between salutation and body, between the paragraphs, and between body and complimentary close. The body of the note is single-spaced.

Space down 6 times
to place the date

Date ↓ November 6, 19--

QS (quadruple-space);
space down 4 times

Salutation Dear Ralph
DS
There is a book that you just must read since you are "into" computers. It is MEGATRENDS by John Naisbitt.
DS
The author traces the impact on people of the high-tech society brought about by the growing use of computers. He also
Body describes the trend toward the offsetting high-touch society that is developing to help us cope with the many changes (not all positive) the computer has brought into our lives.
DS
The book is at the same time frightening and reassuring. Do read it; then let's compare notes.
DS
Complimentary
close Cordially

Dee

QS (quadruple-space); space down 4 times

Typed (printed)
name Dolores

Personal Note on a Half Sheet

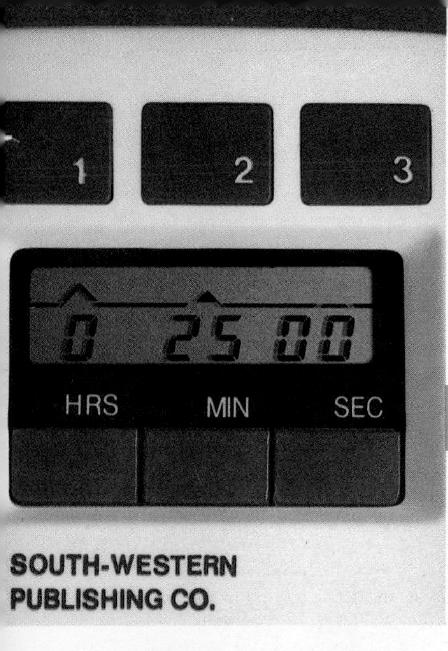

1
2
3
0 25 00
HRS
MIN
SEC
SOUTH-WESTERN PUBLISHING CO.

Unit 25 Lessons 124-125

Measurement Goals

1. To evaluate your table formatting and keyboarding skill.
2. To evaluate your report formatting and keyboarding skill.

Machine Adjustments

Make the usual machine adjustments as required for various activities.

Lesson 124 Evaluate Table Skills

124a ▶ 5 Conditioning Practice

each line 3 times (slowly, faster, in-between rate); as time permits, repeat selected lines

alphabet	1	Most companies emphasize extra valuable jobs for good quality workers.
fig/sym	2	This rug (12′ × 13′6″) was $481.50, but it is now on sale for $317.90.
shift key	3	The salespersons are from Dow & Co., J. & B. Products, and Lynn & Son.
speed	4	When they pay for the land, they may sign the audit form for the firm.

| 1 | 2 | 3 | 4 | 5 | 6 | 7 | 8 | 9 | 10 | 11 | 12 | 13 | 14 |

124b ▶ 45 Evaluate Table Formatting and Problem-Solving Skill

In this activity, you will be evaluated on your ability to arrange and keyboard tables. Only minimum directions are given. You are to make any needed decisions as to placement.

Problem 1

full sheet; DS data; correct errors

Problems continued on page 216.

		words
Main heading:	TEN LARGEST COUNTRIES	4
	IN TERMS OF POPULATION	9
Secondary heading:	(In Millions)	12
Country	Population	17
People's Republic of China	1,042.0	24
India	762.2	26
Soviet Union	278.0	30
United States	238.9	34
Indonesia	168.4	37
Brazil	138.4	40
Japan	120.8	42
Bangladesh	101.5	45
Pakistan	99.2	48
Nigeria	91.2	51
______________		55
Source: Population Reference Bureau, Inc., Washington, DC, 1985.		63 / 68

41b (continued)

Problem 2

Format and key the note given at the right. Use the same directions as you used for Problem 1.

Problem 3

Proofread the note you prepared in Problem 2. Using proofreader's marks, mark any errors for correction. Prepare another copy of the note from your marked copy.

An enrichment problem appears on page 74.

November 8, 19--

Dear Della

The TV people are very unhappy with you. Since I received the trivia game you sent for my birthday, the "pursuit" begins as soon as dinner is over and the TV is OFF. My entire family sends its thanks.

I need one of those "trivia facts" books, though. I play so poorly that I have been nicknamed N. T. for "No Trivia."

Thanks, Della, for helping us learn to play together again. I didn't know mom and dad were so smart.

Cordially

Nelson

Lesson 42	Formatting Simplified Memos	Line length: 60 spaces Spacing: single-space (SS)

42a ▶ 6
Conditioning Practice

1. Each line twice SS.
2. A 1' writing on line 3; find *gwam*.

alphabet 1 Jack Todd will have a quiet nap before his big zoology exam.

fig/sym 2 Our 1987 profit was $53,649 (up 20% from the previous year).

speed 3 The firms may make a profit if they handle their work right.

| 1 | 2 | 3 | 4 | 5 | 6 | 7 | 8 | 9 | 10 | 11 | 12 |

42b ▶ 14
Check/Improve Keyboarding Skill

1. A 1' writing on each ¶; find *gwam* on each writing.
2. A 2' writing on each ¶. If you finish a ¶ before time is called, start over. Find *gwam*; your 2' *gwam* is your 1' *gwam* ÷ 2.
3. A 3' writing on ¶s 1-2 combined; find *gwam*.
4. Proofread your copy and mark it for correction. If time permits, key the ¶s again from your marked copy.

1' Gwam Goals

▽ 25 = acceptable
□ 29 = average
○ 33 = good
◇ 37 = excellent

all letters used | LA | 1.4 si | 5.4 awl | 85% hfw | *gwam* 3'

All of you make an error now and then in performing an   4

act like driving a car, doing the high jump, or playing the   8

piano. Keying is no different. To err is human. The more   12

difficult the activity, the greater the opportunity to make   16

errors. Do not expect all your work to be perfect now.   19

Do not infer from this, though, that the more mistakes   23

you make, the more human you are. A lot of your errors are   27

merely chance; why you make them is a real puzzle. Others,   31

however, are known to be due to lack of attention, improper   35

reading, and bad techniques. Try to reduce the latter.   39

gwam 3' | 1 | 2 | 3 | 4 |

123c ▶ 8
Improve Accuracy: Common Errors

each line 3 times at a control rate

Goal: Not over 1 error in each line. As time permits, repeat any line on which you made an error.

adjacent-key and long-reach errors

Emphasize quiet hands and curved, upright fingers.

1 A number of economic reports predict a bright outlook for the economy.

2 In my opinion, few errors of the covert type were made by the officer.

vowel-confusion errors

Emphasize concentration on copy and continuity of typing.

3 A thief stole a pie from my neighbor during the weird but quiet storm.

4 I tried to seize the foreign piece before it was weighed by the chief.

spacing errors

Emphasize down-and-in spacing with thumb curved and close to space bar.

5 If he is to do the work for us, she may not be able to work with them.

6 Many men and women may share my interest in an exhibit of pop artists.

123d ▶ 15
Measure Basic Skill: Straight Copy

two 5' writings; find *gwam*; circle errors; record better rate

all letters used | A | 1.5 si | 5.7 awl | 80% hfw

	gwam 3'	5'
Information is made up of words, numbers, and symbols that convey	4	3	40
knowledge which can be used in many ways. The mass of information we	9	5	42
have is expanding at a rapid rate. It has caused a paperwork explosion.	14	8	45
One of the major results is a revolution in the way information is pro-	19	11	48
cessed in the office. The most widely used term for such work is word	23	14	51
processing. It is a system that involves workers who are educated to	28	17	54
use specific procedures and electronic equipment.	32	19	56
A word originator dictates or writes input that a word processing	36	22	58
worker types on electronic equipment. It is stored in the system for	41	24	61
later use. The system makes it easy to record, store, recall, and revise	46	27	64
information. For instance, name and address lists can be recalled from	50	30	67
a memory bank to be changed or to send bills, fliers, and other notices.	55	33	70
As you can see, a sizable amount of information stored in the system	60	36	73
can be used in many ways.	62	37	74

gwam 3' | 1 | 2 | 3 | 4 | 5 |
5' | 1 | 2 | 3 |

```
         Space down 6 times
         to place the date



Date  ↓  November 9, 19--

                        QS (quadruple-space);
                        space down 4 times

Addressee  All Students
                    DS
Subject  STUDENT ASSEMBLY
                    DS
         Next week's student assembly will be held in the auditorium on
         Friday, November 16, at 12:45 p.m.  All students are expected
         to attend.
                    DS
Body   Ms. Janet Quinlan of Future Training & Placement Service will
         speak on the topic
                        DS
             COMPUTERS:  INVADERS OF FUTURE CAREERS
                                    DS
         You will want to bring a notebook and pen so that you can take
         notes on this highly informative slide presentation.
                                        QS


Name of writer  Eleanor Sanchez, Assistant Principal
               hb DS
```

Simplified Memo on a Half Sheet

42c ▶ 30
Learn to Format Simplified Memos

3 half sheets, long side at top; 60-space line; block format

Study the model memo above. Its format and spacing are *similar* to those of a personal note.

Problem 1

Format and key the model; center the talk topic on a separate line. Use spacing directions shown in color.

Problem 2

Format and key the memo given at the right. Make placement and spacing decisions.

Problem 3

Format and key Problem 2 again, but address it to **Willis Jones** and change the appointment time to **1:45 p.m.**

An enrichment problem appears on page 74.

November 10, 19--

Jeanne Budka

FOREIGN EXCHANGE STUDY

On Tuesday, December 4, Mr. Adam Doza of Rotary, International, will be here to discuss foreign study with prospective exchange students.

The meeting will be in Conference Room C of Hutchins Library at 11:15 a.m. After the general session, Mr. Doza will visit with each applicant separately. Your appointment is at 2:30 p.m.

Please be prompt for these meetings and bring all your application materials with you.

Joseph M. Quade, Principal

122c ▶ 15
Improve Basic Skill: Statistical Rough-Draft

Two 3' writings on ¶s of 122b, p. 212; then one 5' writing.
Goal: To maintain 3' rate for

5'. Proofread; circle errors; record better 3' rate and 5' rate.

122d ▶ 10
Composing at the Keyboard: Improve Writing Skill

full sheet; DS copy; indent 5 for ¶s

Keyboard the quotation by Hemingway given in the upper-left column, p. 205; then compose a second ¶ in which you try to imitate the writing style of Hemingway.

If time permits, do the same for the Attenborough quotation, p. 205.

Lesson 123 | Keyboarding Speed/Accuracy

123a ▶ 5
Conditioning Practice

each line 3 times (slowly, faster, in-between rate) as time permits, repeat selected lines

alphabet	1	The queerly boxed package of zinc mixtures was delivered just in time.
fig/sym	2	The sale price of P165/8OR138 -- a steel-belted radial tire -- is $172.94.
variable rhythm	3	Did he send a statement to the firm at their new address on that date?
speed	4	He may sign the usual form by proxy if they make an audit of the firm.

| 1 | 2 | 3 | 4 | 5 | 6 | 7 | 8 | 9 | 10 | 11 | 12 | 13 | 14 |

123b ▶ 22
Improve Basic Skill: Speed-Forcing Drill

1. Each line twice at top speed; then:

2. In each set, try to complete each sentence on the call of 15", 12", or 10" timing as directed. Force speed to higher levels as you move from line to line.

3. Move from Set 1 to Set 2 to Set 3 as you are able to complete the lines in the time allowed.

4. Two 1' speed-forcing timings on lines 1e, 2e, and 3e. Compare rates.

5. Take additional 1' timings on the sentence or sentences on which you made your lowest rate(s).

gwam

			15"	12"	10"
	Set 1: High-frequency balanced-hand words emphasized.				
1a	He may also make me go with them to do their work.		40	50	60
1b	They may sign the right amendment form for the auditor.		44	55	66
1c	The firm may make a profit if the men do a quantity of work.		48	60	72
1d	It is their wish to do the right problem and then visit the city.		52	65	78
1e	Both of them may go with me when I go to a city to sign the six forms.		56	70	84
	Set 2: High-frequency combination-response patterns emphasized.				
2a	Send a copy of the statement to me with the check.		40	50	60
2b	Please send the statement to them at their new address.		44	55	66
2c	Nearly all the information enclosed with this report is new.		48	60	72
2d	The quality of the special individual items now in stock is high.		52	65	78
2e	You and I were to go there to do the work before the end of this week.		56	70	84
	Set 3: High-frequency one-hand words emphasized.				
3a	After you rate him, read only a few reserve cases.		40	50	60
3b	After you state a minimum tax rate, give averages only.		44	55	66
3c	Jon regrets that you were referred to him for a tax opinion.		48	60	72
3d	After you state a few tax rates, will you set a tax reserve rate?		52	65	78
3e	In my opinion, you were to refer only a few extra oil tax cases to me.		56	70	84

| 1 | 2 | 3 | 4 | 5 | 6 | 7 | 8 | 9 | 10 | 11 | 12 | 13 | 14 |

Problem 1a
Centered Announcement
Beginning on line 10 of a half sheet (long edge at top), center each line of the announcement horizontally.

Problem 1b
Centered Poem
Beginning on line 10 of a half sheet (long edge at top), center the poem according to the longest line. DS below the title and the author's name; SS the body of the poem.

Problem 1a

SCHOOL OF PERFORMING ARTS

presents

"The Mouse That Roared"

January 21, 22, 23

Marx Theater

All seats: $ 3.50

Problem 1b

OUTWITTED
DS
by
DS
Edwin Markham
DS
He drew a circle that shut me out—
Heretic, rebel, a thing to flout.
But Love and I had the wit to win:
We drew a circle that took him in!

Reprinted by permission of Virgil Markham

Learn to "make" an exclamation mark (!)

If your machine has an exclamation mark key, the left little finger is used to strike it. To "make" the !:

Strike ' (apostrophe); backspace and strike . (period).

Problem 2
Numbered List
full sheet; begin on line 10; 60-space line; SS numbered items, leaving a DS between items

words

SOME POINTS TO REMEMBER ABOUT SPACING   8

1. Space once after , and ; used as marks of punctuation.   20

2. Space twice after . ending a sentence. Space once after .   32
   following an initial (J. W. Mills) or an abbreviation, but   44
   not after . within an abbreviation. (The candidate has a   55
   Ph.D. in English.)   59

3. Space twice after ? at the end of a sentence. (Is the meet-   72
   ing at ten o'clock? If so, please have coffee set up.)   83

4. Space twice after : used to introduce a list, an example,   96
   or a quotation. (He said: "Return my call at 3 p.m.")   107
   Do not space after : used to express time (3:15 p.m.).   118

5. Do not space between a figure and a symbol used with it   130
   ($45, 18%, #75).   134

6. One space should precede (and one should follow), but   146
   no space should follow (nor should one precede). If   157
) is followed by a punctuation mark, no space is left   167
   between them. (See examples in Items 4 and 5.)   177

7. Between a two-letter state name abbreviation and the ZIP   189
   Code, space twice (Dallas, TX 75205-3382). This rule   200
   applies in textual copy as well as in addresses.   210

122b ▶ 20
Key a Report from Statistical Rough-Draft Copy

full sheet; DS copy

1. Format as unbound report. Center main heading:

IMPORTANCE OF KEYBOARDING EFFICIENCY

2. Indent 5 for ¶s.

3. Correct errors. **Goal:** To produce report with maximum keyboarding efficiency: good techniques, continuity of keyboarding, few or no waste motions.

all letters used | A | 1.5 si | 5.7 awl | 80% hfw

	gwam 3'	5'
words in heading	2	1

Keyboarding efficiency is a big part of the *information* production, *process,* it affects as well the *high-tech world* and flow of information in the technological society *the use of the* in which *you and I* we live. A recent study of keyboarding in *firms* business offices in this country shows that key board *workers* *workers* operators (typists, word processing operators, stenos, *, and the like* and secretaries) give 30% of their total keyboarding time *to* producing letters, 20% to reports, 19% to memos, 13% to *to* *rest* forms, and 10% producing tables. The remainder of their *%* keyboarding time (8 percent) *in a day* is given to key- *things* boarding such items as messages, envelopes, itineraries, *as well as other items.* minutes, press releases, and the like. *show*

Quality time studies reveal that the average word processing operator may use 8.17 minutes just to finish *keyboarding* a letter of 176 words, a net keying rate of about 21.5 *This* *capable of typing a* words a minute. An operator may be able to type letter material at a rate of about 40 words a minute, but, when *which relate* all other things relating to the completion of a letter are included (placement, proof reading, correcting spell- *and keyboarding errors* *from* *and* ing, and time lost--pauses, looking up copy, finding palace *and* in copy, checking keyboarding point), the net production *is much lower* *giving* rate falls drammatically. Business people are now putting *a great deal of their attention to* increased emphasis on the importance of the keyboarding *looking for* efficiency and are requiring that keyboarding operators *who are* be able to type at 70 to 80 words or more a minute so as to expand data flow and minimize the costs of information *production.* processing or producing business communications.

7	4
12	7
17	10
20	12
24	14
28	17
32	19
35	21
37	22
41	24
44	26
47	28
51	31
55	33
59	36
62	37
66	40
70	42
76	45
79	47
83	50
86	51
89	54
93	56
97	58
98	59

Problem 3
Personal Note in Script

half sheet (long edge at top);
line: 60; spacing: SS
Format the note in block style, line
for line as shown. Read carefully
to avoid reading errors.

November 10, 19--   4

Dear Marianne   6
On December 18, our Music/Drama Club is sponsoring a special   19
event, "Holiday Sounds," at the Village Center. Instrumental,   31
vocal, and dramatic selections are to be featured.   42

Even though I have only a minor role, I'd like to know that you   54
are in the audience applauding our performance. I really hope   67
that you can be here for the holidays and that you will come to   80
see our show.   83

I have a super ticket for you. You will be seated among people   96
you know and like. We hope to see you on the 18th and through-   108
out the holiday season.   113

Cordially   115

Douglas Mason   117

Problem 4
Simplified Memo in Rough Draft

half sheet (long edge at top);
line: 60; spacing: SS
Format the memo in block style,
line for line as shown. Read carefully to avoid reading errors.

⌃ insert comma
insert space
∿ transpose
𝒮𝓅. spell out
◡ close up space
≡ capitalize

November 10, 19--   4

Junior Achievement Members   9

ORIENTATION MEETING WITH SPONSORS   16

On Thursday evening, November 29, at 7 o'clock, JA members   28
and their sponsors will meet in Emory Auditorium.   39

The purpose of the meeting is to introduce the officers and the   51
sponsor from each company. In addition, a representative of   64
each company will describe its purpose, organization, and plan   76
of operation.   79

The president of each JA company is responsible for planning   91
and conducting her/his company's part of the program.   102

Elliott Richards, ja sponsor   108

xx   109

Note: xx at the end of a document
indicates the keyboard operator's
initials. Substitute your own initials.

121c ▶ 15
Letter Emphasis: Refine Techniques/Improve Speed and Control

each line 3 times (slowly, faster, top speed)

Minimum standard: To complete all lines as directed.

Extra credit: All lines beyond minimum standard.

Goal: To keep hands quiet with keystroking action limited to the fingers.

Emphasize: Continuity and rhythm with curved, upright fingers.

s   Susana was asked to assist us at the session assigned to us in Shensi.

t   Tagett tossed that battered ball into the butter tub without thinking.

u   Your unusual number of unused rubber jugs should be used at our union.

v   Vivian's vivid vocalization of her vowels gave her varied jobs for TV.

w   Wild winter wind will whip powerful waves with force over the wharves.

x   The extra xeroxed copies of next week's taxes would have vexed Xerxes.

y   You may buy yesterday's yield of yams any day; why not buy them today.

z   Zestful Zabrze, eluding tacklers, dizzily zigzagged into the end zone.

alphabet   While Izzy performed exciting jokes, I recited various quaint ballads.

| 1 | 2 | 3 | 4 | 5 | 6 | 7 | 8 | 9 | 10 | 11 | 12 | 13 | 14 |

121d ▶ 15
Transfer Refined Techniques and Improved Control: Guided Writing

1. Two 1' timed writings; find *gwam*; circle errors.

2. Deduct 4 words from better rate; determine 1/4' goals.

3. Two 15" writings; try to reach goal and to keyboard without error.

4. Two 30" writings; try to reach goal and to keyboard without error.

5. Four 1' guided writings at goal rate. **Goal:** Each writing with not more than 2 errors.

Every time you operate the keyboard, make the use of good techniques your goal. This is the way to build your keyboarding efficiency to its highest possible level. Keyboarding efficiency is needed if you are to remain competitive in the world of work, and if you are to use the sophisticated equipment now in use in the technological society in which we live and work.

121e ▶ 10
Composing at the Keyboard: Improve Writing Skill

full sheet; DS copy

1. Prepare a rough draft. Compose a narrative paragraph (tells a story) or two on some fond childhood memory. Do this: Jot down some ideas you want to relate. Arrange ideas in a logical sequence and compose paragraph(s) using your outline.

2. Prepare the final draft. Make any needed corrections in your rough-draft copy; then prepare a final draft. Use as the heading:

A CHILDHOOD MEMORY

Lesson 122   Composing/Report Skills

122a ▶ 5
Conditioning Practice

each line 3 times (slowly, faster, in-between rate); as time permits, repeat selected lines

alphabet 1 The reporters quickly recognized the vexing problems of judging flaws.

fig/sym 2 Use the toll-free number (1-800-632-4759) to call Brown & Jordon, Inc.

shift key 3 Mary Flood, Jack E. Langs, and B. M. Quaile work for O'Brien & Kearns.

speed 4 They may do the problems for us when the city auditor signs the forms.

| 1 | 2 | 3 | 4 | 5 | 6 | 7 | 8 | 9 | 10 | 11 | 12 | 13 | 14 |

Unit 7   Lessons 43-48

Learning Goals

1. To learn how to format business and personal business letters in block style.

2. To learn how to listen for the warning bell and divide words at line endings.

3. To learn how to address large and small envelopes.

Machine Adjustments

1. Paper guide at *0*.

2. Ribbon control to use top half of ribbon.

3. Margin sets: left margin (center - 30); right margin (move to right end of scale).

4. Line-space selector set to SS drills and DS ¶s; set as directed for problems.

FORMATTING GUIDES: LETTERS IN BLOCK STYLE

Block Format

When *all* lines of a letter begin at the left margin, as illustrated in the model, the letter is arranged in *block format* (style). Block format is easy to learn and easy to arrange. It is widely used for both business and personal letters.

Open Punctuation

When no punctuation follows any of the opening or closing lines (except one that may end in an abbreviation), *open* punctuation has been used. Open punctuation is compatible with block format because both save time and reduce errors. All letters in this unit will be formatted with open punctuation.

Model Description

The basic parts of letters written by individuals and businesses to solve business problems are described below in order of their occurrence in a letter.

Heading. On letterhead paper, the printed top portion is the heading or letterhead. It gives the company name, address, and telephone number. On plain paper, often used for personal-business letters, the writer's address appears on the two lines immediately above the date.

Date. When standard letter placement is used -- a practice that is becoming more and more common -- the date is entered or typed on a specified line (line 15 being a common placement) for all letters.

Letter Address. The letter address is begun on the fourth line space below the date. If the letter is addressed to a company, the address *may* include an attention line (the second line of the address) to call the letter to the attention of a specific person, department, or job title.

Salutation. The salutation (greeting) is placed a double space (DS) below the letter address.

Body. The letter body (message) is begun a double space (DS) below the salutation. The paragraphs of the body are blocked and single-spaced (SS) with a double space left between paragraphs.

Complimentary Close. The complimentary close (farewell) appears a double space below the body.

Name of Writer. The name of the writer (the originator of the message) is placed on the fourth line space below the complimentary close. It may be followed on the same line or on the next line by a business or professional title such as Manager, Vice President, Ph.D., or a department name.

Reference Initials. The initials of the typist or machine operator are placed a double space below the writer's name (or the writer's title or department if placed on a separate line).

Enclosure Notation. The enclosure notation, which indicates that something in addition to the letter is included in the envelope, is placed a double space below the reference initials.

Special Letter Parts

A letter may include one or more of the following special parts:

mailing notation (a DS below date)

subject line (a DS below the salutation; a DS above the letter message)

copy notation (*cc* or *pc* a DS below the enclosure notation or the reference initials if there is no enclosure)

postscript (a DS below the last item in the letter)

Because such parts are used sparingly, they will be practiced later in the book.

Letter Spacing Summary

Three blank line spaces (a *quadruple space*) separate date from address and complimentary close from typed name of writer. A *double space* separates *all* other letter parts.

Learn to Format Letters in Block Style

120c ▶ 15
Letter Emphasis: Refine Techniques/Improve Speed and Control

each line 3 times (slowly, faster, top speed)

Minimum standard: To complete all lines as directed in 15'.

Extra credit: All lines beyond minimum standard.

Goal: To keep hands quiet with keystroking action limited to the fingers.

Emphasize: Continuity and rhythm with curved, upright fingers.

j   A jungle jaguar jabbed a paw into the jelly jug as Jon ate the jicama.

k   Kiku and Jack packed a deck keg with krill as Khmer packed a knapsack.

l   Lilly and Polly will fill the old pail with nails for a lake dwelling.

m   Mamie may recommend that Sammy move to Maine to maintain a maple farm.

n   Nancy was naive to think that Ann's name would be on the nylon banner.

o   Otto often looked for gold in the old gold mine near Golden, Colorado.

p   At a political party, Pepe supplied popular apple and pineapple punch.

q   Quen quickly and quietly queued up to buy quince jam in a quaint town.

r   Roberta worked four hours before the morning train arrived from Rugby.

| 1 | 2 | 3 | 4 | 5 | 6 | 7 | 8 | 9 | 10 | 11 | 12 | 13 | 14 |

120d ▶ 15
Composing at the Keyboard: Improve Writing Skill

full sheet; DS copy

1. Prepare a rough draft. Compose a paragraph describing an orange. A paragraph usually has a single main idea (topic sentence) with supporting details. To help you, use the following sentence as your topic sentence:

An orange is a reddish-yellow colored fruit which belongs to the citrus family.

Continue your paragraph by describing the size, shape, texture, and smell of an orange. Then tell what happens when you peel an orange. Describe the peeled orange and the taste of the segments when they are eaten.

2. Prepare the final draft. Make any needed corrections in your rough-draft paragraph; then prepare a final draft. Use as the heading: AN ORANGE.

Lesson 121   Keyboarding/Composing Skills

121a ▶ 5
Conditioning Practice

each line 3 times (slowly, faster, in-between rate); as time permits, repeat selected lines

alphabet 1 Patient quarriers uncovered famous Greek bronzes with onyx-jewel eyes.

fig/sym 2 Lorenzo & Son wrote Check #403 for $310.99 and Check #573 for $862.42.

3d row 3 A reporter tried to write a witty story of Peter Piper for your paper.

speed 4 He may hand me the clay and then go to the shelf for the die and form.

| 1 | 2 | 3 | 4 | 5 | 6 | 7 | 8 | 9 | 10 | 11 | 12 | 13 | 14 |

121b ▶ 5
Build Basic Skill: Control/Speed

1. Two 1' writings, line 1 of 121a. Emphasize accuracy.

2. Two 1' writings, line 4 of 121a. Emphasize speed.

43a ▶ 6
Conditioning Practice

1. Each line twice SS.
2. A 1' writing on line 3; find *gwam*.

alphabet 1   Vicki Jewel can make six quaint prizes for the bridge party.
fig/sym 2   Gene's telephone number in 1986 was (917) 627-4039, Ext. 25.
speed 3   Good form is the key if all of us wish to make the big goal.

| 1 | 2 | 3 | 4 | 5 | 6 | 7 | 8 | 9 | 10 | 11 | 12 |

43b ▶ 14
Learn to Place and Space Letter Parts

2 plain full sheets; line: 60 spaces; date: line 15

1. Study the material on page 75; check each placement point with the model letter on page 77.
2. On a full sheet, arrange and key the opening lines of Drill 1, beginning on line 15 from top edge.
3. After keying the salutation, return 14 times to key the closing lines.
4. Do Drill 2 in the same way, but start the return address on line 13.

Note: Reference initials are not used in personal-business letters.

Language Skills Notes:

1. Note that months, titles, names, abbreviations, and initials (except reference initials) are capitalized.
2. Note that 2 spaces are left between the 2-letter state name abbreviation and the ZIP Code.

Drill 1

November 21, 19--

Miss Rhonda McMahon
2000 Columbus Avenue
Springfield, MA 01103-2748

Dear Miss McMahon

Space down 14 times (using INDEX or RETURN) to allow for body of letter.

Sincerely yours

George C. Ogden
Sales Manager

jr

Enclosure

Drill 2

3899 Norton Avenue
Kansas City, MO 64128-3357
November 21, 19--

Mr. Alan Ditka
Simon & Lowe, Inc.
215 Madison Street, E
Tampa, FL 33602-2936

Dear Mr. Ditka

Space down 14 times (using INDEX or RETURN) to allow for body of letter.

Sincerely yours

Ms. Leona Watkins

Enclosure

43c ▶ 30
Learn to Format Business Letters

1 letterhead (LM p. 29); 2 plain sheets; line: 60; date: line 15

1. Study the letter on page 77 illustrating *block style*, *open punctuation*. Note the vertical and horizontal placement of letter parts.
2. On a letterhead (or plain paper) type line for line a copy of the letter on page 77.
3. Proofread your copy and mark it for correction.
4. If time permits, take a 2' writing on opening lines (date through salutation); then a 2' writing on closing lines (complimentary close through enclosure notation). If you complete the copy before time is called, start over.

119d ▶ 15
Measure and Evaluate Basic Skill: Straight Copy

two 3′ writings; then one 5′ writing

Goal: To maintain 3′ rate for 5′.

Proofread; circle errors; record better 3′ rate and 5′ rate.

After each writing, make a self-evaluation of your technique patterns; reduce rate slightly if you made more than 10 errors.

| all letters used | A | 1.5 si | 5.7 awl | 80% hfw |

	gwam 3′	5′

Several important elements affect fatigue and eyestrain when a — 4 | 2 | 48

computer is operated. A computer monitor should be exactly positioned so — 9 | 5 | 51

you can look directly at it, and there should be little or no reflection — 14 | 8 | 54

from it. The keyboard should be placed in a position that is very com- — 19 | 11 | 57

fortable for you as you are operating it. A good guide is to place the — 24 | 14 | 60

keyboard so that the tips of the fingers, the base of the hand, and the — 28 | 17 | 63

lower arm are in alignment with the angle of the keyboard. This position — 33 | 20 | 66

of the keyboard results in reduced operating fatigue. — 37 | 22 | 68

Another key requirement in relation to position of the keyboard is — 41 | 25 | 71

the need of an adjustable, comfortable chair which may help to make it — 46 | 28 | 73

easy to operate the keyboard and view the monitor. Still another impor- — 51 | 30 | 76

tant element is the color of the screen. Some workers have selected an — 56 | 33 | 79

amber color; others maintain that green produces much less stress and is — 60 | 36 | 82

easier on the eyes. In addition, the copy on the screen must be easy — 65 | 39 | 85

to read. Size of print is important, but of greater importance is the — 70 | 42 | 88

intensity of the print on the screen, a condition of the number of dots — 75 | 45 | 91

that comprise each letter. — 76 | 46 | 92

gwam 3′ | 1 | 2 | 3 | 4 | 5 |
5′ | 1 | 2 | 3 |

Lesson 120 — Keyboarding/Composing Skills

120a ▶ 5
Conditioning Practice

each line 3 times (slowly, faster, in-between rate); as time permits, repeat selected lines

alphabet 1 Liza picked several exquisite flowers which grew by the jungle swamps.

fig/sym 2 Order the 38#, 56#, and 79# packages (untaped) from J. C. Burl & Sons.

adjacent key 3 A sad reporter reported the disaster as he gave his opinion of causes.

speed 4 If he signs the right forms, the auditor may augment the usual profit.

| 1 | 2 | 3 | 4 | 5 | 6 | 7 | 8 | 9 | 10 | 11 | 12 | 13 | 14 |

120b ▶ 15
Improve Basic Skill: Straight Copy

1. Add 4 to 8 words to your 119d *gwam* rate. **Goal:** To reach a new speed level.

2. Two 1′ writings on ¶ 1, 119d, above. Try to reach goal rate.

3. A 2′ writing on ¶ 1. Try to maintain your 1′ rate (2′ *gwam* = total words ÷ 2).

4. Repeat Step 2, using ¶ 2.

5. Repeat Step 3, using ¶ 2.

6. A 3′ timed writing using both ¶s. **Goal:** To maintain your new speed rate for 3′.

Modern Office Systems, Inc.

1049 Michigan Avenue, N • Chicago, IL 60611-2846 • (312) 471-2605

words in parts

total words

		words in parts	total words
Dateline	**November 11, 19--** Line 15	4	4

QS: operate return 4
times to quadruple-
space (3 blank lines)

Letter address	**Mrs. Dorinda O'Neil, Director**	10	10
	Sooner Office Temporaries, Inc.	16	16
	One Williams Center	20	20
	Tulsa, OK 74172-4280	24	24

DS

| Salutation | **Dear Mrs. O'Neil** | 28 | 28 |

DS

| Body of letter | **The block format in which this letter is arranged has grown** | 12 | 40 |
| | **rapidly in popularity for business and personal letters.** | 24 | 51 |

DS

	Users of personal computers, word processors, and typewriters	36	64
	prefer block format because no tab stop settings or indenting	48	76
	motions are required. The result is greater efficiency. In	61	88
	addition, block style avoids the errors that occur in other	73	100
	formats when operators forget to indent certain letter parts.	85	113

DS

	Changes are being made in document formats and placement to	97	125
	simplify the use of modern office machines and to make people	110	137
	more productive. The growing use of block format is just one	122	150
	of many such changes. Some of the other changes are described	135	162
	in the enclosed pamphlet.	140	167

DS

| Complimentary close | **Sincerely yours** | 3 | 170 |

J. T. Bellamah

QS: operate return 4
times to quadruple-
space (3 blank lines)

| Name/title | **Jeffrey T. Bellamah, Head** | 8 | 176 |
| Department | **Work Simplification Unit** | 13 | 181 |

DS

| Initials of operator | **ke** | 14 | 181 |

DS

| Enclosure notation | **Enclosure** | 16 | 183 |

Shown in pica type
on a 60-space line
(camera-reduced)

Block Format, Open Punctuation

Unit 24 Lessons 119-123

Learning Goals
1. To refine and improve your basic keyboarding techniques.
2. To increase your speed and improve your accuracy on basic skill copy.
3. To improve composing skills.

Machine Adjustments
1. Paper guide at *0*.
2. 70-space line and SS unless otherwise directed.
3. Line-space selector on *2* (DS) for all timed writings of more than 1′.

Lesson 119 Keyboarding Technique/Speed

119a ▶ 5
Conditioning Practice

each line 3 times (slowly, faster, in-between rate); as time permits, repeat selected lines

alphabet	1	Just strive for maximum progress by quickly organizing the daily work.
fig/sym	2	Al Jones's order (#30-967) included 248 desks, 15 chairs, and 9 lamps.
space bar	3	If what you say is so, then they should find the work very easy to do.
speed	4	If they do the work for us, I may go to the lake and then to the city.

| 1 | 2 | 3 | 4 | 5 | 6 | 7 | 8 | 9 | 10 | 11 | 12 | 13 | 14 |

119b ▶ 15
Letter Emphasis: Refine Techniques /Improve Control and Speed

each line 3 times (slowly, faster, top speed)

Minimum standard: To complete all lines as directed in 15′.

Extra credit: All lines beyond minimum standard.

Goal: To keep hands quiet with keystroking action limited to the fingers.

Emphasize: Continuity and rhythm with curved, upright fingers.

a As Ada and Anna ate bananas and apples, an aardvark ate many fat ants.
b Bobby bounced a big, bright rubber ball by the babbling abbey cobbler.
c A crane cackled crazily as a raccoon captured the newly hatched chick.
d Don decided on the dark, dreary day to deliver a dog to dad's address.
e Every technique refinement leads to greatly elevated speed rate gains.
f Fifi ate five freshly fried falafels at the fast food efficiency cafe.
g Gregg and Reggie built a garish gargoyle for the gigantic garden gate.
h The highlight of the hike was when Hugh served ham and chips at lunch.
i If it is his to give, I will aid each individual in finding six pails.

| 1 | 2 | 3 | 4 | 5 | 6 | 7 | 8 | 9 | 10 | 11 | 12 | 13 | 14 |

119c ▶ 15
Transfer Refined Techniques and Increased Speed: Guided Writing

1. Two 1′ writings; find *gwam*.
2. Add 4 words to better rate; determine 1/4′ goals.
3. Two 15″ writings; try to equal or exceed 1/4′ goal.
4. Two 30″ writings; try to equal or exceed 1/2′ goal.
5. Two 1′ guided writings at goal rate.
6. Two 1′ speed writings.

    Recognize that the primary element of high-speed keyboarding is to try to type or keyboard with good form and refined technique patterns. In each of the lessons of this unit, your goal should be to fix your mind on the principal keyboarding elements: finger-action keystroking, quick spacing after every word, and a fast return with a very quick start of the new line.

Improve Keyboarding and Language Skills

44a ▶ 6
Conditioning Practice

1. Each line twice SS.
2. A 1' writing on line 3; find *gwam*.

alphabet 1 Joey Knox led a big blitz which saved the play for my squad.

fig/sym 2 Martha ordered 26 5/8 yards of #371 percale at $4.09 a yard.

speed 3 Dorian may lend them a hand with the audit of the soap firm.

| 1 | 2 | 3 | 4 | 5 | 6 | 7 | 8 | 9 | 10 | 11 | 12 |

44b ▶ 9
Improve Language Skills: Word Division

1. Read each rule and type (key) the Learn and Apply lines beneath it.

Note: As you key the Apply lines, insert a hyphen at the point where the word can be divided.

2. Check with your teacher the accuracy of your Apply lines; and if time permits, key again the Apply lines in which you made errors in dividing words.

> Divide a word only between syllables; words of one syllable, therefore, should not be divided.

Learn 1 pro-gram, through, in-deed, straight, pur-pose, con-tracts

Apply 2 decides, brought, control, wonders, thoughts, practice

> Do not separate a one-letter syllable at the beginning of a word or a one- or two-letter syllable at the end of a word.

Learn 3 ideal, prior, ready, enough, ahead, en-try, de-lay, aw-ful

Apply 4 agent, early, party, under, quickly, about, items, fully

> Divide a word between double consonants except when adding a syllable to a word that ends in double letters.

Learn 5 writ-ten, sum-mer, run-ning, sud-den, add-ing, will-ing

Apply 6 gotten, dinner, guessing, thinner, agreeing, dressing

44c ▶ 10
Learn to Use the Line-Ending Bell

1. Set margin stops for exact 60-space line: center − 30; center + 30.

2. Key sentence given at right at a slow pace; stop as soon as bell on machine rings. Instead of keying remainder of sentence, key figures **1234**, etc., until the machine locks. Subtract 5 (the desired warning) from final figure; move right stop one space to the right for each remaining figure (usually 3 to 10 spaces). See the illustrative example under the sentence at the right.

3. Key sentence again to check accuracy of your setting of the right margin stop.

4. Using same margin settings, key the ¶ given at the right. Be guided by bell as cue to complete a word, divide it, key another word, or return.

Copy: Move stop so bell rings 5 spaces before desired line ending.

↓ bell

Example: Move stop so bell rings 5 spaces before desired liB123456789
Move stop so bell rings 5 spaces before desired line en/////.

↑ bell ↓

Set the right margin stop at a point that will cause the warning bell on your machine to ring exactly 5 spaces before the line ending desired by moving the right margin stop 3 to 10 spaces to the right of the exact setting for a specified line length (a 60-space line, for example). You can then key 1 to 7 spaces after the warning bell before the machine locks. By adjusting the number of spaces in the buffer zone (from the bell to the desired line ending), you can complete a word or divide it to maintain a fairly even right margin.

118c ▶ 20
Format and Key a Reference List and a Title Page

Problem 1

Format and key a reference list from the copy below. The top margin is the same as page 1 of the report; the other margins are the same as for the leftbound report. Center heading over line of writing; start first line of each entry at left margin; indent additional lines 5 spaces; SS each entry; DS between entries.

Line 6   11

REFERENCES

QS

American Psychological Association. <u>Publication Manual</u>. 2d ed. Washington, DC: American Psychological Association, 1974.

Attenborough, David. <u>Life on Earth</u>. Boston: Little, Brown and Company, 1979.

Committee on Writing Standards, The National Council of Teachers of English. "Standards for Basic Skills Writing Programs." <u>College English</u>, October 1979, 220-222.

1½" left margin   Cross, Donna W. <u>Word Abuse</u>. New York: Coward, McCann & Geoghegan, Inc., 1979.   1" right margin

Goodlad, John I. <u>A Place Called School</u>. New York: McGraw-Hill Inc., 1984.

Graves, Robert, and Alan Hodge. <u>The Reader Over Your Shoulder</u>. New York: Random House, 1979.

Hemingway, Ernest. <u>In Our Time</u>. New York: Charles Scribner's Sons, 1970.

Lanham, Richard. UCLA Writing Project Lecture, 1979.

Walshe, R. D. "What's Basic to Teaching Writing?" <u>The English Journal</u>, December 1979, 51-56.

Zinsser, William. <u>Writing With a Word Processor</u>. New York: Harper & Row, 1983.

IMPROVE YOUR WRITING

Name of Student
Name of School

Current Date

Problem 2

Format and key a title page for the leftbound report. Using the center point for a leftbound report:

a. Center title on line 16.

b. Center and key your name 8 DS's below title; DS and center the name of your school.

c. Center and key the current date 8 DS's below the name of your school.

44d ▶ 25
Format Letters in Block Style

2 letterheads (LM pp. 31-34);
1 plain sheet;
line: 60; date: line 15

Problem 1
Business Letter

Format in block style the letter given at the right. Return at the color bars in the opening and closing lines. Key the body of the letter line for line as shown. Listen for the warning bell as you approach the line endings.

	words
	parts / total

November 12, 19-- | Mr. Julio M. Perez | 3849 Canterbury Road | — 12 | 12
Baltimore, MD 21218-3365 | Dear Mr. Perez | — 20 | 20

Congratulations! You are now the sole owner of the car you — 12 | 32
financed through our bank. We also want to say thank you for — 24 | 44
choosing us to serve your credit needs. — 33 | 52

The original Certificate of Title and your Installment Loan — 45 | 64
Contract marked "Paid in Full" are enclosed. These papers are — 57 | 77
evidence that you have fulfilled all the obligations of your — 69 | 89
automobile loan. File the papers in a safe place with your — 81 | 101
other important records. — 87 | 106

The promptness with which you made all monthly payments gives — 99 | 119
you a preferred credit rating at our bank. Please let us know — 112 | 131
when we may be of service to you again. — 119 | 139

Cordially yours | Ms. Jennifer Lindgren | Automobile Loan — 11 | 149
Department | hq | Enclosures — 16 | 155

Problem 2
Business Letter

Format the letter given at the right using the directions for Problem 1.

	words
	parts / total

November 12, 19-- | Mrs. Gwendolyn Quade | 7257 Charles Plaza | — 12 | 12
Omaha, NE 68114-3219 | Dear Mrs. Quade | — 19 | 19

In these days of computers and other fancy office equipment, — 12 | 31
the personal and friendly contact with people is sometimes — 24 | 43
overlooked. We want you to know how much we appreciate your — 36 | 55
past orders and this new opportunity to serve you. — 47 | 66

The enclosed acknowledgment lists the four items you ordered — 59 | 78
a few days ago. As in the past, we will carefully follow your — 71 | 90
instructions for processing and shipping. — 80 | 99

Although we appreciate receiving payment with an order, we — 92 | 111
want to remind you that prepayment is not required. If you — 104 | 123
prefer, you may simply enter your personal account number on — 116 | 135
the order form, and we will send a bill later. Your account — 128 | 147
number appears on your catalog address label. — 137 | 156

Cordially yours | Ms. Juanita Miguel, Manager | Mail Order — 11 | 167
Department | jb | Enclosure — 15 | 172

Problem 3

As time permits, take two 1' writings on the opening lines and then on the closing lines of Problem 2 to increase your speed.

5. Preparing the final draft. After many experiences in writing, and as your writing begins to take shape, it is necessary to move to the final phase. All writing needs careful editing and revision. Hemingway is said to have made thirty-nine revisions of the ending of his best seller, A FAREWELL TO ARMS. Mario Puzo, author of the top selling novel of the 1970's, THE GODFATHER, states categorically that "rewriting is the whole secret to writing" (Walshe, 1979, 55).

When you are ready to edit and revise your writing, here are some suggestions that may be helpful:

a. Underline words, phrases, and/or sentences you may want to change or eliminate. (Remove words, phrases, or sentences that really aren't needed.)

b. Use active verbs rather than passive verbs. As Zinsser says, "Passive verbs are the death of clarity and vigor" (1983, 101).

c. Check the sentences. Are they in logical and sequential order? Sentences come in a variety of shapes and sizes which are useful so long as they add interest, not confusion, to your writing. A good suggestion for all writers: Keep your sentences short. Zinsser cautions, "Don't try to make a sentence do too many jobs -- you only confuse the reader and make your writing difficult to follow" (1983, 100).

d. Read your paper aloud. How does it sound? Does it flow smoothly? Is it unified and coherent?

When you edit your work, it is helpful to have your classmates, or others, evaluate and react to your writing. Professor Richard Lanham of UCLA suggests the use of the "CBS Style," CBS standing for Clarity, Brevity, and Sincerity. In writing, he warns us to avoid the "Official or Bureaucratic Style," which often characterizes government publications. To see his point, we have only to read this statement which was written several years ago after the Three Mile Island nuclear accident: "It would be prudent to consider expeditiously the provision of instrumentation that would provide an unambiguous indication of the level of fluid in the reactor vessel." If we translate this statement from the "Bureaucratic Style," it would probably read something like this: We need accurate measuring devices.

When you edit your writing, first check for the more obvious errors -- errors in spelling, grammar, and punctuation. Check to make sure that you have avoided the pitfalls of misplaced modifiers, incorrect verb usage, and fragmented or run-on sentences. Then check your sentence style. Look for long and involved sentences that could be improved by removing nonfunctional words or by dividing them into two shorter sentences. Make sure all words are used correctly in a sentence and that you have not repeated yourself. Stay away from the kind of "confusing wording" we often see in signs on office building doors, such as: EMERGENCY EXIT ONLY -- NOT TO BE USED UNDER ANY CIRCUMSTANCES. (If a door cannot be used under any circumstances, it cannot be used at all!) In other words, check to make sure that what you have said in your writing is logical and makes sense. If you are to convince your reader, what you say must be reasonable and must be supported with convincing evidence. When you have done all or at least some of these things, your paper is ready for the final draft.

Summary Statement

Now what about your writing style? The basic requirement of writing style is to follow the elementary rules of grammar and good usage. Other than that, writing is unique with each of us. Words arranged in one manner in a sentence are capable of stirring the reader deeply. The same words rearranged only slightly may be impotent. Lincoln's Gettysburg Address and the Declaration of Independence are examples of words arranged effectively. Arranged in any other way, the Gettysburg Address or the Declaration of Independence would not be nearly so effective.

The question of writing style, as is true for writing improvement, has no single answer. Each of us must develop a writing style that is unique to us. But we must start somewhere, and that somewhere is to start by writing.

45a ▶ 6

Conditioning Practice

1. Each line twice SS.
2. A 1' writing on line 3; find *gwam*.

alphabet	1	Jack Hud won first prize by solving a tax quiz in less time.
fig/sym	2	We received Marx & Abel's $729.48 check (#1659) on April 30.
speed	3	Suella may row to the small island to dig for the big clams.

| 1 | 2 | 3 | 4 | 5 | 6 | 7 | 8 | 9 | 10 | 11 | 12 |

45b ▶ 9

Improve Language Skills: Word Division

1. Read each rule and type (key) the Learn and Apply lines beneath it.

Note: As you key the words in the Apply lines, insert a hyphen at the point where the word can be divided.

2. Check with your teacher the accuracy of your Apply lines; and if time permits, key again the Apply lines in which you made errors in dividing words.

> Divide a word after a single-letter vowel syllable that is not a part of a word ending.

Learn	1	vari-ous, sepa-rate, usu-ally, ori-ent, situ-ate, edi-fice
Apply	2	holiday, evaluate, gradually, saturate, granulate

> Divide a word before the word endings -able, -ible, -acle, -ical, and -ily when the vowel **a** or **i** is a separate syllable.

Learn	3	prob-able, convert-ible, mir-acle, op-ti-cal, heart-ily
Apply	4	variable, edible, lyrical, handily, manacle, tropical

> Do not divide a word that contains a contraction (a word in which one or more omitted letters have been replaced by an apostrophe).

Learn	5	didn't, haven't, they'll, couldn't, you're, we've, hadn't
Apply	6	aren't, shouldn't, doesn't, you've, you'll, we'll, hasn't

> Divide only between the two words that make up a hyphenated (compound) word.

Learn	7	ill-advised, self-satisfied, well-groomed, self-concerned
Apply	8	ill-mannered, self-contained, well-meaning, self-centered

45c ▶ 10

Identify Word-Division Points

60-space line; DS

1. Clear all tab stops; then starting at left margin, set 3 new tab stops 17 spaces apart.
2. On a full sheet, center **WORD-DIVISION POINTS** on line 12; then DS.
3. Key the first line as shown.
4. In line 2 and following lines, key the words as shown in Columns 1 and 3; in Columns 2 and 4, rekey each word with a hyphen showing the correct division point.

WORD-DIVISION POINTS
DS

strangely	Tab	strangely	Tab	self-help	Tab	self-help
wouldn't				doubtful		
daily				support		
gasoline				physical		
changes				laudable		
getting				policies		

| key | 9 | 8 | 9 | 8 | 9 | 8 | 9 |

There was a tug on the line. Nick pulled against the taut line. It was his first strike. Holding the now living rod across the current, he brought up the line with his left hand. The rod bent in jerks, the trout pumping against the current. Nick knew it was a small one. He lifted the rod straight up in the air. It bowed with the pull (Hemingway, 1970, 201).

It is not difficult to discover the unknown animal. Spend a day in the tropical forest of South America, turning over logs, looking beneath bark, sifting through the moist litter of leaves, followed by an evening shining a mercury lamp on a white screen, and one way and another you will collect hundreds of different kinds of small creatures. Moths, caterpillars, spiders, long-nosed bugs, luminous beetles, harmless butterflies disguised as wasps, wasps shaped like ants...(Attenborough, 1979, 1).

Reading, too, can help us develop our vocabularies, and good vocabularies increase our potentials as writers. In our reading, when we come across words we don't know, we should look them up in a dictionary and then add them to our vocabularies. In order to write, we must use words, and we can't use words we don't have in our vocabularies.

The dictionary, too, can help us pick the right word or the precise word to express thoughts and help us learn to write what we mean. As you study words in the dictionary, you will note that some words are pronounced the same but are spelled differently, e.g., "bare" and "bear." "Bear," used as a noun can mean "a large, furry animal"; it may mean "a person who is clumsy, rude, or gruff"; or it may mean "a person who believes prices on the stock market are going to decline." Used as a verb, "bear" has still other meanings: "to bear fruit," "to support or hold up," "to tolerate," and so on. What we learn as we use the dictionary is that the English language, as William Zinsser has stated, "is rich in words that convey an exact shade of meaning" (1983, 100).

In your reading, learn how to use your library, since it contains the best written words of our culture. As you study and learn the meanings of words, singulars and plurals of nouns, tenses and modes of verbs, the right places to put punctuation, and ways to arrange sentences to show what goes with what, your writing will improve.

4. <u>Writing</u>. That we "learn to write by writing" is an accepted truism; but as Zinsser (1983, 100) has said: "Writing is a deeply personal process, full of mystery and surprise. No two people go about it in exactly the same way." Some writers write carefully and methodically -- their writing is in an almost finished form from the very beginning. Other writers, and this would include most of us, dash off a first draft not caring too much whether it conforms with the mechanics of good English. Research in writing reveals that the "process of writing" (getting thoughts on paper) is the key element; the "product of writing" (the final copy) can be taken care of in the editing and revision phase of writing and that comes later in the learning-to-write cycle.

It may be well to remember that different writing approaches are used for different purposes. There is no one best way to write. The best approach is most often determined by what you are writing. Often, for example, it is necessary to plan carefully what you want to say in a paper before writing it. This is especially true for research papers. Some writers outline what they want to say and then write from the outline. In the research paper, much of the hard work is in the planning, but it must be done if you are to write well. As you make your plan, you can write key ideas and their supporting statements on $6'' \times 4''$ or $8'' \times 5''$ cards. You can give a topic to each card, arrange the cards in logical order of presentation, and write your paper from the cards. Walshe (1979, 54-56) lists these steps in the writing process:

*Selection of a topic

*Pre-writing preparation, including planning

*Draft writing

*Editing, rewriting, with feedback and evaluation from your peer group

*Final writing, publication, or sharing

Use a typewriter or a word processor in preparing your first draft of any writing. Writing on a typewriter or a word processor is the first step in improving the efficiency of writing. Double-space your copy to make it easier to proofread, edit, and revise.

(continued on next page)

Format Letters in Block Style

1 letterhead (LM p. 35); 2 plain sheets;
line: 60; date: line 15

Problem 1
Business Letter

Format the letter in block style on the letterhead sheet. Be guided by the color bars to end lines throughout the letter. Although you will not have to divide words, listen for the bell toward the ends of the lines of the letter body.

	words
	parts / total

November 13, 19-- |Mr. Evan K. Fletcher |910 South Avenue | 11 | 11
Niagara Falls, NY 14305-2267 |Dear Mr. Fletcher | 21 | 21

Did you forget? | 3 | 24

As indicated on the statement you just received, your credit |card 17 | 37
account with us is overdue. More than half the balance |is past due 30 | 51
by over 30 days. | 34 | 55

Because we do not maintain revolving accounts in which partial | 46 | 67
payments can be made, full payment is due each month when you | 59 | 80
receive your statement. Accounts that habitually exceed 30 |days 72 | 93
before payment are subject to cancellation. | 81 | 102

If your overdue and current payments are in the mail, accept |our 94 | 115
thanks. If not, please send us your check for the full |amount today 108 | 128
to assure continued use of your card. | 116 | 136

Sincerely yours |Kyle C. Hoggatt, Manager |Credit Card Center |cp 12 | 149

Problem 2
Personal-Business Letter

Format the letter in block style on a plain sheet, using the directions for Problem 1. Begin the return address on line 13 so that the date will be on line 15.

2905 College Drive |Columbus, GA 31906-3628 |November 13, 19-- | 12 | 12
Mr. Hans Schmidt |Bucherer Watch Company |730 Fifth Avenue | 24 | 24
New York, NY 10019-2046 |Dear Mr. Schmidt | 32 | 32

If anyone can repair a thinline Bucherer watch, you are that |per- 13 | 45
son. So said Olga Melchior, manager of the jewelry repair |depart- 26 | 58
ment of Lorings here in Columbus. | 33 | 65

Ms. Melchior has fixed my watch twice before, but she thinks |it 46 | 78
now needs attention that only a licensed Bucherer shop can |give. 59 | 91
In fact, she believes the entire works may need to be |replaced. 72 | 104
The case and band are of such value that I want to |do whatever 85 | 117
must be done to make the watch useful again. | 94 | 126

Please use the enclosed envelope to send me a rough estimate |of 107 | 139
the cost of repair and to tell me what I should do next. |The watch 120 | 153
case number is 904618 in the event the number may |be of use. The 134 | 166
watch was purchased in Geneva. | 140 | 172

Sincerely yours |David C. Copeland |Enclosure | 9 | 181

Problem 3
Skill Building

As time permits, take a 2' writing on the opening lines and a 1' writing on the closing lines of Problem 2 to increase speed.

in writing needs to be given to self-expression and creative thought, rather than to learning basic language use skills and mastering mechanics -- capitalization, punctuation, parts of speech, and the like. And yet, we must emphasize good sentence structure if what we write is to have meaning.

Further, writing is difficult because it differs greatly from our spoken English. Graves and Hodge (1979, 17) point up this difference as follows:

...there are everywhere obvious differences between written and spoken English. A speaker reinforces his meaning with gestures and vocal inflections, and if people he addresses still do not understand, they can ask for further explanations; whereas a writer, not enjoying either of these advantages, must formulate and observe certain literary principles if he wishes to be completely understood.

Since the writer must rely solely on the written language to get the ideas across to the audience, he or she must write effectively. Written English, unlike spoken English, often has only one shot at getting the reader's interest and attention. And so, we must give it our best shot!

Why Writing Is Important

Writing helps us review and revise our ideas as we think through what it is we want to write. Professor Carlos Baker highlights an important aspect of writing: "Learning to write is learning to think" (Cross, 1979, 226). Dr. S. I. Hayakawa, a semanticist deeply concerned with the meaning of language, says much the same thing when he tells us, "You just don't know anything until you can write it" (Cross, 226).

Writing helps us remember things and so makes us better learners; it contributes to our success, not only in school but also in our jobs and careers. It is a necessary and important skill to master if we are to function in the modern culture.

Further, as pointed out by the Committee on Writing Standards, "Writing can be a deeply personal act of shaping our perceptions of the world and our relationships to people and things in that world" (1979, 220). Writing can be an important means of self-discovery, of finding out what we believe and know.

Some Suggestions to Help You Improve Your Writing

Good writing seems to grow best when all four elements of discourse (listening, speaking, reading, and writing) are constantly woven together. For example, a history class utilizes the elements of discourse when students read textbooks, listen to historical accounts, discuss events, and write reports and essays.

1. Listening. Listening is one of the primary ways we learn: Without listening and learning, we would have little to say in our writing. Our first experiences in listening occur when we are babies. Through these early experiences, we assimilate a vast amount of information in a short time, making it possible to relate to the world and to learn the basics of communication skills. Later, in school, we learn still more as ideas are discussed. Listening is crucial to learning, and thus, crucial to the writing process.

2. Speaking. We can't listen for long without speaking. Basic to good writing is being able to verbalize well -- to put our thoughts into words effectively. Just as we have a "voice" in the classroom when we express our opinions, so do we have our own unique "voice" in our writing. As we learn to convey our thoughts with facility when speaking with others, we find that conveying those same opinions in our writing becomes easier.

3. Reading. Most of us can improve our writing by reading, especially if we read good prose. As we read, we should note how an author captures our attention with words -- words that may stir the imagination. We should study how an author chooses to put these words together to form sentences (sentence structure) for a desired effect. A good writer takes care to choose words with just the correct shade of meaning. He or she takes care to create the best sentence structure. Note how the two authors quoted below have effectively used words and sentence structure to bring about a desired effect. The first author, wishing to capture "present action," uses short sentences and repetition for effect. The second author uses parallel phrases, lists, and figurative language to create a sense of the mysterious or unknown.

(continued on next page)

46a ▶ 6
Conditioning Practice

1. Each line twice SS.
2. A 1' writing on line 3; find *gwam*.

alphabet 1 Five boys quickly mixed the prizes, baffling one wise judge.

fig/sym 2 My income tax for 1987 was $5,320.46 -- up 3% over 1986's tax.

speed 3 Dodi is to handle all the pay forms for the small lake town.

| 1 | 2 | 3 | 4 | 5 | 6 | 7 | 8 | 9 | 10 | 11 | 12 |

46b ▶ 14
Learn to Correct Errors

60-space line; DS

1. Read the ¶ at the right; then watch your teacher demonstrate one or more of the correction methods.
2. As you key the ¶, correct any errors you make and listen for the warning bell as a signal to complete a word or divide it at the end of the line.
3. If time permits, rekey the ¶ to improve skill.

The abrasive typing eraser has "bitten the dust" in thousands of business offices in the country. Other error correcting devices are now replacing it even in schools. These tools include cover-up tape, liquid paper, lift-off tape, and electronic correcting keys. Ask your teacher to demonstrate how to use one or more of these, then use whatever correcting device he or she directs you to use in correcting your work.

46c ▶ 15
Format a Letter from Script

1 letterhead (LM p. 37); line: 60 spaces; format: block style

1. Use **November 14** of the current year as the date.
2. Address the letter to:

Mr. James Sipes, Manager
Huckleberry Square
315 Seneca Street
Seattle, WA 98101-4462

3. Use **Dear Jim** as the salutation.
4. As you key the body of the letter, listen for the bell as a signal to complete a word or divide it at the end of the line.
5. The letter will be signed by **Georgeann Blair** who is **President** of her company. She prefers to use **Cordially** as a complimentary close. Use your own reference initials.
6. Before you remove the letter from your machine (or print out a copy on a computer), proofread it and correct any errors you find.

Your velvety cream-of-peanut soup brought me back to Huckleberry Square yesterday. We were taken to our table promptly, but we waited over ten minutes before menus were presented.

Several times I provided clues to the server that I was hosting the luncheon. Without noting these clues or asking who should receive the check, the server gave it to the man across from me. Had the check been placed upside down in the middle of the table, my client wouldn't have been "put on the spot."

Almost every day of the week someone from Seacom will entertain clients at Huckleberry Square. Will you talk with your staff about greeting diners promptly and about handling checks. But please, Jim, don't disturb the chef!

Format and Key Leftbound Report with Textual Citations

full sheets; center heading over line of writing; DS ¶s; 5 space ¶ indention; errors corrected

Use margins and spacing as given for leftbound report on model page 199, and in guidelines, page 194.

Show page numbers on second and additional pages in upper right corner.

Note. You are not expected to complete the manuscript in this lesson; additional time is provided in Lessons 115-118.

The textual citation form of reference notation is to be used (*as illustrated in manuscript*). This is the preferred form to use in manuscripts prepared for publication.

Guide: Make a light pencil mark at the right edge of the sheet 1″ from the bottom and another 1/2″ above the 1″ mark as a page-end reminder; or, use the page-line gauge provided in LM, p. 7.

IMPROVE YOUR WRITING]— *Center*

QS

All of us have a need to write no mater what we do in life. Writing well is a problem that has concerned our schools *since their beginning*. This report emphasizes the general principles that lead to good writing or composing.

<u>What Is Writing?</u>

Sometime ago, the National Council of Teachers *of English* formed a Committee on writing standards to try to find out what *good* writing is all about. Teh Committee {1979, 220} has given us a definition of writing *that is still useful:* "Writing is the process of selecting, combining, arranging, and developing ideas in *effective* sentences, paragraphs, and often longer units of discourse."

When you or I set *sit* down to write, we tend to follow the writing process that the Committee on writing Standards spoke about. Thoughts *and ideas* flow from the words we use, with *the* words form ing sentences and the sentences growing into paragraphs. The process may be difficult *at first*, but it becomes easier with time and practice. *Eventually,* We *not only* learn to put our ideas on *onto* paper, *but we learn to put those ideas* in a form that effectively conveys *what* we mean to the reader. The reader reverses the process: decoding print into words and words into thought.

Good writing is not a set of rules of writing. And this issue creates one of the problems *of writing*. It is often easier to teach *learn* codified rules than to learn how to write; it is often easier to learn <u>about</u> language than to learn how to <u>use</u> language. Goodlad {1984, 205} supports this point when he indicates that more emphasis *to be memorized*

"Good writing," according to the American Psychological Association (1967, 15), "is clear, precise, unambiguous, and economical."

(continued on next page)

46d ▶ 15 **Learn to Address Envelopes**

1. Study the guides at the right and the illustrations below.

Envelope address Set a tab stop 10 spaces left of center of small envelope, 5 spaces left of center for a large envelope. Space down 12 lines from top edge of small envelope, 14 spaces for a large envelope. Begin the address at the tab stop position.	**Style** Use *block style*, SS. Use all capitals; omit punctuation. Place city name, 2-letter state name abbreviation, and ZIP Code on last address line. Two spaces precede the ZIP Code. **Return address** Use *block style*, SS, cap and lowercase. Begin on line 2 from top of envelope, 3 spaces from left edge.	**Special notations** Place *mailing notations* such as REGISTERED and SPECIAL DELIVERY below the stamp position on line 8 or 9. Place *addressee notations* such as PERSONAL and HOLD FOR ARRIVAL a TS below return address and 3 spaces from left edge of envelope.

Formatting personal and business envelopes as recommended by U.S. Postal Service

small, number 6¾ (6½" × 3⅝")   large, number 10 (9½" × 4⅛")

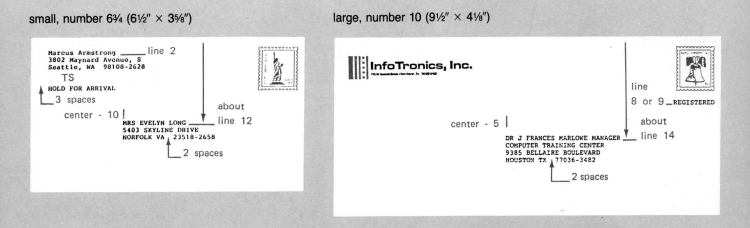

2. Format a small (No. 6 3/4) and a large (No. 10) envelope for each of the addresses given at the right (LM pp. 39-48). Use your own return address on the small envelope.

3. If time permits, practice folding standard-size sheets of paper for both large and small envelopes. (See Reference Guide page RG 7.)

DR LATOYA J HAUSMANN
ROUTE 6 BOX 32
GRAND JUNCTION CO 81501-1177

MISS AIDA HERNANDEZ
BAY CITY OFFICE PRODUCTS INC
ONE POST STREET
SAN FRANCISCO CA 94104-3572

MS ARVELLA BLACKSTONE
8275 DORCHESTER ROAD APT H
CHARLESTON SC 29418-3926

MR HAN SONG KI ASST VP
SATURN ELECTRONICS CORP
110 LOCKWOOD STREET
PROVIDENCE RI 02903-4848

Lesson 47	**Letters/Word Division**	Line: 60 spaces Spacing: SS (or as directed)

47a ▶ 6
Conditioning Practice

1. Each line twice SS.
2. A 1' writing on line 3; find *gwam*.

alphabet 1 Jody Fox left my quiz show and gave back a prize he had won.

fig/sym 2 Installment loan #47293 at 13% is for $5,800 over 36 months.

speed 3 Robby may sign the six forms and work with the city auditor.

| 1 | 2 | 3 | 4 | 5 | 6 | 7 | 8 | 9 | 10 | 11 | 12 |

114a-118a ▶ 5 (daily)
Conditioning Practice

each line 3 times (slowly, faster, top speed); as time permits, repeat selected lines

alphabet 1 Fine cooks brought piquant flavor to exotic foods with zesty marjoram.

fig/sym 2 The purchase price is $14,573.89 plus 6% sales tax and 20% excise tax.

space bar 3 Try to do the work for Jim and then go with me to the city for a week.

speed 4 Sight the visitor, turn the dial to the right, and focus the eye lens.

| 1 | 2 | 3 | 4 | 5 | 6 | 7 | 8 | 9 | 10 | 11 | 12 | 13 | 14 |

114b-115b ▶ 15
Measure and Improve Keyboarding Skill: Straight Copy

two 3' writings; then one 5' writing

Goal: To maintain 3' rate for 5'.

Proofread; circle errors; record better 3' and 5' rates.

all letters used | A | 1.5 si | 5.7 awl | 80% hfw

	gwam 3'	5'
What does it mean to be a good manager and a good leader? Early in	4	3	52
life you learned to manage yourself, your time, and your energies so that	9	6	55
you could accomplish a given task in a given period of time. This is the	14	9	58
initial requirement of a good manager. As you learned self-management	19	11	60
skills, you probably developed leadership skills. A good leader has a	24	14	63
deep respect and just concern for others. He or she can bring out the	29	17	66
best in others by seeking out and encouraging others to develop to their	33	20	69
fullest potentials.	35	21	70
This type of self-confidence may develop from a conscientious effort	39	24	72
to determine one's abilities and weaknesses and zealously to do something	44	27	75
about them. It is tempered by experience and by the acquisition of a	50	29	78
sense of oneself in relation to others and to the world. Next, a good	54	32	81
leader and a good manager needs to plan carefully, to determine the	58	35	84
chance of success or failure of an act, and to give much thought to a	63	38	87
course of action before making a decision to proceed. Such a person is	68	41	89
concerned with a vision of a future that is worthy of achievement. Good	72	43	92
management and good leadership skill, then, is that intangible ability to	77	46	95
motivate yourself and others to perform beyond the ordinary.	81	50	98

gwam 3' | 1 | 2 | 3 | 4 | 5 |
5' | 1 | 2 | 3 |

**Identify Word-
Division Points**
60-space line; DS

1. Clear all tab stops; then starting at left margin, set 3 new tab stops 17 spaces apart.
2. On a full sheet, center WORD-DIVISION POINTS on line 12; then DS.
3. Key the first line as shown.
4. In line 2 and following lines, key each word as shown in Columns 1 and 3; in Columns 2 and 4, rekey each word with a hyphen showing the correct division point.

WORD-DIVISION POINTS
DS

hand-feed	hand-feed	self-made	self-made
increase		greatest	
teletype		tabulate	
agreeing		musical	
plotting		provided	
defend		sharpen	

key | 9 | 8 | 9 | 8 | 9 | 8 | 9 |

**Format Letters in
Block Style**

2 letterheads (LM pp. 49-52);
1 plain full sheet;
line: 60; date: line 15;
address envelopes

**Problem 1
Business Letter**

Format the letter in block style. As you key the body of the letter, listen for the warning bell as a signal to prepare for the return at line endings. Correct any errors you make as you key.

The final figure in the word count column includes the count for the envelope address.

**Problem 2
Business Letter**

Prepare a second letter from Problem 1 copy but substitute for ¶ 3 the handwritten ¶ beneath the letter.

Address the letter to:

**Mr. George C. Sato, Principal
Seven Hills Community College
15000 New Halls Ferry Road
Florissant, MO 63031-4827**

Supply an appropriate salutation.

**Problem 3
Skill Building**

As time permits, take two 1' writings on the opening lines and then on the closing lines of the letter in Problem 1 to increase your speed.

	words	
	parts	total
November 15, 19--	Ms. Phyllis Feldman	Camelback Vocational	12	12
School	6200 Mariposa, W	Phoenix, AZ 85033-2266	Dear Ms.	23	23
Feldman	25	25

If I were to name just two reasons why you should choose the | 12 | 37
Saturn personal computer for use in your school, I would say its | 25 | 50
standard keyboard and user-friendly controls. | 35 | 59

A standard keyboard is vital for keyboarding skill to transfer | 47 | 72
readily from the keyboard used in school to the one most likely | 60 | 85
to be used on the job. A keyboard on which familiar keys are | 72 | 97
located in nonstandard places should be avoided. | 82 | 107

A key used to make a computer perform a special function | 94 | 119
should be labeled to suggest the function it generates. Keys | 106 | 131
labeled with letters or combinations of letters that identify their | 120 | 145
functions are easier for a user to remember than keys labeled | 132 | 157
F1, F2, etc. Thus, they are user-friendly. | 141 | 166

These features, along with a large selection of classroom-tested | 154 | 179
software, are critical in computer selection. | 163 | 188

Cordially yours | Ellis D. Strong, Ph.D. | Educational Services | 12 | 200
Staff | xx* | 14 | 202
*When you see xx, use your own initials for reference. | 220

Function keys should be user-friendly; that is, the labels on the keys should suggest the functions they cause the computer to perform. Words or abbreviations rather than figures should be used because they are easier for the user to remember.

leadership, gently guiding (students) in the right
direction and counseling them when difficulties
occur. Schools will provide a safe environment in
which (students) can engage in many types of learning experiences.[1]

Two very important technologies in education will be video
and computer systems. Videotapes and videodisks will make it
possible for master teachers to produce effective learning
programs that can teach almost any subject. These programs
will be designed to capture the interest of the learner.
Students will be able to check out videotapes from school li-
braries, and they will be able to use them in special instructional cubicles located in the school or in their homes if they
have a videotape player. These new technologies will help to
make education much more effective than it has been in the past.
Students will learn material faster, and teachers will have more
time to deal with individual student learning problems.[2] Beechhold supports the view that the computer in the classroom can
have positive enhancing effects; if used correctly, he feels that
computers can be an invaluable aid to the creative teacher in
the educational process.[3]

Another question frequently raised about computers is the
following: Can computers be so programmed that they will have
a type of artificial intelligence (AI) comparable to human
intelligence? If so, it would mean that computers would have to
define and organize the vast amount of knowledge that we have
stored in the 100 billion nerve cells, known as "neurons,"
that make up our brains. These neurons, when stimulated,
fire electromechanical impulses across the microscopic
gaps called "synapses" at the rate of thousands per second.
This is what "thinking" is all about, and so far even highly
sophisticated computers cannot do that kind of thinking. Nor
do they possess the ordinary sort of knowledge that is called
"common sense." Common sense, together with language skills,
seems to define the essence of what it means to be human and
to have human intelligence.[4]

---

[1] Edward Cornish, "Computer Can't Replace the Teacher,"
Los Angeles Times, 10 May 1985, Part V, p. 2.

[2] Cornish, p. 2.

[3] Henry F. Beechhold, "Computerized Classroom Visions," PC,
May 28, 1985, pp. 303-305.

[4] Frank Rose, Into the Heart of the Mind (New York: Harper
& Row, 1984), pp. 12-23.

*Nevertheless, microcomputers and the new technology are having and
will continue to have a profound effect on everything we do, whether
in school, in ~~our~~ workplaces, or in ~~our~~ homes.*

48a ▶ 6
Conditioning Practice

1. Each line twice SS.
2. A 1' writing on line 3; find *gwam*.

alphabet   1   Kovina will prize six jade chips sent by Marquis for a gift.

fig/sym   2   Order #5647-1839 was shipped August 20 by J&P Freight Lines.

speed   3   Dirk may lend an antique box to the man for the town social.

| 1 | 2 | 3 | 4 | 5 | 6 | 7 | 8 | 9 | 10 | 11 | 12 |

48b ▶ 9
Improve Keyboarding Skill

1. A 1' speed writing on ¶ 1, then on ¶ 2; find *gwam* on each.
2. A 3' writing on ¶s 1 and 2 combined; find *gwam*, circle errors.

1' Goal: At least 24 *gwam*
3' Goal: At least 21 *gwam*

all letters used | A | 1.5 si | 5.7 awl | 80% hfw

gwam 1' | 3'

	1'	3'
A letter message, like any other message, ought to have a	12	4
major purpose. This purpose is usually stated in the opening	24	8
paragraph. A useful way to focus on the primary objective is	36	12
to pose the question: Just why am I writing this letter? Until	49	16
you have answered this question, you are not prepared to write.	62	21
Like any other message, a letter ought to begin with a	11	24
brief statement of its objective. The next paragraph or two	23	28
should convey in a clear, direct manner the ideas, facts, and	36	32
details required to realize the purpose. The final paragraph	48	37
should end the message in a positive, friendly way.	58	40

gwam 1' | 1 | 2 | 3 | 4 | 5 | 6 | 7 | 8 | 9 | 10 | 11 | 12 |
3' | 1 | | 2 | | 3 | | 4 |

48c ▶ 35
Format Letters in Block Style

1 plain full sheet;
2 letterheads (LM pp. 53-56)
  additional plain sheets;
line: 60 spaces;
date: line 15

Problem 1
Personal-Business Letter

Format the letter (shown at the right) in block style with open punctuation on a plain sheet. Correct any errors you make as you key. Before you remove the letter from your machine (or print it out on a computer), proofread the copy and correct any additional errors you find.

Problems 2 and 3 are on p. 86.

words

4026 Eastway Drive│Charlotte, NC 28205-2736│November 16,   12
19--│Sentinel Electronics Company│401 Euclid Avenue│Cleve-   23
land, OH 44144-3561│Ladies and Gentlemen│   32

When I bought a Sentinel clock radio several weeks ago, I   43
was assured of trouble-free service. Further, I was told that   56
repairs could be made locally in the unlikely event something   68
went wrong.   71

About a week ago, severe static developed in the radio, and a   83
recurring click began in the digital clock. I returned the radio   96
to the store where I bought it only to be told that I would have   109
to return it to you for repair.   116

Before being further inconvenienced, I want to be sure that re-   127
turning the radio to you is the proper course of action. I am   141
certain you want to stand behind your products and to be sure   154
that your outlet stores properly represent your products and   166
service. You should have my warranty card on file.   177

Sincerely yours│Miss Gloria Prentice   184

113a ▶ 5
Conditioning Practice
each line 3 times (slowly, faster, top speed); as time permits, repeat selected lines

alphabet	1	The winning team just broke every existing record for playing bezique.
fig/sym	2	Is Check #1576 for $48.90, dated May 23, made out to McNeil & O'Brien?
adjacent key	3	If we are to oppose the oppressive restriction, we must do so quietly.
speed	4	It is a civic duty to handle their problem with proficiency and rigor.

| 1 | 2 | 3 | 4 | 5 | 6 | 7 | 8 | 9 | 10 | 11 | 12 | 13 | 14 |

113b ▶ 10
Improve Language Skills: Kinds of Sentences
Follow standard directions given with 111b, p. 195.

COMPOUND-COMPLEX SENTENCE

> A compound-complex sentence has at least two independent clauses and one or more dependent clauses. (In the examples below, the independent clauses are in color.)

Learn He will go with us if you do his work, but you must do the work today

Learn 2. In Carmel, we spent the morning looking for oil paintings that we would like, but we were unsuccessful.
(Note that Sentence 2 is introduced by the phrase, "In Carmel.")

Apply (Number and compose two compound-complex sentences.)

113c ▶ 35
Format and Key Leftbound Report with Footnotes
full sheets; DS the ¶s; set tab for 5-space ¶ indention; SS and indent quotations of 4 or more lines 5 spaces from left and right margins

MICROCOMPUTERS QS

Microcomputers have now become commonplace. They are used by business offices for information processing, by schools for various educational activities, by medical doctors to interact with medical databases, by attorneys to research case data, and by individuals in the home to perform a variety of special tasks. In schools and in homes, microcomputers have become one of this decade's most potent tools. Yet without software to direct them how to perform, computers can be simply expensive boxes with blank faces. Conversely, with carefully designed software packages or tied into extensive knowledge databases computers can be exciting, stimulating, and effective tools for directing learning.

The key question is: Will the computer take over the business of education with neither teachers nor schools being necessary? The answer is an emphatic No! Computers just cannot provide the many types of learning experiences that can be offered in schools by human teachers. Cornish says:

. . . teachers will continue to be needed in the future and so will schools. Teachers will provide

48c (continued)

Problem 2
Business Letter

Format the letter in block style on a letterhead sheet. Correct any errors you make as you key. Use your own initials for reference in the closing lines. When you complete the letter, proofread it and make any needed corrections before you remove it from the typewriter or print out a copy on a computer. Address an envelope.

November 20, 19-- Miss Gloria Prentice 4026 Eastway Drive | 12
Charlotte, NC 28205-2736 Dear Miss Prentice | 21

¶ We apologize for the inconvenience you were caused | 31
by one of our Sentinel products and for the incorrect | 42
information given you by one of our dealers. | 51
¶ Only on rare occasions does one of our products | 61
malfunction. We regret that you were the victim | 70
of one of these events. I am pleased to tell you, | 81
though, that your Sentinel clock radio will be | 90
repaired free of charge. Just take it and this | 100
letter to Quik Repair Center, our authorized repair | 110
service in your city, and your radio will be put | 120
in like-new condition. | 125
¶ Please accept the enclosed $10 credit coupon | 134
toward your next Sentinel purchase as a token of | 143
our appreciation for your patience and understanding. | 154

Cordially yours Anthony M. Oliver Assistant Vice | 164
President xx Enclosure | 169/**182**

Problem 3
Business Letter

Format the letter in block style on a letterhead sheet, using the directions for Problem 2. Correct all marked errors and any you make as you key.

Computer printers often print copy with distinctive punctuation marks. Study the chart below before you key the letter at the right.

	typewriter	computer
comma	,	ˏ

Proofreader's Marks

ℐ	delete
⌒	close up
∧	insert
¶	paragraph
∿	transpose
/lc	lowercase
sp.	spell out
≡	capitalize
⊙	insert period

November 20, 19-- Ms. Miss Lorraine Helmsley 2398 Hemlock | 11
Way Santa Ana, CA 92704-4628 Dear Ms. Helmsley | 20

¶ I believe you will like the improvements changes we've made in packaging | 33
materials for our Entree royale line of boil-in-the-bag | 44
meals. Please accept our apologies for the dinner that was ruined. | 58
¶ Since we introduced Entree Royale, the factory has had a | 70
problem making bags that protect food from freezer burn and | 82
boiling water and that still permit a variety of foods to | 93
cook within 15 minutes. Three times we have reported com- | 106
plaints about bags that admit let in water as the food is cooked. | 118
The factory has assured us that the problem has been solved. | 130
¶ Help us prove them right. use the enclosed coupons to get | 142
another bag of Shrimp Primavera and to receive a 25 percent | 154
discount on an Entree Royale of your choice. enjoy! | 165

Sincerely yours Brown C. Mills, manager Customer Ser- | 176
vice xx Enclosures | 179/**192**

Line 10 (pica)
Line 12 (elite) ELECTRONIC DATA/WORD PROCESSORS

QS

Electronic data and word processors have become a way of

1½" left
margin life. Almost every area of business and many facets of our

1" right
margin

personal lives have felt their impact.

Indent quotation
5 spaces from
left and right
margins.

Computers are such awesome machines! Their
blinking lights . . . produce a mystique that results in both admiration and distrust. . . . But
whether we like or dislike them, we cannot ignore
them.[1]

Recent technological advances have produced microcomputers

and increased the speed of processing words and data. Govern-

ment agencies, banks, retailers, schools, and homes have found

uses for these mystical wonders. For example:

Indent enumer-
ated items 5
spaces from left
and right margins.

1. after-hour electronic banking
2. automatic scoring devices in bowling alleys
3. electronic controls in home appliances
4. electronic check-out devices in supermarkets
5. electronic information displays in cars
6. electronic patient records in hospitals

Although "fourth generation computers" have personal and

business disadvantages as well as advantages, there is little

doubt that these mystical devices will have increasing impact

on our daily lives in the years to come. "Computers are essen-

tial tools of today's society. . . . Everyone, today, needs

to understand them."[2]

DS
_____
DS

[1]Louis E. Boone and David L. Kurtz, Contemporary Business
(Hinsdale, IL: The Dryden Press, 1976), p. 450.

DS

[2]David R. Adams, Gerald E. Wagner, and Terrence J. Boyer,
Computer Information Systems (Cincinnati: South-Western Publishing Co., 1983), p. 26.

(at least 1" bottom margin)

Leftbound Report with Footnotes

Unit 8 Lessons 49-50

Measurement Goals

1. To demonstrate that you can key straight-copy ¶s for 3 minutes at the speed and control level specified by your teacher.
2. To demonstrate that you can format and key letters, personal notes, and memos in block style.
3. To demonstrate that you can format numbered lists with centered headings.

Machine Adjustments

1. Paper guide at 0.
2. Ribbon control to use top half of ribbon.
3. Margin sets: left margin (center − 30); right margin (center + 30 + bell adjustment).
4. Line-space selector set to SS drills and problems; to DS ¶ timed writings.

Lesson 49 — Letters

Line: 60 spaces
Spacing: SS (or as directed)

49a ▶ 6
Conditioning Practice

1. Each line twice SS.
2. A 1' writing on line 3; find *gwam*.

alphabet 1 Jack Waven dozed off as he quietly prepped for his big exam.

fig/sym 2 I moved from 135 Este Lane to 937-24th Street on 6/10/86.

speed 3 Of the eighty small robot firms, half may make a big profit.

| 1 | 2 | 3 | 4 | 5 | 6 | 7 | 8 | 9 | 10 | 11 | 12 |

49b ▶ 12
Check Keyboarding Skill

1. A 1' writing on ¶ 1; find *gwam*, circle errors.
2. A 1' writing on ¶ 2; find *gwam*, circle errors.
3. A 2' writing on ¶s 1 and 2 combined; find *gwam*, circle errors.
4. A 3' writing on ¶s 1 and 2 combined; find *gwam*, circle errors.

Skill-Building Practice

As time permits, take a series of 1' *guided* writings on each ¶ with the call of the guide each 15 seconds. Use the better 1' writing rate in Steps 1 and 2 as your base rate.

gwam	¼'	½'	¾'	Time
20	5	10	15	20
24	6	12	18	24
28	7	14	21	28
32	8	16	24	32
36	9	18	27	36
40	10	20	30	40
44	11	22	33	44
48	12	24	36	48
52	13	26	39	52

all letters used | A | 1.5 si | 5.7 awl | 80% hfw | gwam 2' | 3'

It is a satisfying feeling to be a winner. Every person   6 | 4
prefers to serve on a winning team. Although the prize might   12 | 8
not be worth either the time or effort involved, the desire to   18 | 12
excel may justify both. Realize that team members must meet   24 | 16
the requirements for a winning exhibition each time they play.   31 | 20

An office work force is a team, also; and the same basic   36 | 24
principles apply there as apply on an athletic field. A major   43 | 28
difference, however, is that in the office the rewards are in-   49 | 32
creased pay and promotions instead of trophies and letters.   55 | 37
Winning is fun on any team, but winning takes effort from all.   61 | 41

gwam 2' | 1 | 2 | 3 | 4 | 5 | 6 |
     3' | 1 | 2 | 3 | 4 |

112a ▶ 5
Conditioning Practice

each line 3 times (slowly, faster, top speed); as time permits, repeat selected lines

alphabet 1 Liquid oxygen fuel was used to give this big jet rocket amazing speed.

fig/sym 2 We bought a 144″ × 96″ drapery, priced at $128.95, on sale for $63.70.

first row 3 Vince named his baby Zana, Ben named his Maxine, and I named mine Ann.

speed 4 If they do the work for us, they then may go to the lake with the men.

| 1 | 2 | 3 | 4 | 5 | 6 | 7 | 8 | 9 | 10 | 11 | 12 | 13 | 14 |

112b ▶ 10
Improve Language Skills: Kinds of Sentences

1. STUDY explanatory rules.

2. Key line number (with period); space twice, and key LEARN sentence(s) DS, noting rule application.

3. Number and key APPLY sentence(s) DS as directed.

COMPOUND SENTENCE

A compound sentence contains two or more independent clauses connected by a coordinating conjunction (and, but, for, or, nor).

Learn 1. Brian Yaeger likes to hike, and Beau James likes to swim.
(contains two independent clauses)

Learn 2. A fire is crackling in the fireplace, the skiers are relaxing, and dinner is being prepared. *(contains three independent clauses)*

Apply (Number and compose two compound sentences.)

COMPLEX SENTENCE

A complex sentence contains only one independent clause but one or more dependent clauses.

Learn 5. The book that you gave Juan for his birthday was lost.
(dependent clause is in color)

Learn 6. If I were you, I would speak to Paul before I left.
(dependent clauses are in color)

Apply (Number and compose two complex sentences.)

112c ▶ 35
Format and Key a Leftbound Report with Footnotes

full sheet

Review the general guidelines for keying leftbound reports and footnotes on page 194. Then, key model on page 199, following the guidelines given there.

Correct errors if your teacher so directs.

Note. The model on page 199 is shown in pica type; if you are keying in elite, your line endings will be different, but your spacing will be the same.

Learning Guide: When formatting manuscripts with footnotes, a simple procedure to remind you to leave a 1″ bottom margin is to do the following:

Make a light pencil mark at the right edge of the sheet 1″ from the bottom. As you key each footnote reference number, add another pencil mark 1/2″ above the previous one. In this way, you will reserve about 3 line spaces for each footnote at the bottom of the sheet. Erase marks when you have completed the page.

If you have a page line gauge (LM, p. 7), use it.

> To position the footnote reference figures: Turn the platen forward a half space if your machine has vertical half spacing; use the automatic line finder and turn the platen forward a half space on machines that do not have vertical half spacing.

49c ▶ 32
Check Formatting
Skills: Letters

1 plain sheet;
2 letterheads (LM pp. 65-68)
  or additional plain sheets;
line: 60; date: line 15;
listen for bell to return; correct
errors; address envelopes

Problem 1
Personal-Business Letter
from Script

plain sheet

4450 Markham, W Little Rock, AR 72205-3674   November 21, 19--   12
Unique Gardens, Inc. 4199 - 57th Street   Des Moines, IA   23
50310-4729   Ladies and Gentlemen   30

Here is my bulb and plant order for the coming spring   41
planting season. A check is attached to the order form.   52

This is the fourth year I have ordered from you. The   63
quality of your plants is excellent, and your service is   75
unequalled. Your location suggestions for annuals and   86
your zone ratings for perennials are quite helpful.   96

If I may offer just one suggestion, a list of soil prepa-   108
ration and planting instructions for each type of plant   119
ordered would be welcomed by those of us who do not   129
have a "green thumb."   134

Cordially   Alexander Wormwood   Enclosures   142/167

Problem 2
Business Letter

letterhead sheet

words

November 26, 19-- | Mr. Alexander Wormwood | 4450 Markham,   11
W | Little Rock, AR 72205-3674 | Dear Mr. Wormwood   21

Thank you for the letter which accompanied your recent order.   33
We humbly accept the praise and welcome the suggestions of   45
one of our valued customers.   51

Instructions for preparing the soil and planting should be in-   63
cluded with each type of bulb and plant we ship. If any of these   77
instructions has been missing from your orders, someone has   89
slipped up. We shall make every effort to see that this omission   101
does not occur again.   106

Would you be willing to let us quote a portion of your letter in   119
our next catalog? If so, will you please sign and return the   131
enclosed Permission to Quote form. We like to let those who   143
receive our catalogs know that our services as well as our prod-   156
ucts bring satisfaction to our customers.   165

As usual, each item you recently ordered will be sent at just the   178
right planting time so you won't have a storage problem.   190

Cordially yours | Miss Elaine Rodriguez | Manager, Customer   201
Service | xx | Enclosure   205/217

Problem 3 (Extra Credit)

Prepare on a letterhead sheet another copy of the letter formatted
in Problem 2. Address it to yourself at your home address; supply
an appropriate salutation.

(DOS. Disk Operating System.

Disk, floppy. An oxide coated plastic disk which can be used for magnetically sorting information.

Flow charting. The process of graphically showing the detailed steps in the solution of a problem.

GIGO. "Garbage In, Garbage Out"--an expression used to describe a poor program when inappropriate data is inputer, or inputted.

Graphics. The use of diagrams or other written symbols and visual displays.

Hard copy. A printed copy of machine output in a good visually readable form.

Icon. A visual image on the display or screen indicating a computer function, such as a miniature file drawer for storage and retrieval.

Input. Information or data transferred or to be transferred from an external source into the internal storage of a computer.

K {Kilo}. Abbreviation denoting 1,024 Bytes.

Menu. A numbered list of choices from which a selection can be made in using a computer.

Modem. A device which converts data from a form which is compatible with data processing equipment to a form which is compatible with transmission facilities, and vice versa.

Output. Information that is produced as a result of processing data.

Printer. Device used for printing of information prepared on a computer.

RAM. "Random Access Memory"--a type of computer memory in which data may be "written in" or "read out."

Scrolling. Moving lines displayed on a terminal screen either up or down.

Software. Programs written for computer systems.

Word processing. The processing, manipulation, and storage of information needed in the preparation of written communications.

This glossary of computer terms is not intended to be all-inclusive. Other terms, and new terms which evolve, will become a part of the basic vocabulary of anyone who learns to use a computer in school, in the home, or in the business world.

50a ▶ 6
Conditioning Practice

1. Each line twice SS.
2. A 1' writing on line 3; find *gwam*.

alphabet   1   Mickie gave Quincy six jigsaw puzzles for his last birthday.

fig/sym   2   Ike asked, "Is the ZIP Code 45208-3164 or is it 45209-2748?"

speed   3   Shana may make a bid for the antique bottle for the auditor.

| 1 | 2 | 3 | 4 | 5 | 6 | 7 | 8 | 9 | 10 | 11 | 12 |

50b ▶ 12
Check Language Skills

full sheet; DS; line: 60 spaces; begin on line 12

1. Read line 1, noting the words that should be capitalized; then key the line, supplying needed capitals.

2. Complete the other lines in the same way. If numbers appear in the lines, express them correctly.

1   you may have the blue sweater. i'll take the brown one.

2   did mr. watts tell us to report to miss knight, the coach?

3   yellowstone national park is located in the state of montana.

4   the local chapter of a m s meets on tuesday, december fifth.

5   the civil war is also known as the war between the states.

6   american electric company gives generously to united appeal.

7   she said that ph. d. means doctor of philosophy.

8   when does the president give the state of the union address?

9   does u p s deliver on saturday or only monday through friday?

10   the play begins at seven fifteen p. m. on sunday, june two.

11   the kendrick building is located at one madison avenue.

12   14 applicants took the test, but only 3 were hired.

50c ▶ 32
Check Formatting Skills

60-space line; listen for bell as signal to return

Problem 1 (half sheet)
Personal Note in Block Style

Format the note using **November 27** and the current year as the date. Use your first name in the closing lines. Correct any errors you make as you key the note.

                          words

                          date   4

Dear Doug   6

Thank you for inviting me to "Holiday Sounds" on   15
December 18. Having been a member of your group   25
for two years, I wouldn't miss it.   32

Our holiday break begins December 13. I have a   42
term paper to complete here before I leave, but I   52
should be home no later than the 16th.   60

It will be great to see all of you do your theatrics.   71
Perhaps there will be time for some skiing, too.   81

Sincerely   83

                          name   84

Format and Key
an Unbound Report

Key an unbound report from rough-draft copy.

full sheets; DS the ¶s; 5-space ¶ indention; SS the definitions, but DS between them (*as indicated*)

Follow standard directions for keying unbound manuscript and paragraph headings as given on p. 194. Stay alert.

Compuer Terminology)center in ALL CAPS
QS

    Any new technology quickly develops a set of terms that are peculiar to that new technology. The field of computer systems is no exception ot this generalized statement. As computers have evolved, such terms as bits, bytes, compatibility, data bases, debug, hard copy, icons, and modems have evolved. Important to computer literacy is to have a knowledge of such terms. The purpose of this report is to introduce a basic vocabulary or working glossary of computer terms that will help to familiarize computer operators with many of the more common terms. The selected glossary is shown below.
DS

BASIC. "Beginner's All-purpose Symbolic Instruction Code"--
a procedure-oriented computer language.
DS

BAUD. A measurement of data transmission rates expressed as "bits per second" or bps. Abbreviation of Baudot.

Bit. The smallest binary unit for storing data in a computer.

Bug. Mistake, or malfunction.

Byte. A term used to indicate a measurable potion of consecutive binary digits, e.g., and 8-bit or 6-bit byte.

Compatability. The ability of one type of computer system to share information or to communicate with another type of computer system.

Cathode Ray Tube {CRT}. Tv-like screen for displaying data.

Computer Program. A set of instructions which directs a computer to perform a sequence or series of task in order to produce a desired output.

Data base. Organized system of data files.

Debug. To test a program to determine if it works properly.

Diskdrive. A device on which a disk can be mounted for use with a comptuer.

(continued on next page)

Problem 2 (half sheet)
Simplified Memo in Block Style

Format the memo using **November 27** and the current year as the date. Use your full name as the writer of the memo. Make the corrections indicated in the memo, and correct any errors you make as you key the copy.

words

date 4

Keyboard Operators ~~s~~   7

Keyboarding Efficiency) ALL CAP   ~ and accuracy   12

You can increase your input speed / by reaching to each ser-   26

vice and function key with the proper finger while keeping   38

the other fingers on ^ their home positions.   49

When

If you move the entire hand to the service / key ^s , you use   - or function   63

more time and increase your chances of making errors. ⌐ You   ## #   75

can increase your productivity with less effort ^ you will   87

reach with the fingers ^ , not the hands.   95

name 98

Problem 3 (full sheet)
Numbered List

Format and key the list. Correct any errors you make as you key. If you do not complete the list before time is called, finish it at a later time and keep it as a convenient reference.

SOME FACTS TO REMEMBER   5

1. Standard-size paper is 8 1/2" wide by 11" long.   15

2. A full sheet has 66 vertical line spaces; a half   26
   sheet, 33 line spaces.   31

3. On a sheet of paper 8 1/2" wide, you can enter   41
   102 elite (12-pitch) or 85 pica (10-pitch) char-   50
   acters and spaces.   54

4. The horizontal center point of an 8 1/2" sheet   65
   is 51 on a 12-pitch machine, 42 on a 10-pitch   74
   machine.   76

5. Many keyboarding machines today have dual   85
   pitch; that is, they can print in either 10- or   95
   12-pitch type.   98

6. To center a heading: From the horizontal center   108
   point of the paper, backspace once for each 2   117
   characters and spaces in the heading; begin   126
   the heading where backspacing ends.   133

111a ▶ 5
Conditioning Practice

each line 3 times (slowly, faster, in-between rate); as time permits, repeat selected lines

alphabet 1 The qualified expert analyzed water from seventy cracked jugs by noon.

fig/sym 2 After May 5, Al's new address will be 478 Pax Avenue (ZIP 92106-1593).

adjacent key 3 To permit emotion to control action seriously limits positive results.

speed 4 He did the work for us, but the city paid for it with their endowment.

| 1 | 2 | 3 | 4 | 5 | 6 | 7 | 8 | 9 | 10 | 11 | 12 | 13 | 14 |

111b ▶ 15
Improve Language Skills: Kinds of Sentences

full sheet; 1″ top margin; 70-space line; DS

1. Study the definitions and explanatory guides.

2. Keyboard the learn sentences DS, noting the application of the guidelines.

3. Compose sentences as directed DS. Number each sentence.

SENTENCES

Phrases are groups of related words used as subjects, adjectives, or adverbs. They do not express a complete thought and cannot stand alone. Most phrases consist of a preposition and a noun or pronoun.

Clauses, on the other hand, have both a subject and a verb; they are either *independent* or *dependent*. An independent clause forms the principal unit of the sentence; it expresses a complete thought and can stand alone. Even though it has both a subject and a verb, a dependent clause does not express a complete thought and cannot stand alone. It needs the independent clause to make sense.

Learn 1. She came from a small town. *(phrase)*

Learn 2. I laughed when I heard him tell the story. *(independent clause)*

Learn 3. I laughed when I heard him tell the story. *(dependent clause)*

Apply (Number and compose three sentences that contain: 1. a phrase; 2. an independent clause; 3. a dependent clause.)

SIMPLE SENTENCE

A *simple sentence* contains a single independent clause. A simple sentence may have as its subject more than one noun or pronoun and as its predicate more than one verb.

Learn 7. Juan has a new bicycle. *(single subject and single predicate)*

Learn 8. Juan and his brother have a new bicycle. *(subject with two nouns)*

Learn 9. Juan washed and polished his bicycle. *(predicate with two verbs)*

Learn 10. Juan and his brother washed and polished his bicycle. *(subject with two nouns and predicate with two verbs)*

Apply (Number and compose four simple sentences that contain(s): 1. single subject and single predicate; 2. subject with two nouns; 3. predicate with two verbs; and 4. subject with two nouns and predicate with two verbs.)

ENRICHMENT ACTIVITY: Timed Writing

Line: 70 spaces
Spacing: double-space (DS)

As time permits during Units 9 and 10, use the ¶s at the right to improve keyboarding skill.

1. A 1' writing on ¶ 1; find *gwam*. Add 2-4 words to set a new goal.

2. Two 1' writings on ¶ 1 at your new goal rate, guided by ¼' guide call.

3. Key ¶ 2 in the same way.

4. A 2' writing on ¶ 1, then on ¶ 2. If you finish a ¶ before time is called, start over.

5. A 3' writing on ¶s 1-2 combined; find *gwam*.

gwam	¼'	½'	¾'	1'
20	5	10	15	20
24	6	12	18	24
28	7	14	21	28
32	8	16	24	32
36	9	18	27	36
40	10	20	30	40
44	11	22	33	44
48	12	24	36	48
52	13	26	39	52
56	14	28	42	56

all letters used | A | 1.5 si | 5.7 awl | 80% hfw   *gwam* 2' | 3'

We live in a society of numbers. From the number of a birth certificate to the number of a death certificate, numbers play a very vital role in the daily life of each of us. Virtually all typed business and personal papers contain figures. Quite often these documents contain some commonly used symbols, also. Therefore, skill in keying on the top row is critical to your future use of the machine.

Data arranged in table form shows a common use of figures and symbols. Although some tables include no figures, the greatest percentage of them do. Just as top skill on a letter keyboard may pay well, expert skill on figure copy may land you a prized job as a data-entry worker that will pay even better. Workers in accounting and data processing offices must know how to operate the number row with efficiency.

ENRICHMENT ACTIVITY: Composing at the Keyboard

Line: 65 spaces, pica; 78, elite
Spacing: double-space (DS)

As time permits during the completion of Phase 3, choose a "Thought Starter" from those listed below. Develop the idea into a 2- or 3-paragraph theme, giving reasons for what you would do.

1 If I had a lot of money, I would...

2 I chose to take a keyboarding course because...

3 During next summer vacation, I plan to...

4 If I had it to do over, I would...

5 I plan to (or do not plan to) go to college because...

6 If I could be the person I want to be, I would...

7 I admire (your mother, father, or someone else of your choice) because...

8 If I could talk with the President of the United States, I would ask...

9 Of my hobbies, I prefer (reading, computer games, swimming, or other hobby choice) because...

10 I want to become a (teacher, data/word processor, salesperson, or other career choice) because...

11 If I could choose my "boss" when I go to work, I would choose one who...

12 Of my personality traits, the three that seem most to attract others are...

13 When I choose my friends, the three most important qualities I look for are...

14 Of all the subjects I have studied in school, the one I have found most useful is (keyboarding, English, mathematics, etc.) because...

15 When I finish this keyboarding course, I want to be able to use my skill to...

Learning Goals

1. To improve your manuscript and report keyboarding skill.

2. To improve language skills (sentence structure).

3. To improve straight-copy keyboarding skills.

Machine Adjustments

1. Paper guide at *0*.

2. 70-space line and DS, unless otherwise directed.

3. Line space selector on *2* or as directed.

FORMATTING GUIDES: REPORTS

Report with Footnotes

Spacing

Reports or manuscripts may be either single- or double-spaced. Double-space school reports, formal reports, and manuscripts to be submitted for publication. Indent the first line of paragraphs 5 spaces. Single-space quoted material of 4 or more lines, indenting 5 spaces from left and right margins. DS above and below quotation.

Margins (Unbound and Leftbound Reports)

Top	Place main heading on: line 10 (pica) line 12 (elite)
Side	1″ left and right margins for unbound 1 1/2″ left and 1″ right margins for leftbound
Bottom	At least 1″ on all pages

Headings and Subheadings

Main heading. Center the main heading in ALL CAPITALS over the *line of writing*. Follow by a quadruple space. **Note:** To find the horizontal center for a leftbound report, add the figures at the left and right margins and divide by 2.

Side headings. Begin side headings at left margin, underline, and capitalize the first letter of all main words. DS above and below side headings.

Paragraph headings. Begin paragraph headings at paragraph indention point, underline, and follow by a period. Capitalize the first letter of the first word.

Reference Notations

Footnotes. If used, place footnotes at the bottom of the page on which the quoted reference appears. Use a divider line (1 1/2″ long) to separate the textual material from the footnotes. DS above and below the divider line. Indent first line of each footnote to the paragraph point and key superior figure about 1/2 line space above footnote line. SS footnotes, but DS between them.

Number footnotes consecutively throughout a report, using superior numbers (raised about 1/2 line space) to refer to the numbered footnotes at the bottom of the page. In planning the placement of footnotes, allow at least a 1 inch bottom margin below footnotes on all pages except the last. Place the footnotes on the last page a DS below the divider line, which separates the footnotes from the report. Footnotes must be arranged in a consistent and acceptable form throughout a report (see illustration on page 199).

Textual citations. Reference citations also may be keyboarded as a part of the text of a report (see page 93). When this is done, footnotes are not used; instead the references are cited by enclosing the author's surname, year of publication, and the page number in parentheses. For example:

(Roberts, 1987, 34)

If the author's name is used in the text of the report, the citation need only include the year and page number. If a reference has no author, the first two or three words of the title are used in place of the author's name. Full information for the textual citations is given in the Reference List at the end of the report.

Page Numbers

The first page may or may not be numbered. The number, if used, is centered and placed on line 62. For second and subsequent pages, place page numbers on line 6 approximately even with the right margin.

PHASE 3

Learn to Format Reports and Tables

In the 25 lessons of Phase 3, you will:

1. Learn to format and process report manuscripts, reference lists, and title or cover pages.

2. Learn to format and process data in columnar or table form.

3. Improve basic keyboarding and language skills.

4. Apply your formatting skills to process a series of documents typical of those prepared in the office of a summer camp.

5. Measure and evaluate your basic/document processing skills.

Drills and timed writings in this phase are to be keyed on a 70-space line. Line length for problems varies according to the format required.

You will work part of the time from model typescript, part of the time from print, and some of the time from handwritten (script) and rough-draft (corrected) copy. Keyboarding for personal and business use is often done from script and rough draft.

Problem 12
Special Table

half sheet, long edge at top; SS and DS data as shown in table; 10 spaces between columns; add following source note:

Source: Rand Youth Poll, December 1983.

(Total words: 53)

	Allowance	Earnings
13-15 Years		
Boys	$11.35	$11.40
Girls	11.70	11.90
16-19 Years		
Boys	$21.80	$31.65
Girls	22.05	32.56

AVERAGE WEEKLY INCOMES
OF 2,500 U.S. TEENAGERS

Problem 13
Unarranged Table:
Learning Transfer

full sheet; SS and DS data in a form similar to table of Problem 12 above; 8 spaces between columns; use 2-line main heading: **MEAN EARNINGS OF MEN AND WOMEN BY EDUCATIONAL ATTAINMENT**; use secondary heading: **(Persons With Income, Aged 18 and Over).**

	Men	Women
Elementary School		
Less than 8 years	$ 8,910	$ 4,333
8 years	11,481	4,897
High School		
1-3 years	11,056	4,988
4 years	14,375	6,750
College		
1-3 years	14,791	7,188
4 years or more	23,833	10,696

Source: Bureau of the Census, Current Population Reports, 1981.

Problem 14
Unarranged Table

Arrange table in attractive format on full sheet. Use main heading: **DOES PRODUCTION STOP AS WE GET OLDER?**

Use secondary heading: **(Some Noteworthy Achievements).** Block column headings.

Age	Achievement
85	Grandma Moses wrote her autobiography
82	Goethe wrote FAUST
79	Benjamin Franklin appointed chief executive of Pennsylvania
76	Margaret Chase Smith served 24th year as U. S. Senator
72	Katharine Hepburn won an Academy Award for ON GOLDEN POND
72	Verdi composed OTHELLO

Learning Goals

1. To learn to format, space, and key topic outlines.

2. To learn to format, space, and key unbound reports, reference lists, and title pages.

3. To learn to align copy vertically and horizontally.

4. To improve basic keystroking skills.

Machine Adjustments

1. Paper guide at *0*.

2. Ribbon control to use top half of ribbon.

3. Margin sets: left margin (center − 35); right margin (center + 35 + 5).

4. Line-space selector set to SS drills; DS ¶s; as directed for problems.

FORMATTING GUIDES: UNBOUND REPORTS

Unbound Report Format

Some reports are placed in protective covers (ring binders or heavy paper covers with clasps or clamps). When reports are to be bound, an extra half inch of space is left in the margin of the binding edge.

Many short, less formal reports are left unbound. If such reports consist of more than one page, the pages are fastened together in the upper left corner by a staple or other fastening device. No extra margin space is left for stapling.

Standard Margins. In unbound reports, as shown in the model, 1-inch (1″) *side margins* are used (10 pica spaces, 12 elite spaces). With the paper guide set at 0 (zero) on the line-of-writing scale, this means that the left margin is set at 10 on 10-pitch machines or at 12 on 12-pitch ones.

A *top margin* of about 2 inches (2″) is customarily used in unbound reports; so place the title on line 12. (In school settings where the same report is done on both pica and elite machines, a 1½″ [line 10] top margin for pica machines may be used so that all students have similar end-of-page decisions to make.)

A 1-inch (1″) *bottom margin* is recommended. Because of variable internal spacing of report items, however, a bottom margin of exactly 1 inch is often not possible. For that reason, a bottom margin of *at least* 1 inch is acceptable.

Internal spacing. A quadruple space (QS) is left between the report title and the first line of the body. A double space (DS) is left above and below side headings and between paragraphs. Paragraphs are usually double-spaced.

Page numbering. The first page of an unbound report is not numbered. On the second page and following ones, the page number is placed on line 6 at the right margin. A double space is left below the page number. This means that the first line of the report body appears on line 8.

Reference citations. References used to give credit for quoted or paraphrased material are cited in parentheses in the report body. This internal citation method of documentation is rapidly replacing the footnote method because it is easier and quicker. Internal citations should include the name(s) of the author(s), the date of the referenced publication, and the page number(s) of the material cited.

All references cited are listed alphabetically by author surnames at the end of the report (usually on a separate page) under the heading REFERENCES. The reference page uses the same top margin and side margins as the first page of the report. Each reference is single-spaced; a DS is left between references. The first line of each reference begins at the left margin; other lines are indented 5 spaces.

Problem 9
5-Column Table
full sheet; DS data; 4 spaces between columns

Alertness cue: Set tab stop for the digit in each column that requires the least forward and backward spacing. To align figures, space forward ▶ or backward ◀ as necessary.

Note: Total lines are usually indented three spaces.

A LOOK AT THE EARTH

Continents	Area (Sq. Mi.)	Percent of Earth	Population*	Percent World Total	
Asia	16,999,000	29.7	2,850,567,000	59.9	38
Africa	11,688,000	20.4	531,000,000	11.2	46
North America	9,366,000	16.3	395,000,000	8.3	56
South America	6,881,000	12.0	264,000,000	5.5	65
Europe	4,017,000	7.0	696,433,000	14.6	73
Australia	2,911,000	5.2	15,500,000	0.3	81
Antarctica	5,100,000	8.9			86
*Estimated World Population			4,762,000,000		95

Source: World Almanac, 1985, p. 625.

Problem 10
Unarranged Table
Arrange table in attractive format on full sheet. Spacing suggestion: 2 spaces between columns.

Learning cue: Backspace once from tab stops for underline that precedes totals; start total figures at this point.

Main heading: **METHODS OF ERROR CORRECTION USED IN THE BUSINESS OFFICE**

Column headings:

Method	Letters	Memos	Reports	Forms	Tables	Total Use
Lift-off	57%	58%	50%	48%	48%	57%
Electronic correction	16	16	18	12	16	16
Correction fluid	13	13	22	24	25	13
Chalk-back paper	11	11	7	8	7	11
Eraser	2	1	2	6	3	2
Other method	1	1	1	2	1	1
Totals	100%	100%	100%	100%	100%	100%

Source: Guffey and Erickson, Monograph 136, South-Western Publishing Co., Cincinnati, Ohio, 1981, p. 13.

Problem 11
Unarranged Table
Arrange table in attractive format on full sheet.

Main heading: NATIONAL STUDY OF LETTER VARIABLES

AS USED IN THE BUSINESS OFFICE

Column headings: Variable / Percent

Length of letter	
125 words or less	57%
126-225 words	26
226-325 words	9
Two or more pages	8
Line length	
Standard 6-inch line	54
Other line lengths	46
Two-letter state abbreviation in address	30
Columnar material in letter	11

Source: Guffey and Erickson, Monograph 136, South-Western Publishing Co., Cincinnati, Ohio, 1981, p. 24.

51a ▶ 7
Conditioning Practice

each line twice SS (slowly, then faster); if time permits, rekey selected lines

alphabet   1   Pat became very quiet just as an extra golf cart zoomed down the walk.

figures   2   They washed 59 cars, 28 vans, 47 campers, and 30 bikes on November 16.

s/es/ies   3   aid aids job jobs car cars do does class classes try tries copy copies

speed   4   Dory may make a fuchsia gown for the civic social to be held downtown.

| 1 | 2 | 3 | 4 | 5 | 6 | 7 | 8 | 9 | 10 | 11 | 12 | 13 | 14 |

51b ▶ 8
Learn to Align Roman Numerals

half sheet (long edge at top)

1. Set left margin stop for a 40-space line.

2. Clear all tab stops; from left margin, space forward to set new tab stops as indicated by the KEY below and the guides above the columns.

3. Center the heading on line 14.

4. As you key the Roman numerals, tabbing from column to column, align them at the right. To do this, space forward or backward from the tab stop as needed.

Margin Release

To begin the numeral III in Column 1, depress the **margin release (6)** with the nearer little finger and backspace once into the left margin.

To key outside the right margin, depress the margin release when the right margin locks and continue to key.

ROMAN NUMERALS

DS (space down twice)

margin	tab	tab
↓	↓	↓
I	IV	VII
		DS
II	V	VIII
		DS
III	VI	IX

KEY | 3   16   2   16   4 |

51c ▶ 20
Learn to Format a Topic Outline

Study the information and outline shown at the right; then format the outline as directed.

full sheet; 1″ side margins (elite, 12 spaces; pica, 10); start on line 12 for elite, on line 10 for pica

• Major headings are preceded by I. and II.

• First-order subheadings are preceded by A., B., etc.

• Second-order subheadings are preceded by 1., 2., etc.

SPACING TOPIC OUTLINES

QS (quadruple-space)-- to leave 3 blank line spaces

2 spaces

Space forward once from margin

I.   VERTICAL SPACING

DS

Reset margin ──→ A.   Title of Outline

1st tab ──→ 1.   Line 12, elite (12-pitch); line 10, pica (10-pitch)

Set 2 tab stops 4 spaces apart.

     2.   Followed by 3 blank line spaces (QS)

B.   Major Headings

2d tab ──→ 1.   First major heading preceded by a quadruple space; all others preceded by 1 blank line space (DS)

     2.   All followed by 1 blank line space

     3.   All subheadings single-spaced

DS

Use margin release; backspace 5 times

II.   HORIZONTAL SPACING

DS

A.   Title of Outline Centered over the Line of Writing

B.   Major Headings and Subheadings

     1.   Identifying numerals at left margin (periods aligned) followed by 2 spaces

     2.   Identifying letters and numbers for each subsequent level of subheading aligned below the first word of the preceding heading, followed by 2 spaces

Language Skills Notes

1. Title in ALL CAPS (*may be underlined*)

2. Major headings in ALL CAPS (not underlined)

3. Important words of first-order subheadings capped

4. Only first word of second-order subheadings capped

Problem 6
Unarranged "Special" Table

Arrange table in proper format; full sheet; DS data; 12 spaces between columns (see note).

Note. In arranging some tables horizontally on a sheet, it may be necessary to use judgment to avoid an off-center appearance of data. In this table, use longest column entry (excluding column headings) to determine horizontal placement. The Column 3 heading is then centered over the longest entry in that column.

Use 2-line main heading:

PRINCIPAL PARTS OF TROUBLESOME
IRREGULAR VERBS

Problem 7

Repeat Problem 6 on half sheet, short edge at top; DS data; 8 spaces between columns. Key column entries as you did in Problem 6.

Present	Past	Past Participle	
see	saw	seen	23
do	did	done	25
go	went	gone	28
break	broke	broken	32
choose	chose	chosen	36
drink	drank	drunk	39
eat	ate	eaten	42
freeze	froze	frozen	46
give	gave	given	49
know	knew	known	53
ring	rang	rung	55
run	ran	run	58
speak	spoke	spoken	61
swim	swam	swum	64
take	took	taken	68
write	wrote	written	72

(Present 6, Past 6, Past Participle 7, 20)

Problem 8
5-Column Table

full sheet; DS data; SS source note; leave 6 spaces between Col. 1 and Col. 2; then, use the following intercolumn spacing between columns: 2-4-2.

Alertness cue: % signs are keyed in intercolumns; see note, page 182.

REASONS OF FRESHMEN FOR ATTENDING COLLEGE

(Percent of Total Responding)

Reasons	1984	Rank	1971	Rank	
Get a better job	75.7%	1	73.8%	1	31
Learn more about things	72.3	2	-	-	38
Make more money	67.8	3	49.7	4	44
Gain general education	65.1	4	59.5	3	52
Meet new and interesting people	56.1	5	45.1	5	61
Prepare for graduate school	47.9	6	34.5	6	69
Improve reading/study skills	41.6	7	22.2	9	80
Become a more cultured person	33.8	8	28.9	7	89
Parental pressure	31.7	9	22.9	8	96
Get away from home	11.1	10	-	-	102
Could not find a job	5.3	11	-	-	109
Nothing better to do	2.0	12	2.2	11	116
Learn more about my interests	-	-	68.8	2	125
Contribute more to my community	-	-	18.7	10	134

Source: American Council on Education/UCLA, The American Freshmen National Norms, 1971, p. 43; 1984, p. 46.

Format an Outline

full sheet; 1″ side margins; start on line 12 for elite, on line 10 for pica; format the outline; correct errors

BASIC TEXT-EDITING FUNCTIONS

I. DELETE FUNCTION

    A. Using Cursor Movement Keys, Locate on Screen Point of Deletion

    B. Delete Character, Word, or Line Using Proper Keys

II. INSERT FUNCTION

    A. Using Cursor Movement Keys, Locate on Screen Point of Insertion

    B. Insert Character, Word, or Line into Existing Text

    C. Replace Existing Text

        1. Delete existing text

        2. Insert new text (character, word, or line)

III. AUTOMATIC CENTERING FUNCTION

    A. Strike Proper Key for Automatic Centering

    B. Enter Copy to Be Centered (Machine Will Center It)

Lesson 52   Unbound Reports

52a ▶ 7
Conditioning Practice

each line twice SS (slowly, then faster); if time permits, rekey selected lines

alphabet 1 Joyce paid the exotic woman a quarter for the three black gauze veils.

figures 2 Can 58 students answer the 37 questions about the dates 1492 and 1066?

d/ed/ied 3 use used form formed work worked reach reached fry fried apply applied

speed 4 The girls cut and curl their hair when they visit their rich neighbor.

| 1 | 2 | 3 | 4 | 5 | 6 | 7 | 8 | 9 | 10 | 11 | 12 | 13 | 14 |

52b ▶ 43
Learn to Format an Unbound Report and Reference List

1. Study the report formatting information on page 93.

2. On two full sheets of plain paper, format the model report shown on pages 96 and 97. Do not correct your errors as you keyboard.

3. When you have finished, proofread your copy, mark it for correction, and prepare a final copy with all errors corrected. (Line endings of elite/pica solutions differ.)

Elite (12-pitch) Layout

Problem 4
3-Column Table

full sheet; DS data; 12 spaces between columns

Learning cue: Remember to TS to Col. 1 heading; DS above and below divider line.

Alertness cue: Set tab stop for the digit in each column that requires the least forward and backward spacing. To align figures, space forward ▶ or backward ◀ as necessary.

POPULATION OF UNITED STATES, 1790-1980

(In Millions)

Year	Population	Percent Increase
1790	3.9	—
1810	7.2	84.6%
1830	12.9	79.2
1850	23.2	80.0
1870	38.6	66.4
1890	63.0	63.2
1910	92.2	46.3
1930	123.2	33.6
1950	151.3	22.8
1970	203.3	34.4
1980	226.5	11.4

Source: World Almanac, 1985, pp. 248-249.

8
11
12
22
24
27
30
33
36
39
42
45
49
52
55
59
67

Problem 5
Unarranged Table

Arrange table in proper format; full sheet; DS data; 12 spaces between columns; SS source note and key full width of table.

Main heading: WORLD POPULATION, 30-2000 A.D.
Secondary heading: (In Millions)

Column headings: Year / Population / Increase

Year	Population	Percent Increase
30	250	—
1650	545	118.0%
1700	623	14.3
1750	728	16.7
1800	906	24.5
1850	1,171	29.2
1900	1,608	37.3
1940	2,170	35.0
1950	2,501	15.3
1960	2,986	19.4
1970	3,610	20.9
1980	4,478	24.0
1990	5,326	18.9
2000	6,246	17.3

Source: Woytinsky and Woytinsky, 1953; United Nations Population Studies, 1984.

6
9
11
20
23
26
29
33
36
39
42
45
49
52
55
58
61
65
68
78
84

Title   ↓ CORRECTION DEVICES

QS (space down 2 DS)

Internal
citation

"To err is human, to forgive divine." So said Alexander Pope more than two centuries ago (Bartlett, 1968, 403). To err in the keyboarding process is human, but failure to correct errors is hardly forgiveable. That is why a variety of correcting devices

Report body
or text

have been invented to remove or cover up inevitable errors made at the input stage of typewriter or computer keyboarding. These devices are of two types: manual devices and electronic devices.

DS

Side
heading

Manual Devices

DS

Manual correcting devices include the typing eraser, cover-up tape, cover-up liquid, lift-off film, and lift-off tape. The most time-consuming and least satisfactory of these devices is the abrasive rubber typing eraser which was used for many years before more effective devices were invented. Of the manual devices available,

1″   the quickest and most satisfactory is lift-off tape which literally   1″

lifts the error off the paper when a special backspace (correction) key is used to position the printing point over the error and the key struck in error is restruck.

DS

Side
heading

Electronic Devices

DS

The use of special correction keys on electronic typewriters, computers, and word processors permits the automatic removal of individual letters, words, word groups, lines, and paragraphs so that all corrections can be made before paper copy printout occurs. Electronic error correction is the most efficient method for producing error-free documents and is being used increasingly to prepare

At least 1″

Shown in pica type (10 pitch)

Unbound Report

Long and Short Column Headings

1. If a table has both long and short column headings, center items according to the longest item in each column, whether a column heading or a column entry.

2. In this drill, use backspace-from-center method to set left margin and tab stop using longest column item. Leave 4 spaces between columns.

Name	Location
Grizzly Bear	USA
Bald Eagle	USA
Brown Pelican	USA

Lessons 107-110   Complex Tables

107b-110b ▶ 45 (daily)

words

Format Complex Tables

In the time period for each lesson, try to complete as many problems as possible, pages 189-193. Unless otherwise directed, center tables using the longest column item, whether a heading or entry.

Problem 1
3-Column Heading

half sheet, long edge at top; DS data; 12 spaces between Cols. 1 and 2; 6 spaces between Cols. 2 and 3; block column headings;
Learning cue: DS between 2-line main heading.

Problem 2
2-Line Column Headings

half sheet, long edge at top; DS data, but SS column headings; 6 spaces between columns

Learning cue: When you space forward, 1 for 2, for longest column entry, note center point of column for use in centering column headings.

Problem 3
Long Column Headings

full sheet; DS data; 4 spaces between columns (review directions, page 188, if necessary).

AVERAGE COST IN CENTS PER MILE			6
TO OWN AND OPERATE A NEW CAR			12
Car Size	1978	1983	19
Subcompact	22.5	34.6	23
Compact	24.8	43.3	27
Mid-Size	28.7	45.5	31
Intermediate	28.9	49.6	35
Standard	32.3	55.4	39
AVERAGE	27.5	45.7	42

IMPROVE YOUR SPELLING			4
Study Each Word	Pronounce by Syllables	Capitalize Trouble Spots	10 / 24
environmental	en-vi-ron-men-tal	enviRONmenTAL	33
existence	ex-ist-ence	ExistENCE	40
guarantee	guar-an-tee	gUARanTEE	46
incidentally	in-ci-den-tal-ly	incidenTALLY	55
miniature	min-i-a-ture	miniATURE	61
miscellaneous	mis-cel-la-ne-ous	misCELLanEOUS	70
omission	o-mis-sion	omisSION	76
pursue	pur-sue	PURsue	80

IMPROVE YOUR SPELLING			4
Study Each Word	Pronounce by Syllables	Capitalize Trouble Spots	29
address	ad-dress	aDdress	34
analyze	an-a-lyze	anaLYZE	40
believe	be-lieve	belIEve	45
convenience	con-ven-ience	convenIence	52
courtesy	cour-te-sy	COURteSY	58
disease	dis-ease	disEASE	63
eligible	el-i-gi-ble	eligIble	69
equipped	e-quipped	equipPed	75
judgment	judg-ment	juDGMent	80
mortgage	mort-gage	morTgage	86
occurred	oc-curred	oCCuRRed	91
unforgettable	un-for-get-ta-ble	unforgetTABLE	100

Line 6   2
DS

Internal citation

"letter perfect" work. As Erickson (1983, 9) points out: "The

number of errors made in keyboarding is relatively unimportant

provided the operator detects and corrects such errors in the proof-

1"   reading." Speed of keystroking, speed of error detection, and speed   1"

of error correction are the critical elements in efficient document

processing.
QS (space down 2 DS)

REFERENCES
QS (space down 2 DS);
then change to SS

List of references

Bartlett, John. *Familiar Quotations*. 14th ed. Boston: Little,
    Brown and Company, 1968.
                    DS
Erickson, Lawrence W. "Typewriting vs. Keyboarding--What's the
    Difference?" *Century 21 Reporter*, Fall 1983.

Lesson 53 Unbound Reports

53a ▶ 7
Conditioning Practice

each line twice SS (slowly, then faster); if time permits, rekey selected lines

alphabet 1 The prize for the eleven-kilometer race was a square gold jewelry box.

figures 2 On June 23 she served 461 hamburgers, 597 sodas, and 80 bags of chips.

ing 3 do doing go going get getting run running shave shaving build building

speed 4 They may visit their pen pal in the small island town by the big lake.

| 1 | 2 | 3 | 4 | 5 | 6 | 7 | 8 | 9 | 10 | 11 | 12 | 13 | 14 |

53b ▶ 8
Learn to Format a Title Page

A title or cover page is prepared for many reports. Using the following guides, format a title page for the report you prepared in Lesson 52.

1. Center the title in ALL CAPS on line 16 of a full sheet (from top edge space down 8 double spaces).

2. Center your name in capital and lowercase letters on the 16th line below the title.

3. Center the school name a DS below your name.

4. Center the date on the 16th line below the school name.

CORRECTION DEVICES

Jane Martin
North Central High School

November 15, 19--

Title Page

Improve Basic Skill: Straight Copy

1. Take two 1′ speed writings on each paragraph.

2. Take two 3′ writings on ¶s combined; proofread and circle errors; find *gwam*. Record better score.

3. Take two 5′ writings on ¶s combined; proofread and circle errors; find *gwam*. Record better score.

all letters used | A | 1.5 si | 5.7 awl | 80% hfw

	gwam 3′	5′
In the word-processing area of work, there is now an increasing	4	3	55
demand for persons who can key with speed on their machines. Keyboarded	9	5	58
errors are not as relevant as they were in the past because of the ease	14	8	61
of correction of such errors with the modern electronic equipment now in	19	11	64
use in many modern-day offices. Along with the speed of keyboarding, the	24	14	67
next most relevant factor is good proofreading skill. A keyboard opera-	29	17	70
tor must be able to proofread the copy well and to spot and correct any	33	20	73
errors that were made. Developing good proofreading skill is not very	38	23	75
easy. Proofreading is learned through zealous effort and much practice.	43	26	78
An individual can become a speedy keyboard operator after an ample	47	28	81
amount of practice. The most important element in building speed is	52	31	84
learning to keyboard with requisite technique or good form patterns.	57	34	87
Good form means that the fingers are kept curved over the keys and the	61	37	89
keystroking action is limited to the fingers. The hands and arms should	66	40	92
be kept in a quiet position. An expert operator also should try to learn	71	42	95
to space quickly after each word and to begin the next word without a	76	45	98
pause or stop. To do this, the expert operator learns to read slightly	81	48	101
ahead in the copy while it is being keyed to anticipate just the right	85	51	104
keystroking or response patterns.	88	53	105

gwam 3′ | 1 | 2 | 3 | 4 | 5
5′ | 1 | 2 | 3

Preapplication Drills

Drill 1

Column Headings Longer Than Column Entries

1. If column headings are longer than column entries, first center and key the column headings horizontally (in this drill leave 4 spaces between headings).

2. Then DS, center, and set margin and tab stops for the longest column entry under each heading. Use forward-space, backspace method.

Study Each Word	Pronounce by Syllables	Capitalize Trouble Spots
mathematics	math-e-mat-ics	mathEmatics

Endangered Mammals	Known Distribution
Manatee	Florida

(Drill 2 on next page)

53c ▶ 35
Format a Book Report in Unbound Style

1. Review the formatting guides for unbound reports (page 93).

2. Format the material given at the right as an unbound report. Substitute your name for the one given. Correct any errors you make as you key.

3. Place the reference below the last line of the report.

4. Staple the pages together across the upper left corner or fasten them with a paper clip.

Title of books or magazines may be shown in all-caps or underlined with only the first letter of important words capitalized (for example, LINCOLN or Lincoln).

words

BOOK REVIEW   2
DS

by   3
DS

Kevin Raintree   6
QS

LINCOLN, a historical novel by Gore Vidal, begins as Abraham Lincoln   20
arrives in Washington, D.C., to be inaugurated as the sixteenth President of   35
a disintegrating United States. He arrives in disguise because there has al-   50
ready been talk of a plot to kill him before the swearing-in ceremony to be   66
held in a few weeks. During the next four years there would be many plots   81
to murder this man who had sworn to unite a nation split apart over the con-   96
troversial issue of slavery.   101

Isolated in the White House in a pro-slavery city, Lincoln tries to preside   117
over a divided government. Even some of the members of his own Republi-   131
can Party view him with contempt, call him "Honest Ape," and accuse him in   146
turn of weakness and vacillation and of high-handedness and dictatorship.   161

In this moving historical novel, Lincoln is observed by his loved ones, his   176
rivals, and his future assassins. The result is a view of the man that is at the   193
same time stark and complex as well as intimate and monumental. It is a   207
portrait of the living Lincoln during the war years.   218

Lincoln emerges as seen by his abolitionist spendthrift wife, Mary, who   232
is going mad; by Seward, his Secretary of State, who first scorns and then   247
worships him; by his intense rival, Salmon P. Chase, who would like to be   262
President; by the druggist's clerk who was central to the plot that would   277
eventually take Lincoln's life; and by his young presidential secretary, John   293
Hay, who realizes as the reader will that there would be no nation had there   308
been no Lincoln.   312

Vidal's LINCOLN deals not so much with the Civil War itself as with the   326
people (politicians, influential businessmen, and generals) whose decisions   341
determine the purpose, scope, and execution of war. Viewed from this   355
perspective, Lincoln is seen as a person of both great conviction and indeci-   371
siveness, of both strength and weakness, of both deep sadness and high   385
humor. Thus, the reader comes to know the legendary Lincoln as a fellow   399
human being.   402

REFERENCE   404

Vidal, Gore. Lincoln. New York: Random House, 1984.   416

Learning Goals

1. To improve skill in formatting complex tables.
2. To improve spelling and word-use skills.
3. To increase straight-copy skill.
4. To improve language skills (punctuation).

Machine Adjustments

1. Paper guide at *0*.
2. 70-space line and SS, or as directed.
3. Line-space selector on *1*, or as directed.
4. Paper bail rollers in proper position.

Lesson 106 Complex Table/Language Skills

106a-110a ▶ 5 (daily)
Conditioning Practice

each line 3 times (slowly, faster, in-between rate); as time permits, repeat selected lines

(In each new lesson, try to increase your speed and control.)

alphabet	1	Joan Zadik, who was piqued by Gail's rude manner, left very excitedly.
fig/sym	2	The new pool (19′ wide × 26′ long × 8′ deep) will cost but $14,235.70.
direct reaches	3	Cecil brought a number of bright nylon flags to a big center ceremony.
speed	4	Big profit is born with a busy hand, a key focus, and proficient work.

| 1 | 2 | 3 | 4 | 5 | 6 | 7 | 8 | 9 | 10 | 11 | 12 | 13 | 14 |

106b ▶ 10
Improve Language Skills: Punctuation

full sheet; 1″ top margin; 70-space line

Study/Learn/Apply/Correct Procedures

1. STUDY explanatory rule.

2. Key line number (with period), space twice, and key LEARN sentence(s) DS, noting rule application.

3. Key APPLY sentence(s) DS, making changes needed to correct sentences.

4. As your teacher reads the corrected sentences, show in pen or pencil any corrections that need to be made in your copy.

5. Rekey any APPLY sentence(s) containing an error, CORRECTING the error as you key. Key the corrected sentence in the space below the APPLY sentence containing the error.

APOSTROPHE (continued)

> Use an apostrophe *plus s* to form the plural of most figures, letters, and words (6's, A's, five's). In market quotations, form the plural of figures by the addition of *s only*.

Learn 1. Your f's look like 7's. Boston Fund 4s are due in 2005.
Apply 2. Cross your ts and dot your is. Sell United 6's this week.

> To *show possession,* use an apostrophe *plus s* after a (a) singular noun and (b) a plural noun which does not end in s.

Learn 3. The boy's bicycle was found, but the women's shoes were not.
Apply 4. Childrens toys are on sale; buy the girls bicycle.

> To *show possession,* use an apostrophe *plus s* after a proper name of one syllable that ends in s.

Learn 5. Please pay Jones's bill for $675 today.
Apply 6. Was it Bess' hat, Ross' shoes, or Chris' watch that was lost?

> To *show possession,* use *only* an apostrophe after (a) plural nouns ending in s and (b) a proper name of more than one syllable which ends in s or z.

Learn 7. The girls' counselor will visit the Adams' home.
Apply 8. The ladies handbags were found near Douglas Restaurant.

54a ▶ 7
Conditioning Practice

each line twice SS (slowly, then faster); if time permits, rekey selected lines

alphabet 1 Tex Quinn just received a sizable rebate check from the wagon company.

figures 2 Order 196 was for 38 vests, 72 jackets, 40 skirts, and 25 plaid suits.

ly/ily 3 apt aptly near nearly great greatly true truly busy busily easy easily

speed 4 They shall amend the form to entitle their heir to half of the profit.

| 1 | 2 | 3 | 4 | 5 | 6 | 7 | 8 | 9 | 10 | 11 | 12 | 13 | 14 |

54b ▶ 43
Format an Unbound Report

words

1. Format the copy shown here and on page 100 as an unbound report. Do not correct your errors.

2. Place the reference list on a separate sheet.

3. Prepare a title page.

4. Proofread all pages and mark errors for correction; then prepare a final copy with all errors corrected.

5. Fasten the pages together across the upper left corner.

EDITING FUNCTIONS OF WORD PROCESSORS   7

Few people can sit down at a keyboard or with pen and paper and compose as a first draft a message they are willing to use as the final draft. From first to final draft, a letter or report usually undergoes substantial change: in sequence of ideas, in word choice, in grammar, in punctuation, and in other elements of written expression. This process of revision is called editing (Meroney, 1984, 5). Editing includes finding and marking routine errors (proofreading) but goes much beyond mere error detection and correction. It may, and often does, involve rewriting.   21 36 52 67 82 96 111 123

The author or word originator may do much of the editing and revising (Casady, 1984, 25). Often, however, a secretary or word processor operator assists in editing and revision. When a standard typewriter is used, each draft of a message requires a retyped copy. When electronic equipment is used, the keyboard operator inputs the message only once and makes revisions electronically on the display screen before a paper printout (hard copy) is made. The speed and ease of on-screen corrections reduce time, effort, and cost in the processing of documents that require heavy editing.   137 152 167 182 196 211 225 241

Some terms you will need to know when you edit copy using electronic media are defined below. Each of these describes a function that is easily performed by a computer, a text-editor, or a sophisticated electronic typewriter.   253 269 284 287

Delete. To remove from text a segment of copy (a character, a word, a phrase, a line, a sentence, a page).   302 310

Insert. To add to text a segment of copy (a character, a word, a phrase, a line, a sentence, a page).   326 332

Block move. To move a block of copy (often a sentence or a paragraph) from one location in a document to another.   348 357

Search. To locate an editing or correcting point within a document by matching a series of characters or words.   372 381

Global search and replace. To direct a word processor to find a repeated series of characters and replace it with a different series of characters automatically throughout a document (for example, find and replace Co. with Company).   401 416 431 433

(continued on next page)

Improve Keyboarding: Speed and Control

Use the two sets of paragraphs to increase your skill. Follow the procedure below.

1. Take two 1' speed writings on each of the three ¶s in a set; find *gwam* and circle errors on each writing.

2. Take two 1' control writings on each of the three ¶s in a set. Pace yourself so that you can key for 1' with no more than 2 errors.

3. Take a 5' writing on the three ¶s combined; find *gwam*, circle errors.

all letters used | A | 1.5 si | 5.7 awl | 80% hfw

gwam 1' | 5'

	1'	5'
Knowing that there are sixty seconds in every minute and sixty min-	13	3	49
utes in each hour, we should be able to schedule our activities into the	28	6	52
available time without difficulty. Why, then, do so many people end up	42	8	55
rushing around in a frenzy, trying to meet deadlines? The answer is in	56	11	58
the psychological nature of time. When we are enjoying ourselves, time	71	14	61
seems to fly away; but time spent on tedious jobs seems endless.	85	17	64
Do you ever "goof off" for an hour or more with a television program	14	20	66
or a visit on the telephone and discover later that you haven't actually	28	23	69
enjoyed your leisure? Each nagging little vision of homework or chores	43	26	72
to be completed always seems to result in taking the edge off your plea-	57	28	75
sure. And you still have to complete whatever you postponed -- probably	71	31	78
in a hurry.	74	32	78
If you fit the situation above, don't waste valuable time feeling	13	34	81
guilty; for you have lots of company. What you should feel is cheated --	28	37	84
out of leisure that you didn't enjoy and study time that didn't produce	42	40	87
results. Check with your companions who always seem ready for a good	56	43	90
time but are also ready for unexpected quizzes. The secret is in the	71	46	92
budgeting of your time.	74	47	93

gwam 1' | 1 | 2 | 3 | 4 | 5 | 6 | 7 | 8 | 9 | 10 | 11 | 12 | 13 | 14 |
5' | 1 | 2 | 3 |

all letters used | A | 1.5 si | 5.7 awl | 80% hfw

	1'	5'
Although the path to success is usually lengthy, you can make it	13	3	46
shorter if you will start at the beginning of your business career to	27	5	49
develop two important skills. The first is the ability to see and to	41	8	52
solve problems; the second, the ability to gather facts and arrange them	56	11	55
in logical order, from which you can draw the correct conclusions.	69	14	57
Surely you can recall occasions when you devoted many hours, even	13	16	60
days, to striving unsuccessfully for a goal, and then you happened to see	28	19	63
the difficult problem from a new viewpoint. Perhaps you exclaimed to a	43	22	66
friend or yourself, "Now I see what the problem is!" And once identified,	57	25	69
the problem was easily solved. As you begin work on a project, make your	71	28	72
initial step that of seeing the actual problem.	81	30	73
To solve problems, use all effectual means to get the data that you	14	33	76
will need. Books and magazine articles give facts and expert opinions,	28	36	79
and a request by mail or phone may offer added aid. Enter the data on	42	38	82
cards, divide the cards into logical groups, review the work, and apply	57	41	85
common sense to reach conclusions that the data support.	68	44	87

gwam 1' | 1 | 2 | 3 | 4 | 5 | 6 | 7 | 8 | 9 | 10 | 11 | 12 | 13 | 14 |
5' | 1 | 2 | 3 |

54b (continued)

Electronic machines differ in the assignment and use of code, command, 447
and function keys that must be operated to direct the machine to perform 461
the various editing functions. An operator's manual which gives step-by- 476
step guides is available for each make and model of equipment. 489

REFERENCES 491

Casady, Mona J. Word/Information Processing Concepts. 2d ed. Cincin- 512
nati: South-Western Publishing Co., 1984. 521
Information/Word Processing Glossary. Willow Grove, PA: International 543
Information/Word Processing Association, 1982. 552
Meroney, John W. Word Processing Applications in Practice. Cincinnati: 575
South-Western Publishing Co., 1984. 582

Remember to DS between references.

Lesson 55	**Report from Rough Draft**

55a ▶ 7
Conditioning Practice

each line twice SS (slowly, then faster); if time permits, rekey selected lines

alphabet	1	The jazz performer quickly ate six large bologna sandwiches every day.
figures	2	Of 1,302 persons who took the test in 1987, 856 passed and 446 failed.
r/er	3	use user give giver drive driver help helper sing singer great greater
speed	4	Cy may be the right man to blame for the big fight in the penalty box.

| 1 | 2 | 3 | 4 | 5 | 6 | 7 | 8 | 9 | 10 | 11 | 12 | 13 | 14 |

55b ▶ 43

Format an Unbound Report from Rough Draft

1. Format the copy shown here and on page 101 as an unbound report, making all corrections marked in the copy and correcting any errors you make as you key.
2. Place the reference list on a separate sheet.
3. Prepare a title page.
4. When the work is completed, proofread again, correct any remaining errors, and fasten the pages together across the upper left corner.

Proofreader's Marks

∧	insert
⌃	insert comma
#	space
∿	transpose
⌐	move right
◡	close up
≡	capitalize

words

Planning and Preparing Reports) ALL CAPS 6

Whether written for personal or business use, Qs
∧A report should present a message that is well organized, 27

stated simply, and clear in meaning (Burtness, 1985, 392). A 42
and Hulbert

report that does not meet these criterion ~~shows~~ *reflects a* lack of care 55

in planning and preparation. # The following suggestions will 67
to *so* *and concise*

help you∧ plan and prepare reports that are∧ clear∧ that the 82

reader will not have ⟨to⟩ puzzle over ~~them.~~ *their intended meaning.* 94

Planning a Report 101
taken

Three steps should be ~~used~~ in planning a report. Selecting 114
important

the topic is not merely the first step but also the most∧ ~~vital~~ 127
topic

one. It is vital that you chose a ~~subject~~ in which you have 139
related

suficient interest to do the necessary∧ reading and research. 153

Next, it is essential that you limit the topic so that you 165
treat

can ~~handle~~ the subject adequately with◡in the space and time 177

(continued on next page)

100

105b (continued)

Problem 2
3-Column Table

half sheet, long edge at top; SS 2-line items in Col. 1, indenting second line 3 spaces; DS between items; 8 spaces between columns; SS source lines

Reminder: Col. 1 heading is started a DS below secondary heading.

{ } = parentheses
¬ = comma

words

RACIAL AND ETHNIC MINORITIES IN U.S.A. IN 1980 — 9

{Percent of Total population} — 15

Group	Number	%	
			21
Blacks	26,487,000	11.7	25
Hispanics	14,606,000	6.5	30
Asians and			33
Pacific Islands	3,501,000	1.5	39
Indians, Eskimos,			43
Aleuts	1,418,000	0.6	47
			51

Source: Bureau of Census, _Supplementary Reports_, — 66
May 1981. — 68

105c ▶ 10
Improve Language Skills: Punctuation

full sheet; 1″ top margin; 70-space line

Key as directed in 103c, p. 182.

SEMICOLON (continued)

Use a semicolon to separate a series of phrases or clauses (especially if they contain commas) that are introduced by a colon.

Learn 1. These are the sales figures: 1987, $5,678,342; 1988, $6,789,020.
Apply 2. The new officers are: Dee O'Brien, President Jay Ford, Secretary.

Place the semicolon _outside_ the closing quotation mark; the period, _inside_ the quotation mark.

Learn 3. Mrs. Jane spoke on "Building Speed"; Mr. Paul, on "Accuracy."
Apply 4. He said, "Don't use sarcasm;" she said, "I'll try".

APOSTROPHE

Use an apostrophe as a _symbol_ for _feet_ in billings or tabulations, or as a _symbol_ for _minutes_. (The quotation mark may be used as a _symbol_ for _inches_ or _seconds_.)

Learn 5 Please deliver ten 2″ × 4″ × 10′ pine boards to my address.
Apply 6. He ran the mile in 3 min. 54 sec. The room is 12 ft. 6 in. × 18 ft.

Use an apostrophe as a symbol to indicate the omission of letters or figures (as in contractions).

Learn 7. Each July 4th, we try to renew the "Spirit of '76."
Apply 8. Use the apostrophe in these contractions: isnt, cant, youll.

limitations*that have been set*.   Finally, you should decide*upon* and list in logical   194

outline
form the major ideas and the subordinate ~~ideas~~ *points* for each idea   208

that you want to use as support (Gonzalez et al., 1981, 499-   220

518).   221

Preparing the report   229

Three steps should be followed in preparing the report*, also.*   242
The first of these is to look for ~~information~~ *data and authoritative statements* to support your   259

prepare
ideas. ~~you want to express.~~ The next step is to ~~write~~ a rough   268
of the report
draft*, *organizing the data in* to *a series of related paragraphs,   283

each with a topic sentence to announce its major theme. The   295
carefully
last step is to read the rough draft*for sequence of ideas,   309
re
clarity*, and accuracy and to prepa~~ir~~ the final draft in correct   322
c
form with all errors corrected. In checking for ac*uracy, be   335

certain that   337

DS {
1. all words are spel*l*ed correctly;   345
2. punctuation rules have been correctly applied;   355
3. proper spacing follows each punctuation mark;*applied*   365
4. capitalization rules have been correctly ~~used;~~   376
5. all numbers are accurate; and   382
6. number expression rules have been correctly applied.   394

Whether the report is typed or printed*, it should be neat   406
format
and arranged in proper*~~style~~. A neat report presented in an   418
m   positive
orderly style makes an im*ediate*impression on the reader.   431

REFERENCES   2

Burtness, Paul S., and Jack E. Hulbert. _Effective_   14
Business Communication. 8th ed. Cincinnati: 28
South-Western Publishing Co., 1985.   35
Gonzalez, Roseann, Ruby Herlong, Mary Hynes-Berry,   45
and Paul Pesce. _Language: Structure and Use_.   61
Glenview, IL: Scott, Foresman and Company,   69
1981.   70

104c ▶ 10
Improve Language Skills: Punctuation

full sheet; 1″ top margin; 70-space line

Key as directed in 103c, p. 182.

QUOTATION MARKS (continued)

Use quotation marks to enclose special words or phrases used for emphasis, or for coined words (words not in dictionary usage).

Learn 1. My problem is that I have "limited resources" and "unlimited wants."
Apply 2. His speech was liberally sprinkled with you knows.

Use a single quotation mark (the apostrophe) to indicate a quotation within a quotation.

Learn 3. She said, "We must take, as Frost suggests, the 'different road.' "
Apply 4. I wrote, "We must have, as Tillich said, the courage to be."

SEMICOLON

Use a semicolon to separate two or more independent clauses in a compound sentence when the conjunction is omitted.

Learn 5. To be critical is easy; to be constructive is not so easy.
Apply 6. We cannot live on past glory we must strive to improve.

Use a semicolon to separate independent clauses when they are joined by a conjunctive adverb (however, consequently, etc.).

Learn 7. You exceeded the speed limit; consequently, you were stopped.
Apply 8. I cannot help you however, I know someone who can.

| Lesson 105 | Simple Table/Language Skills |

105a ▶ 5
Conditioning Practice

each line 3 times (slowly, faster, in-between rate); as time permits, repeat selected lines

alphabet 1 The kind queen received extra jewels from a dozen brave young pirates.
fig/sym 2 The #5346 item will cost McNeil & Company $921.78 (less 10% for cash).
adjacent key 3 Did Bert Werty say he would join Robert or Lasiter before he departed?
speed 4 Eighty of the men may work for the island firms if they make a profit.

| 1 | 2 | 3 | 4 | 5 | 6 | 7 | 8 | 9 | 10 | 11 | 12 | 13 | 14 |

105b ▶ 35
Problem Solving: Table Formatting

Problem 1
2-Column Table

half sheet, long edge at top; DS data; 6 spaces between columns

Alertness cue: Space forward twice after height Items 1, 2, 4, and 5 in Column 1.

(Problem 2 on next page)

		words
NORMAL WEIGHT RANGE		4
Men	Women	8
5′6″ = 142 lbs.	5′0″ = 100 lbs.	14
5′8″ = 154 lbs.	5′2″ = 110 lbs.	21
5′10″ = 166 lbs.	5′4″ = 120 lbs.	27
6′0″ = 178 lbs.	5′6″ = 130 lbs.	34
6′2″ = 190 lbs.	5′8″ = 140 lbs.	40

56a ▶ 7
Conditioning Practice

each line twice SS (slowly, then faster); if time permits, rekey selected lines

alphabet 1 Jacintha expects my crazy quilt to fit nicely on Geneva's new oak bed.

figures 2 The data are given in Figures 26 and 27 of Part 14, Unit 39, page 508.

n/en 3 ox oxen take taken drive driven prove proven less lessen sharp sharpen

speed 4 Did the eight sorority girls clap with vigor for the city bugle corps?

| 1 | 2 | 3 | 4 | 5 | 6 | 7 | 8 | 9 | 10 | 11 | 12 | 13 | 14 |

56b ▶ 8
Check Keyboarding Skill: Straight Copy

1. A 1' writing on ¶ 1, then on ¶ 2; find *gwam* on each writing.

2. A 2' writing on ¶s 1-2 combined; find *gwam*.

3. A 3' writing on ¶s 1-2 combined; find *gwam*.

all letters used | A | 1.5 si | 5.7 awl | 80% hfw   *gwam* 2' | 3'

A great many people alibi that if they could only stop the clock   7 | 4

or hold the hands of time, they could accomplish whatever they desire   14 | 9

to do. Unfortunately, time marches on whether human beings do or not.   21 | 14

The question therefore becomes not how can we acquire more time for   28 | 18

ourselves, but how can we utilize more productively the time allotted   35 | 23

us. Learning to use time wisely is a major step toward success.   41 | 27

Time is a constant, for everyone has an equal amount of it. How   47 | 32

we use time, however, is a critical variable in the equation of ex-   54 | 36

cellence. Thinking requires time, of course; but we can conserve our   61 | 41

time by taking time to plan before beginning our work. The likelihood   68 | 45

of having to do work over is decreased by thinking through all related   75 | 50

problems and planning the project before starting work.   81 | 54

gwam 2' | 1 | 2 | 3 | 4 | 5 | 6 | 7 |
3' | 1 | 2 | 3 | 4 | 5 |

56c ▶ 35
Prepare for Measurement

3 plain full sheets; correction supplies

List on a slip of paper the page numbers and lesson parts given below:

p. 95, 51d
pp. 95-97, 52b

1. Format the outline of 51d as directed there. Correct any errors you make as you key the copy. (See the model in 51c if you need help.)

2. Format and key the report shown as a model on pages 96 and 97. Correct any errors you make as you key. If time permits, format a title page for the report.

104a ▶ 5
Conditioning Practice

each line 3 times (slowly, faster, in-between rate); as time permits, repeat selected lines

alphabet	1	Fools won't likely adopt the unique economizing objectives of experts.
fig/sym	2	Here are the prices: #300/1200, $455; #3878, $695; and #515/20, $159.
long words	3	Systems engineers had complete responsibility in space communications.
speed	4	Vivian may sign the amendment form if they do their work for the city.

| 1 | 2 | 3 | 4 | 5 | 6 | 7 | 8 | 9 | 10 | 11 | 12 | 13 | 14 |

104b ▶ 35
Problem Solving: Table Formatting

Problem 1
Table with Centered Column Headings

full sheet; DS data; 8 spaces between columns; center headings over columns

Column Heading Centering Formula: Forward space 1 for 2 in longest column line; backspace 1 for 2 in heading to be centered.

words

SOME ENDANGERED SPECIES	5

Common Name	Location	
Bald eagle	USA	16
Black-footed ferret	Western USA	22
Blue whale	Pacific Ocean	27
California condor	California	33
Dusky seaside sparrow	Florida	39
Gray wolf	Northern USA	44
Ivory-billed woodpecker	USA	49
Kirtland's warbler	Eastern USA	55
Manatee	Florida	59
Whooping crane	Canada, USA	64

67

Source: U.S. Department of Interior, Washington, DC.   77 / 78

Problem 2
Table with Centered Column Headings

full sheet; DS data; 8 spaces between columns; center column headings

Problem 3
Build Skill

As time permits, repeat Problem 2, half sheet, long edge at top; 6 spaces between columns; SS data; block column headings. **Note:** For Problems 2 and 3, DS between source notes.

WORLD'S LARGEST METROPOLITAN AREAS	7
(In Descending Order)	11

1900	1950	2000*	
London	New York	Mexico City	23
New York	London	Sao Paulo	28
Paris	Tokyo	Tokyo	31
Berlin	Paris	New York	36
Chicago	Shanghai	Shanghai	41
Vienna	Chicago	Peking	45
Tokyo	Los Angeles	Rio de Janeiro	52
Leningrad	Berlin	Bombay	57
Philadelphia	Moscow	Calcutta	63
Manchester	Philadelphia	Jakarta	69

73

Source: World Almanac.   78

*Projected data: The Christian Science Monitor, August 7, 1984, p. 19.   95 / 98

57a ▶ 7
Conditioning Practice
each line twice SS (slowly, then faster), if time permits, rekey selected lines

alphabet 1 Quin just got a dark pink vase from his uncle for my next lawn bazaar.

figures 2 Our group read 45 plays, 178 books, and 203 articles during 1986-1987.

ion 3 act action opt option except exception digest digestion elect election

speed 4 Guthrie may wish to dismantle the antique chair for the busy neighbor.

| 1 | 2 | 3 | 4 | 5 | 6 | 7 | 8 | 9 | 10 | 11 | 12 | 13 | 14 |

57b ▶ 33
Check Formatting Skill: Report
2 plain full sheets; correction supplies

Format and key the report in unbound style. SS the listed items and indent them 5 spaces from the left margin only; DS between items. Format the reference list on a separate sheet. Correct any errors you make as you key.

words

WORD PROCESSING TRAINING   5

Office support personnel must have superior keyboarding skill in order   19
to work with confidence and efficiency. They must use that skill with profi-   35
ciency in processing a wide assortment of business papers and technical   49
documents. These abilities are required of employees who work in face-to-   64
face settings with executives or with supervisors in word processing centers   79
(Beaumont, 1981, 7).   84

In addition to keyboarding skill and formatting knowledge, good work   97
habits are essential. Office support personnel must organize, plan, and   112
complete their job tasks efficiently. They must edit source documents from   127
which they work as well as proofread and correct the copy (output) they   142
produce. They must perform all these tasks with minimal direction and   156
supervision.   159

A keyboarding, formatting, and document processing course, therefore,   172
has several purposes. Those listed below are among the most important.   187

1. Help students reach the keyboarding speeds most often required for   201
   employment: 40, 50, 60, and 70 words a minute (Occupational Outlook   219
   Handbook, 1980-81, 95).   226

2. Help students learn and apply the formatting guides and procedures   240
   for processing a variety of documents.   248

3. Familiarize students with word processing functions and procedures   262
   that are performed on electronic equipment in the modern office   275
   (Occupational Projections and Training Data, 1984, 46-48).   295

4. Ease the transition from school to office by providing students with   310
   sets of simulated office job tasks that closely reflect the real world   324
   of work.   326

REFERENCES   328

Beaumont, L. R. "Typing vs. Keyboarding -- Is There a Difference?"   341
    Century 21 Reporter, Spring 1981.   352
Occupational Outlook Handbook. 1980-81 ed. Washington, DC: Bureau of   372
    Labor Statistics.   376
Occupational Projections and Training Data. 1984 ed. Washington, DC: 398
    Bureau of Labor Statistics.   404

103b (continued)

Problem 3
2-Column Table

half sheet, long edge at top; DS data; 12 spaces between columns

Alertness cue: Reset tab stop for Column 2 as needed; or, remember to space forward.

Problem 4
Build Skill

Repeat Problem 3 on half sheet, short edge at top; DS data; 6 spaces between columns.

Note. When % signs or $ signs appear in the body of a table, they are keyed in the intercolumns; therefore, do not count them as parts of columns.

		words
SUGAR CONTENT OF SELECTED FOODS		6
(Mean percentage of sugar)		12
Life-savers mints (assorted)	68.6%	18
Chocolate (plain)	56.0	23
Chocolate creme cookies and	40.2	30
Dry cereals breakfast	25.1	35
Icecream products	15.1	40
Soft drinks	4.3	43
Canned juices	2.5	47
		51
Source: Newburn, E. Cardiology, 2d ed.		59

103c ▶ 10
Improve Language Skills: Punctuation

full sheet; 1″ top margin; 70-space line

1. STUDY explanatory rule.

2. Key line number (with period); space twice, and then key the LEARN sentence(s) DS, noting rule application.

3. Key the line number (with period); space twice, then key the APPLY sentence(s) DS, making changes needed to correct each sentence.

4. As your teacher reads the correct sentence(s), show in pen or pencil any corrections that need to be made in your copy.

5. Rekey any APPLY sentence containing an error, CORRECTING the error as you key. Place the corrected sentence(s) in the space below the APPLY sentence containing the error.

UNDERLINE

Use an underline to indicate titles of books and names of magazines and newspapers. (Titles may be keyed in ALL CAPS without the underline.)

Learn   1. The book Learning How to Think was condensed in Reader's Digest.
Apply   2. I read the review of Any Child Can Write in the Los Angeles Times.

Use an underline to call attention to special words or phrases (or use quotation marks). **Note:** Use a continuous underline (see preceding rule) unless each word is to be considered separately, as shown below.

Learn   3. She asked us to spell separate, privilege, and stationery.
Apply   4. He misspelled supersede, concede, and proceed.

QUOTATION MARKS

Use quotation marks to enclose direct quotations. **Note:** When a question mark applies to the entire sentence, it is typed outside the quotation marks.

Learn   5. The teacher asked, "Did you do your homework?"
Learn   6. Was it Emerson who said, "To have a friend is to be one"?
Apply   7. He quoted Zinsser, Writing is the logical arrangement of thought.
Apply   8. Did Shakespeare say, All the world is a stage?

Use quotation marks to enclose titles of articles, poems, songs, television programs, and unpublished works like dissertations and theses.

Learn   9. Please read the poem "The Road Not Taken" by Robert Frost.
Apply   10. They enjoyed watching the TV series Dallas.

57c ▸ 10
Check Formatting Skill: Outline

1 plain full sheet; correction supplies

Using the same top and side margins as for an unbound report, format and key the outline shown in rough draft at the right. Correct any errors you make as you key.

Computer printers often print copy with distinctive punctuation marks. Study the charts of computer punctuation marks below before you key the copy.

	typewriter	computer
ampersand	&	&
comma	,	ˑ
parentheses	( )	{ }
question mark	?	?
quotation marks	"	″
semicolon	;	ˑ

If time permits at the end of the class period, take another 3′ timed writing on the ¶s of 56b, p. 102; find *gwam*, circle errors.

COMPOSING
WRITING EFFECTIVE MESSAGES

I. PLAN THE MESSAGE
   A. Determine the Main Purpose and Gist of the Message (Presented
   B. Select All the Pertinent Ideas and Data to Be) Used
   C. Keep the Reader in Mind as You Plan (the Audience)

II. ORGANIZE THE MESSAGE
   A. Decide on the Order of Ideas and Data to Be Presented
      1. List in logical order the major points to make
      2. Jot down pertinent facts under each point
      3. Develop each major idea into a paragraph SS
   B. Present each Main Point Clearly and Concisely
      1. Use simple language; avoid "jargon" words
      2. Use short sentences for simplicity and clarity
      3. Avoid long and involved paragraphs

III. REVISE, REFINE, AND PREPARE AN ERROR-FREE COPY OF THE MESSAGE

ENRICHMENT ACTIVITY: Language Skills

Divide Words at Acceptable Points

full sheet; 70-space line; begin on line 10; DS

1. Clear all tab stops.

2. From left margin, set 3 new tab stops as indicated by the key beneath the copy.

3. Key the first word in Column 1; tab to Column 2 and rekey the word, showing by a hyphen where it may be acceptably divided.

4. Key the first word in Column 3; tab to Column 4 and rekey the word, showing by a hyphen where it may be acceptably divided.

5. Key all other words in the same manner.

ACCEPTABLE WORD DIVISION POINTS

specialist		wraparound	
technique		acceptable	
readily		condition	
computer		printout	
processor		automated	
electronic		delete	
insert		text-editor	
ergonomic		processing	
formatting	for-mat-ting	keyboarding	key-board-ing

KEY | 10 | 8 | 12 | 8 | 11 | 8 | 13 |

Improve Language Skills: Composition

70-space line; SS sentences; DS between sentences; full sheet

From the list of words given in Problem 3, p. 180, use as many as you can in complete sen- tences. If you can use two or more homonyms in the same sentence, do so, as in the example given below.

Example: He remained in a stationary position as he distributed the stationery.

Lesson 103 | Simple Table/Language Skills

103a ▶ 5

Conditioning Practice

each line 3 times (slowly, faster, in-between rate); as time permits, repeat selected lines

alphabet	1	After a wild jump ball, the guards very quickly executed a zone press.
fig/sym	2	The 0-384 MC costs $196.75, and the 300/1200 Baud modem costs $265.89.
shift key	3	Ryan read the articles "Fatigue," "How to Relax," and "Saving Energy."
speed	4	A big firm kept half of the men busy with their work down by the lake.

| 1 | 2 | 3 | 4 | 5 | 6 | 7 | 8 | 9 | 10 | 11 | 12 | 13 | 14 |

103b ▶ 35

Problem Solving: Table Formatting

Problem 1
2-Column Table

full sheet; DS data except where more than one title is given with a name; SS such titles with a DS above and below the group of ti- tles; 16 spaces between columns; space forward twice after each pe- riod given with each number; cen- ter column headings over columns

Learning cue: To center column headings shorter than column en- tries follow these steps:

1. Determine placement of col- umns in usual way.

2. From column starting point, space forward once for each two strokes in longest entry. From this point, backspace once for each 2 strokes in column heading.

3. Keyboard and underline col- umn heading.

Problem 2
Build Skill

Repeat Problem 1 with 8 spaces between columns.

	words
IMPORTANT READINGS FOR THE HUMANITIES	8
(Ranked in Order of Importance)	14

Name	Title	
1. Shakespeare	Macbeth; Hamlet	18 / 24
2. American Historical Documents	Declaration of Independence	34
	Constitution	39
	Gettysburg Address	43
3. Twain	Huckleberry Finn	48
4. Bible	Old and New Testaments	55
5. Homer	Odyssey; Illiad	60
6. Dickens	Great Expectations	66
	A Tale of Two Cities	70
7. Plato	The Republic	75
8. Steinbeck	Grapes of Wrath	81
9. Hawthorne	The Scarlet Letter	88
10. Sophocles	Oedipus	92
11. Melville	Moby Dick	97
12. Orwell	1984	102
13. Thoreau	Walden	106
14. Frost	Collected Poems	112
15. Whitman	Leaves of Grass	117
		121

Source: National Endowment for the Humanities, Washington, DC, 1984.

	134
	135

Unit 10 Lessons 58-64

Learning Goals

1. To learn to format and center 2- and 3-column tables.

2. To improve keyboarding skill on copy containing figures and symbols.

3. To learn to align figures at the right.

4. To improve keyboarding skill on straight copy.

Machine Adjustments

1. Paper guide at *0*.

2. Ribbon control set to use top half of ribbon.

3. Margin sets: 70-space line (center − 35; center + 35 + 5) unless otherwise directed.

4. Line-space selector to SS drills, DS ¶s; as directed for problems.

FORMATTING GUIDES: TABLES

Parts of a Simple Table

Table information is arranged in rows and columns for convenience of reader reference. Tables range in complexity from those with only two columns and a main heading to those of several columns with main, secondary, and column headings; totals; source notes; leaders; and rulings. The tables in this unit are limited to the following parts:

1. main heading (title) in ALL CAPS
2. secondary heading in capital and lowercase letters
3. blocked column headings
4. body (column entries)
5. source note

The first tables you will format consist of only a main heading and two columns of data. The tables progress gradually in complexity so that, finally, they will include three columns and all five of the listed parts.

Spacing Table Parts

Short, simple tables are usually double-spaced (DS) throughout. Double spacing between all parts of a table simplifies the processing of tables on typewriters and, especially, on microcomputers which require the use of special commands to change the spacing within a document.

Horizontal/Vertical Placement of Tables

Tables are placed on the page so that the left and right margins are approximately equal (about half the characters in each line at the left of horizontal center; about half, at the right).

When prepared on separate sheets, tables are placed so that the top and bottom margins are approximately equal (about half the lines above center; about half below). Tables that are placed slightly above exact center (sometimes called "reading position") are considered to look more appealing than those placed at or below exact center.

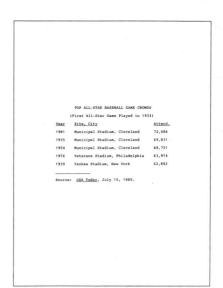

TENNIS CLUB OFFICERS

Joe Chung	President
Laurel Banks	Vice President
Juan Gomez	Treasurer
Sofia Wilkes	Secretary
Mark Devlin	Reporter

WEAKNESSES OF WORD PROCESSING WORKERS
(Reported as % of Responding Supervisors)

Inadequate Language Skills	45
Poor Spelling	39
Inadequate Vocabulary	39
Lack of Experience on WP Equipment	33
Inadequate Keyboarding Skills	27

TOP ALL-STAR BASEBALL GAME CROWDS
(First All-Star Game Played in 1933)

Year	Site, City	Attend.
1981	Municipal Stadium, Cleveland	72,086
1935	Municipal Stadium, Cleveland	69,831
1954	Municipal Stadium, Cleveland	68,751
1976	Veterans Stadium, Philadelphia	63,974
1939	Yankee Stadium, New York	62,892

Source: *USA Today*, July 15, 1985.

102a ▶ 5
Conditioning Practice

each line 3 times (slowly, faster, in-between rate); as time permits, repeat selected lines

alphabet	1	Will Jim realize that excellent skill develops by refining techniques?
figure	2	Just call 1-800-645-3729 for complete information on software systems.
one hand	3	Only after I stated my adverse opinion were better grades agreed upon.
speed	4	If they do the work for the city and me, he may spend the day with me.

| 1 | 2 | 3 | 4 | 5 | 6 | 7 | 8 | 9 | 10 | 11 | 12 | 13 | 14 |

102b ▶ 30
Problem Solving: Table Formatting

Problem 1
2-Column Table

full sheet; DS data; 16 spaces between columns

Learning recall: length of dividing line.

Learning cue: Reset tab stop for Column 2 after keying Item 2.

Problem 2
Build Skill

Repeat Problem 1 on half sheet, short edge at top; SS data; 10 spaces between columns.

Learning cue: Remember to DS above and below divider line even though the body is single-spaced.

Problem 3
2-Column Table

full sheet; DS data; center vertically and horizontally; 20 spaces between columns

Note. Save problem to use in 102c, p. 181.

words

LEADING CAUSES OF DEATH — 5

(Approximate Percent of Total Deaths) — 12

		words
Heart disease	49.6	16
Cancer	29.9	19
Stroke	8.6	21
Accidents	5.3	24
Pulmonary disease	2.8	28
Pneumonia and influenza	2.6	34
Diabetes	1.7	37
Liver disease	1.6	40
Atherosclerosis	1.5	44
Suicide	1.3	47

_____ — 50

Source: Vital Statistics. — 56

WORDS WITH SIMILAR PRONUNCIATION — 7

BUT DIFFERENT MEANINGS (HOMONYMS) — 14

		words
stationary	stationery	18
their	there	20
blue	blew	22
whether	weather	26
would	wood	28
do	due; dew	30
deer	dear	32
sight	cite; site	36
advice	advise	38
farther	further	42
lose	loose	44
principal	principle	48
real	reel	50
two	to; too	52

58a ▶ 7
Conditioning Practice

each line twice SS (slowly, then faster); if time permits, rekey lines 2 and 4

alphabet 1 Mack just questioned the five zoologists about the extra fawn display.

figures 2 We have stores at 396 Hogan Lane, 802 Petri Court, and 4175 Taft Road.

fig/sym 3 There was a credit on 8/19 for $487.23 and a debit on 9/5 for $360.82.

speed 4 Audit the work forms and then pay the six girls for the work they did.

| 1 | 2 | 3 | 4 | 5 | 6 | 7 | 8 | 9 | 10 | 11 | 12 | 13 | 14 |

58b ▶ 8
Review/Improve Use of Backspacer and Tabulator

1. On a plain sheet, center each of lines 1-3 horizontally.

2. For lines 4-6, beginning at the left margin set 3 tab stops according to the key beneath the lines. Key the lines, tabbing from column to column.

Backspacer

1   Find center point of paper;

2   backspace once for each two strokes in line;

3   begin keyboarding where backspacing ends.

Tabulator

4 to do so	Tab	work with us	Tab	all the firms	Tab	make them pay
5 to go to		she may sign		sign the form		kept the form
6 if he is		go with them		they work for		they may lend

KEY | 8 | 8 | 12 | 8 | 13 | 8 | 13 |

58c ▶ 35
Learn to Format a Simple Two-Column Table

half sheet (long edge at top) horizontal center points: elite, 51; pica, 42

1. Study the guides for vertical and horizontal centering given at the right.

2. Using the model table on page 107, set left margin to begin Column 1; set a tab stop for Column 2, leaving 14 spaces between columns.

3. Determine the line on which to place the heading of the double-spaced table. If an odd number results, use next lower even number to raise the table to visual center.

4. Format and key the model table.

5. Proofread and check your completed table, mark it for correction, and prepare a final copy with all errors corrected.

Vertical Centering Steps

1. Count the lines to be keyed and the blank line spaces to be left between them (1 blank line space between double-spaced lines).

2. Subtract *lines needed* from *total lines available* (33 on a half sheet; 66 on a full sheet).

3. Divide remainder by 2 to determine top margin. If the number that results ends in a fraction, drop the fraction. *If an odd number results, use the next lower even number.*

4. From top edge of paper, space down once for each line determined in Step 3 and key the main heading.

Example: lines available = 33
total lines needed = 12
$$\overline{21} \div 2 = 10\frac{1}{2}$$
place heading on line 10

Horizontal Centering of Columns

1. Move margin stops to ends of scale.

2. Clear all tabulator stops.

3. Move printing point to horizontal center point of paper.

4. Decide spacing between columns (if spacing is not specified) -- preferably an even number of spaces (4, 6, 8, 10, 12, 14, etc.).

5. Set left margin stop:

a. From center of paper, backspace once for each 2 characters and spaces in longest line of each column, then once for each 2 spaces to be left between columns. If the longest line in one column has an extra letter or number, combine that letter or number with the first letter or number in the next column when backspacing by 2s, as in check####proofread.

◄ 1 1 1 1 1 1 1 1 1
ch|ec|kp|ro|of|re|ad|##|##

If you have 1 stroke left over after backspacing for all columnar items, disregard it.

b. Set the left margin at the point where all backspacing ends.

6. Set tabulator stops:

a. From the left margin, space forward once for each character and space in longest line in the first column and once for each space to be left between first and second columns.

b. Set tab stop at this point for second column.

c. When there is a third column, continue spacing forward in the same way to set a tab stop for it.

101c ▶ 15
Check Learning: Composition

full sheet; 1″ top, side, and bottom margins

Compose complete sentence answers to the questions listed here. If necessary, refer to the *Table Formatting Guides* on page 177 and 178.

Number your answers as you keyboard them. SS the lines of each answer; DS between answers. X-out or strike over any keyboarding errors you make as you compose.

1. How many line spaces are available on a full sheet (8 1/2″ × 11″)?

2. How many line spaces are available on a half sheet with the long edge at top?

3. How many line spaces are available on a half sheet with the short edge at top?

4. What governs the number of spaces to be left between columns?

5. In your own words, give the steps to follow to determine the vertical placement of a table.

6. In your own words, give the steps to follow in using the backspace-from-center method to determine the horizontal placement of columns.

7. When column entries are double-spaced and a source note ruling is used, how many blank line spaces are left above and below the ruling?

8. How do you find the horizontal center of a sheet of any size?

101d ▶ 10
Improve Language Skills: Punctuation

full sheet; 1″ top margin; 70-space line

Study/Learn/Apply/Correct Procedures

1. STUDY explanatory rule.

2. Key line number (with period); space twice, and key LEARN sentence(s) DS, noting rule application.

3. Key APPLY sentence(s) DS, placing parentheses around the proper words or numbers to make the sentence(s) correct.

4. As your teacher reads the correct sentences, show in pen or pencil any corrections that need to be made in your copy.

5. Rekey any APPLY sentence containing an error, CORRECTING the error as you keyboard. Key the corrected sentence in the space below the APPLY sentence containing the error.

PARENTHESES

Use parentheses to enclose parenthetical or explanatory matter and added information. (Commas or dashes also may be used.)

Learn   1. Enclosed are the contracts (Exhibits A and B).

Apply   2. Nichols' memoirs published by Delta Pi Epsilon are interesting.

Use parentheses to enclose identifying letters or figures in lists.

Learn   3. Check these techniques: (1) keystroking and (2) spacing.

Apply   4. She emphasized two key factors: 1 speed and 2 control.

Use parentheses to enclose figures that follow spelled-out amounts when added clarity or emphasis is needed.

Learn   5. The balance due on the note is five hundred dollars ($500).

Apply   6. I bequeath to my son the sum of five thousand dollars $5,000.

Use parentheses to enclose a name and date used as a reference.

Learn   7. Learning stamps you with its moments (Welty, 1984).

Apply   8. In writing, no rules prevail except to avoid monotony Lanham, 1979.

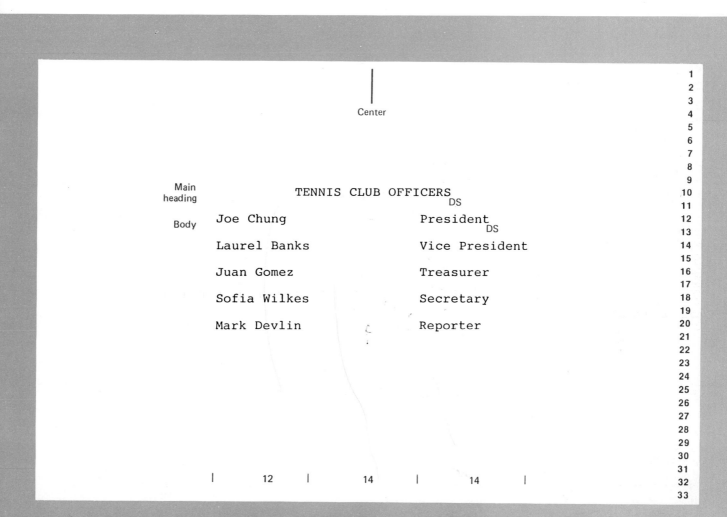

		1
		2
		3
	Center	4
		5
		6
		7
		8
		9
Main heading	TENNIS CLUB OFFICERS DS	10
		11
Body	Joe Chung President DS	12
		13
	Laurel Banks Vice President	14
		15
	Juan Gomez Treasurer	16
		17
	Sofia Wilkes Secretary	18
		19
	Mark Devlin Reporter	20
		21
		22
		23
		24
		25
		26
		27
		28
		29
		30
	12 14 14	31
		32
		33

Two-Column Table Centered Vertically and Horizontally

Lesson 59 — Simple Two-Column Tables

59a ▶ 7
Conditioning Practice

each line twice SS (slowly, then faster); if time permits, rekey lines 2 and 4

alphabet	1	Ray expected a quick quiz on the five women's boring journal articles.
figures	2	On April 6 you ordered 5 TABCO filing cabinets: 2 HC-7850; 3 VC-9146.
s/es/ies	3	age ages win wins run runs go goes reach reaches cry cries rely relies
speed	4	The duty of the auditor is to sign the usual audit forms for the city.

| 1 | 2 | 3 | 4 | 5 | 6 | 7 | 8 | 9 | 10 | 11 | 12 | 13 | 14 |

59b ▶ 8
Review Procedures for Vertical/Horizontal Centering

half sheet; DS

Using the model table above, see how quickly you can make needed machine adjustments and key the copy.

1. Review formatting guides on page 106 if necessary.
2. Double-space all lines.
3. Leave 12 spaces between columns.

4. Check your work for proper placement. Did you place the main heading on line 10? Are left and right margins approximately equal?

101a ▶ 5
Conditioning Practice
each line 3 times (slowly, faster, in-between rate); as time permits, repeat selected lines

alphabet 1 Baryshnikov freely executed with ease the amazingly quick dance jumps.

fig/sym 2 Order 4 color #710 monitors, 6 IBM-POs, 89 Lotus 1-2-3s, and 5 modems.

rhythm 3 Please make the address corrections on all the old computer printouts.

speed 4 The right goal is to work for proficiency when a key problem turns up.

| 1 | 2 | 3 | 4 | 5 | 6 | 7 | 8 | 9 | 10 | 11 | 12 | 13 | 14 |

101b ▶ 20
Problem Solving: Table Formatting

Check solutions with placement cues given below problems.

Problem 1
3-Column Table
full sheet; DS data; 6 spaces between columns; dividing line, 1 1/2"

Problem 2
Build Skill
Repeat Problem 1 on half sheet, long edge at top; DS data; 6 spaces between columns.

Problem 3
Build Skill
Repeat Problem 1 on half sheet; short edge at top; DS data; 4 spaces between columns.

Learning cue: To find horizontal center of half sheet with short edge at top: Add scale reading at left edge of sheet to scale reading at right edge of sheet and divide by 2.

lines used

				words
1	WORDS FREQUENTLY MISSPELLED			6
2				
3	occurrence	permissible	privilege	12
4				
5	conscientious	acknowledgment	conscious	20
6				
7	supersede	questionnaire	precede	26
8				
9	consensus	category	restaurant	32
10				
11	accommodate	maintenance	benefited	39
12				
13		DS		43
14		DS		
15	Source: Shell and Schmidt, DPE JOURNAL, 1984.			52

Vertical Placement of Table

Formula: $\dfrac{\text{lines available} - \text{lines used}}{2} = X$ if X has a fraction, drop it; if X (the resulting number) is: EVEN, space down that number; ODD, use next lower even number.

Full sheet

$\dfrac{66 - 15}{2} = 25.5$ (Begin on line 24.)

Half sheet (long edge at top)

$\dfrac{33 - 15}{2} = 9$ (Begin on line 8.)

Half sheet (short edge at top)

$\dfrac{51 - 15}{2} = 18$ (Begin on line 18.)

Horizontal Placement of Table

Backspace from center of paper 1 space for each 2 strokes in longest line of each column, carrying over to next column any odd stroke. Ignore any odd stroke at end of last column. Then backspace 1 space for each 2 strokes to be placed between columns.

co|ns|ci|en|ti|ou|sa|ck|no|wl|ed|gm|en|tr|es|ta|ur|an + 3 + 3 *(2 + 2 for Problem 3)*

Set left margin stop; then space forward to determine tab stops for Columns 2 and 3.

59c ▶ 35
Format Two-Column Tables with Main Headings
3 half sheets
(long edge at top)

Problem 1
Center table vertically DS; center table horizontally leaving 12 spaces between columns.

MEN'S TEAM CAPTAINS		4
Baseball	Ken Morrison	8
Basketball	Cy Briggs	13
Football	Joe Hererra	17
Gymnastics	Kevin Kwan	21
Soccer	Bo Simpson	25
Volleyball	Greg Diablo	29

Problem 2
Center table according to Problem 1 directions, but leave 10 spaces between columns.

Problem 3
Proofread Problem 2, mark it for correction, and prepare a final copy with all errors corrected.

WOMEN'S TEAM CAPTAINS		4
Basketball	Diana Lindsay	9
Gymnastics	Lili Wong	14
Soccer	Aida Lopez	17
Softball	Fran Hildebrand	22
Volleyball	Glenda Washington	28

Lesson 60 | Simple Two-Column Tables

60a ▶ 7
Conditioning Practice
each line twice SS (slowly, then faster); if time permits, two 1' writings on line 4

alphabet	1	Jack pleased the mayor by awarding the prized onyx plaque for service.
figures	2	The shop is 278.4 meters long, 90.6 meters wide, and 13.5 meters high.
fig/sym	3	Both start today (2/14): Sam Hahn at $98.75/wk.; Tia Dun at $3.60/hr.
speed	4	Both of them may also wish to make a formal bid for the big auto firm.

| 1 | 2 | 3 | 4 | 5 | 6 | 7 | 8 | 9 | 10 | 11 | 12 | 13 | 14 |

60b ▶ 13 Learn to Align Figures
key twice DS; center horizontally according to KEY, 12 spaces between columns

To align whole numbers at right:
Set a tab stop for the digit in each column (after Column 1) that requires the least forward and backward spacing. To align the figures, space forward ▶ or backward ◀ as necessary.

margin ↓	tab ↓	tab ↓	tab ↓
294	1827	10	2619
▶36	▶750	◀305	▶475
110	3046	61	1950

KEY | 3 | 12 | 4 | 12 | 3 | 12 | 4 |

Learning Goals

1. To improve skill in formatting material in table (tabulated) form.
2. To improve spelling and word-use skills.
3. To improve language skills (punctuation).

Machine Adjustments

1. Paper guide at *0*.
2. 70-space line and SS, or as directed.
3. Line-space selector on *1*, or as directed.
4. Paper bail rollers set to divide paper into thirds, or fourths, if your machine has three rollers.

FORMATTING GUIDES: TABLES

Table Spacing Summary

Double-space (DS):

1. Below all heading lines.
2. Above and below column headings.
3. Column entries when so directed.
4. Above and below source note ruling separating column entries from source notes.
5. Above column TOTALS, when used.

Single-space (SS):

1. Column entries when so directed.
2. Multiple-line column headings.

Vertical Placement

Step 1: Count all lines to be used in table (including all blank line spaces).
Step 2: Subtract this figure from total lines available on sheet. **Note.** Most machines have six line spaces to the vertical inch; therefore, paper 8 1/2″ × 11″ has 66 vertical line spaces (11 × 6).
Step 3: Divide remainder by 2 to determine the number of the line on which to key the main heading. If a fraction results, disregard it. If the number that results is

EVEN, space down that number from the top;
ODD, use next lower even number.

Note. This means that the main heading of a table will always begin on an even number.

Horizontal Placement of Columns Using Backspace-from-Center Method

Step 1: Move margin stops to ends of scale and clear all tab stops.
Step 2: From the horizontal center of sheet, backspace once for each 2 strokes in the longest line in each column (carry over to the next column any extra stroke at the end of a column but ignore any extra stroke at the end of the last column); then, backspace once for each 2 spaces to be left between columns. **Note.** As center point of paper 8 1/2″ wide, use 42 for pica; 51 for elite.
Step 3: Set left margin stop at point where backspacing ends.
Step 4: From the left margin stop, space forward once for each stroke in the longest line in the first column, and once for each space to be left between the first and second columns. Set a tab stop at this point for the start of the second column. Continue procedure for any additional columns.

lines used			
1	WORDS FREQUENTLY MISSPELLED		
2			
3	occurrence	permissible	privilege
4			
5	conscientious	acknowledgment	conscious
6			
7	supersede	questionnaire	precede
8			
9	consensus	category	restaurant
10			
11	accommodate	maintenance	benefited
12			
13	_____		
14			
15	Source: Shell and Schmidt, DPE JOURNAL, 1984.		

Spacing Between Columns

As a general rule, leave an even number of spaces between columns (4, 6, 8, 10, or more). **Note.** The number of spaces to be left between columns is governed by the space available, the number of columns needed for the table, and the ease of reading the table.

Column Headings

When used, column headings are often centered over the columns. **Note.** If a table contains single-line column headings and also column headings of two or more lines, the bottom line of each multiple-line heading is placed on the same line as the single-line heading(s).

Computer Placement

Key longest line in first column, plus spaces to be left between first and second columns; then key the longest line of second column. Continue procedure for any additional columns. When line is completed, press CENTER key, then set margin stop and tab stops at points indicated. Delete trial line; then key the table using stops determined with trial line.

Improve Document Formatting Skills -- Simple Tables

60c ▶ 30 Learn to Format Two-Column Tables with Secondary Headings

3 half sheets
(long edge at top)

Problem 1

Center the table vertically DS and horizontally with 8 spaces between columns. DS all headings and entries.

Problem 2

Center the table as in Problem 1, but leave 10 spaces between columns. Align figures at decimal.

Problem 3

Proofread Problem 2, mark it for correction, and prepare a final copy with all errors corrected.

		words
WEAKNESSES OF WORD PROCESSING WORKERS		8
(Reported as % of Responding Supervisors)		16
Inadequate Language Skills	45	22
Poor Spelling	39	25
Inadequate Vocabulary	39	30
Lack of Experience on WP Equipment	33	38
Inadequate Keyboarding Skills	27	44

		words
WHERE ACCIDENTS HAPPEN		5
(Percent at Each Location)		10
At home	38.7	13
At industrial sites	13.0	18
On roads	10.8	20
At recreational sites	8.9	26
In schools	8.9	29
On farms	1.4	31
Other locations	18.3	35

Lesson 61   Three-Column Tables

61a ▶ 7 Conditioning Practice

each line twice SS (slowly, then faster); if time permits, rekey lines 2 and 4

alphabet	1	Luci Kwan said the boutique might have jade, onyx, and topaz for sale.
figures	2	The 405 members voted 267 to 138 to delay the tax increase until 1992.
d/ed/ied	3	tie tied list listed walk walked check checked dry dried reply replied
speed	4	The city auditor is due by eight and she may lend a hand to the panel.

| 1 | 2 | 3 | 4 | 5 | 6 | 7 | 8 | 9 | 10 | 11 | 12 | 13 | 14 |

61b ▶ 8 Build Skill in Formatting and Keying Table Headings

Using the copy of Problem 1 above, see how quickly you can make machine adjustments and key the headings and the first 2 or 3 entries.

1. Review centering guides on page 106 if necessary.
2. Double-space all lines.
3. Leave 8 spaces between columns.
4. Check your work for proper placement. Did you place the main heading on line 10? Are left and right margins about equal?

PHASE 5

Extend Document Processing Skills

The 25 lessons of Phase 5 continue the emphasis on improving your keyboarding and document processing skills. The lessons are designed to help you:

1. Further refine your keyboarding techniques as you make applications of your keyboarding skill.

2. Improve and extend your document formatting skills on simple and complex tables and on reports that include footnotes as well as textual citations (the modern method of showing reference citations).

3. Increase your basic language-skill competency.

4. Increase your keyboarding speed and improve your control.

5. Improve your proofreading competency.

61c ▶ 35
Learn to Format
Three-Column Tables

3 half sheets
(long edge at top)

Problem 1
Table with Blocked
Column Headings

Center vertically DS and horizontally with 6 spaces between columns. Block the column headings at left edge of columns; DS above and below them.

TICKET SALE WINNERS			words
			4
Event	Winner	No.	10
Winter Wonderland	Janelle Lindstrom	408	18
Octoberfest	Sally Williams	372	24
Holiday Sounds	Michel Durate	250	31
Football Festival	Helmud Franks	169	38

Problem 2
Table with Main, Secondary,
and Column Headings

Center vertically DS and horizontally with 8 spaces between columns. DS all headings and entries.

Problem 3

Reformat Problem 1 with 8 spaces between columns. Correct all errors you make as you key.

JANUARY SALES REPORT			4
(In Thousands of $)			8
Salesperson	Goal	Final	17
Amorini, Joseph	23.5	23.75	22
Cartwright, Susan	28.0	28.50	28
Ellington, Maxine	30.2	30.10	34
Hernandez, Eduardo	26.7	26.80	40
Jackson, Della	29.5	30.20	45
McKay, Eldon	31.9	32.00	50
Wang, Howard	34.6	33.90	54

Lesson 62   Tables on Full Sheets

62a ▶ 7
Conditioning
Practice

each line twice SS
(slowly, then faster); if
time permits, two 1′
writings on line 4

alphabet	1	Barth was given a big prize for completing six quick high jumps today.
figures	2	Ozark has a flight at 8:26; Delta, at 9:37; and Continental, at 10:54.
fig/sym	3	Strikes in 1986 delayed delivery of 524,350# (or 7% of all shipments).
speed	4	The firm may wish to bid by proxy for title to the lake and the docks.

| 1 | 2 | 3 | 4 | 5 | 6 | 7 | 8 | 9 | 10 | 11 | 12 | 13 | 14 |

62b ▶ 8
Build Skill in Formatting and Keying Table Headings

Using the copy of Problem 2 above, see how quickly you can make machine adjustments and key the headings and the first 2 or 3 entries.

1. Review centering guides on page 106 if necessary.

2. Double-space all lines.

3. Leave 8 spaces between columns.

4. Check your work for proper placement and spacing. Did you place the main heading on line 6? Are left and right margins about equal?

100a ▶ 5
Conditioning Practice

each line twice (slowly, faster); as time permits, repeat selected lines

alphabet	1	These children were amazed by the quick, lively jumps of the gray fox.
fig/sym	2	The 468 copies (priced at $3.75 each) may be shipped on July 19 or 20.
fingers 3, 4	3	Did Sid say if Ada saw the several polo ponies near the old mill pond?
speed	4	Dudley and the auditor did their work and may wish to sign their form.

| 1 | 2 | 3 | 4 | 5 | 6 | 7 | 8 | 9 | 10 | 11 | 12 | 13 | 14 |

100b ▶ 15
Measure Basic Skill: Statistical Rough Draft

Two 5' writings on 99c, p. 174; find *gwam*; circle errors; record better rate. Compute your percent of transfer by dividing your 100b rate by your straight-copy rate on 98c, p. 172.

100c ▶ 30
Measure Document Processing Skill: Letters

Time Schedule

Plan and prepare	4'
Timed production	20'
Proofread; compute *n-pram*	6'

1. Use letterheads (LM pp. 39-44) or plain full sheets; adjust margins according to letter length.

Letter 1: Modified block, blocked ¶s; mixed punctuation; correct errors.

Letter 2: Block style, open punctuation; correct errors.

Letter 3: If time permits, format Letter 1 with indented ¶s.

2. When time is called, proofread your completed work; mark any uncorrected errors; deduct 15 words for each uncorrected error. Compute *n-pram*.

words

Letter 1

Current date | Dr. L. W. Evans | Jones Graduate School of Education | 300   14
Agnew Avenue | Los Angeles, CA 90045-3116 | Dear Dr. Evans: 27
(¶ 1) I was pleased to have the opportunity to discuss with you your skill   40
learning/writing research proposal when you were in the office last week. I   55
believe the formal proposal you left with me will receive favorable attention   71
by our Board and that it will be considered for funding.   82
(¶ 2) So that I will be able to answer Board questions, I need to know your   96
rationale for the use of the typewriter in the writing program that you out-   111
lined in your proposal. The Board is scheduled to meet at the end of next   126
month. (101)   128
Sincerely yours, | Miss Jan Gilcrest | Vice President-Secretary | xx | 140
   159

Letter 2

Current date | Miss Jan Gilcrest | Vice President-Secretary | The Windsor Foun-   14
dation | 1510 Michigan Avenue | Los Angeles, CA 90033-3600 | Dear Miss   28
Gilcrest   30
(¶ 1) It is my belief that a new approach to the teaching of writing is   43
needed. I suggest that the typewriter can be used effectively to teach writ-   59
ing and other skills needed by everyone. Why the typewriter? First of all,   74
if students are to learn to write, it is clear that we need more powerful inter-   90
vention strategies than are presently being used. Students learn to write by   106
writing, and the typewriter is the most effective writing tool we presently   121
have. Its use in helping students improve their writing or composition skills   137
represents an alternative learning strategy that has great promise.   150
(¶ 2) Handwriting is a cumbersome and slow process. It is relatively easy for   165
most persons to learn to keyboard at least two or three times faster than   180
they can handwrite. All students, therefore, can get much more writing   194
practice as they use the typewriter for their writing.   205
(¶ 3) In addition, a knowledge of and proficiency in the use of the typewriter   220
keyboard has many values -- in writing, in computer applications, in using   235
word processing equipment, and in the employment marketplace.   247
(¶ 4) Please let me know if you need any other information. Thanks, again, for   262
your interest and help. (237)   267
Sincerely yours | L. W. Evans | Professor of Education | xx | 278
   301

62c ▶ 35
Format Tables on Full Sheets
full sheets; DS

Problem 1
Two-Column Table with Source Note
Center vertically and horizontally, leaving 12 spaces between columns. DS above and below the 1½-inch rule (15 underline spaces, pica; 18 underline spaces, elite).

Note: Do not count $ as part of a column.

head in ALL CAPS—Annual Cost of Eating Out DS 5
(Per Person by Region) Tab ↓ 10

Pacific	$673	13
New England	659	16
Mountain	563	18
Mid-Atlantic	501	22
South	478	24
East north Central	473	28
West North Central	441	33

36

DS Source: The Food Institute. 42

Problem 2
Three-Column Table with Blocked Column Headings
Center vertically and horizontally, leaving 4 spaces between columns. DS above and below column headings; begin column headings at left edge of columns.

Problem 3
Reformat Problem 2. Add as a secondary heading: (First All-Star Game Played in 1933).

TOP ALL-STAR BASEBALL GAME CROWDS			
Year	Site, City	Attend.	16
1981	Municipal Stadium, Cleveland	72,086	24
1935	Municipal Stadium, Cleveland	69,831	32
1954	Municipal Stadium, Cleveland	68,751	40
1976	Veterans Stadium, Philadelphia	63,974	49
1939	Yankee Stadium, New York	62,892	56
			60

(heading line: 7)

Source: USA Today, July 15, 1985. 69

Lesson 63   Prepare for Measurement

63a ▶ 7
Conditioning Practice
each line twice SS (slowly, then faster); if time permits, rekey lines 2 and 4

alphabet 1 Marvin, the tax clerk, was puzzled by the quaint antics of the judges.
figures 2 I ordered 36 desks, 49 chairs, 15 tables, 80 lamps, and 72 file trays.
ing 3 be being row rowing hum humming read reading pave paving carve carving
speed 4 The panel may then work with the problems of the eight downtown firms.

| 1 | 2 | 3 | 4 | 5 | 6 | 7 | 8 | 9 | 10 | 11 | 12 | 13 | 14 |

63b ▶ 43
Prepare for Measurement
3 half sheets; 1 full sheet

Make a list of the problems and page numbers given below:
page 108, 59c, Problem 1
page 109, 60c, Problem 1
page 110, 61c, Problem 2
page 111, 62c, Problem 1

To prepare for measurement in Lesson 64, format and key each of the tables according to the directions given with the problems.

Refer to the centering guides on page 106 as needed. Correct any errors you make as you key the tables.

99c ▶ 20
Format a Short Report from Statistical Rough-Draft Copy

full sheet

1. Prepare as an unbound report. Use 1" side margins.

2. Use main heading:

A LOOK AT OUR POPULATION

QS below heading.

3. Indent 5 for ¶s.

4. Proofread copy before removing it from the machine; correct any errors you find.

5. Evaluate and grade your work in terms of neatness and correct division of words at ends of lines.

all figures used | A | 1.5 si | 5.7 awl | 80% hfw

The total population of our ~~nation~~ *country* is continuing to grow.	2
It is estimated that our population will grow from some 230 mil-	5
lion in 1981 to 268 million in the year 2000, and ~~that~~ it will	7
reach an all-time high of 309 million in 2050. ~~An element~~ *a factor* con-	10
tributing to the population increase is the fact that we are	12
living longer ~~growing older~~. Adequate exercise, good nutrition, and better	15
health care are contributing factors *to our longer longevity* At the turn of the	18
century, the *average* life expectancy was only 49 years. today, the *average*	21
life expectancy has increased to 70.7 years for males and to	23
78.3 years for fe males. By the year 2005, life expectancy	26
will increase to 73.3 years, *for* males, *and to 81.3 for females*	28
The total population of our ~~nation~~, *country* too, is growing older. In	31
1970, the *median* age of our population was 27.9 years; in 1980, it was	34
30.2 years; by 1990, it is projected to be 32.8 years; and by	36
the year 2000, the estimated median age will increase to *approximately* 35.5	39
years. This graying of America, as it has been called, *indicates* ~~shows~~	42
that the proportion of our population 65 years and over will	45
in crease from 26.2 million in 1981 to 35.1 million in the year	47
2000, with a startling jump to 67.0 million in 2050. *Additionally,*	50
it means that we will have to discover new ways to	51
use the unique talent and wisdom that are characteristic	54
of the older person.	55

99d ▶ 10
Evaluate Technique

each line 3 times; repeat as time permits (Make a self-evaluation of keyboarding technique; compare with your teacher's evaluation.)

↓ tab set (60)
Try to make a quick return
(Repeat three times)

tab and return   1 **and start of the new line. ——— tab ——→**

keystroking and space bar   2 **If they do the work for us, then I may pay them if they sign the form.**

shift keys   3 **Ms. Sue McCray, President of Dalton & O'Brien, Inc., lives in Chicago.**

continuity and variable rhythm   4 **Send these forms and the statement to them at the address on the card.**

| 1 | 2 | 3 | 4 | 5 | 6 | 7 | 8 | 9 | 10 | 11 | 12 | 13 | 14 |

64a ▶ 7
Conditioning Practice

each line twice SS (slowly, then faster); if time permits, two 1' writings on line 4

alphabet	1	Suzi can equal a track record by jumping twelve feet at the next meet.
figures	2	Their team took some close games: 97 to 96, 84 to 83, and 105 to 102.
fig/sym	3	My statement read: "Payment #36 will be $590.78 plus 12.4% interest."
speed	4	The eighty girls did rush down the field with usual and visible vigor.

| 1 | 2 | 3 | 4 | 5 | 6 | 7 | 8 | 9 | 10 | 11 | 12 | 13 | 14 |

64b ▶ 8
Check Keyboarding Skill: Straight Copy

1. A 1' writing on each ¶; find *gwam*; circle errors.

2. A 3' writing on the 2 ¶s combined; find *gwam*; circle errors.

3. If time permits, take an additional 1' writing on each ¶ to build skill.

all letters used | A | 1.5 si | 5.7 awl | 80% hfw   *gwam* 3' | 5'

If success is vital to you, you have a distinct advantage over many   5   3

people who have no particular feeling one way or the other. The desire   9   6

to succeed is helpful, for it causes us to establish goals without which   14   9

our actions have little or no meaning. Success may not necessarily mean   19   11

winning the big prize, but it does mean approaching a goal.   23   14

It is foolish, of course, to believe that we can all be whatever   27   16

we wish to become. It is just as foolish, though, to wait around hop-   32   19

ing for success to overtake us. We should analyze our aspirations, our   37   22

abilities, and our limitations. We can next decide from various choices   42   25

what we are best equipped with effort to become.   45   27

gwam 3' | 1 | 2 | 3 | 4 | 5 |
5' | 1 | 2 | 3 |

64c ▶ 35
Check Formatting Skill: Tables

2 half sheets; 1 full sheet; DS all lines; format the table at the right and those on page 113; correct errors

Problem 1
Table with Main and Secondary Headings

half sheet; 8 spaces between columns

		words
DEFICIENCIES OF HIGH SCHOOL GRADUATES		8
(Reported as a % of Responding Companies)		16
Do not find and correct errors	77.3	23
Lack of pride in work done	47.7	30
Lack of telephone courtesy	46.6	36
Lack of initiative, drive, and ambition	45.1	45
Lack of respect for work	39.4	51
Poor personal appearance, grooming	28.0	59
Do not accept responsibility	25.0	66

HRS   MIN   SEC

Unit 20   Lessons 99-100

Evaluation Goals

1. To measure and help you evaluate your overall keyboarding skill.

2. To help you identify areas of needed improvement.

Machine Adjustments

Use:

*70-space line and single spacing for drills; DS below each SS group of drill lines

*70-space line and double spacing for ¶ timings of more than 1 minute

*as directed or needed for other copy

Lesson 99 | Evaluate Keyboarding/Language Skills

99a ▶ 5
Conditioning Practice

each line twice (slowly, faster); as time permits, repeat selected lines

alphabet	1	The unique weave of the blue-gray jacket pleased many zealous experts.
figures	2	Is the total charge on Order No. 2384, dated July 10, $57.69 or $5.76?
adjacent keys	3	Opal asked them to weigh and polish a brass pot prior to its delivery.
speed	4	The maps may aid them when they do the work for the town and the city.

| 1 | 2 | 3 | 4 | 5 | 6 | 7 | 8 | 9 | 10 | 11 | 12 | 13 | 14 |

99b ▶ 15
Check Language Skills: Grammar/Punctuation

full sheet; DS; 1″ top margin; 70-space line

1. Keyboard each sentence, including the sentence number, period, and two spaces. Choose the correct word in the parentheses or insert correct punctuation as you keyboard the line.

2. As your teacher reads the corrected sentences to you, circle the number of any sentence in which you have made an error.

3. Reinsert your paper, align it, and rekey correctly any sentence in which you made an error in the blank space below the sentence.

Awareness cue: Remember to reset margin when you reach Figure 10.

1. One of the persons (is, are) here for the interview.
2. Jim and John (is, are) going to the theater to see the musical.
3. Neither the teacher nor the students (has, have) left the school.
4. Neither of the men (is, are) here to do the work.
5. Each of the boys (is, are) doing (his, their) work.
6. Some of the students (is, are) in Room 1134.
7. He (don't, doesn't) like the cafeteria food.
8. They, too, (don't, doesn't) like the cafeteria food.
9. Neither Marc nor Greg (has, have) completed (his, their) report.
10. The committee (has, have) completed (its, their) report.
11. All the books (is, are) new.
12. The number of books in the library (has, have) been increased.
13. The box (is, are) in the storage room.
14. A number of students (has, have) registered for the new program.
15. The data (seems, seem) to be incorrect.
16. Each of the girls (has, have) (her, their) favorite sport.
17. The class planned (its, their) prom.
18. Somsara and Robert (don't, doesn't) have (his or her, their) books.
19. If you go to the market please get milk bread and eggs.
20. He was born in Denton Texas on April 18 1956.
21. During 1987 1249 applications for patents were filed.
22. Seventy six applications were received for the twenty three jobs.
23. These are the items you will need a workbook pencil and pad.
24. A first class ticket is more expensive than a coach class ticket.
25. The teacher said This is my best class.

Problem 2
Table with Main and Column Headings and Source Note
half sheet; 12 spaces between columns

		words
U.S. DOLLARS SPENT IN SPACE		6
Program	Cost to Date	14
Apollo	21.3 billion	18
Space Shuttle	18.8 billion	23
Skylab	2.5 billion	27
Gemini	1.3 billion	31
Mercury	392.6 million	35
		38
Source: NASA, 1985.		42

Problem 3
Table with Main, Secondary, and Column Headings
full sheet; 8 spaces between columns

Punctuation Marks

	typewriter	computer
ampersand	&	&
comma	,	,
parentheses	( )	{ }
question mark	?	?
quotation marks	"	"
semicolon	;	;

			words
LONGEST-RUN BROADWAY PLAYS			5
(As of August 5, 1984)			10
Play	Open.	Perf.	16
A Chorus Line	1974	3,744	21
Grease	1972	3,388	25
Oh! Calcutta! (revival)	1976	3,359	32
Fidler on the Roof	1964	3,242	38
Life with father	1993	3,224	44
			47
Source: Information Please Almanac, 1985, p. 798.			62

ENRICHMENT ACTIVITY: Language Skills

Capitalization and Number Expression

60-space line; DS

1. Read and key each line, making needed changes in capitalization and number expression.

2. Check accuracy of work with your teacher; rekey any line that contains errors in rule applications.

1 the fourteen boys left on may third to hike in lone star park.

2 she bought twelve place settings of oneida flatware.

3 the new marx theater is located at 1 east 10th avenue.

4 ms. jeanne hanna, the manager of edit, inc., has arrived.

5 he told us to study chapter four and to review chapter three.

6 about 20 voted; that's nearly two thirds of the members.

7 jill gave one third to ken, one third to jo, and one third to me.

8 "keep up the good work," he said, "and you'll make the goal."

9 my flight for new york leaves at four ten p.m. on january three.

10 dodi read Pages 1-150 of vidal's lincoln sunday afternoon.

98c ▶ 15
**Measure Basic Skill:
Straight Copy**
two 5′ writings; find
gwam; circle errors;
record better rate

Fingers curved   Keystroke   Spacing stroke

all letters used | A | 1.5 si | 5.7 awl | 80% hfw

	gwam 3′	5′
As you read copy for keyboarding, try to read at least a word or,	4 3	44
better still, a word group ahead of your actual keyboarding point. In	9 5	47
this way, you should be able to recognize the keystroking pattern needed	14 8	50
as you learn to keyboard balanced-hand, one-hand, or combination word	19 11	52
sequences. The adjustments you make in your speed will result in the	23 14	55
variable rhythm pattern needed for expert keyboarding. It is easy to	28 17	58
read copy correctly for keyboarding if you concentrate on the copy.	32 19	61
When you first try to read copy properly for keyboarding, you may	37 22	63
make more errors, but as you learn to concentrate on the copy being read	42 25	66
and begin to anticipate the keystroking pattern needed, your errors will	47 28	69
go down and your keyboarding speed will grow. If you want to increase	51 31	72
your keyboarding speed and reduce your errors, you must make the effort	56 34	75
to improve during each and every practice session. If you will work to	61 37	78
refine your techniques and to give a specific purpose to all your prac-	66 39	81
tice activities, you can make the improvement.	69 41	82

gwam 3′ 1 2 3 4 5
5′   1   2   3

1. Add 4 words to your *gwam* rate of 98c. Take two 1′ guided writings at this new goal rate on each ¶ of 98c.

2. Two 3′ writings on the ¶s of 98c. In each writing, try to improve your speed and/or your accuracy, according to your need.

3. If time permits, take a 5′ writing with a goal of improvement.

Unit 11 Lessons 65-67

Learning Goals

1. To refine your keyboarding techniques.
2. To increase your keyboarding speed.
3. To improve your keyboarding control.
4. To improve your language skills.

Machine Adjustments

1. Paper guide at 0.
2. Ribbon control set to use top half of ribbon.
3. Margin sets: 70-space line (center − 35; center + 35 + 5) unless otherwise directed.
4. Line space selector to SS drills, DS ¶s; as directed for problems.

Lesson 65   Improve Keyboarding/Language Skills

65a ▶ 7
Conditioning Practice

each line twice SS (slowly, then faster); if time permits, two 1' writings on line 4

alphabet	1	Zig will do extra jobs for the antique clock firm if it pays overtime.
figures	2	Our ZIP Code was expanded from 45236 to 45236-1057 on August 18, 1981.
ly/ily	3	low lowly full fully lazy lazily noisy noisily dear dearly glad gladly
speed	4	Both of the girls may go with the busy auditor to visit the auto firm.

| 1 | 2 | 3 | 4 | 5 | 6 | 7 | 8 | 9 | 10 | 11 | 12 | 13 | 14 |

65b ▶ 13 Improve Language Skills: Capitalization

70-space line; DS

1. Read the ¶ at the right, noting words that need to be capitalized.
2. Key the ¶, capitalizing words where appropriate.
3. Check your work, marking all errors for correction.
4. Prepare a final copy with all errors corrected.

in her book, human relations in the workplace, ms. kimberly said: "it is not sufficient to have good office skills." writing on the basis of twenty years' experience with Pro-Tech temporary employee services, inc., she said that "more office workers lose their jobs because of personal and human relations factors than because of inadequate skills." among the factors she mentioned are: lack of dependability, lack of responsibility for the accuracy of work produced, and poor concept of the value of one's job effort.

65c ▶ 13
Improve Keyboarding Technique: Response Patterns

each line twice SS (slowly, then faster); as time permits, a 1' writing on lines 3, 6, and 9; find *gwam* and compare rates

letter response	1	as you are him was ill get oil few ink tax pop set kin ads hip raw pin
	2	as you|you set|as you set|set up|you set up|as you set up|set up rates
	3	Lonny created a great dessert treat: stewed plum in a sweet egg tart.
word response	4	of dot pen lay eye tie bus rug bit key oak map bid via aid got fit air
	5	of the|the world|of the world|to the|the problem|to handle the problem
	6	Did the chair signal the man to name the auditor of the downtown firm?
combination response	7	we the you and are for was may get but tax pay few due him own set men
	8	is up|up to|is up to|he was|was to|he was to|if you|you did|if you did
	9	Di is as aware as they are that the state tree of Ohio is the buckeye.

| 1 | 2 | 3 | 4 | 5 | 6 | 7 | 8 | 9 | 10 | 11 | 12 | 13 | 14 |

97e ▶ 10
Improve Control: Guided Writing

1. A 2' writing (at a controlled pace with fingers curved; quiet hands).

2. Find *gwam*. Subtract 4 from your *gwam* rate. Find ¼' goals for 1' writings at new goal rate.

3. Two 1' writings at goal rate as ¼' guide is called. Work for accuracy; no more than 1 error in each writing.

4. Another 2' writing for control. Maintain goal rate.

			gwam 2'
· 4 · 8 · 12			6 | 48

Failure to concentrate on the copy to be keyboarded often causes   6 \| 48
errors. Looking from the copy to the screen, to the paper in your ma-   13 \| 55
chine, or at your fingers causes still other errors. Faulty techniques   21 \| 62
are another major contributing factor. To reduce errors, concentrate   28 \| 69
on the copy, keep your fingers curved and upright in keyboarding posi-   35 \| 76
tion, and then let your fingers do the keyboarding. Try it and see.   41 \| 83

| 1 | 2 | 3 | 4 | 5 | 6 | 7 |

97f ▶ 10
Improve Basic Skill: Straight Copy

Two 3' writings on 96d, p. 169. Emphasize control.

Goal: No more than 6 errors in each writing.

Lesson 98   Keyboarding/Language Skills

98a ▶ 5
Conditioning Practice

each line twice (slowly, faster); as time permits, repeat selected lines

alphabet 1 As a freezing wave hit them, the explorers quickly adjusted the beams.

figures 2 I reviewed 127 books, 364 magazines, 50 newspapers, and 189 pamphlets.

ny, un, ce, br 3 Many persons were uncertain about swimming under the old brick bridge.

speed 4 She may lend the ancient city map to us if the city pays for the work.

| 1 | 2 | 3 | 4 | 5 | 6 | 7 | 8 | 9 | 10 | 11 | 12 | 13 | 14 |

98b ▶ 10
Improve Language Skills: Punctuation

full sheet; 1" top margin; 70-space line

Follow directions as given in 96c, p. 168.

COLON

Use a colon to introduce an enumeration or a listing.

Learn 1. Please bring the following: a typewriter, a book, and paper.
Apply 2. Add these items to your grocery list bread, butter, and eggs.

Use a colon to introduce a question or a long direct quotation.

Learn 3. The question is this: Are you using good techniques?
Apply 4. This is my concern, Did you really study for the test?

Use a colon between hours and minutes expressed in figures.

Learn 5. The program will start promptly at 7:30 p.m.
Apply 6. Does United Flight 1104 leave at 915 or 1015 a.m.?

65d ▶ 17
Improve/Check Keyboarding Skill

1. A 1' writing on ¶ 1; find *gwam*.

2. Add 2-4 *gwam* to the rate attained in Step 1, and note quarter-minute check points from table below.

3. Take two 1' guided writings on ¶ 1 to increase speed.

4. Practice ¶s 2 and 3 in the same way.

5. A 3' writing on ¶s 1-3 combined; find *gwam* and circle errors.

6. If time permits, take another 3' writing.

gwam	¼'	½'	¾'	1'
24	6	12	18	24
28	7	14	21	28
32	8	16	24	32
36	9	18	27	36
40	10	20	30	40
44	11	22	33	44
48	12	24	36	48
52	13	26	39	52
56	14	28	42	56

all letters used | LA | 1.4 si | 5.4 awl | 85% hfw   *gwam 3'*

Few people know which direction their lives may take or by what   4
road they may travel to their final destination. When they come to a   9
crossroad, many stop to decide which road to take. Many take the easy   14
road and puzzle over what might have happened on the road not taken.   18

Who of us knows exactly what we shall want tomorrow? None of us,   23
hopefully, makes a choice that cannot at some point in the future be   27
changed. All should ask questions of the future for which we have no   32
answers. By always seeking to learn, however, we improve our choices.   37

All of us should pause from time to time and ask ourselves what   41
we desire from life and, if necessary, choose a new road to follow to   45
obtain our goals. Unfortunate, indeed, are those with no purpose in   50
life, people who have set no major goals to investigate or to pursue.   55

gwam 3' | 1 | 2 | 3 | 4 | 5 |

Lesson 66 | Improve Keyboarding/Language Skills

66a ▶ 7
Conditioning Practice

each line twice SS (slowly, then faster); if time permits, two 1' writings on line 4

alphabet	1	Joe very quickly seized the wheel as big cars pulled out from an exit.
figures	2	The 17 jobs will be done by May 30, 1992, at a cost of $465.8 million.
r/er	3	make maker late later dive diver play player deal dealer train trainer
speed	4	She did signal the chair to hand the proxy to the auditor of the firm.

| 1 | 2 | 3 | 4 | 5 | 6 | 7 | 8 | 9 | 10 | 11 | 12 | 13 | 14 |

66b ▶ 13 Improve Language Skills: Number Expression

70-space line; DS

1. Read the ¶ at the right, noting the numbers that should be expressed as words and those that should be expressed as figures.

2. Key the ¶, expressing the numbers correctly.

3. Check your work and mark all errors for correction.

4. Prepare a final copy with all errors corrected.

The fifty most-used words account for 46% of the total of all words used in a study of four thousand one hundred letters, memos, and reports. The first hundred account for 53%; the first 500, 71%; the first thousand, 80%; and the first 2,000, 88%. Of the first 7,027 most-used words, 209 are balanced-hand words and 284 are one-hand words. Balanced-hand words account for 26% of all word uses; one-hand words account for 14%.

97a ▶ 5
Conditioning Practice

each line twice (slowly, faster); as time permits, repeat selected lines

alphabet 1 Frank Carr puzzled over Meg's interest in the exquisitely written job.

figures 2 In 1987, we had 36 office chairs, 42 office desks, and 50 work tables.

one-hand words 3 In fact, a star at rear stage rested as eager casts regarded only him.

speed 4 It is their duty to go downtown to do the work for the six busy firms.

| 1 | 2 | 3 | 4 | 5 | 6 | 7 | 8 | 9 | 10 | 11 | 12 | 13 | 14 |

97b ▶ 5
Improve Accuracy/ Force Speed

1. Two 1′ writings on line 1 of 97a. **Goal:** Not over 2 errors in each writing.

2. Two 1′ writings on line 4 of 97a. **Goal:** To force speed to a new level.

97c ▶ 15
Improve Techniques: Keystroking/Response Patterns/Rhythm

1. Lines 1-6 twice (slowly, faster).

2. Lines 7-12 three times (slowly, faster, top speed).

3. Two 1′ writings on line 10 for speed.

4. Two 1′ writings on lines 11 and 12 for control.

Emphasize fast finger-action keystroking; quiet hands.

third row 1 qua wow with end eke rut for the dot yam jay us usual if it is of pals

first row 2 zoa xyster cod economy vie five bog fob tub name man comb vow but exam

finger emphasis 3 qaza wsxs edcd rfvf tgbg yhnh yjmj ik,k ol.l p;/; aqua aza six wise p;

"b" reach 4 The bright baby boys babbled with joy as the abbey cobbler hurried by.

"y" reach 5 Jay Young may try to carry the yummy yellow yams to their yacht today.

"z" reach 6 Zestful quizzical quiz kids dizzily zigzagged around a buzzing bazaar.

Emphasize high-speed response patterns.

7 and if they|and if they go with me|and if they go with me to the firms

8 she did the work|she did the work for them|six men did the work for me

9 he may go|he may go with them|he may go with them and me to their city

10 If he is to do their work for them, then he may go with me to the bog.

Emphasize variable rhythm; finger-action keystroking.

11 Send the statement on the monopoly case to the union at their address.

12 Ask him to restate the nylon problem as the statement was exaggerated.

| 1 | 2 | 3 | 4 | 5 | 6 | 7 | 8 | 9 | 10 | 11 | 12 | 13 | 14 |

97d ▶ 5
Improve Language Skills: Punctuation

full sheet; 1″ top margin; 70-space line

Follow directions as given in 96c, page 168.

HYPHEN (continued)

Use a hyphen to join compound adjectives preceding a noun they modify as a unit.

Learn 1. The Book-of-the-Month Club lists this book.
Apply 2. The out of bounds catch stopped our first down drive.

Use a hyphen after each word or figure in a series that modifies the same noun (suspended hyphenation).

Learn 3. All 6-, 7-, and 8-foot boards were used during construction.
Apply 4. Please check the rates on first, second, and third class mail.

66c ▶ 13
Improve Keyboarding Technique

1. Key each line twice.

2. Take a 1' writing on each of lines 2, 4, 6, 8, and 10.

Shift keys

1 Robert and Mandy left with Spence and Jacki on a South Pacific cruise.
2 Nan visited Rockland, Maine, and Springfield, Massachusetts, in April.

Space bar

3 Did all the men on the dock go to bid on an oak chair and a clay bowl?
4 The dog is too big to sit on my lap, but he may sit on a cozy fur rug.

Adjacent keys

5 Louisa was aware that the three ponds were polluted with oily residue.
6 The top stagehands were eager to join the powerful new worker's union.

Long direct reaches

7 The recent survey is summarized in a brochure she found in my library.
8 Margaret's unusual gift for the bride was a bright green nylon caftan.

Balanced-hand sentences

9 Dirk may hang the bugle by the antique ornament or by the oak workbox.
10 Eighty firms may bid for the right to make the big signs for the city.

| 1 | 2 | 3 | 4 | 5 | 6 | 7 | 8 | 9 | 10 | 11 | 12 | 13 | 14 |

66d ▶ 17
Improve/Check Keyboarding Skill

1. A 1' writing on ¶ 1; find *gwam*.

2. Add 2-4 *gwam* to the rate attained in Step 1, and note quarter-minute check points from table below.

3. Take two 1' guided writings on ¶ 1 to increase speed.

4. Practice ¶s 2 and 3 in the same way.

5. A 3' writing on ¶s 1-3 combined; find *gwam* and circle errors.

6. If time permits, take another 3' writing.

gwam	¼'	½'	¾'	1'
24	6	12	18	24
28	7	14	21	28
32	8	16	24	32
36	9	18	27	36
40	10	20	30	40
44	11	22	33	44
48	12	24	36	48
52	13	26	39	52
56	14	28	42	56

all letters used | A | 1.5 si | 5.7 awl | 80% hfw

gwam 3'

Words are the major building blocks of written communication, and 4
the keyboard is a very vital tool we use to put those words on paper 9
with speed and ease. To develop an effective message, we must choose 14
our words precisely and arrange them into clear paragraphs. 18

Some communication experts say we think in words; others insist 22
that words follow our thoughts. Quite simply, however, we do not draft 27
really good messages unless we make at least a mental plan first and 31
then select carefully each of the words to execute our plan. 35

All who keyboard with skill can record their ideas at a machine 39
more quickly than in longhand. Therefore, jotting down the main ideas 44
of a message before starting to compose is critical. The prize for a 49
good letter or report depends on planning as well as actual writing. 53

gwam 3' | 1 | 2 | 3 | 4 | 5 |

96d ▶ 15
Measure Basic Skill: Straight Copy

1. Two 5′ writings; find *gwam*.

2. Proofread; circle errors.

3. Record better *gwam* rate on your rate record sheet.

Quarter-Minute Checkpoints

gwam	¼′	½′	¾′	1′
24	6	12	18	24
28	7	14	21	28
32	8	16	24	32
36	9	18	27	36
40	10	20	30	40
44	11	22	33	44
48	12	24	36	48
52	13	26	39	52
56	14	28	42	56
60	15	30	45	60
64	16	32	48	64
68	17	34	51	68
72	18	36	54	72
76	19	38	57	76
80	20	40	60	80

all letters used | A | 1.5 si | 5.7 awl | 80% hfw

gwam

	2′	3′	5′

One of the key advances in computer technology during the last — 6 | 4 | 3

thirty years has been the growth of small computers, which are versatile, — 14 | 9 | 4

reliable, and quite easy to use. Known as microprocessors, these com- — 21 | 14 | 8

puters on a chip of silicon no larger than the tip of a finger are the — 28 | 19 | 11

heart of microcomputers. They can process, store, retrieve, and pass on — 35 | 23 | 14

millions of pieces of information. Such computers are making low-cost — 42 | 28 | 17

computer power available in the home, in the business office, and in our — 49 | 33 | 20

schools. As has often been said, they are an idea whose time has come. — 57 | 38 | 23

Expectations for the uses of the microcomputer are almost without — 7 | 42 | 25

end. Microcomputers in cars have the job of checking mechanical func- — 14 | 47 | 28

tions as well as the speed. Microcomputers and a few other items built — 21 | 52 | 31

into typewriters have become word processing systems. The high speed of — 28 | 56 | 34

the computer along with the ability of the computer for pattern recogni- — 35 | 61 | 37

tion has made possible talking as well as speech recognition machines. — 42 | 66 | 40

Also, machines that read books aloud are now in wide use by the visually — 50 | 71 | 43

handicapped. Many new changes have come about in the field of medicine, — 57 | 76 | 45

and you should realize the effect that the microcomputer has had and — 64 | 80 | 48

will have in the future on your life as well as on the lives of others. — 71 | 85 | 51

gwam 3′ | 1 | 2 | 3 | 4 | 5
5′ | 1 | 2 | 3

96e ▶ 15
Improve Basic Skill: Straight Copy

1. Add 4 to 8 words to your 96d *gwam* rate. **Goal:** To reach a new high-speed rate.

2. Two 1′ guided writings on ¶ 1 of 96d at your new goal rate as the ¼′ guides are called.

3. A 2′ guided writing on ¶ 1. Try to maintain your 1′ rate.

4. Repeat Step 2, using ¶ 2.

5. Repeat Step 3, using ¶ 2.

6. A 3′ writing using both ¶s. **Goal:** To maintain your new speed rate for 3′.

169

67a ▶ 7
Conditioning
Practice

each line twice SS
(slowly, then faster); if
time permits, two 1'
writings on line 4

alphabet 1 Xavier quit pouring cement when jet black clouds filled the azure sky.

figures 2 Joe must sell 27 to 28 tickets for the 19th and 35 to 40 for the 26th.

ion 3 tense tension express expression suggest suggestion protect protection

speed 4 I wish to do the work so the girls may go with them to make the signs.

| 1 | 2 | 3 | 4 | 5 | 6 | 7 | 8 | 9 | 10 | 11 | 12 | 13 | 14 |

67b ▶ 13 Improve
Language Skills

1. Read the ¶ at the right, mentally noting words that should be capitalized and numbers that should be shown in figures.
2. Key the ¶, making the needed changes.
3. Check your work and mark all errors for correction.
4. Prepare a final copy with all errors corrected.

of the forty-five members of the footlight club, 36 were present at the meeting on friday, february 7. the club president, sybil harshman, called the meeting to order at three thirty p.m. the meeting involved a discussion of plans for the big spring show, "footlight serenade." at the suggestion of the vice president, john sparkman, it was decided to stage the show on april thirtieth and may first and second to celebrate may day.

67c ▶ 13 Improve
Keyboarding Speed:
Skill Transfer

1. A 1' writing on each ¶; find *gwam* on each.
2. Compare *gwam* on the 3 writings.
3. Another 1' writing on the slowest ¶.
4. A 2' writing on each ¶; find *gwam* on each. If you finish a ¶ before time is called, start over.
5. Compare *gwam* on the 3 writings.
6. As time permits, take another 2' writing on the slowest ¶.

Recall

∧ insert

♀ delete

⌒ close up

| all letters used | A | 1.5 si | 5.7 awl | 80% hfw | | *gwam* 1' | 2' |

It has frequently been said that talk is cheap, but this — 11 | 6

is not true in a business office. Whether workers are engaged — 24 | 12

in a work-related conversation or in idle chatter, the cost — 36 | 18

per minute to the company is the same. In business, time is — 48 | 24

money. That is why workers who waste time in social conversa- — 61 | 30

tion are often criticized by office supervisors and managers. — 73 | 36

Another work habit that often costs a company — 11 | 6

money is the failure to find and correct errors before work is — 24 | 12

given to the supervisor for approval. A manager is quite — 36 | 18

critical of those who expect others to proof read and mark — 48 | 24

errors. Using highly paid people to find the errors made — 61 | 30

by those at a lower level can't be tolerated. — 70 | 35

Finally, workers who are frequently late getting to work — 11 | 6
and are often absent multiply the cost of getting work done. — 24 | 12
Such employees come in for criticism when an executive is — 35 | 18
asked to identify the prime weaknesses of office workers be- — 47 | 24
cause they are not giving a fair day's work for a fair day's — 60 | 30
pay. Time is money whether a worker uses it wisely or not. — 71 | 36

117

Unit 19   Lessons 96-98

Learning Goals
1. To refine your keyboarding technique patterns.
2. To increase your speed and improve your accuracy.
3. To increase your straight-copy rate.
4. To improve language skills.
5. To improve proofreading skills.

Machine Adjustments
Paper guide at *0*.
Use:
*70-space line and single spacing for drills; DS below each SS group of drill lines
*70-space line and double spacing for ¶ timings of more than 1 minute
*as directed or needed for other copy

Lesson 96   Keyboarding/Language Skills

96a ▶ 5
Conditioning Practice
each line twice (slowly, faster); as time permits, repeat selected lines

alphabet	1	A travel expert frequently amazed them with talks about jungle dances.
figures	2	Please ship Order 1750 for 36 word processors, 49 desks, and 28 lamps.
shift key	3	J. A. Hall, P. C. McLain, and Anzel Paul work for Steinmann & Company.
speed	4	It is the duty of the eight men to fix the bicycle for the city firms.

| 1 | 2 | 3 | 4 | 5 | 6 | 7 | 8 | 9 | 10 | 11 | 12 | 13 | 14 |

96b ▶ 5
Improve Accuracy/ Force Speed

1. Two 1' writings on line 1 of 96a. **Goal:** Not over 2 errors in each writing.

2. Two 1' writings on line 4 of 96a. **Goal:** To force speed to a new level.

96c ▶ 10
Improve Language Skills: Punctuation
full sheet; 1" top margin; 70-space line

Study/Learn/Apply/Correct Procedures

1. STUDY explanatory rule.

2. Key line number (with period); space twice, then key the LEARN sentence(s) DS, noting rule application.

3. Key the line number (with period); space twice, then key the APPLY sentence(s) DS, making changes to correct sentence(s).

4. As your teacher reads the correct sentence(s), show in pen or pencil any corrections that need to be made in your copy.

5. Rekey any APPLY sentence containing an error, CORRECTING the error as you key. Place the corrected sentence in the space below the APPLY sentence containing the error.

EXCLAMATION MARK

Use an exclamation mark after emphatic exclamations and after phrases and sentences that are clearly exclamatory.

Learn 1. What a beautiful view!
Apply 2. That was a great game.

QUESTION MARK

Use a question mark at the end of a sentence that is a direct question; however, use a period after a request that appears in the form of a question.

Learn 3. Do you know how to program a microcomputer?
Learn 4. Will you please see me after this class.
Apply 5. Will you please try to complete the report before the meeting.
Apply 6. Did you finish all the reports.

HYPHEN

Use a hyphen to join compound numbers from twenty-one to ninety-nine.

Learn 7. Their ages ranged from twenty-three to seventy-six.
Apply 8. Spell out these numbers as you keyboard them: 42, 66, and 91.

67d ▶ 17
Improve/Check Keyboarding Skill

1. A 1' writing on ¶ 1; find *gwam*.

2. Add 2-4 *gwam* to the rate attained in Step 1, and note quarter-minute check points from table below.

3. Take two 1' guided writings on ¶ 1 to increase speed.

4. Practice ¶s 2 and 3 in the same way.

5. A 3' writing on ¶s 1-3 combined; find *gwam* and circle errors.

6. If time permits, take another 3' writing.

gwam	¼'	½'	¾'	1'
24	6	12	18	24
28	7	14	21	28
32	8	16	24	32
36	9	18	27	36
40	10	20	30	40
44	11	22	33	44
48	12	24	36	48
52	13	26	39	52
56	14	28	42	56

all letters used | A | 1.5 si | 5.7 awl | 80% hfw   *gwam 3'*

To hear is to perceive or to sense by the ear. To listen means to   4
hear with quite careful attention. Except for those with impaired hear-   9
ing, hearing is easy. Listening, on the contrary, is a difficult and   14
an often undeveloped skill which one can perfect only by practice.   18

To listen effectively, one must intend to hear and understand and   23
must concentrate on what is being said. Do not permit your mind to   27
drift to anything else. As you attempt to listen, think about and em-   32
phasize the idea being presented. Think along with the speaker.   36

Don't let your mind get distracted by the looks or gestures of the   40
speaker or by some noise or activity in the immediate area. Just con-   45
centrate on the message. Don't allow yourself to react too quickly to   50
what is being said. Instead, hear the whole message before you react.   55

gwam 3' | 1 | 2 | 3 | 4 | 5 |

ENRICHMENT ACTIVITY: Aligning Copy

Learn to Align and Type over Words

1. Key the sentence as shown below.

```
I can align this copy.
```

2. Study and follow the numbered steps given at the right.

Your typed line should look like this:

```
I can align this copy.
```

Not like this:

```
I can align this copy.

I can align this copy.
```

3. If time permits, repeat the drill to develop skill in aligning and typing over to make corrections in copy.

Aligning and Typing over Words

It is sometimes necessary to reinsert the paper to correct an error. Follow these steps to do so correctly.

1. Key a line of copy in which one or more *i*'s appear (such as *I can align this copy*, which you have just keyed). Leave the paper in your machine.

2. Locate **aligning scale (26)** and **variable line spacer (9)** on your machine.

3. Move element (carriage) so that a word containing an *i* (such as *align*) is above the aligning scale. Be sure that a vertical line points to the center of *i*.

4. Study the relation between top of the aligning scale and bottoms of letters with downstems (*g, p, y*). Get an exact eye picture of the relation of typed line to top of scale so you will be able to adjust the paper correctly to type over a word with exactness.

5. Remove the paper; reinsert it. Gauge the line so bottoms of letters are in correct relation to top of the aligning scale. Oper-

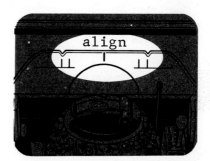

ate the *variable line spacer*, if necessary, to move the paper up or down. Operate the *paper release lever* to move paper left or right, if necessary, when centering the letter *i* over one of the lines on the aligning scale.

6. Check accuracy of alignment by setting the *ribbon control* in stencil position and typing over one of the letters. If necessary, adjust paper again.

7. Return ribbon control to use top half of ribbon.

8. Type over the words in the sentence.

From the desk of John McGee

Mr. Brown wishes this two-page letter prepared as soon as possible. Use modified block style, blocked ¶s, and open punctuation. Refer to the <u>Office Manual</u> before keying the second-page heading. You may wish to put a light pencil mark at the right edge of your paper (about 1½" from the bottom) to remind yourself when to end the first page. Prepare an original copy for each of these addresses:

Mrs. Judith Marx,
Manager
Centek Office Systems, Inc.
Western Regional Office
303 Kings Lane
Santa Maria, CA 93454-0091

Mr. Alberto Valdez,
Manager
Centek Office Systems, Inc.
Eastern Regional Office
2900 Revere Avenue
Manchester, NH 03103-2211

Mrs. Carmen Torres,
Manager
Centek Office Systems, Inc.
Southern Regional Office
450 Crest Lane
Lakeland, FL 33803-1021

John McGee

Use current date
Add address and salutation

As I promised,

Here is the information on the display unit *or monitor*--a basic component of a microprocessor or a word processing system. Please review this information before the divisional meeting. We will need to order the monitors at the same time we order printers.

The display unit is much like a *television* screen. If a word processing software package is used with a microcomputer, or if a *word* processor is being used, the display shows the operator the lines that have been keyboarded. Some monitors have only 40 characters per line--but most have 80 characters. This is a basic necessity if the unit is to be used efficiently for word processing. Vertically a good monitor should display at least 25 lines of text. Some units can display a full page. Still other monitors have a control line which shows the horizontal keystroke number and the number *of vertical lines* remaining on the page.

In *selecting* a display unit, you may have a choice of three types. The cheapest unit is the monochromatic monitor, which works well for word processing. Some operators find green and white displays easier to read than black-and-white displays. So-called composite color monitors are considered best for games and graphics. Composite refers to the way the colors are mixed. In the more expensive range, we have the RGB monitors. These monitors can produce truer colors and sharper images than is true for the composite model.

Another key to a monitor's quality is *referred to as* bandwidth, measured in megahertz (MHz). Bandwidth indicates the frequency level that the monitor can handle. As MHz increase, the resolution becomes better. A monitor's resolution is measured also by what is known as the pixel count. Pixels are tiny picture elements that combine to form the image that appears on the screen. Again, the more pixels there are, the sharper the resolution. A color monitor's pixel count should be listed on the specification sheet accompanying the monitor. Further, the specification sheet should state how many vertical lines--comprised of pixels--will fit on its screen.

Finally, a monitor should be *relatively* glare free. Keyboard operators who use monitors sometimes complain of eyestrain. With a non-glare screen the operator is less apt to experience eyestrain.

I hope the *information which I have supplied here* has given you some basic information about printers and monitors now available. Feel free to call me should you have any questions before the divisional meeting.

I look forward to seeing you there.

Sincerely

Jeff Brown, Division Manager

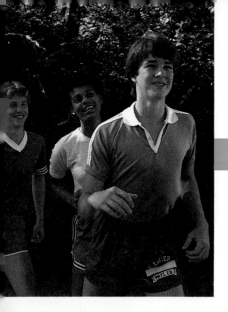

Learning Goals

1. To learn to apply your keyboarding and formatting skills in an office setting.

2. To learn to process a variety of keyboarding jobs in an orderly, efficient manner.

3. To learn to prepare usable business documents with all errors corrected and with only minimum assistance.

Machine Adjustments

1. Paper guide at *0*.

2. Ribbon control set to use top half of ribbon.

3. Margin sets: 70-space line for warm-up practice; as required by formatting guides for various documents.

4. Line space selector as required by formatting guides for various documents.

KILMER YOUTH CAMP (AN OFFICE JOB SIMULATION)

Before beginning the jobs on pages 120-122, read the copy at the right. When planning the assigned jobs, refer to the excerpts from the Kilmer Document Processing Manual to refresh your memory about proper formatting and spacing of documents.

Work Assignment

You have been hired for part-time office work at Kilmer Youth Camp where you are to spend part of the summer.

Kilmer Youth Camp is located near Tapoco, North Carolina, on Lake Santeetlah at the edge of Joyce Kilmer Memorial Forest in the foothills of the Great Smoky Mountains. It is a coeducational camp for youths between the ages of 10 and 16. The camp consists of two villages: the Girls' Village and the Boys' Village. Each village is subdivided by age into Junior Campers (ages 10-13) and Senior Campers (ages 14-16) for housing, training classes, and recreational activities.

The camp is organized and operated by the following people:

Mrs. Alice Lindsay, Camp Director
Mr. James S. Lindsay, Assistant Camp Director
Mr. Neal Adams, Boys' Village Director
Ms. Debra Rountree, Girls' Village Director

The directors are assisted by five boys' counselors and five girls' counselors. Each counselor is assisted by a counselor-in-training (CIT).

As an office assistant, you will work in the office of Mrs. Alice Lindsay. In addition to answering the telephone, filing correspondence and other records, and entering data into the office computer, you will also process letters, memos, and other documents. Because the camp does not yet have a word processor, you will process the documents on a typewriter.

Your keyboarding teacher has verified that you know how to format documents in the basic styles used by Kilmer Youth Camp: letters in block format; reports in unbound format; simplified memos; announcements centered on half sheets; tables centered on full sheets.

To assist you in formatting documents, Mrs. Lindsay gives you the following excerpts from the Kilmer Document Processing Manual.

Letters

1. Letters are prepared on camp letterheads; block format with open punctuation is used.
2. A standard 60-space line is used.
3. The date is placed on line 15.
4. Three blank line spaces (a quadruple space) are left between date and letter address and between complimentary close and typed name of writer. All other letter parts are separated by a double space.

Memos

1. Memos are prepared on camp letterheads; simplified format is used.
2. Side margins of 1″ are used.
3. The date is placed on line 12.
4. Three blank line spaces (a quadruple space) are left between date and addressee lines and between last line of message and name of writer. A double space separates all other memo parts.

Announcements and Tables

1. Announcements are prepared on half sheets; tables, on full sheets.
2. Double spacing is used for announcements and tables. Both are centered vertically and horizontally.

Reports

1. Unbound format is used for all reports: side margins, 1″; top margin, line 10 (pica), line 12 (elite); bottom margin, at least 1″.
2. Three blank line spaces (a quadruple space) separate the title from the body; a double space separates all other lines of reports, including side headings.
3. Page numbers are placed on line 6 at the right-hand margin of all pages except the first, which is not numbered; the report body continues on line 8.

From the desk of
John McGee

Please prepare this second page of a letter for Ms. Stephanie Whitt-- the first page has already been keyboarded. Use block style, blocked ¶s, and open punctuation.

John McGee

Miss Barbara Perez
Page 2
Current date

¶ Further, I'd like to alert you to another of Women In Business' Saturday Conferences for Women. On Saturday, November 14, the conference will be concerned with the topic "Stress Management." Morning speakers will be followed by a buffet luncheon; the afternoon will be devoted to group discussion. The complete agenda is described in the enclosed brochure.

¶ Also, plan now to be with your colleagues in Chicago for the October National Conference. A number of key speakers (see enclosure) will speak on a variety of topics which address current issues affecting today's business woman. Please fill out the reservation request card as soon as possible to assure your registration.

¶ We look forward to seeing you for these upcoming programs.

Sincerely

Ms. Stephanie Whitt
Executive Director

xx

Enclosures

68a-70a ▶ 5 (daily) Prepare for Keyboarding Tasks

Warm up daily before starting job tasks by keying each line twice (slowly, then faster).

alphabet	1	Max Jevon saw a gray squirrel lift up his tail, bark once, and freeze.
figure	2	Ms. Coe bought 976 of the 2,385 new library books; 1,409 were donated.
fig/sym	3	Does Mrs. Ludlow's Policy #304156 for $58,500 expire on June 27, 1992?
speed	4	He may visit the firm to work with the title forms they handle for me.

| 1 | 2 | 3 | 4 | 5 | 6 | 7 | 8 | 9 | 10 | 11 | 12 | 13 | 14 |

68b-70b ▶ 45 (daily) Office Work Assignments

Job 1
Bulletin Board Announcement

Mrs. Lindsay asks you to prepare an error-free copy of an announcement for square dance night. She wants it centered on a half sheet. Miss Renfro will make photocopies to be posted on the bulletin board in each village.

Job 2
Simplified Memo
(LM p. 73)

Mrs. Lindsay hands you handwritten copy for a memo that she wants prepared in final form. She lists these instructions:

1. Use **June 27** of the current year as the date.

2. It is to go to **All Camp Counselors and Directors.**

3. As a subject, use **SPECIAL EVENTS PLANNING MEETING.**

4. Use my name as the writer.

5. Use your initials for reference.

6. Don't forget to indicate the enclosure.

SQUARE DANCE NIGHT
For Junior and Senior Campers
Kilmer Youth Camp Pavilion
8:00 p.m., July 20
Refreshments and Prizes
Sponsor: Miss Julie Renfro

Enclosed is a schedule of special events planned for this summer's group of campers. As you can see, it is a busy schedule that will require careful planning if everything is to run smoothly.

As in the past, each event will be planned and supervised by one of the camp or village directors, two counselors, and two CITs. A general planning meeting will be held at 7 p.m. on July 1 in the guest dining room of the pavilion. All camp directors and counselors should be there. Counselors should leave their CITs in charge of the campers.

Please study the schedule of events, identify the events on which you would most like to work, and come with ideas for organizing and directing the events of your choice. Insofar as we are able, we'll try to honor your choices.

From the desk of John McGee

Jeff Brown, Division Manager of Centek Office Systems, Inc., wants three letters prepared for the three regional managers of his company. Their names and addresses are listed below. Use modified block style, indented ¶s, and mixed punctuation. Use current date and supply an appropriate salutation and complimentary close. Mr. Brown will sign each letter. The three names and addresses are:

Mrs. Judith Marx,
  Manager
Centek Office Systems,
  Inc.
Western Regional Office
303 Kings Lane
Santa Maria, CA 93454-
  0091

Mr. Alberto Valdez,
  Manager
Centek Office Systems,
  Inc.
Eastern Regional Office
2900 Revere Avenue
Manchester, NH 03103-
  2211

Mrs. Carmen Torres,
  Manager
Centek Office Systems,
  Inc.
Southern Regional Office
450 Crest Lane
Lakeland, FL 33803-1021

John McGee

(¶) When we meet next month at the divisional meeting, we will be discussing various printers on the market and the budget allocations each regional division will be given to purchase such printers. There will be various manufacturers on hand to answer any questions you may have about such acquisitions. In the paragraphs below, I have outlined some basic characteristics of the types of printers we will be examining.

(¶) Dot matrix printers--those that use a combination of dots on the paper to form the letters or characters--can print copy at high speed. The speed is usually listed in characters per second (c p s). A high-speed dot matrix printer can produce copy at a rate of 400 characters per second, the equivalent of 80 five-stroke words. With such high-speed printers, the dots are visible and the quality of print is poor. Letter-quality daisy wheel printers are also available. The printing speed varies from 10 to 50 c p s. These printers cost much more than matrix printers.

(¶) Two other technologies--laser and ink jet--can give letter-quality print at extremely high speeds, but such printers may be too expensive for regional budgets. With the first method, a laser beam scorches images onto regular paper. With the second, spurts of ink controlled by a magnetic field are shot onto the paper to form the characters.

(¶) Please familiarize yourself with the enclosed booklets. I will send information about the display unit soon.

68b-70b (continued)

Job 3
Schedule in Table Form

Mr. Lindsay gives you a rough-draft copy of the schedule of special events for the summer. He asks you to prepare the table in final form on a full sheet, all errors corrected. He suggests that you leave 6 spaces between columns. It will be photocopied to be enclosed with copies of the memo you have just processed.

SCHEDULE of SPECIAL EVENTS

Event	Date	Time
Nature trail Campout	July 10-12	10:30 a.m.
Square Dance Night	July 20	8:00 p.m.
Swimming/Diving Competition	July 27	9:30 a.m.
Tennis Tournament	July 31	10:30 a.m.
Soft ball Playoffs	August 1-3	1:30 p.m.
Hot Dog/Marshmallow Roast	August 6	7:30 p.m.
Volleyball Playoffs	August 10-11	1:30 p.m.
Arts and Crafts Exhibit	August 12-15	All Day
Athletics Exhibition	August 14	9:30 a.m.
Sailboat Regatta	August 14	2:00 p.m.
Parents/Awards Banquet	August 14	7:00 p.m.
Bon Voyage Brunch	August 15	11:00 a.m.

Job 4
Form Letter in Block Style
(LM pp. 75-82)

Mrs. Lindsay hands you the body copy for a letter she wants sent to each of the addresses she gives you. She asks you to prepare an original copy for each addressee. She tells you to date each letter **July 14** of the current year and supply an appropriate salutation, complimentary close, and enclosure notation. As the **Camp Director**, she will sign each letter. She asks you to use large business envelopes.

The Kilmer Youth Camp ends its summer activities on Sunday, August 15. Starting at 9:30 Saturday morning, a fun-filled weekend of camper/parent activities is planned.

The directors and counselors at Kilmer cordially invite you to attend the Athletics Exhibition which begins at 9:30 on Saturday morning, the Sailboat Regatta which begins at 2:00 that afternoon, and the Parents/Awards Banquet which starts at 7:00 Saturday evening. And be sure to join us for the Bon Voyage Brunch at 11:00 Sunday morning. All these events are provided with the compliments of Kilmer Youth Camp.

Please check on the enclosed card those events you plan to attend and return the card to me by July 31. I am also enclosing a list of motels and hotels in the Tapoco and Robbinsville area where you may obtain weekend accommodations.

Please join in the final festivities of a successful summer camp experience for your youngsters.

Addresses

Mr. and Mrs. Eduardo Basanez
3100 Wilson Road
Bakersfield, CA 93304-4903

Mrs. Belinda Jamieson
4384 W. Prien Lake Road
Lake Charles, LA 70605-7281

Dr. and Mrs. Lee Chang
One Sage Court
White Plains, NY 10605-2256

Mr. Kermit J. Hendricks
8205 Wasco Street, NE
Portland, OR 97220-8101

From the desk of
John McGee

Prepare this rough-draft memo in simplified format on plain paper. Correct any undetected errors you may find.

John McGee

All Office Personel

ELECTRONIC KEYBOARD

Use current date

Here is additional informaiton about the electronic keyboard or keypad which is to be used with the micro computer or the word processor.

In my previous letter, memo I mentioned to you that the basic keyboard is the same as that now found on the electornic typewriter. The location of the special function keys varies according to the brand name of the manufacturer fo the keyboard or keypad. Never the less it is relatively easy to learn to use the speical functin keys. The operators manual usually gives a detailed explanation of these uses; or, if the keyboard is "user friendly," the function of a key will be is indicated on the key.

The key pad can be tilted from 10 to 15 degrees to accomodate the operator. Here however it is important for the operator to be sure to keep the keypad in proper keyboarding position for maximum keyboarding efficiency, and for the reduction of keyboarding fatigue.

Please review the literature before the workshop.

Marie Cortez, Director of Personnel

xx

Attachment

The rule to follow is this: When the tips of the fingers are on the keyboard, the base of the hand and the elbow should all be aligned with the angle of the keypad for maximum keyboarding efficiency and for reduction of keyboarding fatigue.

The attached literature will give you additional information about the keyboard or keypad. A special workshop will be offered to all interested employees in the near future.

Job 5
Report from Rough Draft

Mr. Adams and Ms. Rountree, directors of the boys' and girls' villages, have prepared rough copy for a page of the brochure that will be used to promote attendance at Kilmer next summer.

Mr. Adams asks you to prepare a final copy in unbound report form. The copy will be sent to a phototypesetter, so he wants letter-perfect copy. Because this copy will be part of the final printed brochure, page numbers will be added when the brochure is typeset.

EXCITING NEW PROGRAMS — *center / main heading*

The ~~D~~ *lc* irectors of Kilmer Youth Camp have under~~way~~, some *development* ~~brand~~ new facilities and programs that ~~we expect~~ will be in operation for next summer's campers.

New Aquatics Facility

Nearing completion is a new facility that permits under-cover swimming *and diving* activities. The Olympic-size pool will also be used for ~~sports like~~ water polo and water volleyball.

New Gymnastics Facility

A new gym is being built ~~housing~~ *to house* ra~~c~~quetball courts, weight-training rooms, indoor volleyball, basketball, and *a* ~~some~~ *variety of* gymnastic equipment such as trampoline, balance beam, parallel bars, *rings,* and side horse.

New Computer-Literacy Center

As part of our "Learning Is Fun" program, we are installing a computer ~~area~~ *center* where formal instruction and supervised informal practice *in the use of* ~~on~~ computers will be provided. In addition to group and tutorial instruction, *software* learning packages will be available to motivate additional practice through electronic games.

New Soccer Field *and Archery Range*

Contributions from several alumni have made possible the a~~d~~dition of a soccer field. *and an archery range* Both soccer and archery will be added to ~~the~~ *next summer's* program of events. ~~next summer~~

¶ Thanks to the fund-raising drive spearheaded by parents of many of our current and former campers, we have been able to expand our facilit~~ies~~ and improve our programs. This kind of support speaks well for the educational and recreational programs we have provided our alumni campers in the 27 years since our camp was founded.

Jobs 3 and 4
(LM pp. 21-24)

From the desk of
John McGee

William Turnage,
President of the
Wilderness Society,
wishes to see this
letter prepared in
both modified block
and block letter
style. Use blocked
¶s and open punc-
tuation with each
letter and correct
any errors Mr.
Turnage may have
overlooked. Pre-
pare 1 carbon copy
of each letter for
the files.

John McGee

Mr. James Bisenius
1633 East Avenue
Haywood, CA 94541-2203

Use current date

Dear Mr. Bisenius

Enclosed ~~you will find~~ *is* your new membership decal along with *ness* your renewal notice. Although your membership in The Wilder Society has not expired, it will soon; and I am writing ~~ine order~~ to ask you to renew at this time. In this way, we can avoid costly membership reminders, and use our limited budget for the public good.

This ~~passed~~ *past* year, The Wilderness Society has been very influ- # ential in working to expand our nations inventory of wildlands-- public lands whose need for protection has never been more ~~urgante~~ *urgent*.

Thank you for your continued support, a reply envelope is enclosed for your ~~conveniance~~. *Convenience*

Sincerely

The Wilderness Society *ALL CAPS*

QS →

William A. Turnage, *President*

xx Enclosure

By renewing now, you can be sure your subscription to The Living Wilderness will continue without interruption.

Job 5

From the desk of
John McGee

Prepare this hand-
written memo for
Carlos Lara, Head
of Transportation
of Fairfield Manu-
facturing. He asks
for simplified for-
mat on plain paper.

John McGee

Use current date

All Employees
Transportation For Company Business } ALL CAP

(¶) The Purchasing Department has recently signed an agreement to lease a variety of cars, vans, and buses. They will be arriving within the next two weeks. (¶) When you need to use such equipment for company business, please place your request at our central garage. At least a forty-eight hour notice will be necessary to reserve any needed transportation. Your authorized budget number should be given when placing your request.

Carlos Lara, Head of Transportation
xx

Unit 13 Lessons 71-72

Learning Goals
1. To improve basic keyboarding skill.
2. To review formatting guides and procedures for letters, reports, and tables.
3. To demonstrate the application of formatting guides and procedures in preparing letters, reports, and tables.

Machine Adjustments
1. Paper guide at 0.
2. Ribbon control set to use top half of ribbon.
3. Margin sets: 70-space line for drills and ¶s; as required for problems.
4. Line space selector to SS drills, DS ¶s; as required for problems.

Lesson 71   Prepare for Measurement

71a ▶ 5
Conditioning Practice

each line twice SS (slowly, then faster); if time permits, rekey line 4

alphabet	1	Jen can get five quiet days off, for she works extra at my plaza club.
figures	2	They replaced at cost 50 plates, 78 knives, 194 forks, and 362 spoons.
fig/sym	3	Boyd & Co. is #307 of 1,648 top firms rated in <u>Fortune</u>, June 25, 1987.
speed	4	Both of us may wish to bid for the antique bicycle or the ivory whale.

| 1 | 2 | 3 | 4 | 5 | 6 | 7 | 8 | 9 | 10 | 11 | 12 | 13 | 14 |

71b ▶ 15
Improve Keyboarding Skill: Skill Comparison

1. A 30" writing on each line; find *gwam* on each writing:

   1' *gwam* × 2

2. Compare *gwam* rates; identify 4 slowest lines.

3. Take a 30" and a 1' writing on each of those lines to improve speed.

balanced-hand	1	The goal of the panel is to handle the big fuel problem for the towns.
double letters	2	Ann will assess the food served at the inn to see if it is acceptable.
combination	3	An audit crew is due at noon; we shall look into the tax problem then.
3d row	4	Terry tried to type the two weather reports with the quiet typewriter.
1st/3d rows	5	Bix quit my new committee on community power to rezone river property.
adjacent-key	6	We built a radio forum on the premise that expert opinion was popular.
outside-reach	7	Alex lost a list of top wallpaper sizes so he will not sell his quota.
direct-reach	8	Brenda checked both number columns twice before she plotted the curve.
one-hand	9	You saw him test a rated water pump on my extra car at a union garage.
shift keys	10	Sumio and Luisa beat Drucilla and Michi in the tournament in San Juan.
figures	11	Of 1,089 pages, 764 were textual pages and 325 were appendix material.
balanced-hand	12	Eighty of the city firms may form a panel to handle the fuel problems.

| 1 | 2 | 3 | 4 | 5 | 6 | 7 | 8 | 9 | 10 | 11 | 12 | 13 | 14 |

71c ▶ 30
Prepare for Measurement

3 full sheets
1 half sheet

Make a list of the problems and page numbers given below:
page 76, 43b, Drills 1 and 2
page 79, 44d, Problem 1
page 110, 61c, Problem 1

Review the formatting guides for letters on page 75 and for tables on pages 105-106.

Format and key the problems on your list according to the directions given with the problems. Correct any errors you make as you key.

From the desk of
John McGee

Joanne Cox, Vice President of United Processing Service, has prepared this draft memo describing the new policy regarding simplified memorandums in the company. Please prepare it in final form on plain paper, using the simplified style discussed in the memo. Ms. Cox asked for 1 carbon copy.

John McGee

Line 10

Febuary 14, 19-- ~~r~~

QS

Janet C. Robertson, *Personnel Manager*

Simplified Memorandum } ALL CAPS

Sumarized here is ~~the~~ our policy ~~on~~ regarding simplified memos. We ~~like~~ have adopted the simplified memorandum not only for our own interoffice memorandums to be prepared within the company, but also for any memorandums which our clients request us to prepare. The only exception will be if clients request that their memo-randums be prepared on their own forms. *printed*

of this policy We will need copies distributed to all of the current word processors and keyboard specialists. Also please review the feaures of this style (listed below) so that you will be able to discuss them in detail *should questions arise.*

1. Prepare simplified memorandums on standard letterhead or plain paper (as specified).

   DS   *side*

2. Use block format with 1" margins.

3. Place the date a double space below the last line of the letterhead or on line 10 if plain paper is used.

4. Double-space below all major parts (name of recipient, ~~the~~ subject line, body paragraphs, reference initials, closing notations) *except* below the dateline and the last para-graph of the body. Quadruple-space (space down 4 times) below ~~the~~ dateline and last paragraph.

5. Single-space the body; double-space between paragraphs.

6. Single-space enumerated items; leave ~~iether~~ a double ~~or single~~ space between ~~them.~~ *items.*

   DS

Because of its streamline*d* format, the simplified memorandum*s* can be processed easily on our microcomputer ~~or~~ word processors. Should ~~and~~ *any* problems arise, please let me know.

   QS ——— *regarding this policy,*

Joanne Cox, Vice Presid*e*nt

xx

72a ▶ 5
Conditioning Practice

each line twice SS (slowly, then faster); if time permits, rekey line 4

alphabet 1 Jacki Veloz hung exquisite paintings on a wall of the academy library.

figures 2 I shall print 850 cards, 173 calendars, 96 leaflets, and 24 circulars.

fig/sym 3 Check #84 (dated 6/5) for $93 covers Invoice #275 less a 10% discount.

speed 4 Is she to pay the six firms for all the bodywork they do on the autos?

| 1 | 2 | 3 | 4 | 5 | 6 | 7 | 8 | 9 | 10 | 11 | 12 | 13 | 14 |

72b ▶ 10
Check Keyboarding Skill: Straight Copy

1. A 3' writing on ¶s 1-3 combined; find *gwam*, circle errors.

2. A 1' writing on each ¶; find *gwam* on each.

3. Another 3' writing on ¶s 1-3 combined; find *gwam*, circle errors.

all letters used | A | 1.5 si | 5.7 awl | 80% hfw

gwam 3' | 5'

Human relations skills on the job are very critical in terms of — 4 | 3

how you will be perceived by peers as well as by superiors. During — 9 | 5

your early weeks at work, you will be sized up quickly by co-workers. — 14 | 8

How they observe and evaluate you will help to determine whether your — 18 | 11

work experience will be pleasant, successful, and valuable. — 22 | 13

Be cautious at first and do not align yourself closely with any — 26 | 16

of the cliques that often develop in the workplace. Show understand- — 31 | 19

ing and be courteous to everybody, but don't take sides in a dispute — 36 | 21

that may occur between members of any group of workers. Show that you — 40 | 24

can think for yourself, but don't convey your ideas too freely. — 45 | 27

Look, listen, and learn before you take an active part in the poli- — 49 | 29

tics of the workplace. Let the older, experienced workers be the agents — 54 | 32

of change. Study and learn from them and carefully notice what seems — 59 | 35

to cause their successes or failures. As you develop on a job, all — 63 | 38

positive human relations skills will be rewarded. — 66 | 40

gwam 3' | 1 | 2 | 3 | 4 | 5 |
5' | 1 | 2 | 3 |

72c ▶ 35
Prepare for Measurement

3 full sheets

Make a list of the problems and page numbers given below:

pages 95-96, 52b
page 97, 53b

Review the formatting guides for preparing reports, reference lists, and title pages on pages 93 and 97.

Format and key the problems on your list according to the directions given with the problems. Correct any errors you make as you key.

91a-95a ▶ 5 (daily)
Conditioning Practice

each line twice (slowly, faster); repeat as many times as you can in 5' at the beginning of each class period

alphabet 1 New equipment will be purchased for the key junior magazine executive.

figures 2 We received 130 chairs, 129 desks, and 75 computers on Order No. 5648.

shift key/lock 3 J. A. Hall, C. McLain, and P. Anzell are experts in BASIC Programming.

speed 4 Sign the form so the auditor may pay their men for their work with us.

| 1 | 2 | 3 | 4 | 5 | 6 | 7 | 8 | 9 | 10 | 11 | 12 | 13 | 14 |

91b-95b ▶ 45 (daily)
Job 1 (plain sheet)

all letters used | A | 1.5 si | 5.7 awl | 80% hfw

From the desk of John McGee

Please take this keyboarding test to give me a gauge of your keyboarding potential. Take two 1' writings on each ¶ and one 5' writing on both ¶s combined. Record your best 5' score at the top of your paper.

John McGee

gwam 5'

The question that may be and often is asked by some persons is this: 3 | 54

What is a computer? A computer is merely a piece of equipment, much like   6 | 57

an electronic typewriter only much more complicated. The heart of the   9 | 60

computer is the microchip, or what is known as the central processing   11 | 63

unit. Computers are designed and programmed to process data at high   14 | 66

speed. With special software programs, the computer can be converted to   17 | 68

a word processor so that it can be used for the preparation of written   19 | 71

documents. The basic parts of a computer system are the keyboard, the   23 | 75

central processing unit, the display unit, and the printer.   25 | 76

Computers can be programmed to do almost any kind of a job. At the   27 | 79

present time, there are as many as fifty or more different programming   31 | 82

languages. Languages are used to change the English-like orders of a   33 | 85

programmer into the binary symbols—ones and zeros—which can be under-   36 | 88

stood by the central processing unit of the computer. BASIC is one of   39 | 91

the common programming languages. It has many benefits. It is very easy   42 | 94

to learn and to use because its English-like commands and organization   45 | 96

are flexible and easy to remember. During your life, you will probably   48 | 99

learn to use many different computer languages. It will be an exciting   51 | 102

adventure for you.   51 | 103

gwam 5' | 1 | 2 | 3 |

Unit 14   Lessons 73-75

Measurement Goals

1. To demonstrate that you can keyboard for 3' on straight copy material at an acceptable speed within an error limit specified by your teacher.

2. To demonstrate that you can format and key (with errors corrected) letters, reports, and tables according to standard formatting guides.

Machine Adjustments

1. Paper guide at *0*.

2. Ribbon control set to use top half of ribbon.

3. Margin sets: 70-space line for drills and ¶s; as required by formatting guides for letters, reports, and tables.

4. Line-space selector to SS drills, DS ¶s; as required for problems.

Lesson 73   Measure Straight Copy and Letter Skills

73a ▶ 5
Conditioning Practice

each line twice SS (slowly, then faster); if time permits, a 1' writing on line 4

alphabet	1	Quite a few men like to do juggling exercises on the very big trapeze.
figures	2	Add 14 meters 25 centimeters, 89 meters 36 centimeters, and 70 meters.
fig/sym	3	The amount of $3,469 I quoted on Order #82071 included a 5% sales tax.
speed	4	Key firms of both towns may risk a penalty if the fuel profit is down.

| 1 | 2 | 3 | 4 | 5 | 6 | 7 | 8 | 9 | 10 | 11 | 12 | 13 | 14 |

73b ▶ 10
Check Keyboarding Skill: Straight Copy

1. A 3' writing on ¶s 1-3 combined; find *gwam*; circle errors.

2. A 1' writing on ¶ 1; find *gwam*; circle errors.

3. A 1' writing on ¶ 2 and on ¶ 3 in the same way.

4. Another 3' writing on ¶s 1-3 combined; find *gwam*, circle errors.

all letters used | A | 1.5 si | 5.7 awl | 80% hfw

	gwam 3'	5'
You have learned a great many things since you began a keyboarding course. Not only have you built good operational technique with speed, you have also grown confident in using a machine with ease and control as you key a letter, report, table, or other document.	4 9 14 18	3 5 8 11
Although you have learned a lot, there is much yet for you to master. For example, you should learn to format additional letter and report styles because they are widely used in business. You can format simple tables; however, you have not attempted a complex one.	22 27 31 35	13 16 19 21
Just as speed and accuracy on straight copy are highly prized, so is the ability to process with efficiency a wide variety of documents that are used for both personal and business needs. Another term of directed practice will push you to higher skill in both areas.	40 44 49 53	24 27 29 32

gwam 3' | 1 | 2 | 3 | 4 | 5 |
        5' | 1 | 2 | 3 |

Excerpts (continued)

Special parts of a letter. The *subject line,* if used, informs the reader of the content of the letter; it is shown in ALL CAPS a DS below the salutation. Begin at left margin or indent to paragraph point if body paragraphs are indented.

The *company name in closing lines,* if used, is shown in ALL CAPS a DS below the complimentary close. The writer's name and title are then placed four lines below the company name.

If more than one *notation* is used in a letter, DS between them and follow this order: typist's initials, enclosure or attachment notation, copy notation, and postscript. Use the abbreviations *cc* (carbon copy) or *pc* (photocopy) for copy notations, leaving one space between the abbreviation and the name of the receiver. Omit the abbreviation (P.S.) for postscript and begin at left margin if body paragraphs are blocked or indent to paragraph point if body paragraphs are indented.

Kingsley Publishers

200 Fairway Drive ● Davenport, IA 52806-1320 ● (319) 642-8811

June 8, 19--

Miss Arlene Douglas
Central Business Academy
666 Walnut Street
Des Moines, IA 50309-2661

Dear Miss Douglas:

LETTER FORMATTING

Enclosed is the booklet, LETTER FORMATTING, that you asked me to send you. It illustrates and describes the letter formats most often used for business letters.

The letter you are reading is an example of the modified block style with indented paragraphs and mixed punctuation. As you can see, a colon is placed after the salutation, and a comma follows the complimentary close when using mixed punctuation. Also, the dateline and closing lines are begun at center point in all modified block letters.

This letter also illustrates the correct placement of special parts: subject line, company name in closing, enclosure notation, copy notation, and postscript. A letter rarely will use more than one or two special parts; many letters have none. We have used them merely to illustrate their placement.

Sincerely yours,

KINGSLEY PUBLISHERS

Mark Greeley, Managing Editor

bx

Enclosure

cc Joan Banks

Should you desire to place an order with us for additional copies of LETTER FORMATTING, let me know.

Special Parts of Letter

ASSEMBLING AND INSERTING CARBON PACKS

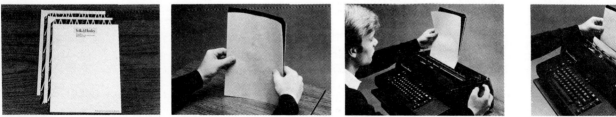

Desk-top assembly method

1. Assemble letterhead, carbon sheets (uncarboned side up), and second sheets as illustrated above. *Use one carbon and one second sheet for each copy desired.*

2. Grasp the carbon pack at the sides, turn it so that the *letterhead faces away from you, the carbon side of the carbon paper is toward you, and the top edge of the pack is face down.* Tap the sheets gently on the desk to straighten.

3. Hold the sheets firmly to prevent slipping; insert pack into typewriter. Hold pack with one hand; turn platen with the other.

Inserting the pack with a trough

To keep the carbon pack straight when feeding it into the typewriter, place the pack in the fold of a plain sheet of paper (paper trough) or under the flap of an envelope. Remove the trough or envelope when the pack is in place.

73c ▶ 35
Check Formatting Skills: Letters

1 plain full sheet
2 letterheads (LM pp. 83-86)
correction supplies

Problem 1
Personal-Business Letter

Using your own return address, format and key the letter on a plain sheet. Use a 60-space line; place date on line 15.

	words
(Your return address) August 25, 19-- Mrs. Alice Lindsay, Director Kilmer	18
Youth Camp P.O. Box 575 Tapoco, NC 28780-8514 Dear Mrs. Lindsay	31

Thank you very much for giving me the opportunity to work in your office | 46
this summer. It was an excellent experience, and I enjoyed working for | 60
money instead of grades! | 66

Although I missed a few of the activities others enjoyed, I felt sort of special | 82
being able to work with you, the other directors, and the counselors. I'm | 97
sure the trade-off was worthwhile. | 104

I'll be returning to Kilmer next summer. If you found my work satisfactory, | 119
perhaps you will permit me to work for you again. With another year of | 134
training, I should be prepared to use the new word processor you expect to | 149
have by then. | 152

Cordially yours (Your name) | 158

Problem 2
Business Letter

letterhead; 60-space line; current date on line 15; prepare an envelope; correct errors

Problem 3
Business Letter

Use Problem 2 directions, but address the letter to:

Mr. Henry S. Ho
Senior Class President
Midtown School of Business
4800 Wilshire Boulevard
Los Angeles, CA 90010-2253

Supply an appropriate salutation.

	words
Miss Paula Nicols, President Business Education Club Waverly Academy	14
of Business 800 S. Rolling Road Baltimore, MD 21228-7801 Dear Miss	27
Nicols	29

Thank you for giving me the opportunity to tell you the main things we look | 44
for in entry-level office workers. | 51

First, we look for graduates who have specific skills we need: in keyboard- | 66
ing, word processing, accounting, filing, and so on. A personal data sheet | 82
will usually provide such information. | 90

Next, we seek people who show pride in themselves--those who dress appro- | 104
priately and are well groomed and who speak positively and forcefully about | 119
their educational background and related experiences. Usually these behav- | 134
ior patterns are observed in the job interview. | 144

Finally, we seek people who show evidence that they can work well with | 158
others. An effective application letter and data sheet will identify group | 174
activities in which the applicant has participated successfully and in what | 189
roles. | 190

People with these qualifications have at least the potential to develop into | 206
valuable members of an office staff. | 213

Sincerely yours Arnold J. Hoffman, Director Personnel Department xx | 227

Training Goals

1. To become familiar with the work of a word processing office.

2. To develop and increase skill in formatting and keying letters in modified block and block styles.

3. To develop and increase skill in preparing simplified memos.

Machine Adjustments

1. Paper guide at *0*.

2. Paper bail rolls at even intervals across page.

Use:

*70-space line and single spacing for drill; DS between each SS group of drill lines

*70-space line and double spacing for ¶ timings

*as directed for jobs

UNITED PROCESSING SERVICE: A CO-OP SIMULATION

Simplified Memo

Work Assignment

Your school in conjunction with various businesses in your community has developed a co-op program to give you actual work experience. You have been assigned to work as a keyboarding trainee for United Processing Service, which provides office services for local businesses. As a co-op trainee you will be assigned work from John McGee, General Office Manager of United Processing Service. You will be preparing mainly correspondence (letters and memorandums).

Each job assignment you receive will be accompanied by instructions stating any particular procedure(s) you will need to follow. When only minimum instructions are given, you are expected to use your own judgment. In some cases, you may be expected to correct undetected errors in grammar or punctuation that have been overlooked by the company submitting the documents.

When completed, all work should be given to your supervisor (your teacher) to examine. You, however, must judge the acceptability of your final work. You should proofread your work carefully, neatly correcting all errors, before submitting it to your supervisor.

United Processing Service has based its office manual on CENTURY 21 KEYBOARDING, FORMATTING, AND DOCUMENT PROCESSING; therefore, use the index of your textbook to check matters of placement when in doubt.

Before beginning your first job assignment, your supervisor gives you a copy of "Excerpts from the Office Manual." You are requested to review them before beginning your work.

Excerpts from the Office Manual

Simplified Memos

A simplified memorandum may be prepared on either letterhead or plain paper.

It is formatted in block style with 1″ side margins. Place the date on line 10 or a DS below the letterhead (if letterhead paper is used). DS below major parts of memo and below paragraphs except after the dateline and the last paragraph of the body. Quadruple-space (space down 4 times) below the date and last paragraph of the body; SS body paragraphs.

Letters

Prepare letters in either block or modified block style, depending on the request of a client. Use 1″, 1½″, or 2″ side margins, depending on the number of words in the letter body (refer to letter placement table, page 149 of your textbook, if necessary).

Second page of letter. For letters requiring a second page, use plain paper of the same quality as the letterhead. Provide a heading on second page and leave at least a 1″ bottom margin on each page. When dividing a paragraph between pages, at least 2 lines of the paragraph must appear on each page.

Heading for second page of letter. The heading for a second page of a letter is started on line 6. DS between heading and body. The two heading styles, as illustrated below, are: (1) *block style* — usually used with block letters; and (2) *horizontal style* — usually used with modified block letters.

> Miss Holly Hudson
> Page 2
> June 15, 19--
>
> in your new position as an account representative for Ernst and Jung Associates. The two-day orientation session will allow you to learn about the company's philosophy and purpose, as well as

Block Style Heading

> Miss Holly Hudson   2   June 15, 19--
>
> in your new position as an account representative for Ernst and Jung Associates. The two-day orientation session will allow you to learn about the company's philosophy and purpose, as well as

Horizontal Style Heading

74a ▶ 5
Conditioning Practice

each line twice SS (slowly, then faster); if time permits, a 1' writing on line 4

alphabet 1 The vote forced the town board to combine six zoning projects quickly.

figures 2 She wired them $365 on May 29 for the items ordered on Invoice 401827.

fig/sym 3 Su & Wong's order (#21473) for 850 sets of 6-ply NCR paper came May 9.

speed 4 It is their duty to sign the amendment if he is to handle the problem.

| 1 | 2 | 3 | 4 | 5 | 6 | 7 | 8 | 9 | 10 | 11 | 12 | 13 | 14 |

74b ▶ 45 Check Formatting Skills: Reports

4 plain full sheets
correction supplies

Problem 1
Two-Page Unbound Report

Format and key the report. Add page number at top of second page. Correct marked errors and any errors you make as you key.

Proofreader's Marks

∧ insert

⌒ close up

✗ delete

space

❝ ❞ quotation marks

/ℓc lowercase

⌄ insert comma

∾ transpose

⊙ period

≡ capitalize

words

HUMAN RELATIONS AT WORK QS   5

The term "human relations" means simply "all interactions 16

among two or more people" (Higins, 1982, 4). The term aplies 29

equally in family school, business, and other organizational settings. 44

Of the many definitions of "work," the most commonly used one is 57

given offered by Buttel (1985 25): "Labor, task, or duty that affords gives 70

one the accustomed means of livelihood." 78

Effective Human relations at work consists of getting along well with others on 94

the job: with supervisors, with peers, and with subordinates. Vir- 108

tually all business operations are group activities that require demand 121

team work of the individuals people who make up the group. Without team- 134

work--each person one contributing his or her share of effort in the right 148

way at the right time --the goals of the group activity are not met. From the 163

personal stand point, it means learning to "fit in," to do one's 176

share, and to be recognized for being as a valued member of the team. 190

As a beginning worker, learning to do the job assigned 201

seems to be the most important immediate goal. Just as important, however, is 217

to learn the status of people around you, the unwritten code of behavior 231

in your work area, what treatment others expect from you, and 244

how you can most smoothly fit yourself into the work group. You do this by 259

studying three groups of people. 266

Supervisors and Other Superiors 278   ← DS this ¶

First, learn who has some control of the work you are to do. Let 291
them guide you into the work patterns they wish you to follow, 304
the formality or informality of the relationship they want to 316
maintain with you, and the chain of command you are to follow 329
to seek help and resolve problems (Reynolds, 1983, 24). 340

90d ▶ 30
Measure Document Processing Skill: Letters

Time Schedule
Plan and prepare .... 4'
Timed production .... 20'
Proofread; compute *n-pram* .... 6'

Use letterheads (LM pp. 17-20) or plain full sheets for the letter problems. Determine placement: See table, p. 149. Correct all errors.

If you complete the letters before time is called, start over on plain sheets. Proofread your work.

Determine total words keyed. Deduct 15 words for each uncorrected error; divide remainder by 20 to determine *n-pram* (net production rate a minute). Compare your *n-pram* with your *g-pram* of 89c. If your *n-pram* is much lower, you may need to try to improve your accuracy or give attention to your error correction skill.

n-pram (net production rate a minute) = total words keyed − (15 × number of uncorrected errors) ÷ time (in minutes) of writing

words

Problem 1
modified block style; blocked ¶s; mixed punctuation

	words
February 3, 19-- |Ms. Stacey Hunnel |Administrative Assistant |Seattle Office	15
Products Company |200 Academy Place |Seattle, WA 98109-2239 |Dear Ms.	29
Hunnel:	30

(¶ 1) I should like to add to the suggestions I sent to you about proofreading. Prevention or reduction of keyboarding errors will reduce the time needed for the detection and correction of errors. — 44 / 59 / 69

(¶ 2) How does a person prevent or reduce keyboarding errors as letters are produced, and as a consequence, increase letter production rates? The first step is to try to keep your eyes on the copy from which you are keyboarding. In this way, you can avoid breaks in your keyboarding rhythm. As you keyboard, keep your fingers well curved and close to the keys; space quickly after each word and start the new word without a pause. When the bell rings, either finish the word you are keyboarding, if this can be done in a few keystrokes, or divide it with a hyphen at a proper division point. Then make the return and start a new line immediately. Concentrate on the copy to be keyboarded. Read ahead; think and keyboard. — 83 / 99 / 113 / 127 / 142 / 157 / 173 / 188 / 203 / 214

(¶ 3) These suggestions will help you increase your letter production rates. They will help you reduce keyboarding errors and thus simplify the proofreading process. Try them and see. (220) — 228 / 243 / 250

Sincerely yours, |Mrs. Jane Denny |Communications Consultant |xx — 262

285

Problem 2
modified block style; indented ¶s; mixed punctuation

Recall: Modified block style with indented ¶s differs from modified block style with blocked ¶s only in that each ¶ is indented 5 spaces.

	words
February 10, 19-- |Mr. Darwin Parsons, President |Domino Technology, Inc. |	14
1511 Pacific View Drive |San Diego, CA 92109-2299 |Dear Mr. Parsons:	28

(¶ 1) Planning for the future is the key element for the continuing success of any business firm. To paraphrase Abraham Lincoln, you can't be sure of getting there unless you determine in advance where it is you are going. — 42 / 57 / 72

(¶ 2) When planning for the future of your company, the definition of goals and objectives is crucial. Without that, it would not be clear when an opportunity was being realized, nor would we know what to do in the face of endless options. — 86 / 101 / 116 / 119

(¶ 3) All this concern with the importance of planning is by way of introducing you to our new publication, EFFECTIVE PLANNING. This book has received rave reviews from all who have read it. The content of the book is described in the enclosed brochure. I know you will want to order a copy for yourself and other key executives in your company. It will be an investment that will pay immediate dividends. (172) — 133 / 147 / 162 / 177 / 192 / 200

Sincerely yours, |Miss Jackie Schaefer |Publications Department |xx | Enclosure — 213 / 215

236

words

Peers 342

Coworkers at *or near* your level of employment are a second group 356

you should study *with care*. Learn to distinguish between those who are 370

merely officious and those who are helpful *,* valued members of the 383

work group in the eyes of other workers *and supervisors*. Be courteous to all, 399

but pattern your behavior after those who have the ear *and respect* of their 414

supervisors. 417

Subordinates 422

Those whose job level is higher than that of others *should* ~~must~~ 434

learn to show courtesy toward and respect for such ~~people.~~ *subordinates.* 447

Give directions clearly to avoid having subordinates *redo* ~~do over~~ 460

work needlessly. Show appreciation for work *done*. If criticism 473

and correction are required, inform the worker in private *,* 484

rather than in front of other workers. 492

In summary, human relations requires an "all for one and 504

one for all" attitude. It means that all pull together *toward* ~~fore~~ 516

a common goal and each member *of the group* aids and supports every other 531

member in all ways possible. 537

Problem 2
Reference Page

REFERENCES *QS* 2

Bittel, Lester R. <u>What Every Supervisor Should Know</u> 5th ed. 21
    New York: McGraw-Hill Book Company, 1985. 30

Daggett, Willard R. <u>The Dynamics of Work</u>. Cincinnati: South- 47
    Western Publishing Co., 1984. 53

Higgins, James M. <u>Human Relations Concepts and Skills</u>. New 72
    York: Random House, 1982. 78

Reynolds, Carolyn. <u>Dimensions *ine* Professional Development</u>. 98
    2d ed. cincinnati: South-Western Publishing Co., 1983. 109

Problem 3
Title (Cover) Page

90a ▶ 5
Conditioning Practice

each line twice (slowly, faster); as time permits, repeat selected lines

alphabet 1 Gymnasts amaze excited fans and judges with very quick leaps on beams.

figures 2 I may buy 15 jackets, 289 blankets, 74 kits, 360 lamps, and 110 tires.

fingers 3, 4 3 Wally saw six wax owls as he and Pris moved about the quaint villages.

speed 4 The city firm may make the audit when they do the work for you and me.

| 1 | 2 | 3 | 4 | 5 | 6 | 7 | 8 | 9 | 10 | 11 | 12 | 13 | 14 |

90b ▶ 7
Measure Basic Skill: Straight Copy

a 5' writing; find *gwam*; proofread; circle errors

Emphasize: Fingers curved and upright; quick finger-action keystroking.

all letters used | A | 1.5 si | 5.7 awl | 80% hfw

	gwam 3'		5'
Just what does it mean to be young and when is a person young? To	4	3	49
be young is perhaps a feeling or disposition, a particular manner of	9	5	52
looking at things and responding to them. To be young is never a chrono-	14	8	55
logical period or time of life, although it might be a young person	18	11	57
examining some material with fascination and pleasure or the composer	23	14	60
Verdi in his eighties writing his best opera. To be young might be a	28	17	63
person "hanging ten" on a surfboard or swinging to a musical composi-	32	19	66
tion. To be young might be Einstein in his seventies still working with	37	22	69
his field theory, sailing his boat, or playing his cherished fiddle.	42	25	71
To be young is never the monopoly of youth. It flourishes every-	46	28	74
where visionaries have stimulated our thinking or amazed us. To be young	51	31	77
in nature is quite desirable whether you are a young person, a middle-	56	33	80
aged person, or a chronologically old person. To be young should be	60	36	83
respected whether the beard is soft and curly or firm and gray. To be	65	39	85
young has no color; it seems always translucent with its own imaginative	70	42	88
light. There is no generation space between the young of any age because	75	45	91
they see things as they ought to be.	77	46	93

gwam 3' | 1 | 2 | 3 | 4 | 5 |
     5' | 1 | 2 | 3 |

90c ▶ 8
Improve Accuracy

1. Three 1' writings of 90b above; start second and third writings at ending point of previous writing. **Goal:** No more than 2 errors in each writing.

2. A 3' writing on ¶s of 90b with a goal of not more than 6 errors. To do this, start slowly and gradu- ally increase your speed as you feel relaxed. Concentrate on the copy and work with continuity.

75a ▶ 5
Conditioning Practice

each line twice SS (slowly, then faster); if time permits, a 1' writing on line 4

alphabet 1 Al criticized my six workers for having such quick tempers on the job.

figures 2 FOR URGENT CALLS: Fire, 561-3723; Police, 461-7022; Doctor, 841-5839.

fig/sym 3 Terms on Devlin & Arnold's order dated 4/6 for $587.90 are 2/10, n/30.

speed 4 It is the wish of all of us to lend a hand to the visitor to the city.

| 1 | 2 | 3 | 4 | 5 | 6 | 7 | 8 | 9 | 10 | 11 | 12 | 13 | 14 |

75b ▶ 10
Check Keyboarding Skill: Straight Copy

1. A 3' writing on ¶s 1-2 combined; find *gwam*, circle errors.

2. A 1' writing on ¶ 1, then on ¶ 2; find *gwam* and circle errors on each.

3. Another 3' writing on ¶s 1-2 combined; find *gwam*, circle errors.

all letters used | A | 1.5 si | 5.7 awl | 80% hfw | gwam 3' | 5'

Few people have enough time to accomplish everything they desire. — 4 | 3

Those who appear to accomplish many of the things they attempt to do — 9 | 5

make choices regarding the most valuable uses of their time. They set — 14 | 8

up a series of major and minor goals and allocate their time to these — 18 | 11

goals on the basis of relative value in terms of time requirement. — 23 | 14

First, determine exactly what it is you desire to have or to do. — 27 | 16

Next, analyze your behavior or actions to see whether they are helping — 32 | 19

or hindering your progress toward your objectives. On the basis of — 37 | 22

this self-analysis, devise a plan for time use that is unique to your — 41 | 25

own situation. Practice self-management until it becomes a habit. — 46 | 27

gwam 3' | 1 | 2 | 3 | 4 | 5 |
5' | 1 | 2 | 3 |

75c ▶ 35 Check Formatting Skills: Tables

2 half sheets; 1 full sheet correction supplies

Problem 1
Two-Column Table with Main Heading and Source Note

half sheet, long edge at top, 6 spaces between columns

		words
WHO BENEFITS FROM SOCIAL SECURITY		7
Retired workers	46.0 million	13
Disabled workers	10.0 million	19
Children of disabled workers	8.0 million	27
Children of deceased workers	5.0 million	35
Spouses of retired workers	2.5 million	43
Widows and widowers	1.5 million	49
—————		52
Source: Social Security Administration.		60

89a ▶ 5
Conditioning Practice

each line twice (slowly, faster); as time permits, repeat selected lines

alphabet 1 The voluble judge quizzes expert witnesses before making any decision.

figures 2 The zoo ordered 785 birds, 4 bears, 20 bison, 9 lions, and 163 snakes.

quiet hands 3 They decided to attend the dedication when the ceremony was cancelled.

speed 4 Pam may pay the firm for the work when they sign the right audit form.

| 1 | 2 | 3 | 4 | 5 | 6 | 7 | 8 | 9 | 10 | 11 | 12 | 13 | 14 |

89b ▶ 10
Improve Language Skills: Punctuation

full sheet; 1" top margin; 70-space line

Key as directed in 88b, p. 154.

COMMA USAGE (continued)

> Use a comma to set off nonrestrictive clauses (not necessary to the meaning of the sentence); however, do not use commas to set off restrictive clauses (necessary to the meaning of the sentence).

Learn 1. The report, which you prepared, was just great.

Learn 2. The report that deals with uses of solar energy was timely.

Apply 3. Unit 13 which you prepared is well written.

Apply 4. Keyboardists who practice with a purpose make speed gains.

> Use a comma to separate the day from the year and the city from the state.

Learn 5. John made the nominating speech in San Francisco, California.

Learn 6. October 12, 1492, is a special day in history.

Apply 7. (Keyboard a complete sentence giving the date, city, and state of your birth.)

> Use a comma to separate two or more parallel adjectives (adjectives that could be separated by the word "and" instead of the comma).

Learn 8. A happy, excited crowd cheered the team to victory.

Learn 9. A dozen large red roses were delivered. *(comma cannot be used)*

Apply 10. The hot sticky humid air made our stay uncomfortable.

Apply 11. The key is in the small square wooden box on my desk.

> Use a comma to separate (a) unrelated groups of figures which come together and (b) whole numbers into groups of three digits each. *Note:* Policy, year, page, room, telephone, and most serial numbers are keyboarded without commas.

Learn 12. During 1987, 3,285 cars were insured under Policy 23-90456.

Apply 13. In 1986 5674 students were enrolled.

Apply 14. Please call 825-2,626 if you need information on Policy #7,304.

89c ▶ 35
Build Sustained Document Processing Skill: Letters

plain full sheets

Time Schedule
Build skill .... 6'
Plan and prepare .... 4'
Timed production .... 20'
Proofread; compute *g-pram* .... 5'

1. Two 1' writings on date through salutation of Problem 1, page 155; then two 1' writings on complimentary close through reference notation of the problem.

2. A 20' sustained production writings on problems listed

below (make pencil notations of the pages and problems):

    page 153, 87c, Problem 1
    page 155, 88c, Problem 1
    page 155, 88c, Problem 3

    If you complete the letter problems before time is called, start over. Work on the control level; do

not correct errors. When time is called, proofread each letter; circle errors. Compute *g-pram* (gross production rate a minute):

    g-pram = total words ÷ 20

75c (continued)

Problem 2
Two-Column Table with
Main and Secondary Headings
and Source Note

half sheet; long edge at top;
20 spaces between columns

SURVIVAL RATES OF CANCER VICTIMS		7
(Five Most Common Types)		12
Lung	13%	13
Breast	75	15
Colonic	53	18
Prostatic	71	20
Rectal	49	22
_____		25
Source: American Cancer Society.		32

Problem 3
Three-Column Table with
Three Levels of Headings
and Source Note

full sheet;
10 spaces between columns

TOP STATES IN DEFENSE PRODUCTION			7
($ Value and % of State Industrial Production)			16
State	$ Value	% IP	23
California	63.1 billion	7.9	29
Texas	24.6 billion	4.4	33
New York	21.7 billion	4.3	38
Virginia	16.5 billion	10.4	44
Florida	13.8 billion	4.6	49
_____			52
Source: Data Resources, Inc.			58

Problem 4

If you complete all tables before
time is called, repeat Problem 1.

OPTIONAL EVALUATION: Language Skills

Capitalization and Number Expression

1. Read the two ¶s given at the right; mentally note needed changes in capitalization and number expression.

2. Key the ¶s, making the needed changes; correct any errors you make as you key.

commerce clearing house, in a usa today story on august fourteenth, 1985, reports that many states are raising sales taxes. oklahoma, for example, has raised sales tax from three % to 3.25%. connecticut's 7.5% sales tax rate is the usa's highest. 21 states plus the district of columbia impose sales taxes of 5% or more. 5 states have no sales tax, so far.

gasoline taxes, too, are on the increase. texas has raised its tax by 5 cents a gallon; arkansas, by four cents; and tennessee, by 3 cents. the state of washington has the highest gasoline tax -- 18 cents a gallon -- followed by minnesota at seventeen cents a gallon.

**Build Document
Processing Skill: Letters**

words

(LM pp. 11-16) or plain full sheets; correct errors; use your initials instead of xx in the reference notation

Problem 1

modified block style; indented ¶s; mixed punctuation

Note: Modified block style with indented ¶s differs from modified block style with blocked ¶s only in that each ¶ is indented 5 spaces.

Problem 2

modified block style; blocked ¶s; mixed punctuation

Indent numbered items 5 spaces from left and right margins. When keying numbered items follow this procedure:

1. Space in 5 spaces, key the figure 1, period, and two spaces. Set left margin at this point. Move right margin to left 5 spaces.

2. After keying the lines of the first item, DS, press margin release, and backspace to the point to key the figure 2. Space forward to key lines of numbered item.

3. Repeat Step 2 for remainder of numbered items. Remember to reset left and right margins for ¶ 2.

Note: Because this letter has a number of unusual parts, start date on line 12.

Problem 3

modified block style; indented ¶s; mixed punctuation

January 25, 19-- | Mrs. Jane Denny | Communications Consultant | Heald	13
Colleges, Suite 1100 | 1255 Post Street | San Francisco, CA 94109-4201 | Dear	28
Mrs. Denny:	30
(¶ 1) My employer, Mr. Henry Seurer, heard you speak at a recent conven-	43
tion. He was impressed with your comments about improving communica-	57
tion skills. He said that if I would write to you, you could give me some	72
suggestions for improving my proofreading skills.	82
(¶ 2) May I hear from you soon. I really do need your help. (63)	93
Sincerely yours, | Ms. Stacey Hunnel | Administrative Assistant | xx	106
	128

January 30, 19-- | Ms. Stacey Hunnel | Administrative Assistant | Seattle Office	15
Products Company | 200 Academy Place | Seattle, WA 98109-2239 | Dear Ms.	29
Hunnel:	30
(¶ 1) I'm pleased to respond to your inquiry about improving your proof-	43
reading skills. In this "high-tech" age, proofreading is an important skill.	59
All keyboarded work should be proofread before you remove it from your	73
typewriter or before you push the print key if you are using a word pro-	88
cessor. Here are some steps to follow when proofreading the letters you	102
prepare:	104
1. The first step is to check the format and placement of the letter.	119
Employers expect keyboard operators to use accepted style and to	132
format letters properly.	137
2. Second, check the accuracy of all figures used in the letter: in the	152
date, in the street address, and in the letter body.	162
3. Third, check to see that all words are divided correctly at the ends	177
of lines.	179
4. As a final step, read carefully the entire letter. As you read the letter	195
for meaning, check to see that grammar is correct and that there are	209
no keyboarding errors. Any errors found must be corrected.	221
(¶ 2) If you follow these proofreading steps, your proofreading skills will	235
improve. (207)	237
Sincerely yours, | Mrs. Jane Denny | Communications Consultant | xx	249
	272

January 31, 19-- | Mr. Tom Stubbs | 3812 Raleigh Avenue | Napa, CA 94558-	14
3311 | Dear Mr. Stubbs:	18
(¶ 1) Today, we must cope with an information explosion and a technological	32
revolution. The one piece of equipment that may be revolutionizing the way	47
we live is the microcomputer.	54
(¶ 2) It is amazing what microcomputers can do. Writing efficiency -- and	67
some say creativity -- can be enhanced with the use of software word pro-	81
cessing programs designed for use with a microcomputer. As a communica-	95
tions device, the microcomputer can be linked online, by telephone, with an	110
extensive list of massive data banks, ranging from Dow Jones to libraries to	126
ERIC centers, as well as to various other special services. As is obvious, the	142
microcomputer can place computer power directly in our hands.	154
(¶ 3) Visit our showroom soon and see our complete line of microcomputers	168
and software packages. We know you will be pleased with our low prices.	183
(165) Sincerely yours, | Miss Virginia Whitacre | Vice President | xx	194
	205

PHASE 4

Improve Keyboarding and Formatting Skills

Here are the Key Steps to improving keyboarding skill:

1. Position: Maintain proper hand-and-finger position.

2. Purpose: Give a purpose to all keyboarding practice.

3. Practice: Use alternating levels of practice speed when keyboarding drill lines -- slowly, then faster, etc.

4. Goals: Set daily and weekly goals -- emphasize improvement.

The 25 lessons of Phase 4 will help you:

1. Refine technique patterns.

2. Build keyboarding skill to new levels.

3. Review Cycle 1 applications.

4. Improve skill on rough-draft and script copy.

5. Improve basic language skills.

6. Improve formatting and production skill on letters.

88a ▶ 5
Conditioning Practice

each line twice (slowly, faster); as time permits, repeat selected lines

alphabet 1 Seven quiet boys extracted juicy chunks from the sizzling pot of stew.

figures 2 Will you enter Machine Nos. 12-93045 and 10-87306 on the repair cards.

shift keys 3 R. H. McNeil, of Smith, Paine & Winnet Company, is visiting in Newark.

speed 4 The maps may aid them when they do the work for the town and the city.

| 1 | 2 | 3 | 4 | 5 | 6 | 7 | 8 | 9 | 10 | 11 | 12 | 13 | 14 |

88b ▶ 10
Improve Language Skills: Punctuation

full sheet; 1″ top margin; 70-space line

Key the lines as directed in 87b, p. 152; however, instead of selecting the correct word from those in parentheses, insert commas where needed.

COMMA USAGE

> Use a comma after (a) introductory words, phrases, or clauses and (b) words in a series.

Learn 1. On our trip, we visited London, Paris, Rome, and Stockholm.

Apply 2. Before you leave please finish the letters reports and memos.

> Do not use a comma to separate two items treated as a single unit within a series.

Learn 3. She ordered ham and eggs, toast, and coffee.

Apply 4. He ordered lox and bagels strawberries and tea.

> Use a comma before short direct quotations.

Learn 5. The teacher said, "If you try, you can reach your goal."

Apply 6. The students said "We'll try."

> Use a comma before and after word(s) in apposition.

Learn 7. Chris, the outgoing president, said to arrive early.

Apply 8. Jean our new president will give the report to the committee.

> Use a comma to set off words of direct address.

Learn 9. I'll look forward, Casey, to seeing you at the meeting.

Apply 10. Please try Letecia to finish this work before you leave.

REMINDER:
When keying drill and problem copy, remember to use good techniques.

Fingers curved and upright

Use quick, snappy keystroking

Space quickly after each word

Unit 15 Lessons 76-80

Learning Goals
1. To improve or refine technique and practice patterns.
2. To transfer improved technique patterns to straight-copy keyboarding.
3. To keyboard and format short reports.
4. To increase speed on straight, statistical, rough-draft, and script copy.

Machine Adjustments
1. Paper guide at *0*.
2. Paper bail rolls at even intervals across page.
Use:
*70-space line and single spacing for drills; DS below each SS group of drill lines
*70-space line and double spacing for ¶ timings of more than 1 minute
*5-space ¶ indention

| Lesson 76 | **Keyboarding/Technique Skills** |

76a ▶ 5
Conditioning Practice

each line twice (slowly, faster); as time permits, repeat selected lines

alphabet 1 Just work for improved basic techniques to maximize keyboarding skill.

figures 2 Type 1 and 2 and 3 and 4 and 5 and 6 and 7 and 8 and 9 and 10 and 123.

adjacent key 3 Did Opal Klen make Quin aware that he was to operate the new computer?

speed 4 He or she may work with us to make a profit for the eighty city firms.

| 1 | 2 | 3 | 4 | 5 | 6 | 7 | 8 | 9 | 10 | 11 | 12 | 13 | 14 |

76b ▶ 15
Improve Techniques: Keystroking

each line twice (slowly, faster); as time permits, repeat selected lines

Home row Emphasize curved, upright fingers, wrists low; quiet hands.

1 fjfj fjfj dkdk dkdk slsl slsl a;a; a;a; a;sldkfj a;sldkfj a;sldkfj jak

2 a jag; a flag; a glass; add a dash; half a jag; add half a flask; lash

3 All lads had half a glass. Ask Sal to add a salad. Sasha had a sash.

4 Dad or Sara had half a dish of salad. Ask Dallas to add half a glass.

Third row Emphasize quick, snap strokes; finger reaches; quiet hands.

5 y yj u uj i ik o ol p p; t tf r rf e ed w ws q qa qpa; wosl eidk rufj;

6 I wrote your quote; you were to try to type it; your typewriter; query

7 Terry wrote our quarterly report; he wrote a witty query to the paper.

8 You were to try to quote proper etiquette to Peter while at the party.

Bottom row Emphasize curved, upright fingers; finger reaches; quiet hands.

9 n nj m mj , ,k . .l / /; b bf v vf c cd x xs z za aza six can vim box,

10 one man and woman; six bison and a zebu; boxes of zinc oxide in a cave

11 Vic Mann can move six or seven boxes of zinc to the cave for Anna Bax.

12 Five or six men can fix many zinc boxes for Maxwell Benjamin Cozzmann.

87c ▶ 30
Build Document Processing Skill: Letters

plain full sheets; modified block style, blocked ¶s; mixed punctuation; current date

Use your name and your home address (with ZIP Code) as the letter address for both problems. Supply an appropriate salutation.

Placement

Use the Letter Placement Table, page 149, to determine margins and dateline placement. The number of words in the letter body is indicated by the number in parentheses at the end of each letter.

Proofread

Proofread your finished copy. Circle all errors.

Problem 1

opening lines 16

(¶ 1) The question you raised about the value of keyboarding skill is one that   31
I am pleased to answer.   36

(¶ 2) In the near future, nearly everyone will need to know how to operate a   50
keyboard, whether that keyboard is a part of a microcomputer, a computer,   65
an electronic typewriter, or a word processor. According to recent fore-   79
casts, approximately 70 percent of the total population of the United States   94
will be using a keyboard in one form or another by 1993.   106

(¶ 3) Today, a microcomputer with a keyboard or keypad is being used in   119
most white-collar jobs, in educational environments, and in the home. If   134
you learn to operate a keyboard, you will have a skill that will be useful to   150
you for the remainder of your life. It is important, therefore, to learn this   165
skill well. (152)   168

Sincerely yours, |Jeff Brown, Director |Public Relations |cm   179

Problem 2

opening lines 16

One application of key boarding skill is the operation of a word   29
processor. Many different models of word processors are being   41
used in the business office. Some machines can perform only   54
word processing functions; others, sometimes called information   66
processors, can do both word and data processing. Most word and   79
information processors have similar features: an electronic key-   92
board or key pad, a display screen, a diskette recording mechanism   114
with a disk drive, and a printer. The keyboard or keypad is not only equipped with a   131
standard letter and number keyboard, but it also has special func-   144
tion keys, and it may have a 10-key numeric pad, all of which are   158
a part of the total key board configuration. The special function   171
keys, as implied by the name, enable the operator to manipulate copy on the display screen   189
in a variety of ways. Among the common uses of these keys are to erase,   204
delete, or otherwise modify the copy. Using these keys, it is easy   217
to move, insert, edit, recall, store, or print out copy as needed.   230
This automation of word and data processing has changed the way   243
in which office work is done, and it has increased dramatically   256
office productivity. some of the skill needed for the automated   269
office can and should be learned in school; still other skills will need   283
to be developed in an on-the-job situation. (276)   297

Sincerely yours, / Jeff Brown, Director / Public Relations / cm   307

a central processing unit that may include

76c ▶ 15
Measure Basic Skill: Straight Copy

1. Two 5' writings; *find gwam*.
2. Proofread; circle errors.
3. Record better *gwam* rate on your rate record sheet (LM, p. 3).

| all letters used | A | 1.5 si | 5.7 awl | 80% hfw |

Snappy
keystroking

Quick
spacing

	gwam 3'	5'
In the lessons of this unit, try to refine your technique patterns	4	3	48
and to improve your overall keyboarding speed by at least six words a	9	5	51
minute. You can accomplish this goal if you work with a purpose and key-	14	8	54
board the various drills at alternating levels of speed. In a signifi-	19	11	57
cant research study, students who followed this plan made greater speed	24	14	60
gains than those who did not. Just remember that it is important to	28	17	62
maintain proper hand-and-finger position, to use snappy keystroking with	33	20	65
the striking action in the fingers, to space quickly after each word,	38	23	68
and to make an immediate return at the end of each line.	41	25	70
You will understand, too, the importance of the several other basic	46	27	73
techniques given in this unit. For example, you will learn to avoid	51	30	76
unnecessary motions, such as bouncing hands and arms, moving hands up	55	33	79
and down the keyboard, as well as the problem of looking away from the	60	36	82
textbook copy. The real secret of high-speed keyboarding is to keep your	65	39	85
hands and wrists very relaxed and let your fingers manipulate the keys.	70	42	87
If you do these things every time you keyboard, you will be amazed with	75	45	90
your speed growth.	76	46	91

gwam 3' | 1 | 2 | 3 | 4 | 5 |
5' | 1 | 2 | 3 |

76d ▶ 15
Improve Basic Skill: Straight Copy

1. Add 4 to 8 words to your 76c *gwam* rate. **Goal:** To reach a new high-speed rate.

2. Two 1' guided writings on ¶ 1 of 76c at your new goal rate as the ¼' guide is called.
3. A 2' guided writing on ¶ 1. Try to maintain your 1' goal rate.

4. Repeat Step 2, using ¶ 2.
5. Repeat Step 3, using ¶ 2.
6. A 3' writing using both ¶s.
Goal: To maintain your new speed rate for 3'.

87a ▶5
Conditioning Practice

each line twice (slowly, faster); as time permits, repeat selected lines

alphabet	1	Freshly squeezed grape juice was served at breakfast the next morning.
figures	2	We proofread 278 letters, 15 reports, 369 invoices, and 40 statements.
space bar	3	Many men and women may be needed to pay for the work down by the lake.
speed	4	They may make the six men pay for the ancient ornament or do the work.

| 1 | 2 | 3 | 4 | 5 | 6 | 7 | 8 | 9 | 10 | 11 | 12 | 13 | 14 |

87b ▶ 15
Improve Language Skills: Grammar

full sheet; 1″ top margin; 70-space line

Study/Learn/Apply/Correct Procedures

1. STUDY explanatory rule.

2. Key line number (with period); space twice, then key the LEARN sentence(s) DS, noting rule application.

3. Key the line number (with period); space twice, then key the APPLY sentence(s) DS, selecting the word (in parentheses) needed to make the sentence(s) correct.

4. As your teacher reads the correct sentence(s), show in pen or pencil any corrections that need to be made in your copy.

5. Rekey any APPLY sentence containing an error, CORRECTING the error as you key. Place the corrected sentence in the space below the APPLY sentence containing the error.

PRONOUN AGREEMENT

> Pronouns (I, we, you, he, she, it, their, etc.) agree with their antecedents *in person* (i.e., person speaking—first person; person spoken to—second person; person spoken about—third person).

Learn	1.	I said I would go if I complete my work early. (*1st person*)
Learn	2.	When you leave to go to the play, bring your ticket. (*2d person*)
Learn	3.	Jay said that he would be taking the troop in his car. (*3d person*)
Apply	4.	All persons who see the exhibit find that (they, you) are moved.
Apply	5.	After you enter a dark room, (one's, your) eyes adjust slowly.

> Pronouns agree with their antecedents *in gender* (masculine, feminine, and neuter).

Learn	6.	Each Girl Scout has her favorite sport. (*feminine*)
Learn	7.	Jack will present his lecture as soon as he arrives. (*masculine*)
Apply	8.	Each boy will vote for (his, its) favorite sport.
Apply	9.	The rose lost (her, its) petals within three days.

> Pronouns agree with their antecedents *in number* (singular or plural).

Learn	10.	The girls discussed their summer vacation. (*plural*)
Learn	11.	Christina lost her book report on the way to class. (*singular*)
Apply	12.	They may complete (his, her, their) assignments this week.
Apply	13.	A pronoun must agree with (their, its) antecedent.

> When a pronoun's antecedent is a collective noun, the pronoun may be either singular or plural depending on the meaning of the collective noun.

Learn	14.	The class planned its next field trip. (*acting as a unit*)
Learn	15.	The class had their pictures taken. (*acting individually*)
Apply	16.	The committee has completed (their, its) report.
Apply	17.	The committee met to cast (their, its) votes.

77a ▶ 5
Conditioning Practice

each line twice (slowly, faster); as time permits, repeat selected lines

alphabet	1	Quick disposal of hazardous toxic waste is governed by major controls.
figures	2	Jan sold 14 rings, 293 clips, 56 watches, 158 clocks, and 70 tie pins.
space bar	3	If they go to the city and sign the form, I may pay them for the work.
speed	4	He may go with me to the big city by the lake to do the work for them.

| 1 | 2 | 3 | 4 | 5 | 7 | 8 | 9 | 10 | 11 | 12 | 13 | 14 |

77b ▶ 20
Improve Technique: Keystroking and Response Patterns

1. Lines 1-4: Each word 3 times (slowly, faster, top speed); when bell rings, complete word, return, and continue.

2. Lines 5-8: Each phrase 3 times (slowly, faster, top speed); when bell rings, complete word, return, and continue.

3. Lines 9-12: Each sentence 3 times (slowly, faster, top speed).

4. As time permits, keyboard lines 5-8 from dictation.

Goal: High speed keyboarding response (think and key each word or word group as a whole).

Finger reaches, quiet hands

Snappy keystroking

Quick spacing

Emphasize fast finger reaches with hands quiet, wrists low and relaxed.

balanced-hand words

1 quay wow eye rut tie yen urn irk own pep aid sod for got hay jay kayak
2 lap and six did fob big ham jam kale land zoa cod vow but nap man lane
3 with they them make then when also work such form than wish paid their
4 them such form right amble amend cubic augment entitle formal downtown

Emphasize high-speed phrase response.

balanced-hand phrases

5 and the|and then|and if they|and if they go|pay for the work|sign them
6 the world of work|make it right|when they sign the form|they may go to
7 sign the form|sign the form for them|the right title for the city firm
8 fight for the land|pay a penalty to the city|dismantle the oak antique

Emphasize high-speed word-level response; quick spacing.

balanced-hand sentences

9 The map of the ancient land forms may aid them when they work with us.
10 Sign the right title forms for the big city firm and then do the work.
11 Pay for the work and then go to the city to sign the usual title form.
12 He may go to visit the ancient chapel and sit by an antique oak chair.

| 1 | 2 | 3 | 4 | 5 | 6 | 7 | 8 | 9 | 10 | 11 | 12 | 13 | 14 |

77c ▶ 10
Transfer Improved Response Patterns

1. Two 1' writings on each of Lines 9-12 of 77b above.

Goal: With each timed repetition, to increase speed by 4 or more words.

To reach this goal, keep your hands quiet and relaxed and let the fingers do the keystroking.

ORCC Office Research & Communication Consultants

30 Lewis Road o Linfield, PA 19468-4353 o (215) 793-8264

words in parts   total words

Dateline   Line 13   January 23, 19--   3   3

                                        4 line spaces
                                        (3 blank lines)

Letter   Mr. Scott Kirkwood, President   9   9
address   Solar Corporation of America   15   15
              1160 Avenue of the Americas   20   20
              New York, NY 10036-2291   27   27

Salutation Dear Mr. Kirkwood: 31   31

              This letter is arranged in the modified block style with blocked 13   44
              paragraphs. The only difference between this letter style and the 26   57
              block style is that the dateline and the closing lines (complimen- 40   70
              tary close and the typed or printed name of the originator of the 53   83
              letter) are started at the horizontal center point.   63   94

Body   Although the block style letter is the most popular letter style   76 107
of letter used in the business world, the modified block style with blocked 90 120
              paragraphs is a popular second choice. As you can see, a letter 102 133
              arranged in this format presents an attractive appearance.   115 145

              Mixed punctuation (a colon after the salutation and a comma after 128 158
              the complimentary close) is used in this letter. Since the origina- 141 172
              tor's name is shown in typed format in the closing lines, only the 155 185
              initials of the typist or the word processing operator need be   167 198
              shown in the reference notation. If an enclosure is mentioned in 181 211
              the body of the letter, the word Enclosure, or Enc., is keyed or 193 224
              typed a double space below the reference notation, flush with the 206 237
              left margin.   209 240

Complimentary   Sincerely yours,   3 243
close

                                        Kaye Banovich

Typed name   Mrs. Kaye Banovich   6 246
Official title   Communications Consultant   11 251

Reference   le   12 252
initials

                                                            Shown in pica type
                                                            1" side margins

Modified Block with Blocked Paragraphs and Mixed Punctuation

77d ▶ 15
Format a Short Report: Rough-Draft Script Copy

full sheet

1. Prepare as an unbound report. Use 1″ side margins.

2. Use main heading:
THE TYPEWRITTEN RE-PORT
QS (quadruple-space) below heading.

3. Proofread finished copy; correct errors.

(Refer to page 93, Cycle 1, if you need to review unbound report format.)

words

Many students in preparing the written work | 13
for their classes often prepare a first draft | 18
which is then revised. This revision of the | 26
work lead to improvement in quality of the | 36
report or other written work. Some students | 45
may write the initial draft and then make | 53
what ever corrections are needed directly on the | 63
handwritten copy so that it looks very | 71
similar to this rough-draft script copy | 79
from which you are now keyboarding. How- | 87
ever, after you have learned to keyboard, | 95
you can save time by keyboarding the | 103
initial draft before revising it. This | 111
initial draft should be double- | 117
spaced to make it easier to read and revise. | 126

As amazing as it may seem, studies | 133
indicate that students get higher grades on | 142
typewritten papers than on hand written | 150
papers. All of us are impressed with the | 158
neatness and easier-to-read characteristics | 167
of typed copy. Teachers are no exception. | 176
You can earn better grades, then, if you | 184
will just take extra time to revise care- | 192
fully your written work and type it in good | 201
form before submitting it to your teachers. | 210

Lesson 78   Keyboarding/Report Skills

78a ▶ 5
Conditioning Practice

each line twice (slowly, faster); as time permits, repeat selected lines

alphabet 1 Ivory silk jacquard banners marked new zoo paths leading to fox cages.

figures 2 Listed were 78 jackets, 293 blankets, 140 kits, 56 lamps, and 8 tires.

continuity 3 Purposeful repetition leads to rapid improvement of stroking patterns.

speed 4 She may go down to the ancient city by the lake to do the work for me.

| 1 | 2 | 3 | 4 | 5 | 6 | 7 | 8 | 9 | 10 | 11 | 12 | 13 | 14 |

86a ▶ 5
Conditioning Practice

each line twice (slowly, faster); as time permits, repeat selected lines

alphabet	1	Forty big jets climbed into a hazy sky at exactly quarter past twelve.
figures	2	What is the sum of 16 7/8 and 23 3/4 and 45 1/2 and 10 8/9 and 90 1/4?
fingers 3, 4	3	Was it Polly who saw Paul quizzing Wally about eating all the loquats?
speed	4	Vivian may pay the men for the work and then go with them to the city.

| 1 | 2 | 3 | 4 | 5 | 6 | 7 | 8 | 9 | 10 | 11 | 12 | 13 | 14 |

86b ▶ 20
Problem Solving: Learn a New Letter Style

1. Arrange the letter on a plain full sheet in modified block style with blocked paragraphs, mixed punctuation.

2. Use the Letter Placement Table, page 149, to determine margins and dateline placement.

(words in body: 92)

3. When you complete the letter, make the check suggested; then make whatever corrections are needed and redo the letter in final form. Correct all errors you make in keyboarding the final draft.

4. In keying the letter, supply the missing parts:
* Address the letter to you at your home address.
* Use the current date.
* Supply an appropriate salutation.

Learning cue: The modified block style letter with blocked ¶s is arranged in the same format as the block style except that the dateline, complimentary close, and the printed or typed name are started at the horizontal center point.

(¶1) In solving problems, you will need to utilize previous learnings in new ways as you attempt to find problem solutions.

(¶2) Recall how you placed letters in block style; then make the needed modifications to arrange this letter in modified block style with blocked paragraphs.

(¶3) When you complete the letter, check your style arrangement with the style letter shown on the next page. If you arranged this letter in the style format shown there, congratulations. / Sincerely, / Robert J. Keller / jm

86c ▶ 25
Reinforcement Learning: New Letter Style

plain full sheets

Step 1

Learn the letter style

Key model letter on p. 151 in modified block style with blocked ¶s as shown (words in body: 209). Use the Letter Placement Table, p. 149.

In arranging the letter in proper format, be guided by the placement and spacing notations given in color.

Key the letter at rough-draft speed (top speed); x-out or strike over any keyboarding errors.

Step 2

Proofread and make rough-draft corrections

Proofread the letter you prepared in Step 1. Show by handwritten corrections any changes that need to be made in the copy.

Where you x'd out or struck over any words or letters, write such words correctly. In making the corrections, use the proofreader's marks you learned (Reference, p. RG 10).

Step 3

Build skill

Using your corrected rough-draft copy, redo the letter. As you key,

make the corrections you have indicated in your copy.

Key on the control level and correct any errors you make. Compare your final draft with the model on p. 151. If you prepared the letter using elite type, your lines will end at different points than those in the model, but spacing between letter parts will be the same.

78b ▶ 15
Improve Technique: Response Patterns

each line 3 times
(slowly, faster, top
speed); as time per-
mits, repeat selected
lines

    To reduce
time interval between
keystrokes (read
ahead to anticipate
stroking pattern).

Technique goals

Fingers
curved
and
upright

Finger
keystroking
action;
hands quiet

Emphasize curved, upright fingers; finger-action keystroking.

one-hand
words

1 as in at my be no we on up are you get him was oil dear only were upon

2 date look data pull best link area jump card lump rate hook case water

3 after union state imply great pupil staff nylon extra plump react jump

Emphasize independent finger action; quiet hands.

one-hand
phrases

4 you are|my case|in my opinion|were you|great pupil|extra jump|are upon

5 after taxes|were you only|my address|minimum decrease|exaggerated poll

6 only after you were|exaggerated opinion|estate tax|you are in|you read

Emphasize continuity; finger action with fingers close to keys.

one-hand
sentences

7 In my opinion, estate taxes decreased only after Junko asserted facts.

8 Only after Wes stated my exaggerated opinion were oil taxes decreased.

9 Only after Ki acted on my reserved opinion were water rates decreased.

| 1 | 2 | 3 | 4 | 5 | 6 | 7 | 8 | 9 | 10 | 11 | 12 | 13 | 14 |

78c ▶ 15
Transfer Improved Response Patterns: Guided Writing

1. Three 1' writings (at a controlled rate with a minimum of
waste motion); find *gwam*.

2. Add 4 words to best rate;
determine ¼' goal rates.

3. Three 15" writings; try to equal
or exceed ¼' goal rate.

4. Three 30" writings; try to equal
or exceed ½' goal rate.

5. Three 1' guided writings at
goal rate.

6. As time permits, take additional 1' writings to increase
speed.

Technique goals

Fingers
well
curved

Fingers
upright

                            •   4   •   8   •   12
        It is no exaggeration to say that the decrease in rainfall has
            •   16   •   20   •   24   •
    resulted in water reserves which are far below the average required for
        28   •   32   •   36   •   40
    safety. We were told to refer this water problem to the committee for
            44   •   48   •   52   •
    attention. New plans probably will be drafted after this committee has
        56   •   60   •   64
    made a minimum study of the water problem.

Unit 17   Lessons 86-90

Learning Goals

1. To develop and increase skill in formatting and keying letters in the modified block (blocked ¶s) and modified block (indented ¶s) styles.

2. To maintain good keyboarding technique patterns when keyboarding and doing applications.

3. To learn and apply basic language skills.

4. To do all work with a minimum of waste time and motion.

Machine Adjustments

1. Paper guide at *0*.

2. 70-space line and SS, unless otherwise directed.

SPECIAL LETTER PLACEMENT POINTS

LETTER PLACEMENT TABLE

Letter Classification	5-Stroke Words in Letter Body	Side Margins	Margin Settings		Dateline Position (from Top Edge of Paper)
			Elite	Pica	
Short	Up to 100	2″	24-78*	20-65*	19
Average	101-200	1½″	18-84*	15-70*	16
Long	201-300	1″	12-90*	10-75*	13
Two-page	More than 300	1″	12-90*	10-75*	13
Standard 6″ line for all letters**	As above for all letters	1¼″	15-87*	12-72*	As above for all letters

*Plus 3 to 7 spaces for the bell cue—*usually add 5* (see p. 78).

**Use only when so directed. Some business firms use a standard 6″ line for all letters.

Placement Table

A placement table will help you place letters properly. With time, you should learn to estimate letter length and place letters properly without using a placement aid.

Stationery

Most business letters are arranged on standard-size letterheads (8½″ × 11″) with the company name, address, and other information printed at the top.

For letters longer than 1 page, plain paper of the same size, color, and quality as the letterhead is used after the first page.

For short letters, smaller letterheads, executive-size (7¼″ × 10½″) or half-size (5½″ × 8½″), may be used; however, most letters, irrespective of length, are placed on standard-size stationery.

Placement Table Guides

1. Vertical Placement. Vertical placement of the dateline varies with letter length. If a deep letterhead prevents placing the date on the designated line, place it on the second line below the last letterhead line.

2. Letter Address and Closing Lines. The letter address is always started on the fourth line (3 blank line spaces) below the dateline. The name of the writer or originator of the letter is placed on the fourth line space below the complimentary close. It may be followed on the same line, or on the next line, by the business title of the writer.

3. Spacing Between Letter Parts. Except after the dateline and the complimentary close, double spacing is used between letter parts.

4. Special Lines. Special lines (attention, subject, company name in closing lines, etc.) or features such as a table, a list, or extra opening or closing lines may require a higher dateline placement than is shown in the placement table.

Letter Formatting Guides

Letter formatting guides are given with the style letter introduced in this unit.

Mixed Punctuation

Mixed punctuation means that a colon is used after the salutation and that a comma is used after the complimentary close.

Extend Document Processing Skills—Letters/Language Skills

78d ▶ 15
Format a Short Report: Statistical Rough-Draft Copy

full sheet

1. Prepare as an unbound report. Use 1" side margins.

2. Use main heading:

THE QUEST FOR SPEED

QS below heading.

3. Proofread finished copy; correct errors.

(Refer to page 93, Cycle 1, if you need to review unbound report format.)

, = comma
{ } = parentheses

	gwam 1'	3'
Cheeta*hs* the fastest of land animals, can run with bursts of #	12	4
speed up to 60 miles per hour. *(mph)* During *the* 1984 olympics, Carl Lewis	27	9
won the 100-meter dash in 9.99 seconds, the equivalent of about	40	13
22.38 mph. specially-built racing cars have travelled at 200 *speeds over*	55	18
mph. In the quest for speed, however, we (had have) to move from	68	22
the ground. *to the air* Jet aircraft, for example, cruising at altitudes of over	83	28
35,000 feet, *to 41,000* fly at equivalent ground speeds of some 535 to 650 *from 8 1,600*	98	32
mph. contrast these speeds with the super sonic speed of the	110	37
Concorde which can fly at a *s*peed of 1,300 mph when it is cruising	122	41
at an altitude of 57,000 feet.	127	42
Moving in to outer space, the speed of the space shuttle is	12	46
18,400 mph, or 5.1 miles per hour. *second* The space shuttle can orbit	25	51
the earth in 1 hour, 10 seconds. *21* Would it fly from Los Angeles	38	55
to San Francisco {358 miles} *statute* in 1 minute, 10 seconds. In the	52	60
physical realm, the speed of sound at sea level is approximately	65	64
1,100 feet per second. {persons have often used this to judge *approximation*	80	69
the distance of a lightening bolt. For example, if you see a	92	73
flash of lightening and approximately 3 seconds elapses before you	105	77
hear the clap of thunder, the lighting bolt was 3,300 feet from *about 3,000* *n*	119	82
the point where you observed it.} None of these speeds, however,	132	86
can compare with the speed of light *which travels 186,300 miles*	145	91
per second.	147	91

Lesson 79 | Keyboarding/Technique Skills

79a ▶ 5
Conditioning Practice

each line twice (slowly, faster); as time permits, repeat selected lines

alphabet 1 Five or six quizzes dealt with the judicial problems in Greek history.

figures 2 The 1987 inventory included 30 office chairs, 46 desks, and 25 tables.

finger action 3 An extra plump polo pony jumped over barriers with ease and good form.

speed 4 It is the duty of the chair to key their amendment to the proxy forms.

| 1 | 2 | 3 | 4 | 5 | 6 | 7 | 8 | 9 | 10 | 11 | 12 | 13 | 14 |

79b ▶ 15
Improve Basic Skill: Statistical Rough-Draft Copy

70-space line

1. Two 1' writings on ¶ 1 of 78d above; find *gwam*.

2. Repeat Step 1 using ¶ 2.

3. Two 3' writings using both ¶s; find *gwam*.

4. Record better 3' rate.

84c (continued)

reactions to us, friends help teach us acceptable social behavior. Further, friends, as Duck (1983, 31) has said, "help cushion our personalities and reassure us about our values as people." Even teacher-student interpersonal relationships have been found crucial to student intellectual growth. The following quote from a study by Block (1980, 178) suggests the importance of a teacher-student friendship:

> Consider the myth that students need only have intellectually resourceful and knowledgeable teachers to grow intellectually. When the data are examined, it is found that teachers who provide a sound emotional relationship with students elicit as much as five times the achievement growth over the course of a year as those who coldly pursue intellectual development.

Friendships, then, require a deep personal involvement with others, being interested in their well-being, in their unique identities, and in their perceptions of the world. Real friends like and accept us for what we are, just as we like and accept them for what they are. To build friendships, we need to be ourselves, take the risk of reaching out, and say "hello" first. We need to show we care. As Henry David Thoreau said, "The most I can do for my friend is just be his friend." Perhaps the following poem, attributed to Albert Camus, best describes the mutual acceptance and closeness that characterize real friendship:

> Don't walk in front of me
> I may not follow
> Don't walk behind me
> I may not lead
> Walk beside me
> And just be my friend.

Lesson 85 | Report Skills

85a ▶ 5
Conditioning Practice

each line twice (slowly, faster); as time permits, repeat selected lines

alphabet	1	Very excited dolphins whizzed quickly by a mako, jellyfish, and slugs.
figures	2	Please order 1,765 pencils, 894 pens, 239 file boxes, and 90 dividers.
space bar	3	Jan and Sam may go to a spa when they come to see me in the late fall.
speed	4	She may make the goal if she works with vigor and with the right form.

| 1 | 2 | 3 | 4 | 5 | 6 | 7 | 8 | 9 | 10 | 11 | 12 | 13 | 14 |

85b ▶ 45
Format and Key Report with Textual Citations

Complete the report you began in 84c, pp. 147-148. Prepare a reference list for your report.

top margin, same as p. 1; other margins as in report; center heading; start first line of each entry at left margin; indent additional lines 5 spaces; SS each entry; DS between entries

If space permits, the reference list may be typed as a part of the last report page. Start it 4 spaces below the last report line; otherwise, use a separate page.

Note. For a longer report (2 or more pages) number the reference page. For a short report, the reference page need not be numbered.

(line 6)   5

REFERENCES

Block, Joel D. Friendship. New York: MacMillan Publishers, Co., Inc., 1980.

Duck, Steve. Friends, for Life -- The Psychology of Close Relationships. New York: St. Martin's Press, 1983.

Fischer, Claude. "The Friendship Cure-All." Psychology Today, January 1983, 74-78.

Webster's New World Dictionary. 2d ed. New York: Simon and Schuster, 1980.

79c ▶ 15
Improve Techniques: Response Patterns/ Space Bar

1. Lines 1-3: Each phrase 3 times; key for speed; when bell rings, complete word or divide it at syllable point, return, and continue typing.

2. Lines 4-6: Each sentence 3 times; key for speed.

3. Lines 7-9: Each line 3 times; space quickly after each word and key next word without pausing.

Color bars (___) under words indicate *word* response. Read and type these words or word groups for speed.

Color dots (. .) under words indicate *letter* response. Read and type these words letter by letter.

Technique goal

Quick spacing with down-and-in motion of right thumb

Emphasize combination or variable response patterns.

phrases

1 and the date |for the address |refer to their address |gave the statement

2 for him |they were |their date |hand weave |she saw |right union |to the tax

3 after the data |are you right |world opinion |address the ancient problem

Emphasize combination or variable response patterns.

sentences

4 Send a statement of the case to the union for an opinion on the taxes.

5 They gave the statement to the union at the address shown on the card.

6 World opinion is a factor in addressing the ancient problem of growth.

Emphasize quick, down-and-in spacing motion with right thumb.

phrases/ sentences

7 and the |and the |and the |and the |and the |and the |and the |and the |and to

8 pay them when they |pay them when they work |pay them when they work for

9 They may pay them when they try to help Jim clean the old storm drain.

79d ▶ 15
Transfer Improved Techniques: Guided Writing

1. Three 1' writings; find *gwam*.

2. Add 4 words to best rate; determine ¼' goal rates.

3. Three 15" writings; try to equal or exceed ¼' goal rate.

4. Three 30" writings; try to equal or exceed ½' goal rate.

5. Three 1' guided writings at goal rate.

6. As time permits, take additional 1' writings.

Goal: To increase speed still more.

Fingers well curved, upright

Quick, snap key-stroke; finger action only

.   4   .   8   .   12

They may send the statement to the address listed on the card. The

.   16   .   20   .   24

union requested that they do this and that the case be referred to the

28   .   32   .   36   .   40

court for further action. The court has promised to consider all the

.   44   .   48   .   52   .   56

facts and the other data of the case. The court will probably be able to

.   60   .   64   66

give us their decision by the end of this month.

84c ▶ 35
Format and Key Report with Textual Citations

full sheets; center heading on line 10 (pica) or line 12 (elite); DS ¶s, indent first line 5 spaces; SS quotations of 4 or more lines, indenting 5 spaces from side margins.

Arrange report in unbound report format (see p. 93, if necessary). Correct errors if directed to do so by your teacher.

Margins:
 side: 1″
 bottom: at least 1″

Place page numbers on line 6 in upper right-hand corner of second and additional pages. DS below page number and continue text.

Note. You are not expected to complete the report in this lesson; additional time is provided in Lesson 85.

Guide. Make two light pencil marks at the right edge of your paper: One 1″ from the bottom and another ½″ above the 1″ mark, as a page-end reminder; or use page-line gauge provided on LM. p. 7.

Note. Center the first line of poem; start remaining lines at this point.

Note. The ellipsis, indicating omission of words from a quotation, is keyed by alternating 3 periods and spaces (. . .) or 4 (. . . .), if the end of a sentence is included in the quotation.

FRIENDSHIP

At some time in our lives, each of us has tossed a pebble into a pool and then watched the ever-increasing concentric circles radiate out from a common center -- the point where the pebble entered the water. Our relationships with others are similar; they can be seen as existing on various levels -- concentric circles radiating out from each of us. The people in the inner circle are our close friends. They are the people to whom we become attached by feelings of deep personal regard; they are the people we refer to as "pals, buddies, chums, sidekicks, sisters, and brothers," and other such words. As we move outward to other circles, we find our casual friends. These are the people who share a common interest with us in such things as sports, clubs, music, and the like. Still farther out in the concentric circles are acquaintances. These are the people who may or may not become our friends.

All friends start out as acquaintances, and it is from this group that we select those who eventually become close or "true" friends. But, how do we choose a friend out of a group of acquaintances? It is easy to say that friendships are built around common interests and values, but as Block (1980, 221) has noted, "That isn't enough to explain close relationships." We could list those kinds of qualities that stimulate friendships -- trust, openness, good humor, sensitivity -- but all of us have acquaintances who have many of these qualities but who fail to ignite in us the spark of close friendship. Over one hundred years ago, Ralph Waldo Emerson lamented that Americans too often mistake acquaintances for true friends. The implication of his statement is that we need to know what friendship is and what it is not.

What, then, is a friend? Webster's New World Dictionary (1980) defines a friend as "a person one knows well and is fond of; an intimate associate."

This definition, however, still does not adequately differentiate between true friendship and casual acquaintanceship. What is the extra ingredient needed for a casual acquaintance to become a real friend? Sometimes real friendships grow out of a shared hardship. For example, a paraplegic veteran, inconsolable, said of his buddy killed in Vietnam: "We were not just fellow victims of the war, you see. He was my best friend. I loved him more than my brother" (Block, 1980, 210).

The Vietnam veteran's statement is about true or real friendship, not a casual acquaintanceship. But, perhaps Emerson came closer to defining true friendship when he said, "A true friend is somebody who can make us do what we can." And further, he said, "The only way to have a friend is to be one." The importance of Emerson's words is that they suggest that although a real friend will make us use our potential to the fullest, a friend also will require us to be a friend to keep the relationship thriving.

A real friendship, then, requires effort to develop and effort to keep alive. As a recent telephone commercial stated, we must "reach out and touch someone" if we are to develop a friendship. Fischer (1983, 74) makes an important statement about friendship, "Friends do not come for free." Just as we must work for anything worthwhile in life, we must work at our friendships. In the final analysis, as Block (1980, 13) has said, "We are each the architects of our own friendships. . . ."

Although friendships require effort to develop, they are also rewarding. As Abraham Lincoln said, "The better part of one's life consists of his friendships." Further, all of us know that our sense of well-being is often enhanced by the quality of our interpersonal relationships with friends. As a result of a friendship, we have often been influenced not only to think differently about things, but also to transform our attitudes about life. By their

80a ▶ 5
Conditioning Practice

each line twice (slowly, faster); as time permits, repeat selected lines

alphabet 1 Jay Wilkert utilized complex formulas for solving this unique problem.

figures 2 The new book contains 926 illustrations, 475 forms, and 1,380 figures.

quiet hands 3 Many union members will expect to receive a maximum salary adjustment.

speed 4 The key to proficiency is to name the right goals, then work for them.

| 1 | 2 | 3 | 4 | 5 | 6 | 7 | 8 | 9 | 10 | 11 | 12 | 13 | 14 |

80b ▶ 10
Format a Short Report: Rough-Draft Copy

full sheet

1. Prepare as an unbound report. Use 1″ side margins.

2. Use main heading:

KEYBOARDING SKILL

QS below heading.

3. Proofread finished copy; correct errors.

(Refer to page 93, Cycle 1, if you need to review unbound report format.)

	gwam 1′	3′
During this decade, it has been predicted that over ⑦⓪	12	4
percent of the polulation of hte United States will operate a	24	8
keyboard of some kind in thier day-to-day activities. Your	37	12
immediate transfer of your keyboarding skill will, in all probability, be	51	17
to a computer key board. You will learn the meaning of such terms	64	21
as bit, byte, chip, CPU, disk, program, and modem. Other computer	77	26
puter words will become a part of your vocabulary. But best of	90	30
all, you will learn through and with a computer. You may use a	102	34
microcomputer, for example, to help you improve your as a word processor composition skills.	121	40
and communication;		
In all likelihood, Many persons will have personal computers in their homes.	12	44
These personal; computers will be portable. Some time ago, a	25	48
copany the in computer industry announced its so-called "computer	38	53
microprocessing d nearly on a chip," a single chip that incorporates all a computer's cir-	56	59
d cuitry on one stamp-size block of silicon. Another computer com-	69	63
your little fingernail pany has develped a chip the size of a collar button that has	83	68
printed half a million circuits on it. Still another innovation is bubble	98	73
of memory, designed to hold hundreds of thousands bits of information	112	77
in a chip even when the power is off. Indeed, the future of	124	82
computers continues to be exciting.	131	84

80c ▶ 10
Improve Basic Skill: Rough-Draft Copy
70-space line

1. Two 1′ writings on ¶ 1 of 80b above.

2. Repeat Step 1 using ¶ 2.

3. A 3′ writing using both ¶s.

4. Find and record 3′ gwam.

Improve Language Skills:
Grammar

full sheet; 1″ top margin;
60-space line

Key as directed in 81c, p. 142.

OTHER VERB GUIDES

If there is confusion whether a subject is singular or plural, consult a dictionary.

Learn   1. The data in your report are interesting.
Learn   2. The world news is encouraging.
Learn   3. The alumni are meeting today.
Apply   4. (Is, Are) the alumni meeting today?
Apply   5. Parentheses (is, are) used in these guides.

When used as the subject, the pronouns I, we, you, and they, as well as plural nouns, require the plural verb *do not* or the contraction *don't*.

Learn   6. They do not want to attend the meeting.
Learn   7. The scales don't work properly.
Apply   8. I (don't, doesn't) think the way you do.
Apply   9. The samples (don't, doesn't) match.

When used as the subject, the pronouns, he, she, it, as well as singular nouns, require the singular verb *does not* or the contraction *doesn't*.

Learn   10. She doesn't want to go with you.
Learn   11. The scale doesn't work properly.
Apply   12. It (don't, doesn't) matter; use either style.
Apply   13. The computer (don't, doesn't) work.

Lesson 84   Outline/Report Skills

84a ▶ 5
Conditioning
Practice

each line twice (slowly,
faster); as time per-
mits, repeat selected
lines for extra credit

alphabet   1   This bright jacket has an amazing weave and is of exceptional quality.
figures   2   The invoice covered 1,398 lamps, 476 chairs, 270 desks, and 115 sofas.
shift key   3   Jane Dodd, President of O'Brien, McNeil & Webber, is in New York City.
speed   4   If it is so, then she may go with me to the city by a lake to do work.

| 1 | 2 | 3 | 4 | 5 | 6 | 7 | 8 | 9 | 10 | 11 | 12 | 13 | 14 |

84b ▶ 10
Format and Key
an Outline

full sheet; 50-space line

Begin on line 12; space parts
of outline properly (see p. 94).

YOUR CAREER

I. CHOOSING A CAREER
    A. Assess Personal Abilities and Interests
    B. Determine Society's Needs
       1. Growth rates of occupations
       2. Possible future trends
    C. Obtain Career Counseling and Guidance
    D. Match Talents with Opportunity
II. PREPARING FOR YOUR CAREER
    A. Need for Formal Education
    B. Need for Specialized Education
    C. Need for On-the-Job Training

80d ▶ 10
Improve Techniques: Shift Keys/Return

1. Lines 1-3: Each line 3 times (slowly, faster, top speed).

2. Lines 4-10: As directed in copy; work for speed.

Technique cue

Manual Return: Use a quick flick-of-hand motion to return carriage.

Electric Return: Make a quick, little-finger reach to the return key.

shift keys

Emphasize little finger reach; keep other fingers in keyboarding position.

left   1 Ja Ja Ja Jan Jan Jan; Jan McNeil, President of McNeil, Inc., resigned.

right   2 F; F; Flo Flo Flo; Dot Ride visited Denver, Cheyenne, and Sioux Falls.

both   3 Flo James, Jack Dowd, and Mario Diaz visited London, Rome, and Berlin.

Emphasize quick return and start of new line.   ↓   tab: center + 10

4 tab ——————————————————————→ and the

5 lake ———————————— tab ———————————→ and the

6 work ———————————— tab ———————————→ repeat 3 times

7 tab ——————————————————————→ A quick return

8 at the end of a line ———— tab ———————————→ with an immediate start

9 of the new line ———————— tab ———————————→ will help you reach

10 new speed goals. ———————— tab ———————————→ repeat 3 times

80e ▶ 15
Measure Basic Skill: Straight Copy

two 5' writings; find *gwam*; circle errors; record better rate

all letters used	A	1.5 si	5.7 awl	80% hfw

	gwam 3'	5'

Are you now keyboarding with stationary hands? Are your wrists — 4 | 3 | 53
low and relaxed but off the border of the keyboard? Do you endeavor — 8 | 6 | 56
to keep your fingers well curved and upright and execute all keyboard — 13 | 8 | 59
reaches with the fingers only? Do you space quickly after every word — 18 | 11 | 61
and begin the next word immediately? At line endings, do you make the — 23 | 14 | 64
return quickly with an immediate start of the new line? Do you remember — 28 | 17 | 67
to keep your fingers close to the keys when operating the keyboard? Do — 33 | 19 | 70
you activate every key with a snap stroke made by the correct individual — 37 | 22 | 73
finger? If you can answer in the affirmative to these questions, you — 42 | 25 | 76
should be making an effective growth in speed. — 45 | 27 | 77

As you remember, your objective in this writing is to increase your — 50 | 30 | 80
overall speed by at least six words a minute. If you followed carefully — 54 | 33 | 83
the purpose given for each technique activity, and then made a diligent — 59 | 35 | 86
effort to make a refinement in your technique pattern and to eliminate — 64 | 38 | 89
all unproductive motions as you operated the keyboard, you should reach — 69 | 41 | 92
this objective. If you do not increase your speed by at least six words — 73 | 44 | 95
a minute, you may want to make a concerned evaluation of your keyboard- — 78 | 47 | 97
ing form, and then do again selected technique drills given in the lessons — 83 | 49 | 100
of this unit. — 84 | 50 | 101

gwam 3' | 1 | 2 | 3 | 4 | 5
5' | 1 | 2 | 3

83a ▶ 5
Conditioning Practice

each line twice (slowly, faster); as time permits, repeat selected lines

alphabet 1   Quickly, zealous Gene Fox jumped over the big hurdles to win the race.

figures 2   ninety-eight, 98; one, seven eighty, 1,780; fifteen thirty-four, 1534.

bottom row 3   Manny Cox and Ada Nixon helped me move six zinc boxes from the cavern.

speed 4   The six busy men may go down to the field to fix an authentic antique.

| 1 | 2 | 3 | 4 | 5 | 6 | 7 | 8 | 9 | 10 | 11 | 12 | 13 | 14 |

83b ▶ 35
Format and Key Personal/Business and Business Letters

4 full sheets

Problem 1

Using your home address in the opening lines, and your name in the closing lines, format the letter in personal/business style (see p. 75) to:

Mr. Mark Gray
Director, Camp Paiviki
c/o Crippled Children's Society
7120 Franklin Avenue
Los Angeles, CA 90046-1211

Use block style, open punctuation. Use a 50-space line and start your address on line 17. Supply all necessary parts for letters (salutation, complimentary close, and your printed name).

Problem 2

Arrange Problem 2 in block style, open punctuation (see p. 75). Use a 60-space line; begin dateline on line 19. Supply an appropriate salutation.

Problems 3 and 4

Format and key the letters as directed for Problem 1.

Problem 1

April 10, 19-- (¶ 1) I wish to apply for the job as counselor at Camp Paiviki, your summer camp for handicapped children.

(¶ 2) During the past two summers, I have worked as an aide in the Crippled Children's Summer Camp Day Program in (give name of your city). I taught arts and crafts and assisted with the swimming program.

(¶ 3) The supervisor of these summer programs, Mrs. Marilyn Graves, said she would be happy to recommend me. Her phone number is (use your area code) 285-3976.

Problem 2

May 9, 19-- (Use your name and home address) (¶ 1) Because Mrs. Graves speaks so highly of your work with handicapped children in the Summer Camp Day Program, I am prepared to offer you a summer job as counselor at Camp Paiviki. You will be working with children in the 9-12 age group.

(¶ 2) If you accept this job offer, I'd like to have you report for work on the afternoon of June 20. I am enclosing a map showing the location of Camp Paiviki in Crestline, California. We will work out the details of clothes you should bring after I hear from you.

Sincerely yours|Mark Gray, Director| jr|Enclosure

Problem 3

May 13, 19-- (¶ 1) Your letter offering me a position as counselor at Camp Paiviki arrived today. I am happy to accept your offer.

(¶ 2) As you requested, I shall report for work on the afternoon of June 20.

Problem 4

August 30, 19-- (¶ 1) Thank you for the opportunity to be a counselor at Camp Paiviki this summer. It was a new and wonderful experience for me to work so closely with handicapped children. Their optimistic approach to life is an example that I shall follow.

(¶ 2) I enjoyed, too, the opportunity to become so well acquainted with you and the rest of your staff. Thanks, again.

Unit 16 Lessons 81-85

Learning Goals
1. To review and improve basic application skill for preparing tables, personal/business letters, and reports.
2. To improve language and word-division skills.
3. To maintain and improve techniques and basic skills.

Machine Adjustments
1. Paper guide at *0*.
2. Paper bail rolls at even intervals across page.
Use:
*70-space line and single spacing for drills; DS below each SS group of drill lines
*70-space line and double spacing for ¶ timings of more than 1 minute
*5-space ¶ indention

Lesson 81 Center/Language Skills

81a ▶ 5
Conditioning Practice

each line twice (slowly, faster); as time permits, repeat selected lines

alphabet 1 Max just amazed that Portland crowd by kicking five quick field goals.

learning* 2 two, 2; fifty, 50; four thirty-two, 432; three, one twenty-four, 3,124

home row 3 Dashall Kagal added all glass sales as Jeff Ladd added all jade sales.

speed 4 He or she may go with us to the city to do the work for the big firms.

| 1 | 2 | 3 | 4 | 5 | 6 | 7 | 8 | 9 | 10 | 11 | 12 | 13 | 14 |

*Read, think, and keyboard figures in combination sequences, as possible.

81b ▶ 30
Recall Centering Skills

Problem 1
half sheet, long edge at top

1. DS copy; determine vertical placement.
2. Center problem vertically and each line horizontally (Reference: page RG 10).

Problem 2
Repeat Problem 1 on full sheet.

BASIC COMPUTER TERMINOLOGY

CPU: Central Processing Unit

ROM: Read-Only Memory

RAM: Random-Access Memory

DOS: Disk Operating System

Problem 3
half sheet, long edge at top
DS; center problem vertically and horizontally (*name of each language to be centered on separate line*).

(Problem 4 on page 142)

SOME COMPUTER LANGUAGES

Basic | Logo | Pascal | Smalltalk | Cobol | Fortran | Forth

Recall Basic Applications/Build Language Skills

Problem 1

half sheet; long edge at top

1. Center problem vertically and horizontally in proper table format.

2. DS table.

3. Decide how many spaces to leave between columns for best appearance.

Problem 2

full sheet

1. Center problem vertically and horizontally; DS table.

2. Decide how many spaces to leave between columns.

3. DS above and DS below the divider line (1½″ long).

Note. SS and key table notation the width of the table.

Problem 3

half sheet, long edge at top

1. Center vertically and horizontally; DS table.

2. Decide how many spaces to leave between columns.

3. Key the words without the periods that show syllabic division.

As time permits, repeat Problem 3; full sheet. Show by hyphens preferred division points for each word at end of a line. Assume bell rings on the first letter of each word.

COMPUTER TERMINOLOGY

micro chip	graphics
software	Main frame
data base	automation
terminal	bug
disk drive	flowchart

WORD DIVISION REVIEW *

(Preferred Division Points at Ends of Lines)

knowl-edge	mathe-matics
study-ing	area
oper-ate	highly
planned	enough
sum-mer	run-ning
starter	begin-ning

* If a word is written without hyphens, it cannot be divided.

WORDS FREQUENTLY MISSPELLED

ac·com·mo·date	li·brar·y	scis·sors
an·swer	li·cense	sep·a·rate
change·a·ble	min·i·a·ture	ser·geant
e·quipped	mis·spell	su·per·sede
fa·mil·iar	mort·gage	syn·o·nym
lab·o·ra·tor·y	oc·curred	ven·geance

81b (continued)

Problem 4

half sheet, long edge at top

1. DS copy; determine vertical placement.

2. Center problem vertically and each line horizontally.

DS ＞ CENTERING STEPS

Find horizontal center of paper; 16
add scale reading at left edge of paper 19
to scale reading at right edge of paper; 20
divide sum by 2 to find center point. 20
From center point, backspace 1 space for 19
each 2 letters and spaces in line; ignore any 22
odd letter; start line at ending point. 19

81c ▶ 15
Improve Language Skills: Grammar

full sheet; 1″ top margin; 60-space line

Study/Learn/Apply/Correct Procedures

1. STUDY explanatory rule.

2. Key line number (with period); space twice, then key the LEARN sentence(s) DS, noting rule application.

3. Key the line number (with period); space twice, then key the APPLY sentence(s) DS, selecting the word (in parentheses) needed to make the sentence(s) correct.

4. As your teacher reads the correct sentence(s), show in pen or pencil any corrections that need to be made in your copy.

5. Rekey any APPLY sentence containing an error, CORRECTING the error as you key. Place the corrected sentence in the space below the APPLY sentence containing the error.

SINGULAR VERBS

Use a singular verb with a singular subject.

Learn   1. The tree has lost its leaves.
Apply   2. A careless driver (is, are) dangerous to pedestrians.

Use singular verbs with indefinite pronouns (each, every, any, either, neither, one, etc.) used as subjects.

Learn   3. Everyone is doing well in this class.
Apply   4. Each of us (is, are) ready to help you.

Use a singular verb with singular subjects linked by *or* or *nor*. Exception: If one subject is singular and the other is plural, the verb agrees with the closer subject.

Learn   5. Either my sister or my brother is to do the work.
Learn   6. Neither the teacher nor the students are here.
Apply   7. Neither the book nor the magazine (is, are) being used.
Apply   8. Either the girl or her parents (is, are) to help us.

Use singular verbs with collective nouns (committee, team, class, jury, etc.) if the collective noun acts as a unit.

Learn   9. The committee is meeting with the president.
Learn 10. The class has been dismissed.
Apply 11. The jury (has, have) returned its verdict.
Apply 12. The board (is, are) in session.

82a ▶ 5
Conditioning Practice

each line twice (slowly, faster); as time permits, repeat selected lines

alphabet 1 With care and vigor, Kim Bass uniquely played the sax for a jazz trio.

figures 2 twelve thirty-four, 1234; fifty, six seventy-eight, 50,678; ninety, 90

3d row 3 A witty reporter wrote quips without error for reports for your paper.

speed 4 Pay them for their work and then go with us to the city for the forms.

| 1 | 2 | 3 | 4 | 5 | 6 | 7 | 8 | 9 | 10 | 11 | 12 | 13 | 14 |

82b ▶ 15
Improve Language Skills: Grammar

full sheet, 1″ top margin; 60-space line

Key the lines as directed in 81c, p. 142.

SINGULAR VERBS (continued)

> Use singular verbs with the pronouns *all* and *some* (as well as fractions and percentages) when used as subjects *if* their modifiers are singular. Use plural verbs *if* their modifiers are plural.

Learn 1. All the food is gone.
Learn 2. All of the supplies were lost or misplaced.
Apply 3. Some of the work (is, are) done.
Apply 4. All of us (is, are) present.

> Use a singular verb when number is used as the subject and is preceded by *the*; however, use a plural verb if *number* is preceded by *a*.

Learn 5. The number of persons requesting information has increased.
Learn 6. A number of visitors are here for the tour.
Apply 7. The number who can qualify for work (is, are) small.
Apply 8. A number of persons (has, have) left for the day.

PLURAL VERBS

> Use a plural verb with a plural subject.

Learn 9. The trees have lost their leaves.
Apply 10. The boxes (is, are) in the storage room.

> Use plural verbs with compound subjects joined by *and*.

Learn 11. The dog and the cat are in the kennel.
Apply 12. The principal and the superintendent (is, are) here.

CAPITALIZATION GUIDES

■ Capitalize

1 The first word of every sentence and the first word of every complete direct quotation. Do not capitalize (a) fragments of quotations or (b) a quotation resumed within a sentence.

She said, "Hard work is necessary for success."
He stressed the importance of "a sense of values."
"When all else fails," he said, "follow directions."

2 The first word after a colon if that word begins a complete sentence.

Remember this: Work with good techniques.
We carry these sizes: small, medium, and large.

3 First, last, and all other words in titles of books, articles, periodicals, headings, and plays, except words of four letters or less used as articles, conjunctions, or prepositions.

Century 21 Keyboarding   "How to Buy a House"
Saturday Review   "The Sound of Music"

4 An official title when it precedes a name or when used elsewhere if it is a title of distinction.

President Lincoln   She is the Prime Minister.
The doctor is in.   He is the treasurer.

5 All proper nouns and their derivatives.

Canada   Canadian Festival   France   French food

6 Days of the week, months of the year, holidays, periods of history, and historic events.

| Sunday | Labor Day | New Year's Day |
| June | Middle Ages | Civil War |

7 Seasons of the year only when they are personified.

icy fingers of Winter   the soft kiss of Spring

8 Geographic regions, localities, and names.

the North   Upstate New York   Mississippi River

9 Street, avenue, company, etc., when used with a proper noun.

Fifth Avenue   Avenue of the Stars   Armour & Co.

10 Names of organizations, clubs, and buildings.

Girl Scouts   Commercial Club   Trade Center

11 A noun preceding a figure except for common nouns such as *line*, *page*, and *sentence*, which may be keyed with or without a capital.

Style 143   Catalog 6   page 247   line 10

NUMBER EXPRESSION GUIDES

■ Use words for

1 Numbers from one to ten except when used with numbers above ten, which are typed as figures. Note: It is common business practice to use figures for all numbers except those which begin a sentence.

Was the order for four or eight books?
Order 8 shorthand books and 15 English books.

2 A number beginning a sentence.

Fifteen persons are here; 12 are at home sick.

3 The shorter of two numbers used together.

ten 50-gallon drums   350 five-gallon drums

4 Isolated fractions or indefinite amounts in a sentence.

Nearly two thirds of the students are here.
About twenty-five people came to the meeting.

5 Names of small-numbered streets and avenues (ten and under).

1020 Sixth Street   Tenth Avenue

■ Use figures for

1 Dates and time, except in very formal writing.

May 9, 1982   10:15 a.m.
Ninth of May   four o'clock

2 A series of fractions.

Key 1/2, 1/4, 5/6, and 7 3/4.

3 Numbers preceded by nouns.

Rule 12   page 179   Room 1208   Chapter 15

4 Measures, weights, and dimensions.

6 ft. 9 in. tall   5 lbs. 4 oz.   8 1/2″ × 11″

5 Definite numbers used with the percent sign (%); but use *percent* (spelled) with approximations in formal writing.

The rate is 15 1/2%.
About 50 percent of the work is done.

6 House numbers except house number One.

1915-42d Street   One Jefferson Avenue

7 Sums of money except when spelled for extra emphasis. Even sums may be keyed without the decimal.

$10.75   25 cents $300
seven hundred dollars ($700)

BASIC GRAMMAR GUIDES

Use a singular verb

1 With a singular subject.
The weather is clear but cold.

2 With an indefinite pronoun used as a subject (each, every, any, either, neither, one, etc.).
Each one is to bring a pen and paper.
Neither of us is likely to be picked.

3 With singular subjects linked by or or nor. If, however, one subject is singular and the other is plural, the verb should agree with the closer subject.
Either Jan or Fred is to make the presentation.
Neither the principal nor the teachers are here.

4 With a collective noun (committee, team, class, jury, etc.) if the collective noun acts as a unit.
The jury has returned to the courtroom.
The committee has filed its report.

5 With the pronouns all and some (as well as fractions and percentages) when used as subjects if their modifiers are singular. Use a plural verb if their modifiers are plural.
All of the books have been classified.
Some of the gas is being pumped into the tank.

6 When number is used as the subject and is preceded by the; however, use a plural verb if number is preceded by a.
The number of voters has increased this year.
A number of workers are on vacation.

Use a plural verb

1 With a plural subject.
The blossoms are losing their petals.

2 With a compound subject joined by and.
My mother and my father are the same age.

Negative forms of verbs

1 Use the plural verb do not (or the contraction don't) when the pronoun I, we, you, or they, as well as a plural noun, is used as the subject.
We don't have a leg to stand on in this case.
The scissors do not cut properly.

2 Use the singular verb does not (or the contraction doesn't) when the pronoun he, she, or it, as well as a singular noun, is used as the subject.
She doesn't want to attend the meeting.
It does not seem possible that winter's here.

Pronoun agreement with antecedents

1 Pronouns (I, we, you, he, she, it, their, etc.) agree with their antecedent in person -- person speaking, first person; person spoken to, second person; person spoken about, third person.
We said we would go when we complete our work.
When you enter, present your invitation.
All who saw the show found that they were moved.

2 Pronouns agree with their antecedents in gender (feminine, masculine, and neuter).
Each of the women has her favorite hobby.
Adam will wear his favorite sweater.
The tree lost its leaves early this fall.

3 Pronouns agree with their antecedents in number (singular or plural).
A verb must agree with its subject.
Pronouns must agree with their antecedents.
Brian is to give his recital at 2 p.m.
Joan and Carla have lost their homework.

4 When a pronoun's antecedent is a collective noun, the pronoun may be either singular or plural depending on whether the noun acts individually or as a unit.
The committee met to cast their ballots.
The class planned its graduation program.

Commonly confused pronoun sound-alikes

it's (contraction): it is; it has
its (possessive adjective): possessive form of it
It's good to see you; it's been a long time.
The puppy wagged its tail in welcome.

their (pronoun): possessive form of they
there (adverb/pronoun): at or in that place/used to introduce a clause
they're (contraction): they are
The hikers all wore their parkas.
There are several reasons for that result.
They're likely to be late because of the snow.

who's (contraction): who is; who has
whose (pronoun): possessive form of who
Who's been to the movie? Who's going now?
I chose the one whose skills are best.

PUNCTUATION GUIDES

◼ Use an apostrophe

1 As a symbol for *feet* in billings or tabulations or as a symbol for *minutes*. (The quotation mark may be used as a symbol for *seconds* and *inches*.)

12′ × 16′   3′ 54″   8′6″ × 10′8″

2 As a symbol to indicate the omission of letters or figures (as in contractions or figures).

can't   wouldn't   Spirit of '76

3 Add *s* to form the plural of most figures, letters, and words. In market quotations, form the plural of figures by the addition of *s* only.

6's   A's   five's   ABC's   Century Fund 4s

4 To show possession: Add the *apostrophe and s* to (a) a singular noun and (b) a plural noun which does not end in *s*.

a man's watch   women's shoes   boy's bicycle

Add the *apostrophe and s* to a proper name of one syllable which ends in *s*.

Bess's Cafeteria   Jones's bill

Add the *apostrophe only* after (a) plural nouns ending in *s* and (b) a proper name of more than one syllable which ends in *s* or *z*.

boys' camp   Adams' home   Melendez' report

Add the *apostrophe* after the last noun in a series to indicate joint or common possession of two or more persons; however, add the possessive to each of the nouns to show separate possession of two or more persons.

Lewis and Clark's expedition
the manager's and the treasurer's reports

◼ Use a colon

1 To introduce an enumeration or a listing.

These are my favorite poets: Shelley, Keats, and Frost.

2 To introduce a question or a long direct quotation.

This is the question: Did you study for the test?

3 Between hours and minutes expressed in figures.

10:15 a.m.   4:30 p.m.

◼ Use a comma (or commas)

1 After (a) introductory words, phrases, or clauses and (b) words in a series.

If you can, try to visit Chicago, St. Louis, and Dallas.

2 To set off short direct quotations.

She said, "If you try, you can reach your goal."

3 Before and after (a) words which come together and refer to the same person, thing, or idea and (b) words of direct address.

Clarissa, our class president, will give the report.
It was good to see you, Terrence, at the meeting.

4 To set off nonrestrictive clauses (not necessary to the meaning of the sentence), but not restrictive clauses (necessary to the meaning).

Your report, which deals with the issue, is great.
The girl who just left is my sister.

5 To separate the day from the year and the city from the state.

July 4, 1986   New Haven, Connecticut

6 To separate two or more parallel adjectives (adjectives that could be separated by the word "and" instead of the comma).

a group of young, old, and middle-aged persons

Do not use commas to separate adjectives so closely related that they appear to form a single element with the noun they modify.

a dozen large red roses   a small square box

7 To separate (a) unrelated groups of figures which come together and (b) whole numbers into groups of three digits each (however, *policy*, *year*, *page*, *room*, *telephone*, and most *serial numbers* are shown without commas).

During 1986, 1,750 cars were insured under Policy 806423.
page 1042   Room 1184   (213) 825-2626

◼ Use a dash

1 For emphasis.

The icy road -- slippery as a fish -- was a hazard.

2 To indicate a change of thought.

We may tour the Orient -- but I'm getting ahead of my story.

3 To introduce the name of an author when it follows a direct quotation.

"Hitting the wrong key is like hitting me." -- Armour

4 For certain special purposes.

"Well -- er -- ah," he stammered.
"Jay, don't get too close to the --." It was too late.

■ Use an exclamation mark

1 After emphatic interjections.

Wow!   Hey there!   What a day!

2 After sentences that are clearly exclamatory.

"I won't go!" she said with determination.
How good it was to see you in New Orleans last week!

■ Use a hyphen

1 To join compound numbers from twenty-one to ninety-nine that are keyed as words.

forty-six   fifty-eight   over seventy-six

2 To join compound adjectives before a noun which they modify as a unit.

well-laid plans   five-year period   two-thirds majority

3 After each word or figure in a series of words or figures that modify the same noun (suspended hyphenation).

first-, second-, and third-class reservations

4 To spell out a word or name.

s-e-p-a-r-a-t-e   G-a-e-l-i-i-c

5 To form certain compound nouns.

WLW-TV   teacher-counselor   AFL-CIO

■ Use parentheses

1 To enclose parenthetical matter and added information.

The amendments (Exhibit A) are enclosed.

2 To enclose identifying letters or figures in lists.

Check these factors: (1) rate of pay, (2) period of time, and (3) nature of duties.

3 To enclose figures that follow spelled-out amounts to give added clarify or emphasis.

The total contract was for six hundred dollars ($600).

■ Use a question mark

At the end of a sentence that is a direct question; however, use a period after a request in the form of a question.

What day do you plan to leave for Honolulu?
Will you mail this letter for me, please.

■ Use quotation marks

1 To enclose direct quotations.

He said, "I'll be there at eight o'clock."

2 To enclose titles of articles and other parts of complete publications, short poems, song titles, television programs, and unpublished works like theses and dissertations.

"Sesame Street"   "The Next Twenty Years"
"Out Where the West Begins"   "Living"

3 To enclose special words or phrases, or coined words.

"limited resources"   "Murphy's Law"

■ Use a semicolon

1 To separate two or more independent clauses in a compound sentence when the conjunction is omitted.

To err is human; to forgive, divine.
It is easy to be critical; it is not so easy to be constructive.

2 To separate independent clauses when they are joined by a conjunctive adverb (however, consequently, etc.).

I can go; however, I must get excused.

3 To separate a series of phrases or clauses (especially if they contain commas) that are introduced by a colon.

These officers were elected: Lu Ming, President; Lisa Stein, vice president; Juan Ramos, secretary.

4 To precede an abbreviation or word that introduces an explanatory statement.

She organized her work; for example, putting work to be done in folders of different colors to indicate degrees of urgency.

■ Use an underline

1 With titles of complete works such as books, magazines, and newspapers. (Such titles may also be typed in ALL CAPS without the underline.)

Century 21 Shorthand   New York Times   TV Guide

2 To call attention to special words or phrases (or you may use quotation marks). **Note:** Use a continuous underline unless each word is to be considered separately.

Stop keying when time is called.
Spell these words: steel, occur, separate.

WORD-DIVISION/LETTER-PLACEMENT/ZIP CODE ABBR.

■ Word-division guides

1 Divide words between syllables only; therefore, do not divide one-syllable words. **Note:** When in doubt, consult a dictionary or a word division manual.

through-out	pref-er-ence	em-ploy-ees
reached	toward	thought

2 Do not divide words of five or fewer letters even if they have two or more syllables.

into	also	about	union	radio	ideas

3 Do not separate a one-letter syllable at the beginning of a word or a one- or two-letter syllable at the end of a word.

across	enough	steady	highly	ended

4 You may usually divide a word between double consonants; but, when adding a syllable to a word that ends in double letters, divide after the double letters of the root word.

writ-ten	sum-mer	expres-sion	excel-lence
will-ing	win-ner	process-ing	fulfill-ment

5 When the final consonant is doubled in adding a suffix, divide between the double letters.

run-ning	begin-ning	fit-ting	submit-ted

6 Divide after a one-letter syllable within a word; but when two single-letter syllables occur together, divide between them.

sepa-rate	regu-late	gradu-ation	evalu-ation

7 When the single-letter syllable *a*, *i*, or *u* is followed by the ending *ly*, *ble*, *bly*, *cle*, or *cal*, divide before the single-letter syllable.

stead-ily	siz-able	vis-ible	mir-acle
cler-ical	but	musi-cal	practi-cal

8 Divide only between the two words that make up a hyphenated word.

self-contained	well-developed

9 Do not divide a contraction or a single group of figures; try to avoid dividing proper names and dates.

doesn't	$350,000	Policy F238975

■ Letter-placement points

Paper-guide placement

Check the placement of the paper guide for accurate horizontal centering of the letter.

Margins and date placement

Use the following guide:

5-Stroke Words in Letter Body	Side Margins	Date-line
Up to 100	2″	19
101-200	1½″	16*
Over 200	1″	13

*Dateline is moved up 2 line spaces for each additional 25 words.

Horizontal placement of date varies according to the letter style.

Address

The address begins on the fourth line (3 blank line spaces) below the date. A personal title, such as Mr., Mrs., Miss, or Ms., should precede the name of an individual. An official title, when used, may be placed on the first or the second line of the address, whichever gives better balance.

Two-page letters

If a letter is too long for one page, at least 2 lines of the body of the letter should be carried to the second page. The second page of a letter, or any additional pages, requires a proper heading. Either the block or the horizontal form may be used for the heading; each is followed by a double space.

Second-page headings
(begin on line 6)

Block form

```
Mr. J. W. Smith
Page 2
June 5, 19--
```

Horizontal form

```
Mr. J. W. Smith        2        June 5, 19--
```

Attention line

An attention line, when used, is placed on the second line of the letter address.

Subject line

A subject line is placed on the second line (a double space) below the salutation. It may be either centered or keyed at the left margin.

Company name

Occasionally the company name is shown in the closing lines. When this is done, it is shown in *all capital letters* 2 lines (a double space) below the complimentary close. The modern practice is to omit the company name in the closing lines if a letterhead is used.

Typed/Printed name/official title

The name of the person who dictated the letter and his/her official title are placed 4 lines (3 blank line spaces) below the complimentary close, or 4 lines below the company name when it is used. When both the name and official title are used, they may be placed on the same line or the official title may be placed on the next line below the typed/printed name.

Unusual features

Letters having unusual features, such as tabulated material, long quotations, or an unusual number of lines in the address or the closing lines, may require changes in the settings normally used for letters of that length.

■ ZIP Code abbreviations

Alabama, AL	Florida, FL	Kentucky, KY	Montana, MT	Ohio, OH	Texas, TX
Alaska, AK	Georgia, GA	Louisiana, LA	Nebraska, NE	Oklahoma, OK	Utah, UT
Arizona, AZ	Guam, GU	Maine, ME	Nevada, NV	Oregon, OR	Vermont, VT
Arkansas, AR	Hawaii, HI	Maryland, MD	New Hampshire, NH	Pennsylvania, PA	Virgin Islands, VI
California, CA	Idaho, ID	Massachusetts, MA	New Jersey, NJ	Puerto Rico, PR	Virginia, VA
Colorado, CO	Illinois, IL	Michigan, MI	New Mexico, NM	Rhode Island, RI	Washington, WA
Connecticut, CT	Indiana, IN	Minnesota, MN	New York, NY	South Carolina, SC	West Virginia, WV
Delaware, DE	Iowa, IA	Mississippi, MS	North Carolina, NC	South Dakota, SD	Wisconsin, WI
District of Columbia, DC	Kansas, KS	Missouri, MO	North Dakota, ND	Tennessee, TN	Wyoming, WY

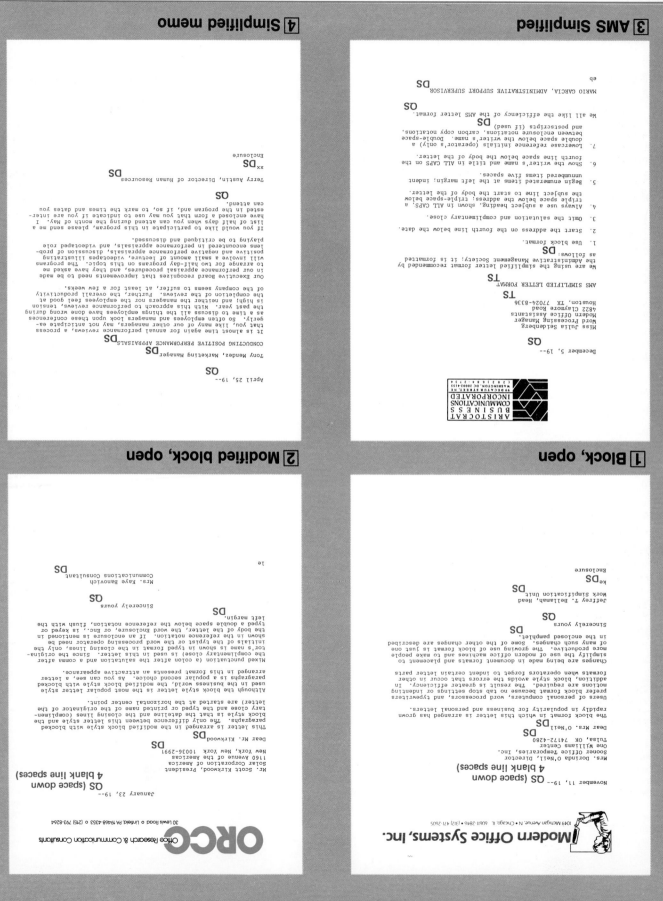

1 Block, open

Modern Office Systems, Inc.
1049 Michigan Avenue, N • Chicago, IL 60611-2846 • (312) 471-2605

November 11, 19--   QS (space down 4 blank line spaces)

Mrs. Dorinda O'Neil, Director
Sooner Office Temporaries, Inc.
One Williams Center
Tulsa, OK 74172-4280   DS

Dear Mrs. O'Neil   DS

The block format in which this letter is arranged has grown rapidly in popularity for business and personal letters.

Users of personal computers, word processors, and typewriters prefer block format because no tab stop settings or indenting motions are required. The result is greater efficiency. In addition, block style avoids the errors that occur in other formats when operators forget to indent certain letter parts

Changes are being made in document formats and placement to simplify the use of modern office machines and to make people more productive. The growing use of block format is just one of many such changes. Some of the other changes are described in the enclosed pamphlet.   DS

Sincerely yours   QS

Jeffery T. Bellamah, Head   DS
Work Simplification Unit   DS
xe   DS
Enclosure

2 Modified block, open

ORCC
Office Research & Communication Consultants
30 Lewis Road □ Linfield, PA 19468-4353 □ (215) 793-8254

January 23, 19--   QS (space down 4 blank spaces)

Mr. Scott Kirkwood, President
Solar Corporation of America
1160 Avenue of the Americas
New York, New York 10036-2991   DS

Dear Mr. Kirkwood   DS

This letter is arranged in the modified block style with blocked paragraphs. The only difference between this letter style and the block style is that the dateline and the closing lines (complimentary close and the typed name of the originator of the letter) are started at the horizontal center point.

Although the block style letter is the most popular letter style used in the business world, the modified block style with blocked paragraphs is a popular second choice. As you can see, a letter arranged in this format presents an attractive appearance.

Mixed punctuation (a colon after the salutation and a comma after the complimentary close) is used in this letter. Since the originator's name is shown in typed format in the closing lines, only the initials of the typist or the word processing operator need be shown in the reference notation. If an enclosure is mentioned in the body of the letter, the word Enclosure, or Enc., is keyed or typed a double space below the reference notation, flush with the left margin.   DS

Sincerely yours   QS

Mrs. Kaye Banovich   DS
Communications Consultant
le

3 AMS Simplified

ARISTOCRAT BUSINESS COMMUNICATIONS INCORPORATED
99 DECATUR STREET, NE
WASHINGTON DC 20003-4134
(202) 688-3734

December 5, 19--   QS

Miss Julia Seldenberg
Word Processing Manager
Modern Office Assistants
4822 Claymore Road
Houston, TX 77024-8336   TS

AMS SIMPLIFIED LETTER FORMAT   TS

We are using the simplified letter format recommended by the Administrative Management Society; it is formatted as follows: DS

1. Use block format.

2. Start the address on the fourth line below the date.

3. Omit the salutation and complimentary close.

4. Always use a subject heading, shown in ALL CAPS, a triple space below the address; triple-space below the subject line to start the letter.

5. Begin enumerated items at the left margin; indent unnumbered items five spaces.

6. Show the writer's name and title in ALL CAPS on the fourth line space below the body of the letter.

7. Lowercase reference initials (operator's only) a double space below the writer's name. Double-space between enclosure notations, carbon copy notations, and postscripts (if used).   DS

We all like the efficiency of the AMS letter format.   QS

MARIO GARCIA, ADMINISTRATIVE SUPPORT SUPERVISOR   DS
eb

4 Simplified memo

April 25, 19--   QS

Tony Mendez, Marketing Manager   DS

CONDUCTING POSITIVE PERFORMANCE APPRAISALS   DS

It is almost time again for annual performance reviews, a process that you, like many of our other managers, may not anticipate eagerly. So often employees and managers look upon these conferences as a time to discuss all the things employees have done wrong during the past year. With this approach to performance reviews, tension is high; and neither the managers nor the employees feel good at the completion of the reviews. Further, the overall productivity of the company seems to suffer, at least for a few weeks.

Our Executive Board recognizes that improvements need to be made in our performance appraisal procedures, and they have asked me to arrange for two half-day programs on this topic. The programs will involve a small amount of lecture, videotapes illustrating positive and negative performance appraisals, discussion of problems encountered in performance appraisals, and videotaped role playing to be critiqued and discussed.

If you would like to participate in this program, please send me a list of half days when you can attend during the month of May. I have enclosed a form that you may use to indicate if you are interested in the program and, if so, to mark the times and dates you can attend.   QS

Terry Austin, Director of Human Resources   DS
xx   DS
Enclosure

ENVELOPES: ADDRESSING, FOLDING AND INSERTING

■ Addressing procedure

Envelope address

Set a tab stop (or margin stop if a number of envelopes are to be addressed) 10 spaces left of center for a small envelope or 5 spaces for a large envelope. Start the address here on Line 12 from the top edge of a small envelope and on Line 14 of a large one.

Style

Type the address in *block style*, single-spaced. Type the city name, state name or abbreviation, and ZIP Code on the last address line. The ZIP Code is typed 2 spaces after the state name abbreviation.

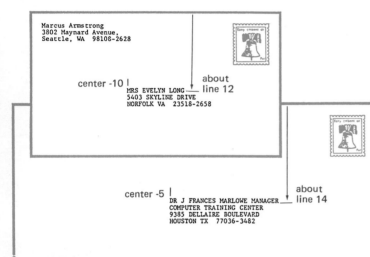

```
Marcus Armstrong
3802 Maynard Avenue,
Seattle, WA  98108-2628
```

center -10 | about
            MRS EVELYN LONG —— line 12
            5403 SKYLINE DRIVE
            NORFOLK VA 23518-2658

center -5 | about
           DR J FRANCES MARLOWE MANAGER —— line 14
           COMPUTER TRAINING CENTER
           9385 DELLAIRE BOULEVARD
           HOUSTON TX 77036-3482

Addressee notations

Type addressee notations, such as *Hold for Arrival, Please Forward, Personal*, etc., a triple space below the return address and about 3 spaces from the left edge of the envelope. Type these notations in all capitals.

If an *attention line* is used, type it immediately below the company name in the address line.

Mailing notations

Type mailing notations, such as SPECIAL DELIVERY and REGISTERED, below the stamp and at least 3 line spaces above the envelope address. Type these notations in all capital letters.

```
InfoTronics, Inc.
115 W. Seventh Street · Fort Worth, TX 76102-2160 · (817) 561-3540

TS
HOLD FOR ARRIVAL

DS
SPECIAL DELIVERY

            BAY CITY CIVIC ASSOCIATION
            ATTENTION MRS SANDRA LUEBBE
            65 POST STREET
            SAN FRANCISCO CA  94104-3572
```

■ Folding and inserting procedure

Small envelopes (No. 6¾, 6¼)

Step 1
With letter face up, fold bottom up to ½ inch from top.

Step 2
Fold right third to left.

Step 3
Fold left third to ½ inch from last crease.

Step 4
Insert last creased edge first.

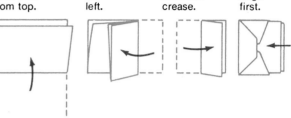

Large envelopes (No. 10, 9, 7¾)

Step 1
With letter face up, fold slightly less than ⅓ of sheet up toward top.

Step 2
Fold down top of sheet to within ½ inch of bottom fold.

Step 3
Insert letter into envelope with last crease toward bottom of envelope.

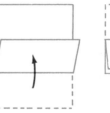

Window envelopes (letter)

Step 1
With sheet face down, top toward you, fold upper third down.

Step 2
Fold lower third up so address is showing.

Step 3
Insert sheet into envelope with last crease at bottom.

① Unbound, page 1

Main head → PLANNING AND PREPARING REPORTS ← line 10 pica; line 12 elite

QS

1″ → Whether written for personal or business use, a report should present a message that is well organized, stated simply, and clear in meaning (Burtness and Hulbert, 1985, 392). A report that does not meet these criteria reflects a lack of care in planning and ← 1″ preparation. The following suggestions will help you to plan and prepare reports that are so clear and concise that the readers will not have to puzzle over their intended meaning.

DS

Side head Planning a Report DS

Three steps should be taken in planning a report. Selecting the topic is not merely the first step but also the most important one. It is vital that you choose a topic in which you have sufficient interest to do the necessary related reading and research. Next, it is essential that you limit the topic so that you can treat the subject adequately within the space and time limitations that have been set. Finally, you should decide upon and list in logical outline form the major ideas and the subordinate points for each idea that you want to use as support (Gonzalez et al., 1981, 499-518). DS

Preparing the Report DS

Three steps should be followed in preparing the report, also. The first of these is to look for data and authoritative statements to support your ideas. The next step is to prepare a rough draft of the report, organizing the data into a series of related paragraphs, each with a topic sentence to announce its major theme.

↑ at least 1″

① Unbound, page 1

② Unbound, page 2

2 line 6

line 8 The last step is to read the rough draft carefully for sequence of ideas, clarity, and accuracy and to prepare the final draft in correct form with all errors corrected. In checking for accuracy, be certain that

1. all words are spelled correctly;
2. punctuation rules have been correctly applied;
3. proper spacing follows each punctuation mark;
4. capitalization rules have been correctly applied;
5. all numbers are accurate; and
6. number expression rules have been correctly applied.

Whether the report is typed or printed, it should be neat and

1″ → arranged in proper format. A neat report presented in an orderly ← 1″ style makes an immediate positive impression on the reader.

QS

REFERENCES

QS

Burtness, Paul S., and Jack E. Hulbert. _Effective Business Communication_. 8th ed. Cincinnati: South-Western Publishing Co., 1985.

DS

Gonzalez, Roseann, Ruby Herlong, Mary Hynes-Berry, and Paul Pesce. _Language: Structure and Use_. Glenview, IL: Scott, Foresman and Company, 1981.

② Unbound, page 2

③ Leftbound, page 1

Main head → ERGONOMICS AND THE BUSINESS OFFICE ← line 10 pica; line 12 elite

QS

1½″ → Ergonomics, simply defined by Springer as "the study of humans at work,"[1] has become a topic of popular interest and ← 1″ concern in recent years. To be more specific, ergonomics deals with the compatibility of people and the other properties in their work environment. According to Popham, ". . . ergonomics integrates both the physiological and psychological factors involved in creating an effective work area."[2] It includes, therefore, the office furniture and equipment; the physical layout; and procedures such as the organization and method of work in the office as well as the worker's attitude toward computer software he or she must use.

Physical Factors DS

Where there are several physical factors that affect workers' productivity, two of the more common ones are the office chair and the video display terminal (VDT). Since most office personnel perform their tasks from a seated position, it is obvious that the chair is the foundation of the workstation. The widespread use of the video display terminal--sometimes

DS
DS
DS

[1]T. J. Springer, "Ergonomics: The Real Issues," _Office Administration and Automation_, May 1984, p. 69.

[2]Estelle L. Popham, Rita Sloan Tilton, J. Howard Jackson, and J Marshall Hanna, _Secretarial Procedures and Administration_ (Cincinnati: South-Western Publishing Co., 1983), p. 31.

↑ at least 1″

③ Leftbound, page 1

④ Leftbound, page 2

2 line 6

line 8 for long periods of time--in today's office makes the VDT another apparent source of ergonomics attention.

Office chairs. Since office personnel vary so greatly in size, it is imperative that office chairs be adjustable. While most chair seats can be moved up or down, most often

1½″ → it is difficult to do and sometimes requires special tools. ← 1″ The ideal is the office chair designed for easy adjustments of both the seat and back so that users can alter their positions as tasks change or fatigue occurs.

VDTs. Problems with VDTs vary from screen glare to posture strain. Glare can be remedied by the use of window coverings, recessed or indirect lighting, and screens that tilt and turn. Designs that separate the keyboard and screen aid both of these problems. DS

Psychological Factors DS

Among the psychological factors that influence worker comfort is the worker's perception of software he or she may use. Even some ergonomically alert people have not considered software to be an ergonomic issue. However, "friendly" software that is designed to be readily usable and that is documented for understanding by nontechnical users is just as much a part of ergonomics as are the hardware and furniture.

④ Leftbound, page 2

Panel 5

CONTENTS ← line 10 pica;
DS   line 12 elite
Page DS

I.   WHAT IS WRITING?   1
II.   WHY WRITING IS IMPORTANT   2
III. SOME SUGGESTIONS TO HELP YOU IMPROVE YOUR WRITING   3

      A. Listening   3
      B. Speaking   4
      C. Reading   4
      D. Writing   6
      E. Preparing the Final Draft   7
          1. Underline copy you may want to eliminate .   8
          2. Use active verbs rather than passive verbs   8
          3. Check sentences   8
          4. Read your paper aloud   8

IV.   SUMMARY STATEMENT   9

1½"   →
                                                      1"

5 Leftbound, contents page

Panel 6

‖ line 6

REFERENCES ← line 10 pica;
QS   line 12 elite

Indent 5   American Psychological Association. *Publication Manual*. 2d ed.
           → Washington, DC: American Psychological Association, 1974.

1½" →   Attenborough, David. *Life on Earth*. Boston: Little, Brown
           and Company, 1979.   1"

           Committee on Writing Standards, The National Council of Teachers
           of English. "Standards for Basic Skills Writing Programs."
           College English, October 1979, 220-222.

           Cross, Donna W. *Word Abuse*. New York: Coward, McCann &
           Geoghegan, Inc., 1979.

           Goodlad, John I. *A Place Called School*. New York: McGraw-Hill
           Inc., 1984.

           Graves, Robert, and Alan Hodge. *The Reader Over Your Shoulder*.
           New York: Random House, 1979.

           Hemingway, Ernest. *In Our Time*. New York: Charles Scribner's
           Sons, 1970.

           Lanham, Richard. UCLA Writing Project Lecture, 1979.

           Walshe, R. D. "What's Basic to Teaching Writing?" *The English
           Journal*, December 1979, 51-56.

           Zinsser, William. *Writing With a Word Processor*. New York:
           Harper & Row, 1983.

6 Leftbound, reference list (bibliography)

Panel 7

Main
head
                MEASURING PRODUCTIVITY OF OFFICE EMPLOYEES   line 12 pica;
                                QS   line 14 elite

        How much work should an office employee be expected to do in
a given period of time? On what basis should an office employee
be paid? These basic questions are almost impossible to answer
for a number of reasons. The classification "office employee" includes hundreds of jobs. One of the major occupational categories
listed in the *Dictionary of Occupation Titles* is "Clerical and
Sales Occupations." "Clerical occupations, which are classified ←
in Divisions 20 through 24, include those activities concerned with
preparing, transcribing, systematizing, and preserving written
communications and records; distributing information; and col-
lecting accounts" (1977, 153). The jobs listed in these divisions
range from social secretary to library page. Because of the diver-
sity of tasks performed by office employees with no standards of
production, these workers traditionally have been paid on a time
basis--by the hour, day, week, month, or year.

        With the adoption of word processing, attempts have been made
to establish standards for those who keyboard materials. In a
study conducted with word processing originators and supervisors
in Tennessee, 41.3% indicated that they measured word processing
production while 53.8% did not. "Typical responses regarding how
production was measured included: (1) keystrokes; (2) line count;
(3) number of pages; (4) weekly logs; (5) number of documents a day;
and (6) quantity and quality of work" (Robinson and West, 1984,

1"   1"

↑ at least 1"

7 Topbound, page 1

Panel 8

Maxwell Nash Corporation
2502 Sycamore Avenue Baltimore, MD 21219-1331 Interoffice Communication

TO: Isabel Garcia

FROM: Sidney Cross, Assistant to Personnel Director

DATE: November 3, 19--

SUBJECT: Insurance Benefit Package DS

As we discussed in your orientation session yesterday, Maxwell Nash
Corporation does provide insurance benefits for its full-time employees. The insurance plans for which you are eligible are:

1. Medical, hospital, and major medical insurance covering the
    prevailing fees charged by participating physicians, hospitals,
    and other health agencies. Employees may elect to participate
    in this insurance plan. DS

2. Life insurance including basic life, accidental death, and dis-
    memberment coverage at a rate of two times the employee's regu-
    lar annual salary. Employees may elect to participate in this
    insurance plan.

3. Disability insurance which becomes effective 90 days after the
    beginning of a disability. This insurance provides monthly
    payments equal to 60 percent of the employee's regular salary
    up to a maximum of $1,800 per month. Participation in this
    insurance plan is required of all employees.

4. Dental insurance covering the entire or a portion of the pre-
    vailing fees charged by participating dentists for dental work
    which is covered in the plan. Employees may elect to partici-
    pate in this insurance plan.

Maxwell Nash will pay 90 percent of the cost of the premium for
each of these four insurance plans. Employees pay the remaining
10 percent through payroll deductions.

Please decide within the next 15 days which of the three voluntary
plans in which you will participate. If you need additional information, contact Mark Harmon in the personnel department.

sjc

1"   1"

8 Memorandum Report

CORRECTION SYMBOLS/CENTERING PROCEDURES

Correction symbols

■ Proofreader's marks

Sometimes typed or printed copy may be corrected with proofreader's marks. The typist must be able to interpret correctly these marks in retyping the corrected copy or *rough draft* as it may be called. The most commonly used proofreader's marks are shown below.

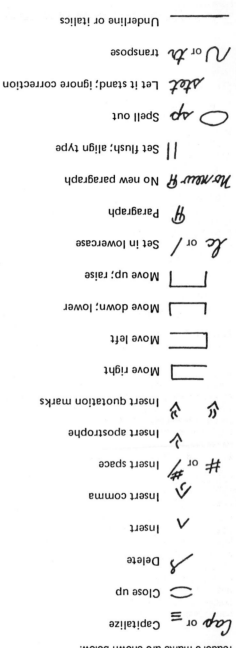

Cap or ≡	Capitalize
⌒	Close up
ℐ	Delete
∨	Insert
⌄	Insert comma
# or ⌄	Insert space
⌃	Insert apostrophe
⌄⌄	Insert quotation marks
□	Move right
□	Move left
⊔	Move down; lower
⊓	Move up; raise
lc or /	Set in lowercase
¶	Paragraph
No new ¶	No new paragraph
‖	Set flush; align type
○ *sp*	Spell out
stet	Let it stand; ignore correction
∿ or ⤸	transpose
_____	Underline or italics

Centering procedures

1 Horizontal centering

1 Move margin stops to extreme ends of scale.
2 Clear tab stops; then set a tab stop at center of paper.
3 Tabulate to center of paper.
4 From center, backspace once for each 2 letters, spaces, figures, or punctuation marks in the line.
5 Do not backspace for an odd or leftover stroke at the end of the line.
6 Begin to key where backspacing ends.

Formula for finding horizontal center of paper

Scale reading at left edge of paper
+ Scale reading at right edge of paper
Total ÷ 2 = Center Point

Example
0
102
102 ÷ 2 = 51

2 Spread headings

1 Backspace from center once for each letter, character, and space except *the last letter or character* in the heading. Begin to type where the backspacing ends.
2 In keying a spread heading, space once after each letter or character and 3 times between words.

3 Vertical centering

Mathematical method

1 Count lines and blank line spaces needed to type problem.
2 Subtract *lines to be used* from *lines available* (66 for full sheet and 33 for half sheet).
3 Divide by 2 to get top and bottom margins. If a fraction results, disregard it.
4 If an even number results, space down that number of times from top of sheet and key the first line. If an odd number results, use the next lower number.

Dropping fractions and using even numbers usually places a line or two above exact center-- in what is often called *reading position*.

Formula for vertical mathematical placement

$$\frac{\text{Lines available} - \text{lines used}}{2} = \text{top margin}$$

Backspace-from-center method

Basic rule

From vertical center of paper, roll platen (cylinder) back once for each 2 lines, 2 blank line spaces, or line and blank line space. Ignore odd or leftover line.

Steps to follow:

1 To move paper to vertical center, start spacing down from top edge of paper.
  a half sheet
    down 6 TS (triple spaces) – 1 SS (Line 17)
  b full sheet
    down 11 TS + 1 SS (Line 34)
2 From vertical center
  a half sheet, SS or DS: follow basic rule, back 1 for 2
  b full sheet, SS or DS: follow basic rule, back 1 for 2; then back 2 SS for reading position.

TABLE FORMATTING PROCEDURES

Prepare

1 Insert and align paper unless you are using a computer.

2 Clear margin stops by moving them to extreme ends of line-of-writing scale.

3 Clear all tabulator stops.

4 Move element carrier (carriage) or cursor to center of paper or line-of-writing scale.

5 Decide the number of spaces to be left between columns (for intercolumns) -- preferably an even number (4, 6, 8, 10, etc.).

1 Plan vertical placement

Follow either of the vertical centering procedures explained on page RG 10.

Spacing headings. Double-space (count 1 blank line space) between main and secondary headings, when both are used. Double-space (count 1 blank line space) between the last table heading (either main or secondary) and the first horizontal line of column items or column headings. Double-space between column headings (when used) and the first line of the column entries.

Spacing above totals and source notes. Double-space (count 1 blank line space) between the total rule and the total figures. Double-space (count 1 blank line space) between the last line of the table and the 1½" rule above the source note. Double-space (count 1 blank line space) between the 1½" rule and the source note.

2 Plan horizontal placement

Backspace from center of paper (or line-of-writing scale) 1 space for each 2 letters, figures, symbols, and spaces in *longest* item of each column in the table. Then backspace once for each 2 spaces to be left between columns (intercolumns). Set left margin stop where backspacing ends.

If an odd or leftover space occurs at the end of the longest item of a column when backspacing by 2's, carry it forward to the next column. Do not backspace for an odd or leftover character at the end of the last column. (See illustration below.)

Set tab stops. From the left margin, space forward 1 space for each letter, figure, symbol, and space in the longest item in the first column and for each space to be left between Cols. 1 and 2. Set a tab stop at this point for the second column. Follow this procedure for each additional column of the table.

Note. If a column heading is longer than the longest item in the column, it *may* be treated as the longest item in the column in determining placement. The longest columnar entry must then be centered under the heading and the tab stop set accordingly.

3 Center column headings

Backspace-from-column-center method

From point at which column begins (tab or margin stop), space forward (→) once for each 2 letters, figures, or spaces in the longest item in the column. This leads to the column center point; from it, backspace (←) once for each 2 spaces in column heading. Ignore an odd or leftover space. Type the heading at this point; it will be centered over the column.

Mathematical methods

1 To the number on the cylinder (platen) or line-of-writing scale immediately under the first letter, figure, or symbol of the longest item of the column, add the number shown under the space following the last stroke of the item. Divide this sum by 2; the result will be the center point of the column. From this point on the scale, backspace (1 for 2) to center the column heading.

2 From the number of spaces in the longest item, subtract the number of spaces in the heading. Divide this number by 2; ignore fractions. Space forward this number from the tab or margin stop and key the heading.

4 Horizontal rulings

To make horizontal rulings in tables, depress shift lock and strike the underline key.

Single-space above and double-space below horizontal rulings.

5 Vertical rulings

On a typewriter, operate the automatic line finder. Place a pencil or pen point through the cardholder (or the typebar guide above the ribbon or carrier). Roll the paper up until you have a line of the desired length. Remove the pencil or pen and reset the line finder.

On a computer-generated table, use a ruler and pen or pencil to draw the vertical rulings.

	MAIN HEADING		
	Secondary Heading		
These	Are	Column	Heads
xxxxxx	*longest*	xxxx	xxxxx
xxxx	*item*	*longest*	xxx
xxxxx	xxxxx	*item*	*longest*
longest	xxxxxx	xxxxx	*item*
item	xxxx	xxx	xxx

longest 1234 longest 1234 longest 1234 longest

CORRECTING ERRORS

1 Electronic correction

Electronic typewriters, word processors, and computers vary in the way keystroking errors may be corrected. All, however, have a correction key that removes errors from the electronic window/screen and/or paper. Use the Operator's Manual for your machine to learn the steps for making corrections electronically.

2 Lift-off tape

1 Strike the special backspace/lift-off key to move the printing element (or carrier) to the point of the error.

2 Rekey the error exactly as you made it. In this step, the lift-off tape actually lifts the error off the page. The printing element stays in place.

3 Key the correction.

3 Correction fluid

1 Turn the paper up a few spaces to ease the correction procedure.

2 Shake the bottle; remove the applicator; daub excess fluid on inside of bottle opening.

3 Brush fluid sparingly over the entire error by a light touching action.

4 Return applicator to bottle and tighten cap; blow on the error to speed the drying process.

4 Correction paper

1 Backspace to the beginning of the error.

2 Insert the correction tape or paper strip behind the ribbon and in front of the error, coated side toward the copy.

3 Rekey the error exactly as you made it. In this step, powder from the correction paper is pressed by force into the form of the error, thus masking it.

4 Remove the correction paper; backspace to the point where the correction begins and key the correction.

Special correction paper is available for correcting errors on carbon copies.

5 Rubber eraser

1 Turn the paper up a few spaces; then move the element carrier (carriage) to the extreme right or left so that eraser crumbs will not fall into the machine.

2 Move the paper bail out of the way. Pull the original sheet forward (if a carbon copy is being made) and place a card (5" × 3" or slightly larger) in front of, not behind, the first carbon sheet to protect the carbon copy from smudges.

3 Flip the original sheet back and make the erasure with a hard eraser. Brush or blow the eraser crumbs off the paper.

4 Move the protective card to a position in front of the second carbon sheet if more than one carbon copy is being made. Erase the error on the first carbon copy with a soft eraser.

5 Remove the card and key the correction.

6 Correcting errors by squeezing/spreading

In correcting errors, it is often possible to "squeeze" a word into less space or to "spread" a word to fill out extra space.

Letter omitted in a word

1 Remove the word with the omitted letter.

2 Move printing element to second space after preceding word.

3 Pull half-space lever forward (or use electronic incremental back-spacer) to move printing element a half space to the left.

4 Hold lever in place as you key the corrected word with the other hand.

5 Release the lever and continue keying.

Error
an omitte letter
Correction
an omitted letter

Letter added in a word

1 Remove the word with the added letter.

2 Move printing element to third space after preceding word.

3 Pull half-space lever forward (or use electronic incremental back-spacer) to move printing element a half space to the left.

4 Hold lever in place as you key the corrected word with the other hand.

5 Release the lever and continue keying.

Error
a lettter within
Correction
a letter within

INDEX

SPECIAL INDEX

Alphabet sentences[1]

Figure sentences[2]

Figure/Symbol sentences[3]

Fluency (speed) sentences[4]

[1]An alphabetic sentence appears in every Conditioning practice, beginning on page 34.
[2]A figure sentence appears in most of the Conditioning practices, beginning on page 47.
[3]A figure/symbol sentence appears in many of the Conditioning practices, beginning on page 62.
[4]Beginning on page 30, an easy sentence, designed for speed building or fluency practice, appears in every Conditioning practice in the book.

Concentration drills

a, 4, 5, 6, 8, 9, 208, 278; **b,** 22, 170, 208, 278; **c,** 16, 208, 278; **d,** 4, 5, 6, 8, 9, 208, 278; **e,** 8, 9, 10, 38, 208, 278; **f,** 4, 5, 8, 9, 208, 278; **g,** 21, 208, 278; **h,** 8, 9, 10, 208, 278; **i,** 13, 208, 278; **j,** 4, 5, 6, 8, 9, 210, 278; **k,** 4, 5, 6, 8, 9, 210, 278; **l,** 4, 5, 6, 8, 9, 210, 278; **m,** 25, 210, 278; **n,** 19, 210, 278; **o,** 9, 10, 210, 278; **p,** 22, 210, 278; **q,** 28, 32, 33, 210, 278; **r,** 9, 10, 210, 278; **s,** 4, 5, 6, 9, 11, 278; **t,** 13, 211, 278; **u,** 16, 211, 278; **v,** 31, 32, 33, 211, 278; **w,** 19, 211, 278; **x,** 25, 32, 211, 278; **y,** 27, 32, 170, 211, 278; **z,** 27, 170, 211, 278; **ed,** 38; **er,** 43, 280; **ce/ec,** 43; **ik/ki,** 38; **io/oi,** 43, 80; **ft/ju,** 38; **ny/yn,** 43; **ol/lo,** 38; **po/op,** 43, 280; **q/a,** 43; **r/b,** 280; **r/v,** 280; **sa/as,** 43; **ui/iu,** 43, 280; **um/mu,** 43, 280; **un/nu,** 43, 280; **we/ew,** 43, 280; **ws/sw,** 38; **za/az,** 38, 43; **apostrophe,** 62; **colon,** 31; **comma,** 28, 33; **diagonal,** 56; **exclamation mark,** 73; **period,** 15, 32, 33; **question mark,** 33; **quotation marks,** 62; **semicolon,** 4, 5, 6, 8, 9; **#,** 59; **$,** 56; **%,** 58; **&,** 59; **(),** 61; ***,** 64; **- (hyphen),** 58; **-- (dash),** 58; **___ (underline),** 64, 182.

Guided writing copy

Letters: 222, 224, 252.
Paragraphs: 37, 39, 42, 44, 47, 54, 66, 87, 91, 115, 116, 118, 133, 136, 138, 169, 171, 172, 208, 209, 211, 218, 242, 256, 281, 282, 283, 284.
Sentences: 134, 168, 170, 210.

Models illustrated in text

Application for employment, 241.
Block style letter, open punctuation, 77.
Data sheet, 238.
Interoffice memorandum, formal, 229.
Interoffice memorandum, simplified, 72.
Leftbound report with footnotes, 199.
Letter with special features, 221.
Modified block style letter, blocked ¶s, mixed punctuation, 151.
Numbered list with centered heading, 69.
Personal note on half sheet, 70.
Two-column table, 107.
Unbound report, 96.

Preapplication manipulative activities

Addressing envelopes, large, 83; small, 83.
Aligning Arabic numerals, 108; Roman numerals, 94.
Aligning/typing over words, 118.
Assembling/inserting carbon pack, 160.
Attention line, 220.
Automatic line finder (ratchet release), 233, 234.
Backspacer, 67, 106.
Bell cue, 78.
Centering on special-size paper, 233, 245.
Centering column headings, 188, 189, 255.
Erasing, 82.
Footnotes, 199.
Headings, main/secondary, 106, 141, 178.
Horizontal centering, 68, 141, 178.
Line-space selector, setting, 7.
Margin release, 94.
Margin stops, planning and setting, 5, 7, 106.
Second-page headings, letters, 166.
Spacing a tabulation, 235.
Spreading headings, RG 10.
Squeezing/spreading letters, RG 12.
Superscripts/subscripts, 199.
Tab mechanism, 106.
Vertical centering, 106, 178.

Problems in rough-draft and script

Rough-draft: 74, 90, 100, 101, 104, 111, 113, 117, 121, 122, 127, 128, 137, 139, 144, 153, 162, 163, 164, 167, 174, 182, 185, 191, 193, 196, 197, 200, 201, 203, 212, 246, 247, 248, 250, 251, 257, 263, 268, 270, 271, 276.
Script: 73, 74, 82, 86, 89, 90, 101, 109, 117, 120, 135, 142, 144, 150, 163, 165, 166, 167, 191, 193, 223, 229, 234, 245, 247, 249, 253, 255, 269, 272, 273, 275, 277.

Related communication activities

Capitalization: 39, 40, 41, 44, 59, 60, 63, 89, 113, 114, 117, 130.
Composing at the typewriter: 91, 179, 181, 210, 222, 224, 239, 240.
Ellipsis: 147.
Grammar: 142, 143, 146, 152, 154, 156, 173, 195, 198, 200, 254, 257.
Number expression: 53, 54, 60, 89, 113, 115, 117, 130.
Proofreader's marks: 55, 67, 127.
Punctuation: 16, 81, 171, 173, 179, 182, 184, 185, 187.
Spacing with figures/symbols: 69, 73, 235, 255, 257.
Spacing after punctuation: 9, 16, 73.
Special symbols: feet, 185; number, 59; pounds, 59; seconds, 185.
Spelling: 144, 214, 232, 233.
Word division: 78, 80, 84, 104, 144.

Skill-transfer timed writings

Rough-draft: 1', 117, 137, 139. 2', 3', and 5', 117, 137, 139, 175, 213.
Script: 1', 58', 117. 2' and 3', 117.
Statistical: 1', 58, 60, 254. 2', 3', and 5', 60, 213, 254.

Straight-copy timed writings

1': 29, 32, 35, 39, 48, 52, 55, 58, 60, 64, 71, 85, 102, 112, 124, 125, 129, 157, 161, 186, 188, 218, 230, 235.
2': 39, 44, 52, 54, 55, 60, 64, 66, 71, 87, 91, 102.
3': 52, 54, 55, 64, 66, 71, 85, 87, 91, 102, 112, 115, 116, 118, 124, 125, 129, 157, 171, 172, 188, 202, 209, 218, 242, 256.
5': 133, 140, 157, 161, 169, 172, 186, 188, 202, 209, 214, 218, 225, 242, 259, 260, 262, 263.

Technique drills

Keystroking:

adjacent keys, 55, 57, 61, 63, 68, 116, 123, 173, 184, 195, 209, 214, 222, 239.
double letters, 68, 123.
fingers: 1st/2d, 29, 36; 3d/4th fingers, 29, 36, 150, 175.
first row, 21, 132, 145, 170.
home row, 9, 11, 14, 132, 141, 198.
home/first rows, 36, 47.
home/3d rows, 36, 47.
long direct reaches, 55, 57, 61, 63, 116, 123, 187, 224, 225, 240.
outside reaches, 63, 68, 123.
third row, 11, 14, 15, 21, 123, 132, 143, 170, 210, 239.
third/1st row, 17, 18, 23, 26, 27, 123.

Machine parts:

automatic line finder (ratchet release), 233, 234.
backspacer, 67, 106.
carriage (element) return, 4, 5, 17, 23, 26, 51.
margin release, 94.
shift keys, 15, 18, 20, 21, 24, 29, 30, 35, 51, 57, 116, 123, 140, 146, 168, 174, 181, 211, 215.
shift lock, 33, 35, 40, 51, 57.
space bar, 14, 18, 24, 26, 27, 29, 30, 31, 34, 35, 36, 39, 46, 51, 57, 116, 138, 148, 152, 174, 202, 208, 214, 240.
tabulator, 34, 35, 51, 57, 140, 174, 235.

Response patterns

combination, 36, 41, 43, 50, 53, 61, 65, 68, 114, 123, 170, 213, 228, 230, 235.
letter (stroke), 36, 40, 41, 43, 50, 53, 55, 61, 65, 68, 114, 123, 136, 170, 180, 213.
word, 36, 40, 41, 43, 50, 53, 55, 61, 65, 68, 114, 116, 123, 134, 170, 213, 228, 230, 235.